KT-148-506

CHILDHOOD DISORDERS
Second Edition

WITHDRAWN

Childhood Disorders

Second Edition

Philip C. Kendall
Temple University, Philadelphia, USA

Jonathan S. Comer
Columbia University, New York City, USA

Psychology Press
Taylor & Francis Group

HOVE AND NEW YORK

First published 2000 by Psychology Press
27 Church Road, Hove, East Sussex BN3 2FA

Second edition published 2010 by Psychology Press
27 Church Road, Hove, East Sussex BN3 2FA

Simultaneously published in the USA and Canada
by Psychology Press
270 Madison Avenue, New York, NY 10016

Psychology Press is an imprint of the Taylor & Francis Group, an Informa business

Typeset in Palatino by Garfield Morgan, Swansea, West Glamorgan
Printed and bound in Great Britain by TJ International Ltd, Padstow, Cornwall
Cover design by Jim Wilkie

British Library Cataloguing in Publication Data
A catalogue record for this book is available from the British Library

Library of Congress Cataloging-in-Publication Data
Kendall, Philip C.
  Childhood disorders / Philip C. Kendall and Jonathan S. Comer. – 2nd ed.
    p. cm.
  Originally published: 2000
  Includes bibliographical references and index.
  ISBN 978-0-415-48641-5 (hardback) – ISBN 978-0-415-48642-2 (pbk.) 1. Child
psychiatry. 2. Child psychopathology. 3. Mental illness. 4. Child psychotherapy.
I. Comer, Jonathan S. II. Title.
  RJ499.K393 2010
  618.92'89–dc22
                                                                    2009047334

ISBN: 978-0-415-48641-5 (hbk)
ISBN: 978-0-415-48642-2 (pbk)

Contents

Series preface

Clinical Psychology: A Modular Course was designed to overcome the problems faced by the traditional textbook in conveying what psychological disorders are really like. All the books in the series, written by leading scholars and practitioners in the field, can be read as standalone text, but they will also integrate with the other modules to form a comprehensive resource in clinical psychology. Students of psychology, medicine, nursing, and social work, as well as busy practitioners in many professions, often need an accessible but thorough introduction to how people experience anxiety, depression, addiction, or other disorders, how common they are, and who is most likely to suffer from them, as well as up-to-date research evidence on the causes and available treatments. The series will appeal to those who want to go deeper into the subject than the traditional textbook will allow, and base their examination answers, research projects, assignments, or practical decisions on a clearer and more rounded appreciation of the clinical and research evidence.

Chris R. Brewin

Other titles in this series:

Depression, Second Edition
Constance Hammen and Edward Watkins

Stress and Trauma
Patricia A. Resick

Childhood Disorders, First Edition
Philip C. Kendall

Schizophrenia
Max Birchwood and Chris Jackson

Addictions
Maree Teesson, Louise Degenhardt and Wayne Hall

Anxiety, Second Edition
S. Rachman

Eating and Weight Disorders
Carlos M. Grilo

Personality Disorders
Paul M.G. Emmelkamp and Jan Henk Kamphuis

Getting to know the children 1

One unassuming fact is true of all of us—we have all been children. However unwittingly, each of us has completed the journey from newborn to young adult or beyond. Whether it is easy to recall the memories of favorable or unfavorable emotional experiences or barely remember going through several years of elementary school, all adolescents and adults have successfully charted the ever-changing waters of childhood.

For many reasons, although we can learn from retrospective reports of childhood experiences (Brewin, Andrews, & Gotlib, 1993; Kessler, Berglund, Demler, Jin, Merikangas, & Walters, 2005b; Nock, Kazdin, Hiripi, & Kessler, 2007), a complete understanding of childhood and the psychological disorders of childhood can not rely solely on children's own reports (Comer & Kendall, 2004), or on retrospective self-reports of adults about their childhood (Hardt & Rutter, 2004). Memories of past childhood experiences can be useful, but may not always be accurate or complete. Also, children are not consistently aware of the psychological difficulties associated with their behavior or with the reality that their behavior is aberrant.

A third simple fact: Although some of the disorders of childhood are severe and difficult to treat, many of the childhood disorders represent extensions or extremes of behavior and emotion that all of us have done or felt at some time in our lives. What can under some circumstances be considered a disorder when it is extreme and inter-fering with the adjustment of the child may, under other circum-stances, be a routine struggle within normal development.

These several simple facts aside, the causes, nature, course, and treatments of childhood disorders are highly complex. The complexi-ties of clinical work with children are evident when considering the following questions: Is it optimal to work with the child or should the treatment include members of the child's family? Under what circumstances is it best to work with the child alone and when is it best to work solely with the child's parents? What role should be played by the child's peers, by the school? Should treatment be provided in a mental health setting, or as part of the routine school day? Is there a place for medication in the management of child problems?

What we hope to accomplish in this book is not to fashion you into an expert or a professional, but instead to provide you, the reader, with the current information about childhood disorders, and a discussion and evaluation of the major models that guide psychological thinking about these disorders. To do this, we provide a description of each of the major childhood disorders, a consideration of the criteria used to make diagnoses, a presentation of the latest research findings on the nature of the disorder, and an overview of the treatment of the disorders. Throughout, the range of normal behavioral variations is set as the backdrop against which to make judgments about psychological disorders. Within the coverage of the treatments of childhood disorders, emphasis is placed upon those treatments that have been empirically evaluated and found to be effective in producing beneficial change. Treatments that have been proffered but not supported by empirical research will be mentioned only minimally if at all.

Introducing some of the children

Plainly, and to the great satisfaction of many parents, the majority of children do not have psychological disorders. The pleasing truth is that although there are large numbers of disordered youngsters, many children experience and enjoy their childhood without serious psychological distress and mature into reasonably well-adjusted adults. For present purposes, however, we need to pay attention to those children whose psychological conditions are not satisfactory. Select cases of children with psychological difficulties will be described. Although some of the behavior may seem familiar or even commonplace, you will, once you know the diagnostic criteria, recognize why these youngsters are outside the acceptable range of behavior.

Consider the following examples of children—pay special attention to their behavior, their emotional well-being, and the quality of their adjustment. The children are merely introduced here—brief descriptions to excite your curiosity and whet your interest. In later chapters we provide more detailed information and offer insights into the children and their situation as well as hypotheses about the etiology of the problems and strategies for their remediation.

Jamie lives nears you. You don't know him well but you have seen him "hanging out" and playing with other kids in the neighborhood.

As you sit with a friend and talk with neighbors, the police race by and a fire alarm sounds. Your concern mounts and you begin to sweat as you notice that the police cars have stopped and the fire trucks have arrived at a house just two doors from where you live. You and your friend start to walk quickly toward your home. Jamie, a tough and troublesome 11-year-old, lives with his mother in the house that is now ablaze. You know that Jamie has been in trouble for excessive fighting and temper outbursts at school, and for vandalism at the park. You also recall seeing him being searched by the police at the shopping mall, and you recall seeing the police bringing him home very late one night during the summer. Although you have no evidence in the present case, you begin to wonder, might Jamie have intentionally started the fire? You think to yourself "I wouldn't be at all surprised if this fire is Jamie's doing." You don't want to blame him, and you feel disappointed in yourself for rashly thinking him responsible, yet you also trust your initial judgment. Again you wonder . . . might an 11-year-old intentionally start a fire?

Sarah was a relatively young and once-attractive woman. Presently, she works as a waitress and appears older than her years. You met her last summer while you were working a part-time job at a local restaurant. Although both you and Sarah were busy most of the time, there were quiet hours after work when the staff would share a bite to eat and a bit of conversation. It was during these after-hours calming conversations that you got to know personal information about several of the other staff, including Sarah. For example, you have heard Sarah describe her two young children. Her tone and manner disclose her genuine love for the children. Even when they upset her, her manner betrays her true maternal care. You have also heard her complaining, almost constantly, about her conflictive marriage. She often comes to work angry following her husband's outbursts, she has missed days off work because she is too upset to show her tearful eyes, and she has lied to cover up incidents where it was suspected that she might have been physically beaten. Secretly, she has been seeking and planning a divorce.

Today, Sarah reports that her divorce is complete. Moreover, she discloses that she is both very worried and very hopeful—worried about keeping her ex-husband away from her and the children and hopeful that the fighting will end and that things will be better for her children. Will divorce be a solution to the conflictive marriage, or will the divorce add to the children's emotional turmoil? What effect does marital dissolution have on children? Are the effects different for children of different ages? Of different gender?

In the eighth grade, Joseph was a clever and sometimes offbeat boy who loved to smile, was well liked, and enjoyed playing soccer, trading baseball cards, and mastering video games. But by the middle of the ninth grade, the kids in his class noticed he seemed somewhat different. He was smiling less often and appeared increasingly tired. Although previously known as a "model" student, Joseph began arriving tardy to school on a regular basis. He started turning in homework assignments late, often with holes worn through the pages—seemingly due to excessive erasing. He would ask to go to the bathroom almost every period, and many students noticed that the skin on his hands appeared chapped and cracked.

At home, Joseph's mom had grown concerned about his increased rigidity and the excessive amount of time he would spend arranging and rearranging things in his room. She was surprised at how upset he would get when she put his socks in the wrong dresser drawer, and she noticed he would spend extraordinary amounts of time in the bathroom, scrubbing his hands to the point where they were red and raw. He would flush the toilet 10 to 15 times after using the bathroom, stating that he was waiting until it flushed "just right." Before Joseph would get into his bed at night he would engage in a number of time-consuming rituals, such as setting and resetting his alarm clock up to 15 times and checking that the locks were locked, that the refrigerator door was shut, and that the appliances were all shut off. These rituals were taking longer and longer each night, considerably cutting into his sleep. He would often lie awake thinking long after he had gotten into bed, burdened by intrusive concerns that he may have gotten someone at school sick by spreading germs. Joseph's mother also noticed he was getting up earlier and earlier each day to ensure he had sufficient time to attend to an increasing repertoire of morning rituals, which already included a 45-minute shower and making sure there were no extraneous markings on his homework. Once during an uneventful car ride, Joseph's mother was caught off guard and alarmed when he demanded that they retrace their route to check that they had not hit a pedestrian.

Although Joseph's mother always thought of her son as "a bit quirky," she was now convinced that there was "something more" and that his condition was getting considerably worse. She decided to consult a psychologist with a number of questions: Was Joseph just a "quirky" kid? Was this just a phase? Or was he suffering from an identifiable psychological disorder? Could his condition worsen if left untreated? Were there effective treatments for his condition?

Not long ago, for a brief period, you volunteered at a community mental health center, answering the telephone of the "hotline." You met and got to know several of the professional staff and bonded with a few of the youthful callers.

The hotline was set up for anyone in the community to call in whenever they feel troubled. Ads in businesses and schools, on the radio, and at concerts and athletic events were successful in bringing the service to the attention of members of the community. Recent calls had to do with suicide attempts, child abuse, and runaways. On one otherwise quiet weekend morning, you answer the phone and a woman states that her daughter is having troubles. Without much introduction, she puts her daughter, Nora, on the phone. Nora speaks haltingly, "Uh, can I like talk to somebody who knows about being crazy?" You reply, "Perhaps I can help you." Nora stumbles, "I need to talk to somebody because . . . well, because I don't think straight.

But I really do. Nobody understands. I don't know, I just don't fit."

Nora—a lonely and depressed youngster who is seeking relief from the psychological pain of feeling useless, alone, and unloved—reports that she is 12 years old. She recognized that she had a problem but did not know what to do . . . did not know where to turn.

Most parents in your community are in favor of providing social gatherings for young teenagers. There is some question, however, about just when—at what age—children should have unsupervised dances at school or at community centers.

One evening, when the 13-year-olds are having a social dance, the loud music and dancing can be heard at several nearby homes and stores. It isn't deafening, but it does annoy some of the members of the neighborhood. Those who were in attendance at the event reported that the event was great—and that the loud music contributed to a lively and engaging party. The loudness is annoying but not the source of psychological concern.

As the hour gets late the partygoers get hungry, and pizzas are ordered and delivered. The food is wolfed down by everyone, especially Sheila. Soon after the food, you notice Sheila, who has told you that she doesn't want to gain weight, in the bathroom making herself vomit. She says other kids do it too, and that it helps her not to gain weight. Her parents do not know about the vomiting, and her girlfriends help her keep it a secret. Is her behavior putting her health at risk?

A classmate discloses to you that her younger brother was recently diagnosed with Asperger syndrome. She goes on to tell you that he has poor social skills, a very narrow range of interests, terrible handwriting, and is poorly coordinated. Although he is said to be very bright, you learn, he has great difficulty on a number of nonverbal tasks in school, and consequently his academic marks may not accurately reflect his intelligence. His difficulties have also greatly impaired the quality of his social life, as he has great difficulty in making and keeping friends. You remember that your mother once told you that your second cousin, who you always found to be somewhat awkward at family gatherings, was given the very same diagnosis.

Out of curiosity, you decide to look up "Asperger syndrome" on the internet and find reports suggesting that the rate of this condition is steadily rising in the population. What could explain this rise? You find one website charging that increases in environmental pollution, which can have neurotoxic effects on the young child's developing brain if exposed, are responsible. Intrigued, you ask your childhood pediatrician for her thoughts about this. She informs you that clinical recognition of the condition has improved tremendously in the last 10 years, and she believes that the increased rates simply reflect improved identification of Asperger syndrome, rather than an actual increase in the number of true cases. Improved assessment methods, she argues, are identifying cases of the condition that would have gone undetected in years past. You mention this to a neighbor, who is a school administrator, and learn that he has a very different opinion on the subject. Having seen in recent years a great number of schoolchildren with minimal impairments carrying the diagnosis, he believes that a number of professionals may now be over-diagnosing Asperger syndrome.

People clearly hold strong and diverging opinions about increasing rates of childhood psychological disorders, such as Asperger syndrome, in the general population. Do such data reflect actual increases in the prevalence of childhood disorders? Or do such data simply reflect improved clinical recognition and assessment methods? Could there be a recent tendency to over-diagnose psychological disorders in children?

At the nursery in the hospital, when relatives and friends gather for the birth of a child, everyone wishes for the good health of the mother and of the newborn. Often, the child and mother are healthy and the parents emerge to begin to fill their roles as parents of the newborn. Such a preferred outcome is, unfortunately, not always the case.

When you met your new neighbors, and got to chat with them about their family, you learned about one of the children: David, a 4-year-old. David's mother apologetically stated that he "was late to walk and slow to learn." She added that his preschool teacher reported that he appeared to be unable to organize and plan his work. "He isn't a contrary child," the teacher said, "he just doesn't understand the lessons." David's mom didn't suggest that he had a disorder, and she seemed to describe him in euphemistic terms—using mild terms to describe behaviors that seem severe even to you. What was David's situation? He was noticeably impaired, but did he have a specific disorder? How will he adjust in adulthood? Psychological testing conducted at the time he entered preschool indicated that David's IQ score was 62. What does all of this mean?

Everyone seemed to know that Bernie was a "disturbed" child. He was variously described as "different," "stiff," and "nonresponsive."

Bernie never seemed to hear or respond to other people—not even when you looked him in the eye and spoke to him directly. He didn't socialize with other children, he didn't show interest in group activities, and he didn't seem to want to be near his parents.

Bernie was playing at the park and seeing him sparked you to ask some questions. Your mom knew Bernie's mother and his history and she was able to answer some of your queries. She stated that Bernie wasn't "cuddly" as an infant, and she recalled that he didn't enjoy playing with other children. She said that Bernie's mom told her that, as a baby and infant, he hadn't developed normal communication. You also learned that although Bernie's parents once thought he was deaf, he was recently tested and found to have normal hearing. Testing also revealed that Bernie was identified as having a pervasive developmental disorder called autism. What is autism?

The various cases that you have just read illustrate several of the psychological disorders that cause anguish in the lives of children and their parents. But do specific child behaviors automatically mean that a child has a disorder? Do nondisordered children display troubled behavior on occasion? Consider the following example, where no one specific disorder is being illustrated, but the behavior pattern is disturbed nonetheless.

Ginger, like most of the girls in her neighborhood, went to a summer camp organized by the local community athletic program. The girls had various likes and dislikes about the camp, but on average they felt that it was one of the great fun activities of their summer. The adults who ran the camp had been given special instructions regarding Ginger. All sharp objects, especially pins, paperclips, and needles had to be kept away from her. It wasn't to protect others from harm, but because Ginger would "stick" herself. During the spring just before this year's camp, inch-long pins were found in her thumb. One needle had entered a vein in her leg and required that she be taken to the emergency room. Besides keeping pins and needles away from Ginger, what else can be done about such self-injurious behavior?

Childhood disorders are widespread, and examples of children with psychological problems are easy for us to recall and recount. Indeed, after over 35 combined years in the field—providing psychological assessment, diagnosis, and therapy for children in private practice, clinic, and hospital settings, and conducting research on childhood disorders—and after 20 years for one of us (PCK) volunteering as a coach with community youth sports programs, it would be easy to provide many more illustrations of both mild and extreme maladaptive child behavior. It would also be easy to provide examples of what might appear to be a disturbing behavior but which, on closer inspection, is merely a transient adjustment issue for an otherwise nondisturbed child. Indeed, it is one of the themes of this book that, although there are many disorders of childhood and many children who suffer from these disorders, there are many more youngsters who may temporarily experience emotional distress, display defiant behavior only on occasion, evidence transient scattered and impulsive thinking, or otherwise disturb teachers and parents only quite intermittently. It is essential to note that not all of these transient outbursts reflect psychological disorders—it is part of normal development to face and wrestle with emotional and social demands. To label all distress as a disorder is to over-pathologize normal variations in behavior and normal struggles with developmental challenges. Consider this one last example.

Steve, a 12-year-old basketball player, sat on the bench while his teammates struggled to try to come from behind.

His team was losing the important playoff game by 12 points, with only 3 minutes left to play. On any given day, it would be unanimous among the coaches that Steve should be in the game, playing guard. He is one of the best defensive players with a knack for stealing the ball and making the breakaway lay-up. His teammates too wanted to have him in the game for the last 3 minutes. This day, however, was different. He had received two technical fouls and was therefore ineligible to play. In the first quarter, when he was called for a foul, he turned to the referee and chided him with a comment and a "face." Referees may tolerate such acts in the professional sports, especially from the stars, but the referees in youth sports try to build good sportsmanship and they do not tolerate such antics. At halftime, in front of many spectators, Steve yelled to his coach, "That ref hates me, 'cause I made his kid look bad in a game a few weeks ago . . . The ref stinks, we should protest." A spectator who saw only this game might think that Steve is a "hot head" or that he has a problem controlling his anger. In fact, the spectator would be wrong. Steve plays aggressively, as one should in the game of basketball. He also plays "smart"—he knows the rules and works within them to give his team an advantage. For the entire season, he had a total of zero technical fouls and had not previously fouled out of a game. Today, unlike other days, Steve was frustrated and tired. He was at a sleepover the evening before the game, had been teased mercilessly by his friend's older brother, and, missing his mother's cooking, he didn't eat well. Steve's behavior on this day was not a model of ideal adjustment, but neither was it a sign or signal of serious disturbance.

Introducing some of the questions

Our journey through the psychological disorders of childhood provides information about what such disorders may look like to observers or feel like for the child, about the possible causes of the problems, the course of the disorders across the life span, as well as the treatments that are used to help rectify the childhood disorders. Some of the topics that we address will help to clarify and answer some of the questions that may have come to mind as you read the examples just presented. If you haven't yet made a list of questions, you may want to do so. The following may spark your thinking. Perhaps some of these questions will sound familiar to you.

- Do children act out their psychological problems? Does their behavior reflect the quality of their inner psychological adjustment?
- Does divorce typically reduce the distress of a troubled marriage and will it help the children? Does divorce have differential effects for children at different ages?
- Can children become depressed; how do they display dysphoria; and how do they handle feelings of sadness?
- Are psychological disorders the product of genetics, without concern for the quality of their parenting or living environments? Stated simply, are children with disorders born that way?
- To what extent are the child-rearing practices of caregivers responsible for the psychological well-being of their children?
- Unlike adults, children do not seek psychological help for themselves. What brings them to treatment?
- Can someone really lose weight by vomiting after eating? Is it safe? Is it healthy?
- What level of psychological adjustment can children with low IQs attain as they grow older?
- What is autism, and what causes it?
- Are rates of childhood disorders increasing? What factors might explain the increased prevalence of a childhood disorder?
- To what length can caregivers go to prevent a child from hurting him- or herself?
- Many troublesome behaviors or outbursts are transient—part of mastering the challenges of development. How do we differentiate between genuine disorders and routine struggles with adjustment?

Our discussion of the psychological disorders of youth is divided into several chapters. In Chapter 2 we overview the models that are offered to help organize and understand psychological disorder. We then examine several of the issues that impinge on our study of the disorders of childhood (Chapter 3). In the next two chapters we consider separately two behavior disorders—conduct disorder and attention-deficit hyperactivity disorder. The chapters that come after these behavior disorders address, separately, the emotional disorders of anxiety (Chapter 6) and depression (Chapter 7). Eating disorders, due to their initial appearance in the early years, are considered disorders of youth and are addressed in Chapter 8. The disorders associated with intellectual and learning performance are examined in Chapter 9. The pervasive developmental disorders are considered in Chapter 10. A discussion of tics and the elimination disorders is presented in Chapter 11. Challenging questions are posed in the closing chapter, where you are asked to consider not only the questions and their potential answers, but also the implications of the various possible answers for you in particular, and for society in general.

There are a few emphases that will be evident as you progress through this book. First, it is important that we use knowledge about normal development to make decisions about the presence of abnormality. The descriptions of the disorders provide a sense of the disturbance, but judgments of disorder require comparisons against normal variations in behavior.

Second, the role of the family will be given emphasis. The family is the child's most powerful social context and as such plays an important role in the onset and course of psychological difficulties. Third, there is a strong emphasis on the empirical research literature: the studies that have been conducted and published are the basis for the information provided. This holds true for the descriptions of the nature of the disorders as well as the presentation of the interventions used to treat the disorders (Hibbs & Jensen, 2005; Kazdin & Weisz, 2006; Ollendick, King, & Chorpita, 2006). Although the research base will be apparent, it does not take away from the fact that the children we are discussing are real people with real lives—numerous cases are presented to communicate the needed sensitivity to human struggle often associated with psychological distress. The names have been changed, but the authenticity of the struggles remains.

Models of childhood disorders 2

Researchers have been conscientious, and the psychological literature abounds with the results of studies of the nature of the various childhood disorders. How can we organize our information about childhood disorders to guide future studies and applications? What is needed is a guiding framework—a model—to help conceptualize and organize the data about the onset and development of maladaptive behavior. Models stimulate hypotheses, and research tests the validity of the model's assumptions.

Several models pertinent to the study of the childhood disorders will be overviewed: the biological, behavioral, cognitive, psychodynamic, and systems models (see also Sonuga-Barke, 1998). No one grand model will explain all child psychopathology. However, focused versions of the models often do provide a satisfactory framework for understanding a specific disorder, and models that integrate features of these models are most promising. For example, a cognitive-behavioral model integrates learning theory with human information processing, and a diathesis-stress model involves the interaction of biological predispositions and environmental stressors. Integrative models, especially those focused on specific disorders, offer useful frameworks for understanding many of the child disorders.

Biological models

Biological models suggest that the symptoms of psychological disorders are caused by biological factors. Such models are variously referred to as medical, organic, biomedical, or disease models. Biological models may identify or suggest abnormalities in brain structure or function, infectious transmission, neurotransmitter dysregulations, and genetic predispositions as possible sources of psychological disorders.

The brain

The brain plays an important role within the biological model. Two major ways that the brain is suspected of producing psychopathology concern abnormalities in the *structure* of the brain and in *communication* across the brain structures. Advances in non-invasive neuro-imaging technology now provide windows into the living brain in ways previously unimagined (Gerber & Peterson, 2008). In particular, magnetic resonance imaging (MRI) produces high-resolution images without any radiation exposure. MRI provides cross-sectional anatomical images that reveal the physical appearance of the brain, including physical abnormalities such as inflammation, tissue damage, bleeding, and tumors. One variant of MRI, called functional MRI or fMRI, produces images of time-dependent neuronal changes that are linked with an individual's performance on a cognitive or behavioral task. These images approximate the brain "in motion" by comparing the appearance of the brain during a target behavior (e.g., reading) and a baseline/control task (e.g., looking at dots), offering both structural and functional information about the brain. Another variant of the MRI, diffusion tensor imaging or DTI, reveals the connectivity of the brain by identifying and characterizing white matter pathways central to communication across brain regions (Cascio, Gerig, & Piven, 2007; Marsh, Gerber, & Peterson, 2008).

Consisting of billions of cells, the brain is the most complex of all body parts. Different collections of neurons in different regions of the brain are responsible for certain functions. For example, the cerebral cortex is primarily responsible for sensory processing, motor control, and higher mental functioning involving complex information processing, learning, memory, planning, and judgment. The brain has three sections: the forebrain, the midbrain, and the hindbrain. The forebrain consists of the two cerebral hemispheres, the thalamus, and the hypothalamus. The thalamus, for instance, is important in the processing and relaying of information between other regions of the central nervous system and the cerebral cortex, and the hypothalamus regulates hunger, thirst, sex drive, and body temperature. The limbic system, which includes parts of the cortex, the thalamus, and hypothalamus, provides homeostasis, or constancy of the internal environment, by regulating the activity of endocrine glands and the autonomic nervous system. These structures all play critical roles in emotions and drives (Kalat, 2007).

Below the forebrain is the midbrain, a way station that coordinates communications between the forebrain and the region just below it called the hindbrain. The hindbrain contains the pons, medulla, and reticular activating system and is connected to the spinal cord. The pons is involved in sleeping, waking, and dreaming; the medulla regulates breathing and heart rate. The pathways from other regions of the brain pass through the pons and medulla. The reticular activating system is a network of neurons that screens incoming information and arouses other areas of the brain.

Biological abnormalities in these structures can arise in numerous ways. A child might be born with an inordinately small or oddly formed brain structure. An injury resulting from complications at birth or a severe blow to the head might disturb a part of the brain and/or disrupt its development. More subtle processes such as prenatal exposure to toxins (e.g., drugs, alcohol, pollutants, viruses) can also alter the growth and development of the brain (Buka, Cannon, Torrey, & Yolken, 2008). Increasing evidence shows that early trauma and stress can have adverse effects on the developing brain (DeBellis et al., 1999). Whatever their source, anatomical abnormalities have been linked to some psychological disorders.

Interest in the biological model of psychopathology focuses not only on abnormalities in neural structures, but also in neural communication (Breedlove, Rosenzweig, & Watson, 2007). For human behavior to take place there must be communication in the brain.

The billions of neurons in the brain communicate by transmitting chemical signals, known as neurotransmitters, to one another (Kolb & Whishaw, 2008; Sejnowski, Koch, & Churchland, 1988). In a process known as neurotransmission, a neuron receives a chemical signal or message in the form of a neurotransmitter and, if the signal is excitatory, transforms the chemical message into an electrical impulse that passes through the neuron. In colloquial terms the neuron is said to be "firing." When the electrical impulse reaches the end of the neuron, it prompts neurotransmitters to be released. They cross the synaptic cleft at the synapse (i.e., the spatial gap between each neuron) and thereby pass on the signal to the next cell. Neurons receive messages from up to 10,000–20,000 other neurons at a time, sending either excitatory signals (which encourage the receiving neuron to fire) or inhibitory signals (which discourage the neuron from firing). Whether a neuron releases neurotransmitters and effectively propagates a message "down the line" is determined by a process known as summation, in which the excitatory and inhibitory signals received in the neuron are integrated. If the net excitatory effect is sufficiently greater than the net inhibitory effect, the neuron will propagate the signal to other neurons. Neurotransmitter substances are hot topics for research and scientists have so far discovered more than 50 different types of neurotransmitters in the brain—and these different neurotransmitters serve different functions in different regions of the brain.

Neurotransmission is not an elementary process. It can go awry in many ways because the processes governing both the release and reabsorption of a particular neurotransmitter substance are highly complex. Neurotransmission problems can involve dysregulated production and/or availability of neurotransmitters, release of neurotransmitters across the synaptic cleft, binding of neurotransmitter on receptors, or the presence or absence of neurons that inhibit neural connections and the interrelationships between the different neurotransmitters. These neurotransmission problems can contribute to psychopathology. Moreover, the effects on behavior can emerge when environmental forces such as stress inhibit synaptic transmission, or when medications used to treat the symptoms of certain mental disorders affect the neurotransmitter process.

Genetics

Chromosomes carry codes for the potential expression of characteristics in their basic units, genes. Each human cell normally contains 23 pairs of chromosomes. Genes control innumerable characteristics such as eye color, hair color, male baldness, and color blindness. Do genes carry a code for psychological disorders?

The idea that mental disorders might be inherited is a very old one, and clinicians have long observed that some forms of psychological disorder run in families. Some argue that the heritability of certain traits and even specific disorders is indisputable (Bouchard, Lykken, McGue, Segal, & Tellegen, 1990; State, Lombroso, Pauls, & Leckman, 2000). Monozygotic (identical) twins who share the same genetic makeup are more likely to share the same disorder than are dizygotic (fraternal) twins who share only 50% of their genes—like any other sibling pairs. For example, consider the data on the typically adult disorder schizophrenia (see Chapter 10). The average rate for adult schizophrenia in the full population is 1%. Yet studies have shown that when one monozygotic twin has schizophrenia, in about 40–50% of cases the other twin will also have schizophrenia. In comparison, under these same circumstances only 5–15% of dizygotic twins will have the disorder (Gottesman & Erlenmeyer-Kimling, 2001; Gottesman, McGuffin, & Farmer, 1987; Gottesman & Shields, 1972). Although none of the childhood disorders show such a conspicuous genetic contribution, schizophrenia is a sound illustration that genetics can play a meaningful role in psychological disorders. But genes are not autonomous over behavior: Genes are influenced by other factors and, often, these factors are environmental (Nelson & Bloom, 1997).

Evaluating the biological model

Advocates of the biological model have identified how infectious agents, structural abnormalities, neurotransmitter dysregulations, and genetic predispositions might contribute to or produce psychological disorders. Schizophrenia, for example, has a genetic component. In addition, the biological model of psychological disorder has stimulated advances in medical treatments that have had positive effects. Psychoactive medications have helped countless thousands of youngsters to better manage their conditions.

As biological influences are identified, however, it is important that they are not automatically deemed to be the sole cause of disorder. Instead, they should be recognized and placed among the several causal factors. As noted, the monozygotic twin of an individual with schizophrenia—who shares 100% of the twin's genetic makeup—has only up to a 50% chance of having schizophrenia as well. An attempt is made throughout this book to stipulate the need for integrated models linking biological vulnerability with social and psychological factors that lead to disorder in some individuals but not in others.

The biological model also has several potential shortcomings. First, an exclusive focus on biological processes does not appear relevant to most problems, and may lead us to ignore or downplay the important contributions of personal learning histories, ongoing interpersonal conflicts, or cognitive misperceptions of interpersonal events in the search for defective genes.

A second area of concern is the quality of brain images. Despite the improved resolution of images of the live brain provided by current imaging technologies, the pictures offered are still crude when compared to the seemingly infinite detail and complexity of the human brain (see Peterson, 2003). In addition, with current technology individuals must lay relatively still in a laboratory when undergoing magnetic resonance imaging, and thus our window into the functioning brain does not reveal brain functioning in naturalistic settings while performing complex, "real world" tasks.

Third, research in molecular and population genetics has made it increasingly clear that childhood mental disorders do not exhibit single-gene inheritance patterns. Research has shifted to the search for multiple susceptibility genes that may, under specific circum-stances, increase vulnerability for the development of psychopathol-ogy (Sanders, Duan, & Gejman, 2004; State et al., 2000). For example, the inheritance for autism likely involves the interaction of more than 15 genes, with each contributing only a relatively small risk (Happe, Ronald, & Plomin, 2006; State et al., 2000).

Finally, the scientific status of biological factors as causal agents in disorder is far from established. The discoveries of neurochemical or other biological differences between people with disorders and normal (nondisturbed) people, for example, do not indicate whether the biological difference is the cause or merely a by-product of the presence of the disorder. Similarly, the success of medications in treating disorders is not itself evidence that the disorder arose from biological causes. We can successfully treat a fever with aspirin, for example, but that does not mean that the lack of aspirin was the underlying cause of the fever.

Behaviorism: The learning models

Rapidly growing since the 1960s, behaviorism concerns the manner in which human behavior is acquired or learned. Behavior occurs as a consequence of its having been learned in the past. Behaviorally oriented psychologists underscore the role of reinforcement, pleasant events, and a person's learning history, as well as the role of the current social and interpersonal environment, as forces contributing to adaptive as well as maladaptive (disordered) behavior.

The behavioral model emphasizes the observable behavior of the child and the environmental factors that maintain the action. Beha-viorists believe that when other influencing factors are constant, the differences that exist among children are the result of learning. Beha-vior patterns, both normal and abnormal, are influenced greatly by the existing environment, and changes in the environmental influences will change the behavior pattern (Masters, Burish, Hollon, & Rimm, 1987; O'Leary & Wilson, 1987). Three forms of learning that can con-tribute to our understanding of psychological disorders are classical conditioning, operant conditioning, and observational learning.

Classical conditioning

A basic form of learning, classical conditioning involves once neutral stimuli that come to evoke involuntary responses. Classical conditioning (Pavlov, 1928) involves both conditioned (learned) and unconditioned stimuli and responses. If you found yourself stuck in a dangerous location, such as on the center lines dividing traffic on a major highway, then your being afraid would be perfectly normal and adaptive. However, people can learn to be afraid of things and situations when it is not normal or adaptive to be fearful. Classical conditioning helps us understand the development of these fears.

To begin, a realistically dangerous situation produces fear without prior learning or conditioning. Because this fear occurs without learning or conditioning, the dangerous situation is called an unconditioned stimulus (UCS) and the reaction, fear, is the unconditioned response (UCR). They occur naturally. A neutral stimulus does not itself produce a response. However, a neutral stimulus that is repeatedly paired with a dangerous situation becomes a conditioned stimulus (CS) and can itself lead to the UCR, fear. When the neutral situation itself becomes capable of producing fear, the fear it produces is called a conditioned response (CR). It is the conditioned (learned) responses that are of particular interest in psychopathology. For example, a specific piece of music played repeatedly in a dangerous situation becomes capable of producing fear. Think of the two-note theme from the movie *Jaws*. The music is a CS because it has acquired the fear-producing properties via conditioning, and the fear it produces is a CR.

Through conditioning processes, each of us has developed preferences and other reactions, and possibly even fears. Many researchers have used classical conditioning to explain the development of the psychological disorders called phobias, which are specific fears of a specific object or situation (e.g., fear of dogs). Fortunately, the principles of classical conditioning can and have been applied as a treatment to reduce and eliminate maladaptive fears.

Operant conditioning

Operant conditioning is concerned with the consequences of behavior—the probability that a response will be increased or decreased when it is followed by reinforcement or punishment (Thorndike, 1898). When responses lead to satisfying consequences, the responses are strengthened and more likely to occur in the future. When responses lead to unsatisfying consequences, they are not strengthened and are less likely to occur again in the future; this, then, was Thorndike's law of effect.

Skinner (1953) further developed the theory of behavioral consequences and used the principle of reinforcement to describe how behavioral consequences can strengthen the probability of behaviors recurring. There are numerous contingencies that have been described and researched, and Skinner's operant conditioning has had significant effects on psychological research and theory (see *American Psychologist*, 1992).

Punishment occurs when a response leads to a negative outcome. A dog who jumps on a visitor might be swatted on the rump, and a misbehaving student could be corrected in front of peers in class. Each of these illustrates the principle of punishment. Following an unwanted behavior with a negative outcome will reduce the likelihood of the unwanted behavior in the future. Although punishment can have desirable effects, it can also be detrimental. When harsh or excessive, punishment can cause serious inhibitions. A child who is punished too often may become overly withdrawn, unwilling to do anything, aggressive, and potentially depressed.

When positive consequences follow a behavior, the behavior is positively reinforced (rewarded) and is more likely to occur again in the future. Maladaptive behaviors, as well as desired patterns of behavior, can be acquired through their consequences. When a child screams or has a tantrum about a cookie, she may get her way because the parent simply wants to quiet her. But the child is also learning that tantrums (or the screaming behavior) produce rewards. More tantrums will follow.

What about more complex behavior? After all, human existence is not simply one behavior or another. Complex behaviors need not be directly reinforced for the behavior to be learned. The process of rewarding successive approximations, called shaping, does not require the learner to produce an entire new response pattern to receive the reinforcement. The shaping process is gradual, providing reinforcement for several interim steps. As the learner masters a new step, reinforcement shifts so that it is provided only after this new last step. Thus, an individual does not learn all at once to be verbally loud and vulgar—the undesirable behavior can be the result of a shaping process that has taken years to complete.

The shaping of behavior has important implications for child development (Gewirtz & Peláez-Nogueras, 1992) and for understanding and treating childhood disorders (Mash, 2006). For instance, complex, disturbed behavior patterns need not themselves be reinforced. The maladaptive pattern can be shaped over time as small portions of the disturbed pattern are reinforced. A pattern of aggression, for example, might be shaped by rewards for successive approximations of violence:

> Matt was sloppily dressed and wore a sneer on his face. He sat quietly, slumped in a chair and gazing out a window, as the Principal dialed his mother's work phone number. It was his third visit to the office for disciplinary action, and he knew that he was about to be suspended from school for having been involved in a fight in the hallway. His year in school was not going well—grades were poor, he didn't do well in sports, and he wasn't exactly popular—but he really didn't care. Although there were many and varied reasons for Matt's situation, and many factors that contributed to his aggressive behavior pattern, a few of the early learning experiences described by his mother, Anita, stood out. It seems that Matt, as early as age 3, was being encouraged and taught by his father (Jerry) to "fight for his rights." Anita noted that when Matt was 7 and was roughed up by a neighborhood boy who was a year older, Jerry was really upset and taught Matt how to fistfight. Anita also recalled that Jerry wouldn't discipline Matt or try to limit his fighting; instead he would pat him on the back for being tough. Matt wasn't a very thoughtful boy and he couldn't express his emotions well—instead, it seemed that he had learned from his father that fighting was the solution to problems.

Another type of reinforcement is negative reinforcement, in which the likelihood of a behavior increases by the removal of a negative (unpleasant) stimulus or situation. For example, if you politely ask a roommate to turn off the television so you can study, and your roommate does so immediately, the likelihood of your making a similar polite request in the future is increased. The polite request was reinforced by the removal of the unwanted (aversive) television distraction.

Additional stimulus–response relationships include escape and avoidance. An escape response stops a negative condition, whereas an avoidance response prevents a negative condition. Consider the following example:

> Sue had procrastinated on some tasks and had been up late the night before. Now she is sleeping with an alarm

clock set to go off at 5:30 am. When the loud and aversive alarm rings, Sue reaches out of bed and hits the snooze button. The snooze button "stops" the aversive alarm (an escape response) for 10 minutes. Sue returns to bed but in a few minutes realizes that the alarm will sound again at 5:40. When it does she slaps the snooze button again (escape response) for another 10 minutes of rest. The alarm will sound again at 5:50, only this time Sue looks at the clock at 5:49 and presses the snooze button to "prevent" the alarm from sounding—an avoidance response.

In this case, the avoidance response works. However, people can learn avoidance responses that are not functional. As will be discussed in Chapter 6 on anxiety disorders, anxious people make responses that they believe will prevent an aversive situation, but which, in fact, do not. The avoidance response offers a remarkable explanation for some of the anxiety disorders. For example, a young girl attends a school dance and is teased by a group of students. The teasing soon becomes harshly delivered ridicule, and it badly hurts her feelings. To stop the pain, she leaves the dance (an escape response). Because of this experience, in the future she will be more likely to run away from peers and potential ridicule, and will perhaps leave the presence of peers sooner. Eventually, staying away from peer interaction becomes associated with anxiety reduction—an avoidance response that prevents the experience of unwanted emotions. The avoidance response may continue despite the fact that students are no longer likely to tease and ridicule her. Patterns of behavior such as these are the result of avoidance learning. They occur, for example, in children and later adults with social phobia, in which individuals avoid feared social or performance situations, even though these behaviors may interfere with social and work relationships. Avoidance responses are persistent and, unfortunately, individuals who have acquired avoidance habits often continue to use them when they are no longer needed.

Observational learning

Modeling, or observational learning, is another manner of learning. Why was the first author of this book embarrassed when his then 5-year-old son dunked his croissant in his milk at a somewhat formal brunch? The answer: He knew where his son learned to dunk breakfast pastry! Dunking is not genetic, nor did the author ever reward his son for dunking. He has simply watched me dunk various pastries into my morning coffee and has, through observation, learned to do the same. Modeling is the process of learning behavior by observing others (Bandura, 1969). A tennis trainee who watches the coach demonstrate (or model) the desired motions of a serve and then practices what she has seen is learning through observation.

Many behavior patterns can be traced to observation experiences. For instance, how little or how much alcohol a person consumes can be influenced by the drinking behavior that the individual observes from others. True, alcohol consumption can have many diverse causes, but modeling effects exist nonetheless. Alcoholics who observed several confederates consume wine at high or low rates adjusted their own wine consumption according to the models' consumption (DeRicco & Niemann, 1980; see also Borsari & Carey, 2001). Children can acquire fearful and avoidant patterns of behavior simply by observing anxiety in their parents and peers (Askew & Field, 2008; Gerull & Rapee, 2002). Aggressive acts such as karate kicks or chops can increase as a result of popular television programs or movies that model and highlight such attacks.

Observational learning is a part of social learning theory (Bandura, 1986), which proposes that behavior is the product of both external stimulus events and internal cognitive processes. An individual's social context is important because it provides many opportunities for behaviors to be observed and imitated. When researchers report that certain disorders run in families, it is often difficult to separate the effects of genetics from the effects of the shared social learning environment. Social learning explanations would discount brain abnormalities and downplay genetics, underscoring instead the role of what has been modeled for and observed by the child. If a child has witnessed his parents use aggressive solutions to problems, and has spent time with his uncle who is loud, vulgar, and aggressive and who has been arrested several times, then the child has been exposed to and may have learned a troublesome pattern of behavior.

Evaluating the behavioral approach

To its credit, the behavioral approach has produced voluminous research, including explanations for the development of certain types of abnormality, and specific methods for treating childhood disorders. Because the model focuses on the child's environment, it is especially sensitive to cultural and social factors. Similarly, by being concerned with the learning history and environment of individuals, there is an implicit concern with ethnic and gender influences.

Learning explanations of psychological disorders, however, have been criticized as oversimplified. For instance, behavioral studies of aggression and violence often rely on a count of aggressive acts. Critics argue that aggression results from complex causes including biological, familial, and cultural factors, and to explain them solely in terms of prior learning is too delimiting.

A second criticism of behaviorism is that its attempt to explain maladaptive behavior without considering the unobservable aspects of human experience downplays the role of cognition in abnormality. For many, we are more than simply the sum of our experiences and observations. Critics of an exclusive focus on environmental determinants of behavior are quick to point out that different people can have widely divergent responses to the very same experience. Have you ever watched a horror movie with a friend and discovered that only one of you found it frightening? In addition, learning can often occur in the absence of any direct experience or observation (Dwyer, 2003; Field, 2006). Such criticisms, however, have been addressed in large part by the modern, integrative model (discussed later) called cognitive-behaviorism.

Cognitive model

How human beings perceive, recognize, attend, reason, and judge has come to play an important role in attempts to understand the development of disorders. Cognitive models emphasize that cognitive functioning contributes to emotional or behavioral distress. Misperceptions of social situations, a tendency to think negatively without sufficient data, and a habit of inaccurately blaming oneself for mishaps are examples of dysfunctional cognitive processing (see also Ellis & Harper, 1975):

> Jonathan is a 10-year-old who lives with his mother, has few friends, and stays in his home most of the time, every day. Jonathan has developed a characteristic way of evaluating the world—a cognitive structure—based on the potential of threat. Jonathan can't do anything without thinking of and worrying about threat and danger, even in what appear to us to be the most innocuous and appealing

activities. As a result, he perceives as threats the very situations and events that are not stressful for most people. When Jonathan is introduced to someone, he sees the experience not as a chance to make a friend, but rather as a risk that puts him in jeopardy. He frequently says to himself, "What will he think of me or do to me? Will he try to hurt me?" When at an amusement park, amusement does not come to Jonathan's mind so much as the risks of accidents on the rides, the possibility of getting separated or lost, and the risk of eating foods that will upset his stomach. Jonathan hardly notices the numerous opportunities for widespread fun.

Distortions and deficiencies

The cognitive processing of children can be differentiated in an important manner—distinguishing between cognitive distortions and cognitive deficiencies (Kendall, 1993). Cognitive deficiencies refer to the absence of thinking—such as when a child's responses and emotional states do not benefit from careful thinking or planning. In contrast, cognitive distortions refer to thought processes that are dysfunctional, such as active misperceptions and misconstruals of the environment.

The different types of cognitive processing mistakes have been linked to different types of childhood disorders (see Kendall & MacDonald, 1993). Distortions in information processing have been implicated in adult depression (Alloy, Abramson, Murray, Whitehouse, & Hogan, 1997; Beck, 1976; Ingram, 2003; Ingram, Miranda, & Segal, 2006; Safren, Heimberg, Lerner, Henin, Warman, & Kendall, 2000), anxiety (e.g., Beck & Emery, 1985), and several other psychological abnormalities (see Dobson & Kendall, 1993; Ingram, 1986), as well as in childhood depression and anxiety (Leung & Wong, 1998; Muris & Field, 2008; Sood & Kendall, 2007; Vasey & MacLeod, 2001; Weems, Costa, Watts, Taylor, & Cannon, 2007). Deficiencies in active information processing are linked to other childhood disorders, such as the interpersonal problem-solving deficits and information-seeking deficits evident in impulsive children, and the problems seen in related types of child psychopathology (Bijttebier, Vasey, & Braet, 2003).

An example of a cognitive model is the one proposed by Beck to help explain depression. This model has received substantial research and clinical attention. According to Beck (1967, 1976, 1987), individuals, early in life, begin to formulate rules about how the world works, and that, for depressed persons, these rules are based on erroneous ideas and beliefs. An individual continues to distort life experiences through characteristic errors in perceiving and thinking about events, event outcomes, personal attributes, and interpersonal relations. These features define the cognitive model of depression. Accordingly, in depression, thought content centers on the experience of major loss, the anticipation of negative outcomes, and the sense of being inadequate.

Evaluating cognitive models

Criticisms have been leveled at the cognitive models. For example, "thought" is only part of the complex system in which people exist. What about the biological, emotional, and interpersonal factors that influence people's lives? Still others have commented that it is not yet clear whether cognitive factors are causally linked to disorder (e.g., Coyne, 1982). They have suggested that the cognitive dysfunctions that are found may be consequences or correlates of disorder rather than causes. These criticisms have led cognitive researchers to examine the role of dysfunctional thinking as a vulnerability factor (e.g., Ingram, 2003): People with maladaptive cognitive processes are at risk for psychological disorder (Abela & Hankin, 2008; Alloy, Abramson, Walshaw, & Neeren, 2006; Riskind & Alloy, 2006; Ingram, 2003).

Critics of the cognitive model point out that many psychologically disturbed people live under objectively horrible life circumstances that are not easily reduced to "irrational" or distorted thinking. Another concern voiced about cognitive factors has to do with the difficulty of verification. People report their thoughts, but reporting one's beliefs is fraught with difficulties (Smith & Allred, 1986; Westen & Shedler, 2007). A person who holds irrational beliefs, for instance, may not be aware that they are irrational. As the cognitive models of psychological disorder continue to make advances, these criticisms deserve further attention.

Cognitive-behavioral model

The cognitive-behavioral model emphasizes the learning process and the influences of the environment, while underscoring the importance of cognitive-mediating and information-processing factors in the development and treatment of psychological disorders (Kendall,

1993). Accordingly, this model proposes treatments aimed at modifying the client's perceptions, evaluations, and processing of events, while employing behavioral performance-based procedures, modeling, and rewards (e.g., Meichenbaum, 1985).

The cognitive-behavioral model is therefore an integrated model (Alford & Norcross, 1991). Cognitive-behaviorism is the result of movement from two perspectives (Kendall & Hollon, 1979; see also Craighead, Meyers, & Craighead, 1985). Behavioral theorists have shown increased interest in the cognitive aspects of psychopathology, and psychodynamic and cognitive theorists have shown greater concern for the performance-based learning aspects of psychological disorders. Not all members of each camp have come together, but there has been sufficient and noticeable movement from both sides towards a middle ground, and the cognitive-behavioral model has served as a functional vehicle to encourage such integration (Mahoney, 1977, 1993; Meichenbaum, 1977, 1993).

Over the past several decades, there has been a tremendous amount of research supporting a cognitive-behavioral approach to childhood disorders. There has also been an increasing acceptance of this integrative model among mental health professionals. Consistent with this approach, major efforts have been made to identify and examine those psychological treatments that can be deemed "empirically supported" according to rigorous research criteria (Chambless & Ollendick, 2001). The majority of psychological treatments found to be empirically supported (efficacious) are cognitive-behavioral in nature (Ollendick & Davis, 2006; Silverman & Hinshaw, 2008). The increasingly popular cognitive-behavioral model has made great strides towards integrating the seemingly conflicting cognitive and behavioral theories that had previously been influential, but less dominant in the study of psychopathology.

Psychodynamic model

The psychodynamic model has historical significance. Toward the end of the 19th century, Freud broke new theoretical ground by offering the first truly psychological account of abnormal behavior (Freud, 1914, 1917/1943). His psychodynamic model emphasized that an understanding of psychopathology lay in the analysis of mental structures in conflict, levels of consciousness, defense mechanisms, and stages of psychosexual development.

Freud's theory is called psychodynamic because it is based on the belief that personality and psychological disorders are the outcome of dynamic interactions among mental (psycho) structures. According to Freud, thoughts, attitudes, and behaviors result from conflict among three mental structures—the ego, the id, and the superego (called intrapsychic conflict).

The part of you that wants satisfaction immediately was called the id. The id is an unorganized reservoir of wishes and passions of our basic sexual and aggressive drives; it strives for immediate gratification that bypasses the demands of reality, order, and logic. The superego is the storehouse of the moral and ethical standards taught by parents and culture (what we generally think of as "conscience"). When these standards are violated, the superego as conscience generates guilt.

Freud attributed finding a realistic means to resolve conflicts to the ego. The main function of the ego is to mediate the wishes of the id, the demands of reality, and the strictures of the superego. By regulating internal conflict and stress, the ego promotes adjustment. But, according to Freud, when the ego is not mediating effectively, conflict erupts and psychological abnormality emerges.

The conflicts Freud described may occur at various levels of awareness. Conscious material is that which we are aware of at any given time, and it changes constantly. Preconscious thoughts are those that are easily made conscious by the effort to remember or by the spark of a related idea. You may now be conscious that you are reading a book and, with a prompt, you could become conscious of the placement of your right foot. Some thoughts or memories are less accessible than others, but preconscious thought can potentially become conscious.

A major portion of mental activity such as the id is unconscious—that is, mental activity outside a person's normal awareness. Thoughts and ideas that are unconscious, according to Freud, press for expression, but may be withheld from consciousness because they are unacceptable to the ego or the superego. Sometimes, the ego is unable to gratify impulses or even unwilling to allow them access to consciousness. When these id impulses press for gratification or consciousness, the ego experiences intense anxiety.

When the ego experiences anxiety or the guilt induced by the superego, it protects itself with defense mechanisms. Defense mechanisms are said to be unconscious processes that try to protect the ego from anxiety provoked by unwanted or unacceptable impulses. These processes are defensive because they defend the self. As Brewin

(1997, p. 107) noted in his discussion of the distortion of meaning: "The impact of unsettling thoughts and memories may be much reduced by mental operations that suppress or transform them." By avoiding our unwanted feelings we avoid looking unacceptable and having our security undermined, and we make ourselves look better and put ourselves in a more flattering light. Yet these mechanisms may not be true to reality or true to another observer.

For instance, repression is the unconscious but purposeful exclusion of painful thoughts or unacceptable desires or impulses from consciousness. A person might, for example, fail to recall—or repress—being mistreated as a child. Repression is often regarded as the primary defense mechanism. Denial is another defense mechanism. In denial, the person simply does not accept or admit the presence of the threatening condition. Projection is a defense mechanism in which the person with the problem attributes their own unacceptable impulses or thoughts to others. When someone makes a socially acceptable explanation for a socially unacceptable behavior, this can be the defense mechanism called rationalization. Other defense mechanisms have been described by scholars of this theory.

According to Erdelyi (1985), defensive processes are the foundation on which the structure of psychodynamic theory rests. But experimental research on defense mechanisms has produced ambiguous results. For example, Erdelyi's (1985) review of the evidence regarding repression concluded that there can be selective rejection of information from awareness, that organisms tend to avoid aversive stimuli and defend themselves against pain, and that some psychological processes can occur outside of a person's awareness. However, although each of these separate features has some support, there still is no clear-cut demonstration of the entire phenomenon taking place all at once. Thus, although psychological studies have helped us to understand complex mental processes, unconscious defensive processes remain a challenge for research. The interested reader is referred to a contemporary "cognitive science" account of the unconscious (Power & Brewin, 1991).

According to Freud, if a person's defense mechanisms are unable to reduce or prevent unwanted anxious arousal, a neurosis may result. The term neurosis is of historical note (it is no longer used to label disorder) but it is still used on occasion to describe the conflicts seen in some persons. Neurotic individuals are said to exhibit intense infantile wishes and impulses. These impulses are so strong that they drive the individual to excessive and rigid use of defense mechanisms to contain them. Excessive repression, for example, keeps facts from awareness and can intensify personal conflict and interpersonal distress.

Although it was not central to Freud's theory, it is important to keep in mind that moderate use of numerous defense mechanisms is not abnormal. They can help us contain our own unwanted feelings, and they can keep us from behaving in less socially acceptable ways. However, defense mechanisms are maladaptive, and abnormal, when a few defenses are relied on excessively or used extensively.

For Freud, the idea of sexuality includes all sensual striving and satisfactions (Brennan, 1955). As a person develops from infancy to young adulthood, the focus of sexual or sensual pleasure changes from the mouth, to the anal area, to the genitals. In Freud's theory of personality development, he proposed five phases for psychosexual development.

In the oral stage, during which the major source of pleasure is the mouth, the infant seeks gratification through sucking, biting, and feeding. The oral stage covers the first year of life. The anal stage extends to about three-and-a-half years of age, through the period of toilet training. During this phase the child derives pleasure from the retention and expulsion of feces. Boys and girls differ in their experience of the next phase, the phallic stage. From about 3 to 5 or 6 years of age, the child's interest centers on the genitals and on masturbatory activities. Borrowing from the theme of the Greek tragedy, *Oedipus Rex*, Freud proposed that the phallic-aged boy develops a sexual attachment to his mother and views his father as his rival—the Oedipal dilemma. He wishes to see his father gone, and fears that his father wishes the same toward him. These wishes and fears conflict with the young boy's genuine love for his father. An adjusted individual resolves his dilemma by renouncing his desire for his mother and identifying with his father.

The Electra dilemma is the phallic-aged girl's experience of the analogous situation with her parents. According to Freud, the girl's shift away from mother and toward father is facilitated by her belief that it was her mother who deprived her of a penis and her subsequent development of what Freud called penis envy. The theory holds that if the child—either boy or girl—is unsuccessful in resolving these dilemmas, the conflict will linger unconsciously and form the basis of maladjustment in adulthood.

The child then enters a latency stage, from 6 or 7 to 11 years of age, during which the sexual drives seem to be inactive. The next phase, the genital stage, begins with puberty and is characterized by a reawakening and maturation of the sexual drives.

With each successive phase, functioning is increasingly mature. Experiencing inordinate gratification or frustration at any given phase can cause psychological difficulties at a later stage. Fixation refers to an excessive attachment to someone or something that is appropriate to an earlier level of development. A regression is a reversion to an earlier, and therefore more immature, form of behavior, usually as the result of some external stress or in response to internal conflict. Regression can occur in both normal and disturbed persons.

Modern neo-Freudian reconsiderations

Few would dispute that Freud's views have been stimulating and provocative, yet his theory is more historical than contemporary. Some writers, although maintaining features of the initial theory, have made changes to modernize it. For example, whereas Freud saw sexual impulses as the basis for neurotic anxiety, the neo-Freudians shifted away when ascribing centrality to the role of sexuality.

One modern spin-off from psychodynamic theory is object relations theory (Kernberg, 1976; Kohut, 1977; Mitchell, 1988). This perspective, which is derived from the idea that people are often the object of others' drives, de-emphasizes *intra*personal forces and counterforces and focuses instead on the influences of early *inter*-personal relationships. Contemporary object relations theorists are concerned with the role that human relationships play in the development of psychological abnormality. They believe that the early mother–child relationship is crucial to the child's development, self-concept, conceptions of others, and the quality of human relationships. Severe disturbances in early relationships can result in poor, if not chaotic, interpersonal relationships. Thus, the child's early interactions and impressions greatly influence later object relations.

Evaluating psychodynamics

Despite the impact of psychodynamic models, some have not withstood the test of time and many have not stood the tests of scientific study. After suggesting that there are only a few enduring contributions of the model, we note several of the weaknesses.

Some of Freud's observations were powerful and accurate. He recognized that a child's early experiences influence adult behavior and that internal conflict is an important source of psychological difficulty. The specific ideas about the dynamics of the conflict may not be correct, but there is widespread acceptance that human dysfunction can arise from the stress and conflict with which a person cannot cope effectively.

In perhaps one of his most enduring contributions, Freud described the unconscious and proposed that unconscious motives play a role in human behavior (see Freud, 1912/1984, 1915/1984). There is considerable agreement that human beings engage in behavior that appears to reflect processes they are not aware of, but exploring unconscious processes presents special problems for researchers.

Contemporary researchers are studying complex cognitive processes and their association to psychological disorders (see Dalgleish & Brewin, 2007; Dalgleish & Watts, 1990; Greenwald, McGhee, & Schwartz, 2008). Today, some researchers refer to unconscious processes whereas others refer to nonconscious processes (see Power & Brewin, 1991, for a discussion of this topic). Nonconscious processes have to do with the ways our learned experiences are organized and function without awareness (Kihlstrom, 1987). Well-learned and practical behaviors become automatic, and we may organize and implement our expectations, beliefs, and even memories without fully understanding or being aware of them.

Several items from Freud's original model have not been verified. First, regarding the universality of sexual and aggressive instincts as the basis for all human behavior—although these biological motives are powerful, other learned motives are powerful as well. Second, there is no evidence that human development unfolds according to Freud's psychosexual stages. Third, there is no compelling evidence that the hypothesized psychic structures (id, ego, superego) are needed as explanations of human disturbance.

Freud's theory was based on a sample of 20- to 45-year-old upper-middle-class women living in Vienna at a time when sexual expression was discouraged. Because his ideas were based on a sample that lacked the representativeness required for a comprehensive theory of human behavior, many have questioned whether the theories can be applied universally or generalized beyond the initial sample. Also, there is sexism in Freud's views, and this has been a source of criticism (Lips, 1988). He depicts women as inferior and suggested, for example, that they experienced envy or jealousy because they have no penis. Further, Freud theorized that a girl's belief that she had been castrated would produce feelings of inferiority in subsequent psychological development. Critics are quick to point out that Freud was not in a position to know what developing girls think as he did not study children—only the retrospective reports of frustrated adult female patients. When the theory is revised in a modern feminist fashion (Chodorow, 1978; Miletic, 2002), some of the strengths of the theory can be sifted from its inherent sexism.

Systems models

Most models of psychological functioning address the individual. But what about applying models of ongoing collections of or systems of people? Different perspectives have advanced different ideas about how a primary social system might contribute to childhood and to later psychological disorders. Often, a systems theory holds that the locus of pathology is not within the individual, who is designated the "patient," but within the family members' interrelationships (Nichols & Schwartz, 2007; Rothbaum, Rosen, Ujie, & Uchida, 2002).

Behaviorists emphasize the environment as a controlling and contributing factor in human behavior and identify the family system—especially the parents—as one of the most important environments (Braswell & Bloomquist, 1991; Brinkmeyer & Eyberg, 2003; McMahon & Forehand, 2005; Patterson & Bank, 1989). Behaviorally, parents can be influential in several ways: (1) through their own behavior, where they serve as models; (2) through their selectively rewarding activities within the family; and (3) through their creation of a social climate—parents may be hostile and rejecting or warm and accepting. Parents are central players within the family system and carry a great deal of influence.

With less emphasis on the parents' behavior but more emphasis on interpersonal relations, the object relations model also sees pathology as within the context of family relationships. One example of a psychodynamic family model addresses the eating disorder anorexia (see Chapter 8). Briefly, anorexia involves a preoccupation with "feeling fat" and accompanying efforts to lose weight—sometimes to the point of starvation. Anorexia typically occurs in female adolescents. Operating from what was once called the Philadelphia Child Guidance Clinic, Minuchin and his colleagues (Minuchin, Roseman, & Baker, 1978) described the characteristics of the family system with an anorexic child. These families were generally overprotective, rigid, and enmeshed, and tended to lack skills for conflict resolution.

Enmeshment in a family system refers to a situation in which no member can have a separate identity. There is an insistence that everyone in the family must be together, with a resulting absence of privacy. Rigidity is evident in an unwillingness to tolerate change, and overprotection is evident in an expression of concern at the least sign of discomfort. When a family denies that conflict exists, or changes the topic of conversation to avoid it, conflict is not resolved. Minuchin's family systems view of anorexia places the abnormality in the family—the female adolescent cannot achieve separation from the family, is denied privacy, feels overcontrolled, and strives for independence by controlling eating. The anorexia isn't her disorder!

Systems models of psychopathology are beginning to receive research evaluation, and family systems notions are being included in integrated models of psychopathology. What remains of central importance is that, unlike other models of psychopathology, systems approaches do not place the locus of the disorder within the individual, but within the system. An individual does not have a disorder; instead, he or she has a problem with patterns of interaction within the social system. Because the family is the primary social network for children, it is the interaction pattern within the family that is seen as dysfunctional and it is often this same interaction pattern that is the target for change in family therapy.

Diathesis-stress model

In the example of schizophrenia cited earlier, recall that genetic forces were influential, but the genetic factors did not account for all of the cases of schizophrenia. If the disorder were entirely genetic, then both members of an identical twin pair would receive an identical diagnosis. Therefore, nongenetic factors, such as environmental influences and stress, must also play a causal role.

The diathesis-stress model proposes an active interaction between genetic and other biological predispositions and stressful environmental influences. Diatheses are predisposing vulnerability factors, which include biological determinants and characteristic manners of responding. Stress is the current environmental factors that can, but do not always, contribute to the development of abnormal behavior. Common stressors for youngsters may include school, peer conflicts, loss of loved ones, physical accidents, exposure to family or community violence, or simply taking on too much responsibility or too many activities. According to this model, diatheses and stress are complementary; neither is sufficient by itself to cause abnormal behavior.

To further elucidate the diathesis-stress model, return to the example of schizophrenia where predisposing factors are involved, but they do not account for all of the data. The development of abnormality depends in part on the contribution of stresses and related environmental influences. As noted diathesis-stress theorist Meehl described in 1962, only those persons with a genetic makeup conducive to schizophrenia will develop the disorder, but they will become schizophrenic only if exposed to a detrimental learning environment and stressful life experience. This statement was designed for schizophrenia specifically, but has application to disorders in general: Complex interactions between the individual and the environment contribute to the behavior of the person (see also Cicchetti, 2007; Ogren & Lombroso, 2003; Rutter, Silberg, O'Connor, & Simonoff, 1999).

Changing times

Historically, models of psychopathology, including models of the childhood disorders, sought to explain all of human pathology and adjustment—they were universal models. One need not go beyond Freud's model to see the attempt to be all-encompassing. Such thinking is no longer advanced. Rather, grand and universal theories (models) are seen as so broad that they can never be adequately tested as a whole. Modern models of the development of childhood disorders do not expect universal applicability. Rather, there is an increase in the advancing of focused models—models that strive to explain single disorders. As will be evident throughout this book, certain models have been more or less successful in explaining some but not other disorders. Models specific to individual disorders are discussed in those chapters devoted to the specific disorders.

Another noteworthy trend is that models are becoming integrated. Although a full and comprehensive integration that receives uniform acceptance has not yet appeared, there are identifiable trends to support the view that modern integrative efforts, not unlike early integrations of psychodynamic and learning theories (Dollard & Miller, 1950), are reasonable and desirable. Both the diathesis-stress model and the cognitive-behavioral model, two models with fairly widespread acceptance, illustrate this integration.

Broad models of disorder have been offered as explanatory systems that hold true for boys and girls, and for majority as well as minority ethnic groups. Future developments, however, may witness greater gender and ethnic specificity.

Summary

Models are guiding frameworks to organize information. The biological, behavioral, cognitive, psychodynamic, and systems models have been influential in understanding childhood disorders. Currently, integrative models such as the diathesis-stress and cognitive-behavioral models are receiving increased attention.

Biological models are concerned with the role of disease, individual biochemistry, and human genetics in psychological disorders. Biological models examine the genetics of behavior and how neurotransmitter substances influence behavior.

Behaviorists emphasize the observable behavior of the person and the environmental factors that maintain the action. The behavioral models are concerned with maladaptive learning and use the outcomes of laboratory research as the cornerstone for this understanding. Classical conditioning describes how a behavior called a conditioned response is acquired through the pairing of unconditioned and conditioned stimuli. Operant conditioning refers to the strengthening of responses that occurs when they are followed by rewarding experiences. Modeling refers to observational learning—when an individual's behavior is influenced by having observed and imitated the behavior of someone else.

The cognitive model emphasizes that an individual's cognitive functioning contributes to any emotional or behavioral distress. Cognitive functioning influences psychological maladjustment. Cognitive deficiencies are the lack of forethought when it would be useful, and cognitive distortions are dysfunctional thought processes. Although cognitive models are sometimes difficult to assess, data suggest that cognitive functioning is associated with various disorders.

The cognitive-behavioral model is integrative—emphasizing both the process of learning behavior and the cognitive information-processing factors that influence such learning.

Freud's theory suggested that psychological disorders result from intrapsychic conflict. This model places important weight on the unconscious causes of behavior. Contemporary revisions of this theory include the object relations approach: a theory that refers to persons as objects of drives and places greatest emphasis on the interpersonal relationships and their role in individual psychopathology. One of Freud's lasting contributions was his identification of the unconscious. However, the nonrepresentativeness of his original subjects and the nonempirical features of the bulk of the theory are sources of concern.

Systems models suggest that an individual's symptoms are the result of a disturbed social system. For behaviorists, learning paradigms operate within the system. For psychodynamic theorists, it is the interpersonal dynamics that contribute to maladjustment.

The diathesis-stress model is a model of combined influences. Diatheses and stress interact. Diatheses are predisposing factors, whereas stress is current environmental factors. The model emphasizes the interaction of the predispositions and environmental stresses in psychological disorder.

The diathesis-stress model and the cognitive-behavioral model illustrate the current efforts to integrate models of psychopathology. Indeed, these models offer conceptualizations that have promise not only for understanding childhood disorders, but also for guiding its treatment. Researchers and practitioners have given these integrated approaches widespread endorsement.

Issues facing the disorders of childhood 3

There is a truism that is worth restating: Children are not "little adults." Obviously, they are often physically smaller, but they are also emotionally less mature, socially and cognitively still in the process of development, and, in terms of sheer experience, they are not yet fully seasoned. Not surprisingly, it is extremely difficult for children to recognize their own psychological problems.

Children also differ from adults in how they make contact with a mental health professional: the problems that bring them into treatment, in their response to certain therapies, and in the course of their disorders. Thus, the psychological difficulties of childhood require special study to be correctly understood and treated.

Researchers have estimated that 13–22% of the children and adolescents in the United States have problems severe enough to need treatment (e.g., Costello, Mustillo, Erkanli, Keeler, & Angold, 2003), but fewer than 20% of youngsters with current problems actually receive services (Tuma, 1989). And, as was found in a 20-year follow-up of children in London (Champion, Goodall, & Rutter, 1995), many of these troubled children go on to become adults with psychological disorders. In several disorders, the median age of onset is between 13 and 25; other disorders can be identified before age 7. Research shows that across the range of disorders, anxiety disorders and impulse control disorders show the earliest median onset (Kessler, Berglund, Demler, Jin, Merikangas, & Walters, 2005b). Regrettably, after onset of disorder the median delay in initiating treatment for those who eventually seek help ranges from 4 to 23 years, depending on the disorder (Wang, Berglund, Olfson, Pincus, Wells, & Kessler, 2005). Among those who do eventually seek care, earlier onset of disorder is associated with longer delays in initiating treatment.

Addressing childhood disorders is very important to both the individual and to society. In fact, disorders that typically onset in childhood are among those ranked highest in terms of global burden (Costello, Egger, & Angold, 2005), an estimate of the overall public health impact of disorders that incorporates associated reduced life quality, disability, functional impairment, lost productivity, and economic costs to the community. If left untreated, children do not outgrow serious problems, but instead can develop into adults with psychological disorders. For example, adults who are diagnosed as having an anxiety disorder have a very high frequency of having had anxiety disorders when they were children (e.g., Last, Hersen, Kazdin, Francis, & Grubb, 1987). Also, a grave psychological disorder in a child, even if transient, is likely to have serious consequences—often more serious than in an adult—because the disorder may encroach on the child's ability to successfully navigate challenges of normal development and meet critical developmental milestones (Cicchetti, 2006). A psychologically impaired child may fail to master key tasks that are faced at different ages such as developing self-esteem, establishing relationships with peers, resolving interpersonal conflict, and acquiring academic skills. These inadequacies may in turn lead to increased frustration and rejection. Moreover, once the critical developmental window for the establishment of self-esteem and other skills has passed, it may be difficult for some children to be given other opportunities to master the particular developmental challenges.

Almost all mental health professionals, across all of the models and theories that have been offered to explain human behavior, agree to one uniform tenet: the early formative years are important to later adjustment and difficulties during these years are the precursors of later maladjustment. The boy is father to the man. For example, once children learn to be unsociably aggressive, a substantial proportion tends to remain aggressive. Left untreated, aggression is a stable aspect of human behavior. In fact, the level of antisocial behavior in childhood has been found to predict the level of antisocial behavior in adulthood (e.g., Kokko & Pulkkinen, 2005; Robins & Price, 1991).

In the chapters that follow, we describe the symptoms of disorders, provide information about their prevalence, discuss research findings, and examine the nature and status of treatments for the disorders. However, before we address the nature and treatment of the specific disorders, four general issues facing childhood disorders in general will be discussed: developmental psychopathology, parenting and family factors, assessing and classifying childhood disorders, and treating disorders of childhood.

Developmental psychopathology

The human organism completes many changes over the life span. Many of these changes occur during childhood. These changes include cognitive, emotional, social, sexual, and biological elements, to name just a few. One branch of psychology, developmental psychology, studies these and other changes as a part of the course of normal human development. Knowledge from the study of normal development plays an important role in the determination of what constitutes a deviation in adjustment.

Emerging from the study of normal child development and its interface with child maladjustment (Cicchetti, 1993, 2006), developmental psychopathology views psychological maladjustment in relation to the major changes that occur across the life cycle. Developmental psychopathology integrates multiple theories and perspectives from across a host of disciplines to examine the complex interplay among biological, psychological, and contextual aspects of development and maladjustment, placing greatest emphasis on the rapid development that occurs between birth and maturity (Achenbach, 1990).

The importance of the interaction between the child and the social context is recognized and emphasized within developmental psychopathology. There are different behavioral styles as well as different beliefs about acceptable behavior, and if the "fit" between the person and the context is not good (e.g., an energetic child in a setting that is intolerant of even normal amounts of activity), maladjustment in the child may be what is seen by adults (Lerner, Hess, & Nitz, 1990). The person–context interaction of developmental psychopathology is embodied in the child's adjustment to the challenges of normal development (Sroufe & Rutter, 1984). For instance, consider the following developmental challenges. During ages 3 to 5, children face the developmental challenges of acquiring self-control, self-reliance, and peer contacts; ages 6 to 12 involve challenges of social understanding, whereas the challenges of adolescence address flexible thinking, emancipation, and identity. Success or failure in facing issues at one point in development are seen as laying the groundwork for success or failure when facing the issues that will need to be addressed later in life.

When evaluating the impact of various life stressors and circumstances on child adjustment, it is critical to consider the child's developmental level. A younger child with less advanced coping resources and emotional competencies may be less equipped to endure in the face of an adversity that may have minimal impact on an adolescent. Moreover, given that each acquired competency builds on the successful mastery of prior developmental achievements, experiencing a trauma early in life is likely to have a broader and more disabling life-course impact than experiencing that same trauma later in life. For example, child maltreatment can be associated with a host of negative consequences—including depression, anxiety, and substance use—but maltreatment experienced during the preschool years can interfere with satisfactory development of the most fundamental processes of memory, perception, and identity (Macfie, Cicchetti, & Toth, 2001). Indeed, such dissociation, thought to represent a potentially protective failure of information processes in the face of trauma (Bower & Sivers, 1998; Dalenberg et al., 2007; van der Kolk, van der Hart, & Marmar, 1996), is said to occur at higher rates among youth who experience very highly traumatic events prior to early developmental competencies in cognition and emotion.

The disorders of childhood are best seen against the backdrop of normal development. An important feature of developmental psychopathology is that it judges child disorders using the backdrop of what is normal for a given age (Campbell, 1986; Cicchetti, 2006). A specific behavior pattern is or is not considered maladaptive depending upon when in the child's development the behavior pattern is seen. A specific example will bring life to this point. Is it a disorder when a 4-year-old reports a specific fear—an extreme fear—such as fear of the dark? The parents are abashed and self-conscious about the child, and the child seems very distressed by even the mention of being in the dark. Normative data indicates that approximately 90% of children between the ages 2 and 14 reported at least one specific fear and that fear of the dark is a common fear for a child this age. It would hardly be appropriate to call such a fear abnormal when it appears instead to be a routine part of the challenges of normal development. In fact, it can be argued that it is through the overcoming of this fear or others like it that the child develops mastery and confidence for future encounters with novelty, the unknown, physical danger, or threat to self-esteem. In contrast, the same fear in a 22-year-old might be abnormal. Defining fears as abnormal depends on the age at which the fear is expressed, on the developmental atypicality of the fear, and on the disruption that results in daily functioning caused by such fears.

Parenting and family factors

The notion that the developing child's social context is important in psychological adjustment has been often stated and well ingrained, as noted in our earlier discussion of the systems and behavioral models of psychopathology. Not surprisingly, the child's family is considered a key social context.

Early—and now known to be incorrect—explanations of certain severe disorders blamed the mother. The childhood disorder autism was once thought to be the result of a cold and unloving mother. Although such an extreme explanation is now known not to be accurate (see Chapter 10), it nevertheless illustrates the prior tendency for mental health professionals, as well as nonprofessionals, to resort to early child rearing for explanations of psychological adjustment. Although this example was a fruitless path, other investigations have been more productive.

Some areas of research have been successful in identifying parenting styles that contribute to the development and maintenance of behavioral and emotional disorders of children. Later, in several chapters in this book, we review studies of the role of parenting behavior in the expression of conduct problems in the children, and the benefits of parent training to reduce child problems. Other research programs have identified biological causal factors, such as in Down syndrome, a form of mental retardation. Because the conclusions that can be reached vary across the different childhood disorders, detailed discussions and comments about the role of parenting practices are presented within the specific chapters on the specific disorders. For now, let's consider one general parenting topic— divorce—and what we know about its effects on children.

Divorce: Solution or detriment for children?

Divorce is a worldwide phenomenon: Although the frequency and acceptance of divorce varies across cultures and generations, the dissolution of marriage occurs at alarming rates. Consider, for example, the data on divorce in the US. Roughly half of the marriage contracts do not last (Bramlett & Mosher, 2002) and approximately 40% of children grow up in a divorced family. Divorce in Europe is also quite high, with roughly 30–45% of marriages resulting in divorce (Eurostat, 2001).

How do children adjust to the changes that come with divorce? In short, the answer is: "It depends." Parental divorce does show a modest, but significant association with short-term child maladjustment (Amato, 2001; Summers, Forehand, Armistead, & Tannenbaum, 1998), but children are not homogeneous on this issue and their responses depend in part on their age, gender, predivorce functioning, and their postdivorce environment. Our understanding of divorce has evolved from conceptualization of divorce as a single, monolithic event, to the current conceptualization of divorce as a complex process that unfolds across time. Divorce does not begin abruptly at marriage dissolution, but rather involves a long and complex sequence of predivorce experiences (Furstenberg & Kiernan, 2001). Moreover, divorce is more likely to occur in families marked by adversities that in themselves predispose children to subsequent maladaptation—such as economic stress and parental psychopathology. Accordingly, historical evaluations of divorce and its impact on children have been overstated.

Early accounts of divorce noted many preschool children experience a 2- to 3-year period of readjustment following divorce. They may show aggression, depression, noncompliance, acting out, and problems in peer relationships (Wallerstein, Corbin, & Lewis, 1988; Weiss, 1979). After the initial distress, however, such research showed that young children's adjustment appears to improve. Based on interviews with preschool and older children 10 years after the parents' divorce, researchers have reported that the younger children exhibited fewer problems than children who were older (Wallerstein & Blakeslee, 1989). Early accounts found that postdivorce response among adolescents is often characterized by acting out and difficulties in school and by early withdrawal and disconnection from the family (Hetherington, 1987; Wallerstein et al., 1988). Findings suggesting older children fare worse than younger children following divorce may reflect true developmental differences in the effects of divorce—but it is also important to note that such differences may simply reflect the likelihood that older children confronted with parental divorce may have been exposed to a longer predivorce history of troubled family relations. Many parents considering marriage dissolution choose to wait until their children are older to divorce, perhaps believing it is in the best interest of their developing children. However, postponing divorce can have the unintended effect of exposing youth to greater "doses" of family conflict, increasing their risk for the development of psychopathololgy.

Early work also noted that the gender of the child may influence postdivorce adjustment. For preschool boys, it has been noted that problems are more intense and enduring than for girls. Why might this be the case? Perhaps boys tend to find the breakup more distressing, perhaps they are less adept at coping with divorce, or perhaps they tend to show their distress more overtly than do girls. Another possibility is that girls fare better after divorce because mothers have custody in most single-parent homes and there is some evidence that children who are in the custody of a parent of the same gender show healthier emotional adjustment after divorce (Camara & Resnick, 1988; Zill, 1988).

Based on other data, it is reasonable to speculate that the child's style of processing information—how a child makes sense of the social environment—contributes to postdivorce adjustment. Children who catastrophized about their social environment showed more symptoms, whereas children who perceived high personal control and were optimistic about the future showed fewer symptoms (Mazur, Wolchik, & Sandler, 1992; see also Kerig, 1998). One's attitudes about the event can influence one's adjustment to the event.

Why do many children whose parents divorce show behavioral and emotional difficulties? Could it be that the divorce is a trauma, that the sense of family stability is forever disturbed, or that the parenting practices of the divorcing adults are severely disrupted. It could also be that the children are, before the divorce, doing less well than others. Methodologically, it is important to take into account the quality of the children's predivorce adjustment before examining any potential variations in their postdivorce adaptation. More recent research has followed families longitudinally across time, finding that problems in child well-being are often evident far in advance of marital disruption, and may account for a great deal of the reduced well-being found in snapshot assessments of children following divorce (Peris & Emery, 2004). Important family variables—such as marital discord—appear to account for the majority of differences between children of intact families and children of divorced parents at both pre- and postdivorce. Cherlin and his colleagues (1991) reported on the outcomes of two longitudinal studies, one conducted in the UK and the other in the US. The results indicated that, for boys, the effect of separation or divorce on behavior and achievement was sharply reduced when one took into account the behavior problems, achievement levels, and family difficulties that were present earlier—before the divorce. The reduction in the apparent effect of divorce occurred for girls as well, but to a slightly lesser extent. Thus, conditions before the separation or divorce play a role in the prediction of childrens' adjustment postdivorce.

Perhaps the most difficult situation for the child is when the parents place the child in the middle of their conflicts. The following clinical case provides an illustration:

> Lisa was seen in therapy for severe separation anxiety—she was almost unable to be away from her mother. Indeed, on most nights, she slept in the same bed as her mother. When taken to school, she experienced inordinate distress. Her social life was affected as well. She would not go to sleepovers at friends' homes, and she often would exhibit amorphous physical complaints, as well as more severe symptoms, especially when her parents tried to force her to interact with peers or to sleep in her own bed. Lisa was 13 years old, and Lisa's parents had divorced when she was 11.
>
> Perhaps a main factor exacerbating Lisa's distress, and a factor that affects many children of divorce, was the degree to which the parents placed her in the middle of their conflict. Lisa's mom would disclose to Lisa that her father had been terribly mean . . . and Lisa's father would complain to her about how her mother was taking all his money and not using it for the children as she was instructed to do by the courts. Mom would confide in her daughter, disclosing personal matters that put her father in a bad light. When Lisa didn't want to spend time with her father, her father would express anger and blame the mother. The child was in the middle of the parents' conflict.

Belittling of the other parent's character, trying to sabotage Lisa's relationship with the other parent, and even trying to seduce Lisa in conspiracies with one parent against another were features of her parent's divorce that contributed to, exacerbated, and maintained her psychological distress. As is evident, the amount and quality of postdivorce contact with both parents can be an important factor in children's adjustment.

Given the high rate of divorce in families with children, researchers have increasingly questioned whether different approaches to settling divorce and navigating child custody disputes are associated with differential child outcomes. In particular, Emery and colleagues (e.g., Kitzmann & Emery, 1994) examined the effects of divorce mediation versus adversarial divorce procedures (e.g., attorney negotiation, litigation) among families petitioning courts for a custody hearing. Families randomly assigned to undergo mediation, relative to those assigned to litigation, are considerably more likely to specify joint legal custody, report more satisfaction with the resulting arrangement, exhibit less coparenting conflict, and are less likely to pursue relitigation regarding the custody arrangement. Follow-up data show that 12 years after divorce families assigned to mediation show greater involvement and child contact by both parents than families who undergo litigation (Emery, Laumann-Billings, Waldron, Sbarra, & Dillon, 2001).

Assessing and classifying childhood disorders

Psychologists and other mental health professionals have designed and evaluated numerous methods for the measurement of human behavior. Like behavior in general, psychological disorders can be assessed by using methods such as self-report inventories, observations, structured interviews, and performance on laboratory tasks. With children, similar assessment procedures are used as with adults, but there are some important differences because young people may be inarticulate or uncooperative, or lack awareness about their emotions or actions. Accordingly, the psychological assessment of children includes ratings of the child's behavior by parents and teachers, structured interviews of the child and the child's parents, as well as self-report questionnaires and the use of structured behavioral observations.

Psychological assessments are useful to the extent that they are reliable and valid. Reliability and validity are the way psychologists test the merits of tests! For instance, reliability refers to the consistency of a test or measure. A reliable instrument is one that would be scored similarly by different examiners (interscorer reliability), and would produce scores that do not change dramatically over time (temporal stability or retest reliability). Reliability is necessary but not sufficient—validity is also required before a psychological assessment can be said to have utility.

A valid test or measure is one that actually assesses what it claims to measure. For example, if a test is said to measure aggression and scores on it correlate highly with scores on other valid tests of aggression it can be said to have concurrent validity. Moreover, if scores on the measure are found to predict the likelihood of aggressive actions, then it can be said to have predictive criterion-related validity.

Assessments involve the gathering of data, and it is preferred that reliable and valid psychological measurement instruments be used. These assessment data are then used by psychologists and other mental health professionals to help make informed decisions. The assessment process is complex, often including data gathered using multiple methods and data from multiple sources, such as from parents and teachers in addition to children themselves.

Assessing childhood disorders

The Children's Depression Inventory (CDI; Kovacs, 1981) is one example of a self-report measure used with children. It is noteworthy because of its widespread use with clinically referred and non-referred children and because the scale includes a wide range of symptoms other than depressed mood (Compas, 1997). Parents may provide ratings using the Child Behavior Checklist (CBCL; Achenbach & Rescorla, 2001), whereas the Diagnostic Interview for Children and Adolescents (DICA; Herjanic & Reich, 1982) and the Anxiety Disorders Interview Schedule-Child Version (ADIS-C; Albano & Silverman, 1996; Silverman & Albano, 1998) characterize the method of assessment using a structured diagnostic interview. The Response Class Matrix (Mash, Terdal, & Anderson, 1973) illustrates structured behavioral observations. More on each of these approaches as we proceed into this chapter.

Children are asked to report about themselves on the CDI—a 27-item scale that assesses depressive symptomatology in children (Kovacs, 1981). To respond to the items on the CDI, the child selects from among alternatives the one option that reflects the degree of the child's depressive symptoms. Consider these sample items from Kovacs (1991).

> Pick out the sentences that describe your feelings and ideas in the past 2 weeks.
>
> 1. ____ I am sad once in a while
>   ____ I am sad many times
>   ____ I am sad all of the time
> 2. ____ I hate myself
>   ____ I do not like myself
>   ____ I like myself

3. ____ Nothing will ever work out for me
   ____ I am not sure if things will work out for me
   ____ Things will work out for me OK

Importantly, a specific interval of time is assessed. Children are asked to report how they felt over the last 2 weeks. Adequate reliability and validity data have been reported (Compas, 1997; Kendall, Cantwell, & Kazdin, 1989; Saylor, Finch, Spirito, & Bennett, 1984b; Timbremont, Braet, & Dressen, 2004). Although a cutoff of 17 (Smucker, Craighead, Craighead, & Green, 1986) suggests maladjustment, more than the child's self-report on one questionnaire is typically needed to make an accurate determination of the presence of a disorder (see Comer & Kendall, 2005). Nevertheless, there is general agreement that for internalizing disorders, such as depression, there is great value in the child's perspective on the degree and intensity of his or her own emotional distress and this information can be gathered on a self-report instrument.

The CBCL (Achenbach & Rescorla, 2001) is a rigorously developed and standardized rating scale, available for both parents and teachers (Teacher Rating Form, TRF). These scales are widely used for assessing the most common dimensions of psychological disorder in childhood (for example, social problems, aggressive behavior, anxiety, or depression). The CBCL presents parents with 118 descriptors—features of behavior problems. An additional 20 descriptors measure social competence. The scores of each child are based on the parent ratings of these descriptors and are then judged against a distribution of scores obtained by a normative sample of children with backgrounds representing the range of social and economic status. The normative data provide the backdrop for the profile of scores received by the target child. A sample CBCL report is presented in Figure 3.1. As can be seen, the parents of this child rated him as low on the first 5 dimensions and high (i.e., T score over 70) on the Delinquent behavior and Aggressive behavior scales, with the scores reflecting that the child is more delinquent and aggressive than 98% of male children of the same age.

The CBCL profile shown in Figure 3.1 belongs to Gar, a 12-year-old boy who meets criteria for conduct disorder. The boy has been reported to engage in petty thefts, repetitive lying, fighting, bullying, disobedience, and arguing. His mother reports that he has "cut school," and that she also

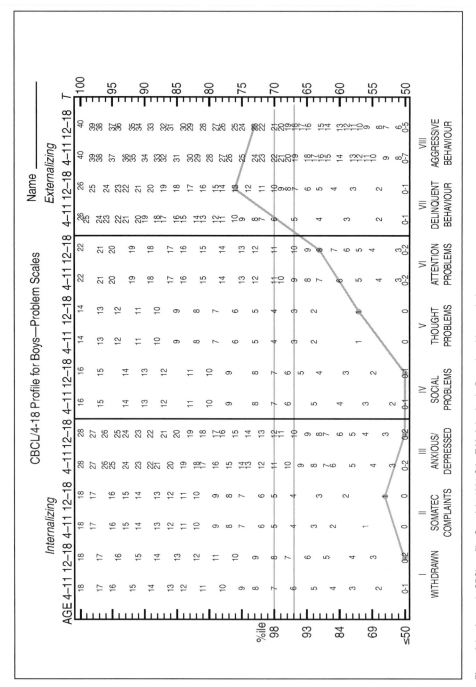

Figure 3.1. A sample CBCL profile. Copyright 1991 © by T.M. Achenbach. Reproduced by permission.

thinks that he has vandalized and started a fire in a nearby park. Although these behaviors are noteworthy in their own right, an advantage of the CBCL is the presentation of the data against a backdrop of the normal range of behavior (reflected in *T* scores). Thus, one can see that Gar's problems are well above that which would fall within the normal range of troubling behavior.

The Response Class Matrix is a method for observing and assessing parent–child interactions (Mash et al., 1973), and represents the effort to assess child behavior as part of a family system (Mash & Terdal, 1997). Trained observers record an observation every 10 seconds. They record both parent and child behaviors by placing a single check mark in one of the cells of a matrix. The rows of the matrix can be for different child behaviors (such as play and negative behavior), and the columns can be for different parent reactions (such as praise and commands). Thus, the matrix for one observation session might show that each negative child behavior was tied to a parental command and that desired child behaviors received no praise from the parent. By providing data about the pattern of interactions, the Response Class Matrix is helpful in identifying specific patterns that the therapist can target for change.

Information from direct observational methods, such as the Response Class Matrix, has the advantage of being representative of actual behavior in the real world. However, normative information about these interactions and behavior are lacking. That is, we do not yet know exactly what constitutes the healthy patterns of "good" parents and "well-adjusted" children. As a result, although observations are helpful to identify target behaviors for treatment, and useful to identify family influences (Mash & Terdal, 1997), they may be of limited utility when used in the absence of structured interviews or checklists for classifying abnormal child behavior or making a diagnosis.

The face-to-face interview can help establish rapport with children and families and permits asking questions that are geared to reaching designated diagnostic decisions. Structured diagnostic interviews are the preferred method of interviewing because the questions are arranged in advance, and the criteria needed to reach a diagnosis are delineated in the interview format. Most of the structured diagnostic interviews for use with youngsters follow an established diagnostic system (such as the *DSM-IV*, or *ICD-10*) and include the full range of childhood disorders.

One structured diagnostic interview, the Anxiety Disorders Interview Schedule-Child (ADIS-C; Albano & Silverman, 1996; Silverman & Nelles, 1988) has received widespread application for use with children—especially children who may be suspected of suffering from an anxiety disorder. This structured interview, like the others that are available, provides the interviewer with specific questions in an organized sequence and format that can lead directly to decisions about the presence or absence of a disorder. The ADIS-C has adequate reliability over time (Silverman & Rabian, 1995) and interrater agreement (Rapee, Barrett, Dadds, & Evans, 1994; Silverman & Ollendick, 2005). The instrument, when used before and after a psychological treatment, has also been found to be sensitive to treatment-produced gains (e.g., Kendall, Hudson, Gosch, Flannery-Schroeder, & Suveg, 2008).

In addition to the ADIS-C, there has been considerable effort in recent years to improve other structured interviewing procedures for use with children and adolescents. For example, the Diagnostic Interview for Children and Adolescents (DICA; Herjanic & Reich, 1982) assesses 185 symptoms and can be conducted in 40–45 minutes with parents or children 6 years of age and older. As is true for structured interviews in general, the DICA has specific questions and scoring procedures that use a branching system to lead to diagnoses. Favorable reliability and validity data are available to support the use of structured diagnostic interviews (Edelbrock & Costello, 1988; Shaffer, Fisher, Lucas, Dulcan, & Schwab-Stone, 2000).

Although the child and the child's parents are typically interviewed separately, there is not yet a uniform method for the integration of these two sources of information. For some disorders, the parent report is given more emphasis, whereas for other disorders the child's perspective is given a major role. Researchers are working to provide specific methods for the integration of child and parent interview data for use in reaching optimally accurate diagnoses (e.g., ADIS) (see Comer & Kendall, 2004; De Los Reyes & Kazdin, 2005).

A diagnostic system for childhood disorders

Perhaps the most widely used classification system for disorders of childhood is the *Diagnostic and Statistical Manual*, 4th edition (*DSM-IV*), published by the American Psychiatric Association (APA, 1994). This system is largely in agreement with another often used system developed in conjunction with the World Health Organization (WHO, 1992)—the *International Classification of Diseases*, 10th edition

(*ICD-10*). Both systems use a categorical approach with specified criteria. There are categories of disorders each with their own criteria and a child who displays a sufficient number of the criterion behaviors (symptoms) is said to have the disorder. Although these systems are widely used, interesting and important points suggest that childhood disorders do not fall neatly into categories (Sonuga-Barke, 1998). For example, there is a high degree of co-occurrence of disorders (comorbidity) and symptoms of one disorder often overlap with symptoms of other disorders.

Conceptual considerations aside, much progress has been made with regard to the diagnosis of child disorders. For example, consider the fact that in the original *DSM* (APA, 1952), children were diagnosed using the adult categories because there were no categories specifically for childhood disorders. Over the years, the classification scheme has become increasingly data based and responsive to input from researchers. The present version, *DSM-IV*, has a separate section for disorders usually first diagnosed in infancy, childhood, or adolescence. Box 3.1 provides an overview of the *DSM* classification of the disorders specific to youngsters. Also, children can receive other diagnoses (such as depression or generalized anxiety disorder) from

---

BOX 3.1   Classification of disorders of young people

Some of these disorders are among the adult disorders, others are specific to youth.

The diagnostic system permits children to receive some of the same diagnoses as adults, but it also includes disorders that are first identified in infancy, childhood, or adolescence. Here is a brief overview of these various disorders with some examples.

- *Disruptive behavior disorders.* These disorders are associated with acting out, such as destructive and dangerous behavior (conduct disorder), and extreme inattentiveness and restlessness (attention-deficit hyperactivity disorder, ADHD).
- *Emotional disorders.* These disorders involve disturbances associated with anxiety and depression. Within anxiety, there are several types of disorders such as generalized anxiety disorder, social phobia, and separation anxiety disorder. Depression, in varying degrees, can also be diagnosed for youngsters.
- *Eating disorders.* Disorders associated with feeding, such as anorexia nervosa and bulimia nervosa.
- *Mental retardation.* Substantial limitations in present functioning characterized by significantly subaverage intellectual functioning and limitations in adaptive living skills.
- *Learning disorders.* Achievement substantially below that expected given age, intelligence, and education.
- *Pervasive developmental disorders.* Impairment in communication and social interaction, together with restricted and stereotyped patterns of behavior. An example is autism.
- *Tic disorders.* Sudden repetitive motor movements or utterances. For example, Tourette's disorder, which involves both motor and verbal tics that occur many times a day.
- *Elimination disorders.* Encopresis, the repeated passage of feces into inappropriate places, and enuresis, the repeated voiding of urine into bed or clothes.

the adult disorders sections of the *DSM*. For example, an early adolescent who displays symptoms of depression would be diagnosed and classified within the system as having a mood disorder, just as an adult. The *DSM-IV* includes developmentally informed modifications for such disorders to facilitate diagnosis in children. For example, the definition of posttraumatic stress disorder (PTSD), which characterizes the development of a specified set of symptoms following exposure to an extreme traumatic event, is defined for individuals of all ages, but includes a number of developmentally sensitive qualifiers. These include specification that: (a) children may exhibit disorganized or agitated behavior during a traumatic event, rather than experiencing fear and helplessness (as is seen in adults); (b) rather than experiencing intrusive nightmares about a traumatic event (as often seen in adults), children may experience generalized nightmares of monsters or of unrecognizable content; (c) reliving a traumatic event may be seen in children via repetitive play (e.g., banging toy cars together following an automobile accident); (d) children may be more likely to complain of various physical symptoms, such as stomach aches and headaches, after a traumatic event.

As suggested earlier, not all psychologists endorse a categorical approach to defining childhood disorders. A related but contrasting approach for childhood disorders comes with an imposing title— multivariate statistical taxometric system—but the basic idea behind the system is actually straightforward. The basic idea is to classify disorders along various continua by using statistical procedures to determine what symptoms occur together with what other symptoms (Drabick, 2009). In this manner, human judgments are much less influential in determining the symptoms of disorders. Using correlations between pairs of symptoms or pairs of behavior ratings, the researcher then examines these relationships to look for patterns of co-occurring characteristics (Achenbach & Rescorla, 2006). This statistical approach to classification describes children in terms of their standing along several different continua of behavior—rather than as "in" or "out" of a category. Recall Figure 3.1 depicting the CBCL profile—it provided a picture of the degree to which the rated child was "extreme" on various dimensions of child behavior.

This method of assessment has led researchers to describe childhood disorders as falling into two broad categories: (1) internalizing disorders and (2) externalizing disorders (Achenbach & Edelbrock, 1978). Internalizing disorders are psychological difficulties that are considered inner directed; core symptoms are associated with overcontrolled behaviors (Reynolds, 1992). Internalizing disorders include such psychological disorders as anxiety, depression, social withdrawal and isolation, and the eating disorders. Externalizing disorders are maladaptive behavior patterns in children, across several situations that create problems for others. In these undercontrolled disorders, which are also called behavioral disorders, the child's behavioral problems result in conflicts between the child and the social context. Conduct disorder, discussed in Chapter 4, is an example.

Studies of adolescents (Costello, Erkanli, & Angold, 2006a; Nock, Kazdin, Hiripi, & Kessler, 2006; Rescorla et al., 2007) suggest a gender distinction: more females report internalizing disorders, whereas more males are identified with externalizing difficulties. By a ratio of 2:1 or 3:1, boys show more problems linked to externalizing than girls (Quay, 1986). For instance, boys, by a ratio of between 2:1 and 9:1 (Barkley, 1997b), are more likely to be diagnosed with attention-deficit hyperactivity disorder (ADHD). Somewhat surprisingly, however, when boys and girls aged 9–13 are studied, the incidence of one internalizing disorder—the anxiety disorders—is equally represented across gender.

Some critics of the distinction between internalizing and externalizing disorders hasten to point out that many externally disordered children also have very tormented inner lives—if not because of their own internal personal turmoil, then perhaps because of the punishment, ridicule, or unwanted attention that their externalizing behavior generates. In response, advocates of the distinction have suggested that children with externalizing disorders display their problems outwardly, but may still experience some inner distress and that these variations can be seen in the profile describing the child's level of distress on each of the dimensions. When there are elevations in the externalizing dimensions, and less elevation on the internalizing dimensions, for example, the child suffers less internally relative to the problems that are discharged on to the environment. As discussed in later chapters, the taxometric approach and its distinction between internalizing and externalizing disorders has led to valuable and informative cognitive and behavioral distinctions that have important implications for psychological therapy.

Are rates of childhood disorders on the rise?

Attention has been paid, in both academic and public outlets, to concerns about the increasing diagnosis of childhood disorders (e.g.,

Costello, Erkanli, & Angold, 2006a; Costello, Foley, & Angold, 2006b; Moreno, Laje, Blanco, Jiang, Scmidt, & Olfson, 2007). For example, clinical diagnosis of autism spectrum disorders has increased significantly (e.g., Gillberg, Cederlund, Lamberg, & Zeijlon, 2006), epidemiologic surveys of adults are showing increasing lifetime rates of major depression reported in later born cohorts (e.g., Kessler et al., 2003), and the diagnosis of childhood bipolar disorder in outpatient settings increased 40-fold over the past 10 years (Moreno et al., 2007).

Do such findings reflect "true" changes in the prevalence of childhood disorders? Is there an epidemic of childhood disorders, or might a number of methodological factors explain the rising rates? It seems as though changes in diagnostic practices may play a role in explaining the changes. First, methods of assessing childhood disorders have improved over the past decade, and youth who may have historically gone unrecognized are now being recognized and receiving needed services. Second, as our diagnostic systems evolve, there are changes in the "thresholds" used for a diagnosis and this change influences prevalence rates. Consider the case of autism spectrum disorders (see Chapter 10)—changed thresholds have resulted in greater numbers of youth meeting criteria for disorder. Moreover, findings of increasing rates of disorder in later born cohorts have typically been based on retrospective recall from adults (e.g., Kessler et al., 2003). In sum, media reports suggesting rising rates of childhood disorders have been overstated, and the changes may more accurately reflect historical underdiagnosis of childhood disorders, evolving diagnostic thresholds, and methodological artifacts of survey research.

Treating disorders of childhood

As noted earlier, children typically come to the attention of the mental health system when parents, teachers, or officials of some type decide that the youngster needs professional assistance—the children themselves do not self-refer. The fact that children are sent for or brought to treatment, whereas adults may seek it, is an important distinction with implications for treatment.

A variety of theories and types of therapy have been applied to children and adolescents (Kazdin & Weisz, 2006; Kendall, 2006). For example, young persons may be treated individually using behavioral procedures, a cognitive-behavioral approach (Kendall, 2006), or psychodynamic (Target & Fonagy, 1994) strategies, or within the family using any of the various theoretical approaches. In other instances, child behaviors may be targeted indirectly through parent training that aims to reshape parenting practices serving to maintain child problems. Which of the various treatments should be used? How does one decide which treatment to implement?

One way to select an intervention is to refer to the empirical literature on the efficacy of the different treatments for specific child problems. Numerous research studies—referred to as treatment outcome studies—have been conducted and reported, and we will discuss several of them in some detail within our consideration of each of the disorders. For now, the general and overall reviews of the full complement of research studies about the effectiveness of therapy with children can be used to draw suggestions about which treatments to use. These reviews often indicate that several of the interventions based on a behavioral or cognitive-behavioral perspective tend to be the more effective (Weiss & Weisz, 1995; Weisz, Weiss, Hans, Granger, & Morton, 1995), although there does not appear to be any one treatment that is consistently more effective than all of the others. The absence of a universally effective treatment, however, is to be expected. It is unlikely that one method of treatment would be effective for all childhood behavior disorders (Shirk & Russell, 1996). Other reviews of the literature, such as those that apply specific criteria for the determination of efficacious treatments (e.g., Eyberg, Nelson, & Boggs, 2008; Kaslow & Thompson, 1998; Kazdin & Kendall, 1998; Lonigan, Elbert, & Johnson, 1998; Ollendick, King, & Chorpita, 2006; Silverman & Hinshaw, 2008) find several treatments to meet the criteria/standards and thereby earn the designation of "efficacious" or "probably efficacious." Interestingly, an examination of these treatments yields some consistencies. The efficacious treatments are time limited and focused on a specific problem with a relatively homogeneous sample of children. The treatments include behavioral components, attention to cognitive processing and emotional experience, and have an action-oriented infrastructure. With regard to the action orientation, the efficacious treatments generally include role plays, practice exercises, exposure to distressing situations, or behavioral experiments as ways for the child to test ideas and learn and practice new skills. Like the earlier mentioned reviews, treatments with a behavioral or cognitive-behavioral orientation can be said to meet the criteria for being classified as probably efficacious or efficacious. Later in this book, when treatments for specific disorders are described, you will recognize the features listed here as they will likely be a part of the treatments that have been found in methodologically sound empirical evaluations to be effective.

Are child therapy and adult therapy alike? Yes, to a degree, child and adult psychological treatments have like-minded theoretical orientations, schedules and structures, and professional ethics. But there are three important differences between adult and child therapy: (1) the role of parents; (2) the use of play in therapy; (3) the relevance and efficacy of psychoactive medications.

Parents play a central role in children's lives, and the degree to which parents and other family members are involved in the problem or the treatment requires consideration. Instead of working one to one with the child, therapists who work with children often choose to spend at least some time teaching the parents to work with the child. Such parent training is often used with younger children. In other instances, the family may be seen together in family therapy (Fauber & Kendall, 1992).

Recall that children did not seek treatment on their own, and recognize that, in the beginning, they may not want to be there. Play is used by a variety of therapists as a means to involve children in the tasks of treatment. One specific form of "play therapy" follows psychodynamic theory and uses play as a means for the child to express thoughts and emotions. This method remains somewhat popular despite a lack of data to support its use. In contrast, the treatments that have received empirical support use play not as a means of child expression, but as a way to engage the child in the action-oriented experiences that are designed to be therapeutic. For example, parent training programs use play in session as a way of maximizing the extent to which treatment gains generalize to natural child activities and settings.

Biomedical treatments, specifically medications, have also been used for childhood and adolescent disorders. A literature documents the efficacy of psychotropic medications for use with children and adolescents suffering with several of the disorders we discuss. The medications may be similar to those found to be helpful for related adult disorders, but therapeutic dosages for children are typically lower and side effect profiles associated with these medications tend to differ across ages. For example, stimulant medications, (e.g., Ritalin), have received support in the treatment of attention-deficit hyperactivity disorder (ADHD; see Chapter 5) in both child and adolescent populations, but some research has found modest but significant short-term side effects on growth when used with children

(Faraone, Biederman, Morley, & Spencer, 2008). Although these side effects appear to attenuate over time, and some data suggest that ultimate growth is not affected, it is nonetheless important that physicians prescribing stimulant medication to children carefully monitor the child (Faraone et al., 2008). Needless to say, when prescribing stimulant medications in adult populations, monitoring growth is not a concern. Throughout this book, you will see that for many disorders, both psychological and pharmacological approaches have shown efficacy in alleviating suffering, and for many disorders—such as childhood anxiety disorders (Walkup et al., 2008)—a combination of psychological and pharmacological approaches shows a superior response rate over either form of treatment alone. When the research evidence provides a basis for their use and tolerability, medications can play an important role in child treatment. In the absence of empirical evaluation and support, use of certain psychoactive medications with children can be questioned.

Summary

Normal development offers an important perspective for understanding psychological disorders in children. In developmental psychopathology, maladjustment is seen in relation to the major changes that normatively occur across the life span. Those assessing and diagnosing child disorders use assessments often similar to those used with adults (e.g., self-reports, structured diagnostic interviews). Some assessments are specific to use with children such as the Child Behavior Checklist (CBCL) and the Response Class Matrix. Psychological disorders of childhood can be classified into categories or described along several continua in an effort to guide treatment. Child problems can be treated individually, in school- or clinic-based programs, in families, or using medications.

Conduct disorders 4

Adults typically seek help for depression and anxiety, but the majority of difficulties in childhood that are brought to the attention of mental health professionals have to do with externalizing, undercontrolled behavior problems. Our focus in this chapter will be on one of these behavior problems—conduct disorder (CD). In the next chapter we will address attention-deficit hyperactivity disorder (ADHD).

> Large for his age, physically strong, and aggressive, Josh was not bullied by the other children, even though he associated with kids several years his senior. Josh was 12 when he was brought home at 1:30 am by the police. He had run away from home, slept in a parked car that he had broken into, and was identified as the perpetrator of a theft at a neighborhood convenience store. He had also been sought by school officials because he had been in fights and had skipped school for several consecutive days. Josh's mother claims that she can't control him, and his teachers report that he is defiant and uncooperative in class, and cruel to some of the other children. Josh did not report feeling emotional distress—"I ain't got no problems"—but the reports indicated that those around him had suffered from his lack of socially appropriate behavior. Indeed, Josh's mother reported several bouts of emotional distress exacerbated by Josh's misbehavior.

Phenomenology and classification

Many if not all children have broken social or familial rules or been disobedient to adults in authority. But, certainly one cannot categorize all children as conduct disordered. What level of defiance is needed for a child to be deemed conduct disordered (see also Hinshaw & Zupan, 1997)?

According to *DSM-IV* (APA, 1994), the essential features of conduct disorder are a repetitive and persistent pattern of behavior that involves violation of the basic rights of others and of the major age-appropriate social norms. The problem is not situation specific: the problems are evident at school, in the home, within the community, and with peers. A common feature of conduct disorder is physical aggression, taking the form of cruelty, damage to the property of others, or starting fires. For example, Jamie, described in Chapter 1, was considered by some to be a suspect in setting fire to his home. Stealing, lying, and cheating are also common among children with conduct disorder. To warrant a diagnosis of conduct disorder, the behavior pattern must include 3 or more of the criteria, listed in Box 4.1, during the past 12 months, with at least one present in the last 6 months. Conduct disorder has been described as an "acting-out" behavior problem (McMahon & Frick, 2007) and, as seen in Box 4.1, represents a variety of serious antisocial acts.

BOX 4.1 DSM criteria for a diagnosis of conduct disorder

Conduct disorder involves a repetitive and persistent pattern of behavior in which the rights of others or societal rules are violated. At least three of the following must be present within the past 12 months, with at least one present in the last 6 months.

- aggression to people and animals:
  - often bullies, threatens, or intimidates others
  - often initiates physical fights
  - has used a weapon that can cause serious physical harm
  - has been physically cruel to people
  - has been physically cruel to animals
  - has stolen while confronting a victim
  - has forced someone into sexual activity
- destruction of property:
  - deliberately set fires with intent to cause serious damage
  - deliberately destroyed others' property
- deceitfulness or theft:
  - has broken into someone else's house, building, or car
  - often lies to obtain goods or favors or avoid obligations
  - has stolen items of nontrivial value without confrontation
- serious violations of rules:
  - often stays out at nights despite parental prohibition (beginning before age 13)
  - has run away from home overnight at least twice while living with parents/guardians
  - often truants from school (beginning before age 13).

DSM distinguishes between childhood onset (prior to age 10) and adolescent onset (after age 10) and specifies three levels of severity: mild, moderate, or severe.

Reprinted with permission from the *Diagnostic and Statistical Manual of Mental Disorders, Text Revision*, Fourth Edition, (Copyright 2000), American Psychiatric Association.

There is a less serious expression of acting-out behavior disorder that is referred to as oppositional defiant disorder (ODD). In several ways, oppositional defiant disorder resembles conduct disorder. However, whereas conduct disorders are essentially concerned with serious violations of the basic rights of others, oppositional defiant disorder involves a pattern of negativistic, hostile, and defiant behavior that has lasted a minimum of 6 months. A diagnosis of oppositional defiant disorder requires evidence of a pattern of behavior (lasting 6 months) during which there is evidence of the presence of at least four of the following behaviors:

- often loses temper
- often argues with adults
- often defies rules, or refuses to comply with adult requests
- often intentionally annoys people
- often blames others for mistakes or misbehavior
- is often touchy or easily annoyed by others
- is often angry and resentful
- is often spiteful and vindictive.

As is evident, the construct of oppositionality is a central feature of this disorder.

When conduct disorder is present, the behaviors associated with oppositional defiant disorder are also likely to be present. Therefore, a diagnosis of conduct disorder preempts a diagnosis of oppositional defiant disorder. Although the category of conduct disorder does reflect a coherent pattern of behavior, the actual children in this diagnostic group are heterogeneous. One child might be a firestarter, whereas many others have never started a single fire. There are cases with and without significant aggression. Not all youngsters receiving a diagnosis of conduct disorder engage in physical fighting. There are still others with and without illegal activities, with and without the presence of family psychopathology, and with and without comorbid diagnoses such as ADHD or learning disabilities. In general, conduct disordered youngsters are often impulsive, have a high need for stimulation, are low in empathy and moral development, and have troubled interpersonal relationships (Martin & Hoffman, 1990). Not surprisingly, substance abuse is also a common concern.

Nock and colleagues (2006) analyzed a nationally representative US sample and identified five overlapping classes of conduct problems: (1) Rule Violations; (2) Deceit/Theft; (3) Aggressiveness; (4) Severe Covert problems, characterized by symptoms common in both the Rule Violations and Deceit/Theft classes, as well as more severe symptoms not present in these two classes; (5) Pervasive Conduct Disorder, characterized by the presence of roughly 8 conduct symptoms. Among these classes of conduct problems, aggressive behavior is associated with the earliest age of onset (~8.5 years), with the other four classes of behavior onsetting on average around 11 or 12 years of age. Pure aggressive behavior is the least prevalent class of conduct problems (~2%), whereas Rule Violations is the most prevalent (~60%). Although many readily associate conduct disorder with aggression, Nock and colleagues' data indicate that pure aggressive behavior is only one subcategory of conduct problems. Aggression can take different forms. Physical aggression is common, but kids can harm each other without raising a fist. Those of us who have worked in schools have overheard children say cruel words to one another, such as "You're not my friend anymore" or "You're not invited to my birthday party." Although many parents teach their children that "Sticks and stones may break my bones, but words will never hurt me," do researchers who study aggression in childhood agree? It turns out, a form of aggression—referred to as *relational aggression*— can have considerable negative effects on a child's well-being. Relational aggression, defined as the removal or threat of removal of relationships with the intent to cause harm and/or negative social consequences, can include malicious gossip, ignoring or "silent treatment," spreading lies, or intentionally excluding a peer from an activity (Crick, Casas, & Ku, 1999). Forms of relational aggression are seen as early as the preschool years but escalate during adolescence, and occur far more frequently among girls than boys (Crick, Ostrov, Burr, Cullerton-Sen, Jansen-Yeh, & Ralston, 2006). Children who engage in relational aggression show serious relationship problems across the life span, including excessive jealousy, intimacy impairments, loneliness, lack of trust, and are at elevated risk for the development of personality disorders in adulthood (Crick, 1996; Murray-Close, Ostrov, & Crick, 2007).

How can we better understand noncompliant acting out? Loeber and colleagues (Loeber, Van Kammen, & Maughan, 1993; Loeber & Farrington, 2000) studied about 500 boys aged 3 to 16 over a 3-year period and identified 3 developmental pathways or trajectories that lead to disruptive behavior problems. According to Loeber et al., the *overt behaviors pathway* consists of those antisocial actions that are confrontative such as fighting, arguing, and temper tantrums. The *covert behavior pathway* consists of concealed actions such as stealing, truancy, and lying. A third pathway—an *authority conflict pathway* (e.g., stubborn, defiant)—was also identified. The lowest rates of offending were seen in boys in the overt and authority conflict pathways, whereas those with highest delinquency and most violent offenses showed escalation over the years on scores on all three pathways. Researchers may come to further identify different etiological pictures and, eventually, distinctions such as these may produce subgroups of children who are differentially responsive to interventions.

Who are the conduct-disordered youngsters?

Conduct problems are prevalent in the general population and especially so in the samples seen in child clinics. Conduct problems are among the most frequently occurring child disorders, with prevalence ranging from 2% to 9% for CD and from 6% to 10% for ODD (Costello et al., 2003; McMahon & Frick, 2007; Nock et al., 2007). When teenagers are asked to self-report their experiences with the specific behaviors that comprise conduct disorder, the results are alarming. More than 50% admit to theft and 45% admit to having caused property destruction. Based on a review of several studies of the prevalence of conduct disorder conducted with clinic-referred children, Wells and Forehand (1985) noted that 33–75% of the referrals were for conduct-disordered behaviors.

Boys and girls differ in the prevalence of conduct disorder. The precise gender ratio in the prevalence of the disorder is difficult to determine because of the varied diagnostic criteria and the varying types of assessments that have been used. Nevertheless, estimates that vary from 3:1 to 7:1 (males–females) are common (Costello et al., 2003; Earls & Mezzacappa, 2002; Nock et al., 2007), with biological and psychosocial theories offered to explain the observed difference (Eme & Kavanaugh, 1995; Zahn-Waxler, Shirtcliff, & Marceau, 2008). Gender differences are apparent in the age of onset of conduct disorder—whereas most boys had an onset before age 10, the onset of conduct disorder in girls was concentrated in the early teens (ages 13–16). Some gender differences are noticeable in symptoms as well: theft is more common among males, and sexual misbehavior is more common among females. Early age of onset is also seen as a poor prognostic indicator (Werry, 1997).

Are these gender differences important in determining the cause or designing the optimal treatment? What can be said about the meaning of these gender differences? Clearly, one cannot determine the causes of the observed differences without further investigation.

However, one speculative explanation is that the socialization process, in both families and schools, shapes boys and girls in different directions. For example, in most western cultures, aggressiveness is tolerated more in boys than in girls, and boys are expected to discharge their tensions in more physical ways. There is also some evidence that, whereas girls may be less likely to engage in serious and persistent conduct problems, they may be at risk for a broad range of other behavior problems including internalizing disorders (Loeber & Keenen, 1994; Zoccolillo, 1993). Others have speculated that there are biological differences, as well as biological predispositions, toward different types of behavior problems.

Although culture and socialization play a role in the development and expression of conduct disorders, they are to be found around the globe (see Rutter, Tizard, Yule, Graham, & Whitmore, 1976). In a sample of youngsters in New Zealand, 9% of boys and 4.6% of girls were found to have chronic antisocial behavior patterns (McGee, Silva, & Williams, 1984). Conduct problems are more prevalent among those of low socioeconomic status, and from urban (8–12%) rather than rural (~4%) settings (Barclay & Hoffman, 1990; Lambert, Wahler, Andrade, & Bickman, 2001; Nock et al., 2006), although an urban–rural difference was not found in one study (Offord, Boyle, & Racine, 1991).

Causes

Are conduct disorders the product of genetics? Of social and peer influences? Of biology? Of parental child-rearing practices? What accounts for the onset of conduct disorder? Although no one factor can provide a full explanation of the cause of conduct problems, there are several types of influence that have been identified and supported by research. We will discuss cognitive factors, biological forces, and the role of the family.

Cognitive processing in conduct disorders

The factors most often associated with risk of conduct disorders include features of the individual child, the child's parents, and the interaction patterns between child and parent. Investigators have found that academic and intellectual difficulties, for example, predict conduct disorder (West, 1982), although many children with limited academic abilities do not display antisocial actions. Other aspects of the child that are possible risk factors include cognitive and biological characteristics. Let's look more closely at the child's manner of making sense of the environment—cognitive processing—as a contributor to problems of conduct.

Aggressive youngsters often show cognitive deficiencies (e.g., Seguin, Pihl, Harden, Tremblay, & Boulerice, 1995). They lack problem-solving skills, scoring low on measures of the ability to generate multiple solutions to problems. Also, conduct-disordered children seem more likely than nondisordered children to think of solutions that others would rate as aggressive, and less likely to think of socially appropriate solutions to interpersonal problems (Fischler & Kendall, 1988).

Aggressive children also display cognitive distortions when thinking about social interactions. Dodge (1985) documented this tendency in a series of studies. He presented children with videotaped vignettes that showed one child doing something that caused a negative outcome for another child. In some of the tapes the intention of the actor who caused the negative outcome was ambiguous. The children who participated in the research were then asked to choose an explanation for the actor's behavior. The studies showed that relatively aggressive children were more likely than nonaggressive children to believe that the actor in the ambiguous tapes had hostile intentions—as if the actor had caused the negative outcome on purpose! In contrast, nonaggressive youngsters were likely to see the ambiguous actions as having been accidental. To illustrate this cognitive distortion, suppose that you have a new iPod. While en route to a school activity you loan it briefly to a friend and, when it is returned, the headphones no longer work properly. The cause of the damage is uncertain. Why did this happen? A greater percentage of aggressive than nonaggressive children are likely to say that the damage was done on purpose, perhaps offering an explanation akin to "He did it to get me mad" or "He did it because he was jealous." Nonaggressive youngsters are more inclined to attribute the headphone damage to causes other than the hostile intentions of the other child (e.g., "It was probably an accident") and seem more willing to accept that "stuff happens."

Research findings have led to the conclusion that, in short, aggressive children have a hostile attributional bias: When a situation is ambiguous, they tend to attribute negative motivations to others. This distortion may then prompt the aggressive child to retaliate ("It was on purpose, so I can fight back"), and a vicious cycle can result.

Over 100 empirical studies have identified associations between attributions of hostile intent and aggressive behavioral patterns (see Dodge, 2006). Some data suggest that all children exhibit a hostile attribution bias in early life, but that most children soon acquire a benign attributional style as they develop more sophisticated capacities to infer others' intentions. Those children who fail to develop a stable pattern of inferring benign intent in response to ambiguous provocations are at greatest risk for developing aggressive behavioral patterns (Dodge, 2006).

Another line of research has identified a pattern of "callous" traits among youth with conduct disorder. Frick and colleagues (e.g., Frick, Bodin, & Barry, 2000; Frick, Cornell, Bodin, Dane, Barry, & Loney, 2003) found that children who go on to develop conduct problems often show a lack of empathy, an absence of guilt (often accompanied by a general constriction of emotion), and view themselves as more important than others. Children who show these callous-unemotional traits early on in life are at elevated risk for the development of severe, aggressive, and chronic conduct problems and antisocial behaviors across the life span (Frick & Dantagnan, 2005; Frick, Stickle, Dandreaux, Farrell, & Kimonis, 2005).

Genetic factors

To determine the contribution of genetic factors it would be necessary to have longitudinal data on numerous sets of monozygotic and dizygotic twins, raised together and raised apart. At present, such twin studies specifically reporting on conduct disorders as currently conceptualized are rare (Earls & Mezzacappa, 2002; Gelhorn et al., 2006; Slutske et al., 1997). Regrettably, the many labels used to describe externalizing behavior problems (e.g., conduct disorder, aggression, antisocial behavior) have clouded our ability to better understand the causes. A recent meta-analysis of 51 twin and adoption studies that included assessment of antisocial behavior (Rhee & Waldman, 2002), however, sheds some light on the issue. This work identified that there are genetic influences on the development of antisocial behavior, the magnitude of this genetic contribution does not differ across males and females, and genetic influences on antisocial behavior seem to decline with age. Twin research conducted by Gelhorn, Stallings, Young, Corley, Rhee, and Hewitt (2005) suggest that individual symptoms of conduct disorder may be differentially heritable. In particular, destruction of property, lying, stealing, use of weapons, and fighting all show moderate heritability, whereas breaking and entering and truancy show no heritability. In recent years, research in molecular genetics has begun to study precise genetic polymorphisms—such as an interaction among dopamine DRD2 and DRD4 (Beaver et al., 2007)—associated with the expression of conduct problems in youth.

The role of the family

The family is the primary context for the socialization of children and many research findings have supported the idea that the family is a major factor in the cause of conduct disorders (e.g., Jouriles, Bourg, & Farris, 1991). Four alternative patterns are common in the families of youngsters with conduct disorders: parental deviance, parental rejection and coerciveness, lack of discipline or supervision of children, and marital conflict and divorce (see Greene, Anderson, Hetherington, Forgatch, & DeGarmo, 2002).

The parents of children with conduct disorders are themselves often deviant, displaying maladjustment, anger, and sometimes criminal behavior. Overt marital conflict can contribute to oppositional behavior in children (Mann & MacKenzie, 1996; Webster-Stratton & Hammond, 1999) and many children with conduct disorders have a parent with antisocial personality disorder or antisocial traits (Frick & Loney, 2002; Rhule, McMahon, & Spieker, 2004; Rutter & Quinton, 1984). More extreme patterns, such as criminal behavior and alcoholism, particularly in the father, put the child at an especially high risk for conduct disorder (Robins, 1966; West, 1982). Separation from an antisocial father does not seem to protect the child from this risk, perhaps suggesting a genetic causal pathway, or perhaps because with the father absent discipline may weaken.

Parenting practices are said to contribute to behavior problems. Parents of conduct-disordered children tend to respond coercively and often negatively to their children. Although precise measurement of parental practices is difficult, there seems to be a strong association between negative parent–child relations and antisocial conduct in youngsters (see Loeber, 1990). An extreme form of parental negativism is physical abuse. In a US study of 584 Caucasian and African-American youth (grades 1 to 4), those who had been physically abused had significantly more conduct problems than those not abused (Dodge, Pettit, Bates, & Valente, 1995). Follow-up evaluations found early physical maltreatment predicted aggression and delinquent behavior in youth 12 years later (Lansford, Dodge, Pettit, Bates, Crozier, & Kaplow, 2002). Findings regarding the relationship between early child maltreatment and the development of conduct problems appear to be universal. In a study of Danish sons of alcoholic fathers, a past history of severe physical abuse by the father was a significant predictor of antisocial traits in the son (Pollock et al., 1986).

The occurrence and observation of the use of weapons in inter-parent violence could be a powerful contributor to child conduct disorder (see Widom, 1997). Jouriles and colleagues (Jouriles, McDonald, Norwood, Ware, Spiller, & Swank, 1998) studied knives, guns and interparent violence and its relationships with child behavior problems. The sample consisted of youngsters from families characterized by interparent violence. Some children had observed the use of weapons when used, others did not witness weapons but they were reported to have been used, and the third group consisted of families where the mother did not report the use of weapons. Interestingly, children from families where weapons violence had occurred and children who had observed violence involving weapons had higher levels of behavior problems than the group where violence did not involve weapons. Marital violence contributes to the likelihood that children will have behavior problems, and the situation seems to worsen when the interparent violence involves weapons.

Let's take a closer look at a specific pattern of parent–child interactions that are said to be related to antisocial activity. Such a close-up is made possible by the work of Patterson and his associates (Patterson, Chamberlain, & Reid, 1982). His research included observations of parents and their conduct-disordered children, and the results indicated that these parents had difficulties appropriately disciplining their offspring. According to Patterson's analysis, the parents of children with conduct disorder tended to reward positive and negative behaviors inconsistently. In particular, the parents often reinforced—such as by attention, laughter, or "giving in"—coercive child behaviors, such as demanding, defying, yelling, and arguing. Thus, consequent to the reinforcement provided by parental attention, the child learns to use coercive behaviors. Over time, the child learns to be even more coercive, possibly escalating to hitting and verbally attacking. Meanwhile, positive behaviors by the child were often ignored or responded to inappropriately by the parents. In effect, the youngster was rewarded for displaying antisocial actions and failed to learn alternate adaptive behavior. Thus, according to Patterson et al., families with children with conduct disorder are characterized by coercive interactions. Poor parenting skills, he argued, produce and promote antisocial behavior.

Research has provided support for this conceptualization of the role of parents in child conduct problems. The coercive interaction parenting style was studied in 708 families, some of which had monozygotic (93) and dizygotic (99) twins (Reiss et al., 1995). These authors reported that almost 60% of the variance in adolescent anti-social behavior could be accounted for by conflictual and negative parenting behavior directed toward the adolescent.

Finally, high rates of divorce have been found to be associated with persistent and late-onset conduct problems (Marmorstein & Iacono, 2005; Rutter & Quinton, 1984) but, as discussed earlier, the divorce itself may not be the sole contributing factor to the problem. Instead, there is some evidence that divorce is frequent among parents and families with certain characteristics, and that those characteristics—not divorce itself—contribute to the onset of conduct disorder. Independent of the cause of conduct disorder, what happens to these children when they reach adulthood?

The course of conduct disorder

A large number of youngsters engage in single behaviors that may resemble some of the actions listed as criteria for conduct disorders. But, it should be highlighted, one incident or one brief conflicted experience does not make a disorder! Of those children who continue, and who show wider ranges of conduct problems, there is increased likelihood of antisocial behavior in adulthood. However, the pattern is not simplistic. Those adults identified as severely antisocial have long histories of disruptive behavior in their childhood, but most conduct-disordered children do not grow up to be severely antisocial adults (Maughan & Rutter, 1998).

There is some evidence of transgenerational consistency in anti-social and aggressive behavior. Indeed, perhaps the most troublesome feature of conduct disorder—not the occasional act of a nondisturbed child—is its stability over time (Lahey et al., 1995). Early evidence of conduct disorder in a child is related to later aggression, antisocial behavior, and other adult difficulties (see Robins, 1978). As argued by Eron and Huesmann (1990), aggressive behavior, if untreated, has been shown to be stable over a 30-year period of time. However, as noted by Maughan and Rutter (1998), when details of the studies are examined there are both continuities and discontinuities across time. For example, male gender, hyperactivity, aggression, poor verbal skills, low achievement at school, peer problems, and family disruption are risks for child-onset conduct disorder (e.g., Dishion, French, & Patterson, 1995). Age of onset is a strong predictor of continuities in disruptive behavior problems (Moffitt, 2006). Broadly speaking, research suggests two courses of antisocial behavior: (1) life-course-persistent, and (2) adolescence-limited (Moffitt, 2006). Life-course-persistent antisocial behavior begins earlier, is associated with serious delinquency in adulthood, and tends to be more associated with biological origins, whereas adolescence-limited antisocial behavior is far more common, has its origins in social processes, and fades in young adulthood. For adolescent onset, gender differences are less marked, aggression and learning problems are not central, and adolescent-onset offending is sometimes associated with peer popularity, close peer orientations, and peer delinquency (e.g., Stattin & Magnusson, 1998).

Although there are many factors that influence the relationship of child conduct problems and adult antisocial behavior (e.g., age of onset, gender, presence of other disorders, intervening treatment), the presence of conduct disorder in childhood carries predictive information for a wide variety of later adjustment problems (including antisocial activities and alcohol and substance abuse). Identification of the mechanisms that account for these trajectories is a major challenge facing the field (Maughan & Rutter, 1998, 2001).

Treatment

From several vantage points the conclusions appear consistent: Family conflict and poor parenting skills characterize the family relations of children with conduct disorders, and the children themselves display cognitive as well as behavioral difficulties. These characteristics suggest several possible approaches to treating these children, and recent reviews have suggested that treatments for young children with emerging conduct disorders can be beneficial. Many of the more effective methods involve system-wide programs in schools or communities (e.g., Hawkins, Arthur, & Olson, 1997), behaviorally oriented parent training (see Southam-Gerow & Kendall, 1997; Webster-Stratton, 2005), cognitive-behavioral therapy for the children themselves (e.g., Kazdin, 2005; Lochman, 1992; Lochman, Powell, Whidby, & Fitzgerald, 2006), or for the child–parent interaction (e.g., Eyberg, 1988; Brinkmeyer & Eyberg, 2003).

Wouldn't it be great if interventions, implemented at a school-wide level, could catch the problem early and prevent the emergence of conduct disorder? One example of a school-based program (Caplan, Weissberg, Grober, Sivo, Grady, & Jacoby, 1992; see also Braswell, August, Bloomquist, Realmuto, Skare, & Crosby, 1997) taught broad-based problem-solving skills and included specific applications of problem solving to problems facing inner city youth (12- to 13-year-olds). After the program, the youngsters were rated as improved in handling personal problems, impulse control, and popularity. Excessive alcohol use was also reduced. Long-term follow-ups and rigorous research designs are needed, including measurement of delinquent and criminal acts, but prevention is a first and worthwhile step in dealing with aggressive and antisocial behavior problems.

Parent training is another oft-used and oft-studied approach to the treatment of conduct problems (Brinkmeyer & Eyberg, 2003; Eyberg, Nelson, & Boggs, 2008; Foote, Eyberg, & Schuhmann, 1998; Webster-Stratton, 2005). Such an approach is suggested and justified by the association between conduct disorders and ineffective, punitive, and inconsistent parenting practices. In action-oriented family therapy, parents are directly taught skills for managing their children (see McMahon & Forehand, 2005; Sexton, Alexander, & Mease, 2003). These treatments aim to undermine the coercive family interactions associated with antisocial behavior. The family and the therapist set goals in terms of changes in target behaviors. Through written manuals, practice with the therapist, and homework assignments, parents learn to identify problem behavior, to observe and record the frequency of the behavior, to reward proper behavior effectively, and to stop rewarding unwanted behavior (see also Henggeler & Borduin, 1990).

Sundry studies have indicated that action-oriented family therapy can lead to improvements in children's functioning, reductions in antisocial behavior, and continuing improvements for at least brief follow-up periods. For example, in one of the early studies in this line of work, Patterson (1974) documented that after treatment the frequency of a target unwanted behavior dropped to a level within the range found in nondeviant families. In another later study (Patterson et al., 1982), the changes in parental discipline were accompanied by reductions in children's antisocial behavior, whereas there was no change in antisocial behavior in families whose discipline practices were found not to change. Though not always measured, home-based parent training programs have sometimes been associated with improvements in child behavior in the classroom and even with reductions in siblings' deviant behavior (see also McMahon & Forehand, 2005). A more recent example is the multisystemic family therapy evaluated by Henggeler and colleagues (Henggeler, Melton, Brondino, Scherer, & Hanley, 1997; Henggeler, Sheidow, & Lee, 2007; Saldana & Henggeler, 2006). This work provided coordinated interventions for juvenile offenders and their families and the effects were reported to be superior to routine care.

Despite promising results, much more research is needed to identify the specific types of antisocial conduct and specific groups of children and families that benefit from various parent training programs (Dumas, 1989). Studies of the effectiveness of these programs are often marred because some families drop out before completing the therapy. Treatment success is greater when the problem children are identified early and is probably also better for families that are less stressed and relatively better off socioeconomically. The published data are supportive, yet the outcomes do not reveal an eradication of conduct problems but a reduction in them. These programs tend to be relatively brief, and it may be the case that antisocial conduct problems represent a long-term problem requiring long-term treatments.

Another approach to treatment focuses on the child's cognitive processing. The therapy targets the deficient and distorted thinking tied to conduct disorders. Cognitive-behavioral treatments, for instance, aim to teach children to stop, think, and engage in reflective problem solving before impulsively engaging in an action. These programs often teach problem-solving skills and provide role play or real experiences to help the child rectify social misperceptions such as the hostile attribution bias. In one program that aims to train children to cope with their anger, the therapist teaches the children the process of problem solving and models how to manage arousal without getting upset (Lochman et al., 2006; see also Nelson & Finch, 1996). The therapist assigns out-of-session homework tasks, provides the children with opportunities to practice their new skills in provocative situations, and gives rewards for improvements.

The empirical studies of cognitive-behavioral treatments have examined various measures for evidence of success, such as ratings by parents and teachers, number of behavior problems, progress in school, participation in social activities, and amount of cooperative play. These studies, and follow-up reports of the effects of booster sessions (for example, see Lochman, 1992), testify to the value of teaching children cognitive and behavioral skills for solving interpersonal dilemmas. For example, cognitive-behavioral treatments

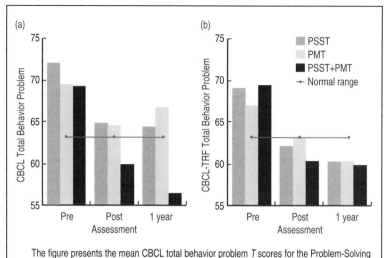

FIGURE 4.1.
Outcomes from cognitive-behavioral skills training and parent management training in the treatment of antisocial behavior in children. Adapted from Kazdin, Siegel, & Bass (1992, p. 744).

The figure presents the mean CBCL total behavior problem *T* scores for the Problem-Solving Skills Training (PSST), Parent Management Training (PMT), and their combination. The left graph (a) is the parent–completed CBCL, the right graph (b) is the teacher-completed CBCL (TRF, the Teacher Report Form).

have shown some success in decreasing aggressive behavior and increasing prosocial behavior (see data in Figure 4.1).

In one study, 20 sessions of a program that taught impulse control and problem-solving skills produced significant improvements in social behavior (Kendall, Reber, McLeer, Epps, & Ronan, et al., 1990b), but some youngsters continued to display conduct-disordered behavior even when their prosocial interactions increased. The outcomes offer some encouragement but additional treatment development and outcome research is needed to enhance and fine-tune the interventions for children of different ages, to foster widespread changes in behavior, and to ensure the longer term maintenance of any gains from the treatment.

Promising leads for future treatment of children with conduct disorders come from programs that improve either parents' behavior-management skills or the child's cognitive processing. In addition, we have learned that preventive efforts are best directed toward younger children who have not yet become immersed in delinquent or anti-social behavior patterns. One prime example is the work of Tremblay and colleagues in Montreal, Canada (Tremblay et al., 1990). This research team provided a 2-year intervention program to opposi-tional and aggressive kindergarten boys from low-income families. The intervention included parent training and child social skills development. At 3-year follow-up, the program, compared to control conditions, resulted in some crucial changes. The treated participants showed less fighting and delinquent behavior, as well as less frequent grade retention (see also Webster-Stratton, Reid, & Stoolmiller, 2008). Early intervention is pivotal because once the problematic behavior patterns become more entrenched, they are also more resistant to treatment.

Summary

Conduct disorder involves behavior that violates the basic rights of others and of the age-appropriate social norms. Aggression, property damage, stealing, and cheating occur among conduct-disordered youngsters. Conduct disorder is more common among boys and evident worldwide. Research indicates that conduct-disordered youth evidence a hostile attributional bias by which they tend to attribute negative motivations to others. Genetic influences, family distress, and ineffective parenting are also implicated in the development of conduct disorder. Although treatments such as action-oriented family therapy, school-based prevention, and cognitive-behavioral therapy have produced beneficial outcomes, the effects are greater for younger participants. Problems with conduct disorder can persist into adult life, particularly when onset occurs early in life.

Attention-deficit hyperactivity disorder 5

Even at age 6, Zach was, according to each of his parents, "unpredictable" and "antsy." His mother, a real estate agent, reported that "he's always on the go, but I'm not sure where he is going. He's into so many things." Zach's father, an attorney, described Zach as "rash and impetuous" and "having his engine running constantly." Both parents were distressed when Zach's school performance suffered because of his impulsivity and poor attention. He was determined to be a bright child, but his teacher suggested that Zach might have ADHD and that the ADHD was interfering.

Phenomenology and classification

Hyperactivity is the common or popular term for the psychological problem of childhood that is technically known as attention-deficit hyperactivity disorder (ADHD). Other terms that professionals have used over the years include hyperkinetic reaction and attention deficit disorder. Today it is formally designated attention-deficit hyperactivity disorder (ADHD), a disorder of limitations in behavioral inhibition that has three essential features: developmentally inappropriate levels of inattention, impulsivity, and hyperactivity, with onset before age 7 (Barkley, 2006b; Iaboni, Douglas, & Baker, 1995; Smith, Barkley, & Shapiro, 2007). Cross-cultural consistency has been supported by research (Leung, Hung, Ho, Lee, Liu, Tang, & Kwong, 2008).

Few if any childhood disorders have received the degree of widespread attention from professionals, teachers, and parents as has ADHD, which remains one of the most widely observed, described, studied, debated, and treated childhood disorders. *DSM-IV* (APA, 1994) provides criteria for different types of ADHD:

- ADHD—predominantly inattentive type
- ADHD—predominantly hyperactive type
- ADHD—combined type.

Descriptively, these conditions are different, but the possibility that these are separate disorders requires additional research.

No doubt you have experienced a time when your interests or your attention shifts from one activity to another, or the topic of your conversation, or the theme of your thinking changes from one idea to another. Is this a sign of disorder? What constitutes an attentional or hyperactive problem? Is it a diagnosable problem and, if so, can it be treated? Should the 3–5% of children who receive this diagnosis be medicated? Discussions of these and other questions have made "hyperactivity" a topic of substantial scholarship and considerable controversy.

Assessing and diagnosing ADHD

One of the advances over the years of scrutiny is that researchers and practitioners have come to recognize that the problem is not simply excessive levels of motor activity (hyperactivity). Difficulties in the three essential features of inattention, impulsivity, and hyperactivity need to be seen across situations—at school, at home, and in social contexts—before one can declare the presence of ADHD.

Inattention

Inattention is observed in behaviors such as seeming not to listen and failing to complete tasks. More specifically, a short attention span is seen in rapid shifts from one activity to another before the first activity is completed (Alessandri, 1992). The child goes from one toy to another without focused play with either toy. In the classroom, the child is easily distracted and fails to pay attention to directions. Is the problem tied to an inability to pay attention, or to difficulty in sustaining attention? Attentional difficulties are required, but the exact nature of the attentional problems seen in ADHD children is still a theme of debate, requiring further research.

Impulsivity

Impulsivity is acting without thinking. Although many children can be impulsive (especially at younger ages), ADHD children routinely interrupt others, blurt out responses to questions, and fail to wait their turn. ADHD youngsters are impaired in their ability to inhibit inappropriate responding (Jennings, Van der Molen, Pelham, Brock, & Hoza, 1997; Schachar, Tannock, Marriott, & Logan, 1995). They have problems organizing schoolwork and have a general need for greater supervision. The problem can be seen in different contexts. Consider the following example which comes from an actual experience with children engaged in athletics. When joining a game of soccer, the impulsive child runs on to the field and chases the ball, eager to kick it. Unfortunately, the child did not yet know the team he was on or which goal to shoot toward. In another context, such as the classroom, the impulsive child tries to answer questions before the question is completely stated by the teacher.

Hyperactivity

Hyperactivity is often reported by parents and teachers who cannot keep up with these children. The children are described as fidgety, restless, and unable to sit still. Using direct observations and mechanical recordings, researchers have substantiated an excess of activity among diagnosed hyperactive children (e.g., Milich, Loney, & Landau, 1982). These children are "on the go," unable to play quietly, and inept at shifting from free to structured activities such as from recess to a classroom activity.

Peer relationships are increasingly identified as central difficulties for the ADHD child (Nijmeijer, Minderaa, Buitelaar, Mulligan, Hartman, & Hoekstra, 2008), with the rule violations and aggression often linked to ADHD children's behavior being viewed negatively by their peers. In school, ADHD youth are rejected more often than their non-ADHD peers (Hoza et al., 2005) and are rated as less well liked (Hodgens, Cole, & Boldizar, 2000). Moreover, the social rejection experienced by children with ADHD appears to develop after only brief periods of interaction with others (Bickett & Milich, 1990). Erhardt and Hinshaw (1994) explored factors contributing to the peer status of children with ADHD and found aggression and child noncompliance to be sizably associated with unfavorable peer impressions. Observational research finds that children with ADHD are more socially intrusive than their non-ADHD counterparts (Frankel & Feinberg, 2002), perhaps contributing to less favored peer acceptance.

Poor academic achievement, perhaps not surprisingly, can be a serious difficulty faced by children with ADHD (Barry, Lyman, & Klinger, 2002; DuPaul, McGoey, Eckert, & Vanbrakle, 2001). Children with ADHD often score slightly lower on intelligence tests than their non-ADHD peers (Frazier et al., 2004), although this is likely due to slightly slower motor speed and reduced vocabulary associated with poor school learning. There is evidence that inattentive symptoms are more associated with academic deficits than are hyperactivity and impulsivity symptoms (Frazier, Demaree, & Youngstrom, 2004). ADHD youth also show discrepancies between their intelligence and their actual academic achievement (Barry et al., 2002). After controlling for intelligence, ADHD at the ages of 4 to 6 predicts subsequent academic achievement 8 years later (Massetti et al., 2008).

In a different line of research, one that focuses on family relationships, ADHD children showed less compliance and more opposition to their parents than non-ADHD children. Interactions between ADHD children and their parents were marked by greater than normal levels of parental commands, reprimands, and punishment (Barkley, Fischer, Edelbrock, & Smallish, 1991).

The difficulties associated with ADHD quite commonly do not exist by themselves. Rather, there is a high degree of comorbidity among ADHD children. According to some sources, up to 44% of children with ADHD have at least one other disorder (Barkley, 2006a, 2006b; Szatmari, Offord, & Boyle, 1989). It has been estimated that up to 60% of ADHD children have poor motor coordination, and 20–25% have difficulties learning (Barkley, 2006a, 2006b). Other problems co-occur as well. Children with ADHD have higher than typical co-occurring anxiety, depressive, and conduct disorders (Costello et al., 2003). An important distinction may be between ADHD youth with and without co-occurring conduct disorder (Hinshaw, 1987).

Making a diagnosis about the presence of ADHD is not simplistic. Identifying ADHD in children should involve several separate assessments:

- *Ratings of the child's behavior by parents and teachers.* The Child Behavior Checklist (CBCL) can be used to place the level of the child's problem in comparison with other children (recall Figure 3.1). Other parent rating forms are also available, such as the Conners Rating Scales (Conners, 1990; Conners, Sitarenios, Parker, & Epstein, 1998a, 1998b) and the ADHD Rating Scale— Home version (DuPaul, Barkley, & Murphy, 1994, cited in Smith et al., 2007).
- *Interviews with the child, parents, and teachers.* The details of the child's behavior or social context that may be lost with rating scales can be gathered through interviews. Interviews with

parents and teachers can be especially helpful in assessing whether the child's behavior is consistent across different situations, and what conditions exacerbate or reduce the problematic behaviors. For instance, the presence of certain classroom peers or a certain classroom seating arrangement may be associated with a worsening of an ADHD child's symptoms in the classroom.

- *Direct observation of behavior and task performance.* Observing the child provides valuable information in assessing ADHD. For example, trained observers can reliably distinguish hyperactive from nonhyperactive children by observing and recording behavior—such as out of seat activity and disruptiveness (e.g., Milich, Loney, & Roberts, 1986).

Most assessments of ADHD employ a combination of data-gathering techniques and strive to determine if the child meets the criteria needed for a diagnosis. Structured diagnostic interviews, for example, are typically used to gauge the child against the diagnostic criteria (see Box 5.1).

Who are the children with ADHD?

Up to 5–8% of youth suffer with ADHD (Polanczyk, de Limas, Horta, Biederman, & Rohde, 2007), with roughly 3% of preschool children meeting current criteria for the disorder (Eggers & Angold, 2006). Although gender differences are routinely recounted, ADHD has been identified in both boys and girls. A male–female ratio of between 4:1 and 8:1 is typical (Barkley, 2006a, 2006b). Gender differences have also been reported in the expression of ADHD. Among clinic-referred children, girls with ADHD have fewer behavior and conduct problems (less aggression) and more social withdrawal and anxiety and depression than boys with ADHD. However, diagnosis of ADHD in girls is associated with considerable higher rates of co-occurring internalizing symptoms (Gershon, 2002) and predicts continued disruptions in social and emotional functioning, as well as in achievement, across the life span (e.g., Hinshaw, Owens, Sami, &, Fargeon, 2006; Owens, Hinshaw, Lee, & Lahey, 2009).

No one culture breeds ADHD. It has been identified in a variety of ethnic groups and across cultures, with some cross-cultural differences emerging. For instance, there is a lower prevalence of ADHD in the UK (Taylor, 1994) and a high rate of hyperactivity in China (Luk & Leung, 1989). Because of inconsistent diagnostic practices, however, interpretations of these rates must be made with caution.

Several methods are typically used to assess ADHD, and the DSM criteria are often used to reach a diagnosis.

Assessments:

• Teachers and parents provide ratings of the child's behavior in the classroom and at home, respectively.
• Psychologists conduct interviews with the child, the parents, and other relevant individuals as needed.
• Psychologists conduct structured diagnostic interviews with the child and the parents.
• Psychologists make observations of the child in certain situations.
• Psychologists have children perform certain tasks.

Diagnostic criteria:

• INATTENTION, as seen in at least six of the following.
  • Often fails to give close attention to details or makes careless mistakes in school, work, or other activities
  • Often has difficulty sustaining attention in talks or play activities
  • Often does not seem to listen to what is being said to him or her
  • Often does not follow through on instructions and fails to finish schoolwork or chores
  • Often has difficulties organizing tasks and activities
  • Often avoids or strongly dislikes tasks that require sustained mental effort
  • Often loses things necessary for tasks
  • Is often easily distracted by extraneous stimuli
  • Is often forgetful in daily activities
• HYPERACTIVITY/IMPULSIVITY, as seen in at least six of the following.
  • Hyperactivity:
    • Often fidgets with hands or feet or squirms in seat
    • Often leaves seat in situations when remaining seated is expected
    • Often runs about or climbs excessively in situations when it is inappropriate
    • Often has difficulty playing or engaging in leisure activities
  • Impulsivity:
    • Often blurts out answers to questions before the questions have been completed
    • Often has difficulty awaiting his or her turn
    • Often interrupts or intrudes on others.

Reprinted with permission from the *Diagnostic and Statistical Manual of Mental Disorders, Text Revision*, Fourth Edition, (Copyright 2000), American Psychiatric Association.

Although ADHD children come from urban and rural as well as rich and poor families, socioeconomic status differences have also been reported: There is a somewhat greater frequency of children with ADHD among families of lower socioeconomic status (Biederman, Faraone, & Monuteaux, 2002). Several possible explanations have been suggested. Mothers of lower socioeconomic status are more likely to have poor nutrition and less access to prenatal care during their pregnancies, as well as a higher incidence of complications, perhaps affecting the developing brain of the as yet unborn child. Second, the troubled environment of families characterized by low socioeconomic status might account for higher rates of family instability and parental psychological disorders (Biederman et al., 1995), which in turn could affect rates of ADHD. Last, the high incidence of reported ADHD among children of lower socioeconomic backgrounds may be due to a predisposition on the part of teachers and others to expect ADHD behavior among them.

Causes

There is no one single cause of ADHD. Rather, there is general consensus that many factors contribute to its onset. Genetically determined predispositions, problems in brain structure and function, diet and toxic substances, and environmental forces (e.g., inconsistent environmental consequences and controls) have all been implicated. What does the research tell us?

It is now well established that problems of attention and behavioral inhibition are heritable (Faraone et al., 2005b). For starters, it is accepted that genetic transmission influences individual differences in general activity level. But do genetics contribute to the disorder? A large body of data suggests that the answer is yes—an individual may genetically acquire a predisposition to develop ADHD in response to environmental events. For monozygotic twins, the concordance rate is roughly 80%, but only 30% for dizygotic twins (Gilger, Pennington, & DeFries, 1992), and ADHD occurs more often in first-degree biological relatives of those with the disorder than would be expected in the general population. Approximately 25% of the biological parents of ADHD children, compared with 4% of adoptive parents, have histories (gathered retrospectively) of ADHD (Deutsch, 1987). In all, it is believed that genetic factors contribute to the variance in ADHD in the general population (Thapar, Holmes, Poulton, & Harrington, 1999).

Siblings of a person with ADHD are at greater risk for ADHD, especially when parents have a history of ADHD, and monozygotic twins are more likely to be concordant than dizygotic twins (McMahon, 1980). The data also suggest that the more serious the symptom picture, the greater the genetic contribution to the disorder. The evidence supports a genetic contribution, but a specific mechanism for the genetic transmission of ADHD—although there is mounting evidence—has yet to be completely identified (Banaschewski et al.,

2005). Several studies have identified an association between the dopamine transporter gene and ADHD (e.g., Cook et al., 1995; Gill, Daly, Heron, Hawi, & Fitzgerald, 1997), and it is accepted that ADHD, in part, depends on dysfunctional and hypoactive dopamine transmission (Sikstrom & Soderlund, 2007; Solanto, 2002). Waldman and colleagues (1998) reported stronger relationships for the hyperactive-impulsive symptoms than for the inattentive symptoms of ADHD. The fact that the results of several studies replicate the relationship of the gene to the psychological disorder is an exciting step toward understanding. However, given that ADHD is often comorbid with other childhood disorders, more research is needed to determine if the genetic link is specific to ADHD. Importantly, as with the other childhood disorders (see Chapter 2), research in molecular and population genetics has made it increasingly clear that childhood ADHD does not exhibit simple, single-gene inheritance patterns. Rather, there are likely multiple susceptibility genes that, under specific environmental circumstances, together increase vulnerability for the development of ADHD (Banaschewski et al., 2005).

What about child brain structure and function? Researchers have studied the possible role of brain damage, brain dysfunction, and delayed brain maturation in ADHD. Several decades ago the label "minimal brain damage" was used for the behaviors currently seen as ADHD. Consistent with the label, researchers were eager to try to document a link between brain damage and ADHD. The results, however, did not often fall in line. In studies of identified ADHD patients, only 5–10% were found to have histories suggestive of brain damage, and most children with well-documented brain damage did not develop ADHD (Rutter, 1977). The use of computerized axial tomography (CAT) scans also failed to reveal anatomical brain differences (Shaywitz, Shaywitz, Byrne, Cohen, & Rothman, 1983) and brain metabolism differences (Zametkin et al., 1993) between ADHD children and non-ADHD controls. Some recent work, however, suggests reduced brain volumes in ADHD youth evident in early life—particularly in the right frontal regions, caudate, corpus callosum, and cerebellum, as well as the parietal, temporal, and occipital regions (Castellanos et al., 2002; Durston et al., 2004; Krain & Castellanos, 2006; Sowell, Thompson, Welcome, Henkenius, Toga, & Peterson, 2003).

Studies have also suggested that brain functioning of children with ADHD may be impaired. ADHD children show performance deficits on tasks sensitive to brain function (e.g., August, 1987; Douglas, 1983), and they perform less well on measures requiring vigilance and impulse control (e.g., Homatidis & Konstantareas, 1981). ADHD youth struggle with tasks that require *executive functioning*—brain-related processes needed for applying a problem-solving set to attain future goals, such as planning, cognitive flexibility, abstract thinking, rule acquisition, initiating appropriate actions, and inhibiting inappropriate actions (Sergeant, Geurts, & Oosterlaan, 2002; Willcutt, Doyle, Nigg, Faraone, & Pennington, 2005). Performance domains with less executive components—such as processing speed, memory retrieval speed, fine and gross motor coordination, timing functions, and motor disinhibition—are also highly associated with ADHD (Banaschewski, Brandeis, Heinrich, Albrecht, Brunner, & Rothenberg, 2003a; Banaschewski et al., 2005; Nigg, 2001; Sheridan, Hinshaw, & D'Esposito, 2007; Smith, Taylor, Rogers, Newman, & Rubia, 2002). Specific parts of the brain, such as the frontal and frontal-limbic areas, have been implicated in these processes and in ADHD. The "so-called" neurological immaturity of ADHD children refers to their being chronically delayed relative to same-aged peers. The attention span, social behavior, and even EEG patterns of ADHD children suggest delayed patterns of brain maturation. Brain imaging studies suggest that circuitry in the temporal and frontal lobes—regions that integrate sensory information with higher order functions—show maturational delays in ADHD youth, lagging up to 5 years behind their non-ADHD counterparts (Shaw et al., 2007). Motor regions of the brain, in contrast, may actually mature faster among ADHD youth. Although research results are consistent with the hypothesis that brain function is involved in ADHD, poor task performance and delayed functioning could be due to other influences.

Have you read or heard the notion that a person's diet may cause ADHD? This hypothesis holds that hyperactivity is related to the child's food choices, such as consumption of large quantities of sugar. In fact, the idea that excessive sugar can cause ADHD is properly considered a myth. Also, eating foods with artificial dyes and pre-servatives is likewise a nonsupported notion about the etiology of ADHD. In the early to mid-1970s, however, after claims that a change in diet could reduce hyperactivity were published (Feingold, 1975), parents eagerly implemented changed diet programs. Concurrently, scientists undertook rigorous tests of the diet hypothesis. Overall, the accumulated evidence was a bit equivocal but generally failed to support the hypothesis that diet, or diet modifications, could have a significant impact on ADHD (Banerjee, Middleton, & Faraone, 2007; Conners, 1980). After reviewing several studies, Swanson and Kinsbourne (1980) made a very informative observation—they noted that the more rigorous the investigation, the less support it provided for the diet hypothesis.

How about television? Is there any truth to the notion that heavy television use interferes with the child's developing attentional abilities and causes ADHD? Supporting this notion, cross-sectional work shows that high television consumption is associated with psychopathology and attention problems (Ozmert, Toyran, & Yurdakok, 2002). However, it is important not to confuse correlation with causation. Does longitudinal research support the notion that television use leads to ADHD? Obel and colleagues (2004) followed a birth cohort in Denmark, and found no support for the notion that television use in early childhood predicted attention problems at age 10–11. Much like concerns about diet, it appears as though television use and related media do not cause ADHD.

Others have hypothesized social and environmental causes for ADHD, particularly the child's failure to learn adequate cognitive and behavioral skills. Like socially appropriate behavior, ADHD behaviors can be shaped by the social environment (O'Leary, 1980). A lack of a structured learning environment, observing inappropriate behavior by others, receiving rewards for fast guessing, not being taught cognitive strategies for modulating attention, and disruption and disorganization in the home can contribute to a child's failure to acquire sufficient self-control. For example, Wahler and Dumas (1989) viewed a variety of childhood problems as the result of dysfunctional parent–child interactions (see also Barkley, Guevremont, Anastopoulos, & Fletcher, 1992b). Research supports a link between social environments and ADHD, but longitudinal work does not indicate that social environmental factors are solely causal in the development of ADHD. Data have suggested that parents of ADHD children provide more direct commands and supervision than others, but these actions may be the result rather than the cause of the ADHD behavior. Also, following effective use of stimulant medication, mothers show a diminished pattern of control (Barkley, Karlsson, Pollard, & Murphy, 1985). As Braswell and Bloomquist (1991) astutely noted and registered, environmental factors seem to play a more important role in the course and ultimate outcome of ADHD than in its initial cause.

Controversial if not bizarre explanations for ADHD have also been offered. Are the soft X-rays emitted from fluorescent lighting to blame? Although one study (reported by Mayron, Ott, Nations, & Mayron, 1974) claimed that children exposed to full-spectrum lighting systems showed greater reduction in hyperactivity than did children who were exposed to standard cool-white fluorescent lamps, the study had several flaws. The observational period was quite brief, and the authors did not control for the level of illumination produced by the two lighting systems. Another study (O'Leary, Rosenbaum, & Hughes, 1978) alternated broad-spectrum and standard cool-white fluorescent systems at the end of each week of an 8-week period. This research team took care to ensure equivalent illumination and brightness during the study and their findings were clear: Lighting conditions had no significant effect on hyperactive behavior.

What then is the accepted etiological explanation for ADHD? In general, the accepted explanation of ADHD invokes a multiple pathways model, not unlike the diathesis-stress model that was described in Chapter 2. The growing consensus is that persons with ADHD have a biological predisposition and that the disorder can be exacerbated by environmental forces. The predisposition is necessary but not sufficient, and there is no single environmental factor, alone or in combination, that is unique or specific to ADHD. Both causes—biological disposition and environmental forces—are implicated in the disorder.

The course of ADHD

But, you might be saying to yourself, "Don't all children show difficulties in attention and impulsivity?" And "Aren't lots of kids really active?" "Isn't it a part of normal development for children to run about and play spontaneously?" In part, your thoughts are accurate and the implications for ADHD are real. Importantly, diagnoses of ADHD should be made in terms of the developmental appropriateness of the behavior. Only those children whose attention and/or activity problems are judged to be excessive relative to what is appropriate for the child's level of development should contribute to a diagnosis of ADHD. Certainly, children's ability to exercise selective attention improves with age (Hagan & Hale, 1973); a 4-year-old is not expected to have the attentional focusing skills of a 12-year-old. The impulsivity of a child just beginning school (6 years old) may be evident in fast and inaccurate responding to assigned math problems, whereas an impulsive adolescent is more likely to display impulsiveness in an increase in accidents (Barkley, Guevremont, Anastopoulos, DuPaul, & Shelton, 1993). Indeed, evidence supports the association between dangerous driving and disorders such as

ADHD (Jerome & Segal, 1997). For a well-reasoned diagnosis, the developmental inappropriateness of the behavior that is thought to be symptomatic is an essential element in an accurate determination of the presence of ADHD.

Segments of the population believe that hyperactive children will "outgrow" the problems. Some parents therefore refrain from seeking help and wait, and hope, for a natural change to occur at puberty. In fact, some ADHD children do show a decrease in excessive motor activity at puberty, but the other ADHD problems do not seem to go away with time (Cantwell, 1987; Faraone, Biederman, & Mick, 2006; Weiss & Hechtman, 1986). In approximately one-half of the children with ADHD, and some suggest in as many as three-quarters, the problems of attentional focus and related academic and social difficulties persist into adolescence (Fischer, Barkley, Edelbrock, & Smallish, 1990; Gittelman, Mannuzza, Shenker, & Bonagura, 1985) and some have argued that roughly 50% of ADHD cases persist into adulthood (Faraone, Biederman, & Mick, 2006). Longitudinal work shows that inattentive symptoms in the preschool years predict poorer reading, spelling, and mathematics scores 8 years later, even after controlling for child intelligence (Massetti et al., 2008). One follow-up report indicated that even when young adults with ADHD appear to overcome some of the educational and legal difficulties experienced during high school, they continue to report psychological problems and continued to seek mental health services (Hansen, Weiss, & Last, 1999). Ten-year follow-up evaluations suggest that ADHD youth are at higher risk for a range of adverse outcomes in later life, including elevated rates of antisocial, addictive, mood, and anxiety disorders. Longitudinal research has also investigated the characteristics of children with ADHD that may predict later problems by following up ADHD youngsters years later when they are adolescents (see Greene, Biederman, Faraone, Sienna, & Garcia-Jetton, 1997). Marked impairment in social functioning of ADHD children was found to predict later conduct disorder and some substance abuse in these same youngsters. In a study conducted in New Zealand, however, attentional difficulties were unrelated to juvenile offending or substance use (Fergusson, Lynskey, & Horwood, 1997).

A longitudinal look at adolescents and adults

A diagnosis of ADHD is typically made at about age 6, when a child begins formal schooling. Do ADHD children become ADHD adolescents, and then grow to be ADHD adults? To determine the adolescent and adult outcomes of children with ADHD, longitudinal research is required. But even this desirable research strategy has potential problems.

Barkley and his associates (see Barkley et al., 1991) studied 100 ADHD and 60 non-ADHD children 8 years after their initial diagnosis. Ratings of behavior problems and family conflicts as well as direct observations of mother–child interactions were taken in childhood and again at adolescence. The hyperactive children were rated by their mothers as having more numerous and intense family conflicts than the non-ADHD controls, although the adolescents themselves did not differ in their own ratings of family conflict. Observations of mother–adolescent interactions revealed more controlling and negative behaviors and less positive and facilitating behaviors among the hyperactive dyads than the controls (Barkley, Anastopoulos, Guevremont, & Fletcher, 1992a). Interestingly, the presence of conduct-disordered behavior was associated with the persistence of the conflictive family situation—a finding that suggested that at least part of the persistence of ADHD can be explained by the comorbid existence of other behavior problems.

There is clear value in prospective longitudinal research. Nevertheless, certain problems emerge whenever researchers try to measure the same psychological dimension at two different points in time. For example, observations of mother–child interactions are different at age 6 and age 14. At age 6 mother–child interactions are observed within a free play situation. At age 14, however, mother–child interactions are observed while the participants engage in neutral and conflictive verbal discussions. Different behavioral observation coding systems are needed for these two different interaction situations. The Barkley study used age-appropriate interaction situations, and the findings nevertheless evidenced meaningful consistencies. Children who were noncompliant as youngsters (in the free play situation) continued to be difficult with their parents at adolescence (in the discussion situation).

A different approach could have been chosen. Barkley and colleagues could have opted to use the same assessment situation at both points in time (e.g., parent–child interactions in free play), but such a choice, while creating equivalence of measurement at different ages, would have reduced the meaningfulness and relevance of the second assessment. Reviewers could have criticized the work for having used a developmentally inappropriate context for assessing mother–adolescent interaction. As it turned out, the use of the developmentally appropriate situation provided the opportunity to observe and record behavior that permitted reasonable tests of the hypotheses. It also permitted reasonable confidence in the conclusion that the mother–child interaction conflicts continue to be significantly greater in hyperactive than nonhyperactive children at 8-year follow-up.

The likelihood that ADHD will persist into adolescence depends on several factors. First, how were the children with ADHD first identified? When ADHD is first seen in clinic-referred children, 50–80% may continue to have the disorder into adolescence (Barkley, 2006a, 2006b). This estimate is lower when the ADHD children are first identified via a school screening procedure. Also, the persistence of ADHD problems into adolescence is associated with other features of ADHD children at the time of the initial identification: the presence of conduct problems, the presence of oppositionality, and poor family relations. When these factors are present, ADHD is more likely to persist.

According to recent reports, roughly half of ADHD cases persist into adulthood (Lara et al., 2009). When the problems persist, they are associated with a decreased quality of life, poorer work performance, less positive mood, and higher rates of injury (Kessler, Lane, Stang, & Van Brunt, 2009; Knouse et al., 2008). Persistence of ADHD into adulthood is consistent across gender and across predominantly inattentive and predominantly hyperactive/impulsive types (Kessler et al., 2005a). Cases of ADHD combined type are the most likely to persist into adulthood. Although issues in the prevalence and course of ADHD await further research, efforts to alter the trajectory have been developed and evaluated. We now turn our attention to these treatments.

Treatment

Currently, the foremost treatments for ADHD are medications and psychosocial programs employing behavioral and cognitive-behavioral strategies (see AACAP Work Group on Quality Issues, 2007; Abikoff & Hechtman, 1996; Anastopoulos, Shelton, & Barkley, 2005; Hinshaw, 2005b; Pelham, Fabiano, Gnagy, Greiner, & Hoza, 2005). Both pharmacological and psychological treatments for ADHD have received considerable application and study. In many instances, the approaches are combined, and the efforts of parents, professionals, and schools are included and integrated.

Medications for ADHD typically involve stimulants, although nonstimulant medications, such as atomoxetine (Straterra), are prescribed to treat ADHD as well. Stimulants, in proper dosage, have what has been described as a temporary "focusing" effect. A review of over 150 studies (Spencer, Biederman, Wilens, Harding, O'Donnell, & Griffin, 1996) concluded that use of psychostimulants (typically methylphenidate [Ritalin], but also pemoline [Cylert] and dextroamphetamine [Dexedrine]) by children with ADHD can increase their ability to sustain attention, decrease impulsiveness, and improve performance on fine motor tasks. Although the outcomes are not always consistent for ADHD children with co-occuring internalizing symptoms (e.g., DuPaul et al., 1994), research over the past 3 decades shows that roughly four-fifths of youth with ADHD treated with stimulant medication are considered "responders," compared to 4% to 30% of those treated with placebo (AACAP Work Group on Quality Issues, 2007; Greenhill, 2002). Also, numerous investigations have indicated that children's performances on a wide variety of cognitive tasks improve while on stimulants (Klorman, Brumaghim, Fitzpatrick, Borgstedt, & Strauss, 1994), and some research suggests that ADHD adults benefit from methylphenidate (Rosler, Fischer, Ammer, Ose, & Retz. 2008; Spencer et al., 2005). Although potentially controversial because of the age of the participants, some have reported that stimulant medications are helpful for preschool ADHD symptoms. It is also worth noting that the symptom reductions are less pronounced than those found in school-aged children treated with stimulant medication (Greenhill et al., 2006).

Initially, stimulant medications were designed for immediate release, and thus the effects would wear off after several hours. At that time, the medication was given two or three times a day. Over the past few years, long-acting forms of stimulant medication (i.e., extended release) have appeared on the market. In addition to convenience, extended release tablets provide children more confidentiality as they do not need to report at midday to a school nurse for medication administration (AACAP Work Group on Quality Issues, 2007). Research suggests that the long-acting stimulant medications are safe and effective among school-aged youth and older.

Although we are not fully certain of the mechanisms involved, stimulants increase norepinephrine and dopamine release in the prefrontal cortex, having a positive effect on attentional symptoms, which in turn can lead to a decrease in physical hyperactivity. However, the attentional focusing does not always translate into increased academic performance. Moreover, although there has been reservation about the use of medications for ADHD children who have tics (involuntary rapid stereotyped motor movements), data suggest that medications did not alter tic frequency (Gadow, Sverd, Sprafkin, Nolan, & Ezor, 1995).

History has been witness to changing information about ADHD. For example, it was once believed that because stimulant medications have a quieting effect on ADHD children the effects were "paradoxical." Indeed, for some years parents and professionals alike thought a paradoxical effect occurred when an ADHD child was quieted by a stimulant. Moreover, the quieting effect was thought to be evidence of the presence of attentional hyperactive problems. We know now that this belief is false. Stimulant medications have a quieting and focused effect on all children, both ADHD and non-ADHD (Arnsten, 2006; Rapoport et al., 1978; Weingartner et al., 1980). Relatedly, it would be an error in reasoning to assume that because a child is more focused on even a trial dose of stimulant, he or she has ADHD. Such thinking—using a positive response to the medications to confirm a diagnosis—is not supported by the data.

Despite positive effects linked to stimulant medications, there are shortcomings that are worth noting. Researchers have estimated that four-fifths of children with ADHD show a positive response to stimulants (AACAP Work Group on Quality Issues, 2007; Greenhill, 2002), but stimulants also have potential, unwanted side effects—including anxiety, insomnia, irritability, weight loss, increased blood pressure and heart rate, and occasional motor tics (Barkley, McMurray, Edelbrock, & Robbins, 1990). Also, not all children can be given these medications, nor do all who take them improve (Whalen & Henker, 1991). In the majority who improve, the effects are short-lived, persisting only as long as the drugs are taken. Moreover, increasingly, long-term follow-up evaluations of stimulant-treated youth are showing that these medications may lead to suppressions of growth in height and weight (Faraone, Biederman, Monuteaux, & Spencer, 2005a; Faraone et al., 2005b; Spencer, Faraone, Biederman, Lerner, Cooper, & Zimmerman, 2006; Swanson et al., 2007).

In the recent past, the number of children given the diagnosis of ADHD rose considerably. Correspondingly, increasing numbers of children were being placed on medications (e.g., Ritalin; Olfson, Gameroff, Marcus, & Jensen, 2003a). Based on biannual surveys conducted in Baltimore since 1971 (Safer & Krager, 1988), the prevalence of medication treatment for ADHD doubled every 4 years in the 1970s and 1980s, with approximately 6% receiving such treatment in 1987. The trend continued in the 1990s, resulting in widespread and increasing use of medications for inattention and hyperactivity (Olfson et al., 2003a). In recent years, the rate of medication use for ADHD youth has leveled off somewhat, although it continues to climb in adults.

How can we explain the increase in ADHD diagnoses and in the use of medications? Some suggest that 30–50% of those taking Ritalin may not even have ADHD (Bocella, 1995). In the US, misidentification of ADHD is said to be on the rise, perhaps in part because government regulations now provide special education services for children with ADHD. Thus, there is an incentive for some parents to seek and receive an ADHD diagnosis for their child.

There is a rising emergency problem. Because of the heightened sense of well-being produced by the drug, there are increased reports of children selling their ADHD medicine, with some youngsters breaking the pills and snorting the drug. Additional monitoring, and preventive intervention, may be needed to quell this trend.

Psychosocial approaches to treating ADHD emphasize teaching children the skills necessary to pay attention, engage in self-control, and reduce or better modulate excessive motor activity. Following the statement of O'Leary (1980) that hyperactive children need skills, not just pills, these methods have continued to modify the environment and provide structured opportunities for children to learn the self-control skills that they can take into new situations. Psychological treatments characteristically teach behavioral management and may feature parent training, structured classrooms, and training in cognitive skills (see Anastopoulos, Shelton, & Barkley, 2005; Bloomquist, 1996; Carter, 1993; Goldstein & Goldstein, 1998; Hinshaw, 2005a, 2005b; Pelham et al., 2005; Pelham & Sams, 1992).

Independent of the type of treatment provided to the child, programs that provide parent training are considered worthwhile. Comprehensive parent-training programs typically provide parents with some basic education about ADHD and teach them behavior management skills to use with their child (e.g., Anastopoulos, 1996; Anastopoulos & Farley, 2003; Anastopoulos et al., 2005; Braswell, 1991; Sonuga-Barke, Daley, Thompson, Laver-Bradbury, & Weeks, 2001). As Barkley (2006a, 2006b) argued, many of the interpersonal difficulties associated with hyperactivity come from the child's noncompliance and lack of self-control. Accordingly, parents are taught skills to reduce noncompliance (see McMahon & Forehand, 2005) and to help the child develop self-control (e.g., Braswell & Bloomquist, 1991; Kendall & Braswell, 1993). Parents learn to reward appropriate behavior, shape desired responses, and reduce and eliminate inappropriate behavior. In addition, use of a brief "time out" from desired activities can be effective. Parents are taught how to ignore unwanted actions, provide nonabrasive commands, and pay attention to positive behavior. Based on the positive outcomes of a comparison between parent training and a wait-list condition, researchers have stated that parent training increased parents' self-esteem, reduced their stress, and produced overall improvements in their children's ADHD symptoms (Anastopoulos et al., 1993). Not all skills that are evident during parent training, however, are maintained after the program is completed.

Because a child's ADHD has an unwanted impact that is evident in school, classroom management programs are designed to develop the child's ability to benefit from classroom instruction, decrease activity levels, and increase focused attention. For example, in one 10-week program, teachers first determined academic and behavioral goals and reinforcers for each child (O'Leary, Pelham, Rosenbaum, & Price, 1976). The teachers completed a daily checklist rating the child's behavior in the classroom, and the child could receive reinforcers according to the results of the checklist at the end of the day and at the end of each week. Compared with untreated children, the children who completed this program were rated as being less hyperactive and as showing improved behavior. Behavioral classroom management programs have demonstrated considerable efficacy in producing short-term gains in the treatment of school-aged ADHD symptoms (see Pelham & Fabiano, 2008). Like parent training, however, classroom skill training is effective while the program is operating, but diminishes in effectiveness after the program is discontinued. Pelham has further developed the classroom approach and employs a research-supported version of it in summer camps for children with ADHD (Pelham et al., 2005).

Programs strive to produce change that persists across settings, but this does not always occur. Overcoming this backsliding—by shaping and encouraging the child to internalize and take to other situations the skills trained in behavioral management programs—has been one of the goals of cognitive-behavioral treatments. Thus, cognitive-behavioral treatments combine behavioral management training with direct efforts to teach both self-control skills, such as self-evaluation and self-reward, and attention-focusing skills. The treatment strives to instill problem-solving skills that the child can apply in the classroom and with parents and peers, but the goal of generalization outside and after the program is quite challenging and has not always been met (Abikoff, 1985, 1991). For clinical cases of

ADHD, generalization of behavior change has not been reported. Only a few research reports have shown generalization of one aspect of ADHD (impulsivity) but other reports have been disappointing. In the absence of continued treatment, gains may not be sustainable across contexts.

Recall that many children with ADHD may have other problems, and that these other difficulties can be associated with an oppositional quality. Recognizing the central role of anger management for ADHD youth, Hinshaw, Henker, and Whalen (1984a, 1984b) provided and compared a cognitive-behavioral anger control program and Ritalin. Relative to the ADHD childrens' behavior before treatment, children in all conditions displayed less fidgeting and verbal aggression. The children receiving the cognitive-behavioral treatment were rated as having higher degrees of self-control and displaying more appropriate coping behaviors than the children receiving just medication. Although medications did not alter the content of the child's response, they did produce changes in the intensity of the child's behavior. Unfortunately, no follow-ups were done to determine if these beneficial gains were lasting.

Although there are inconsistencies, the findings generally indicate that stimulants and behavioral programs can have desirable effects on ADHD. But how do these treatments compare to one another? And what effect does combining stimulant medications and behavior therapy—referred to as a multimodal treatment strategy—have on childhood ADHD?

In an NIMH-funded evaluation, the Multimodal Treatment Study of Children with ADHD (abbreviated MTA study), researchers across the United States concurrently evaluated the progress of 579 ADHD-diagnosed children at six different sites. The youth had been randomly assigned to receive one of four treatments:

1   Medication management.
2   Multicomponent behavior therapy, which included parent training, classroom administered behavior management, and an 8-week summer camp.
3   A combination of Treatments 1 and 2.
4   Usual community care.

Immediately following a 14-month treatment, children in all treatment conditions showed improvements, but children treated with medication management or the combination of medication management and behavior therapy showed better responses than those children treated with behavior therapy alone or with usual community care (MTA Cooperative Group, 1999). Further medication management and the combination of medication management and behavior therapy produced similar gains to one another in the treatment of ADHD symptoms, but the combination strategy produced better gains than medication management alone in improving parent–child relations, reading achievement, teacher-rated social skills, and mood and anxiety symptoms.

Although the initial MTA outcomes suggested that medication or a combination of medication and behavior therapy were the best two options in treatment childhood ADHD, subsequent follow-up evaluations offer a more complicated and nuanced picture. For example, 10 months after treatments were discontinued, many of the initial advantages of these two treatment strategies disappeared (MTA Cooperative Group, 2004a, 2004b), and at 3 years post-treatment there were no longer any significant treatment differences in ADHD symptoms (Jensen et al., 2007). Similar results were found at 6-year and 8-year follow-up evaluations (Molina et al., 2009), during which time analyses showed that the initial response to treatment—any treatment—is most predictive of long-term benefits.

Additional research will help to determine what treatments work best for which subgroups of children with ADHD, but to date the conclusion seems to be that, on average, treatments incorporating stimulant medication (alone or with behavioral therapy) offer better initial outcomes, but that the differential efficacy across treatments dissipates with time. Medications are considered fast acting and effective, but the effects are gone when the medications are discontinued. Psychological treatments are not as fast acting, and the effects may be less apparent initially. However, when the effects are observed, and to the extent that the skills taught were learned and were continued to be applied, they are said to have the potential for persistence over time. The combination of medication and psychological treatment offers a reasonably favorable prognosis.

Summary

Attention-deficit hyperactivity disorder (ADHD) is characterized by inattention, impulsivity, and overactivity. Seen more in boys than girls, the symptoms of ADHD affect academic and social arenas and may persist into adolescence and adulthood. Multiple causal pathways are implicated in the onset of ADHD and there have been some positive results from treating ADHD with psychostimulant medications as well as with behavioral approaches.

Anxiety disorders 6

Emotional development is a challenge for all human beings. Over the course of less than a decade, children move from a state of limited emotional understanding to become complex emotional individuals. With age, the number and complexity of emotional experiences, as well as the demands for modulating emotional expression, all increase. It is not surprising that some children are overwhelmed by these challenges and experience emotional disorders. Anxiety disorders have a chronic course (Costello et al., 2003; Keller, Lavori, Wunder, Beardslee, Schwartz, & Roth, 1992), can produce severe interference in the lives of adults (Mendlowicz & Stein, 2000; Rachman, 1998; Rapaport, Clary, Fayyad, & Endicott, 2005), and are among some of the most prevalent emotional problems of childhood (Comer & Olfson, in press; Costello et al., 2003). Children with anxiety disorders show increased somatic complaints (Hughes, Lourea-Waddell, & Kendall, 2008) and poorer emotion regulation (Southam-Gerow & Kendall, 2000; Suveg & Zeman, 2004), and are rated by their peers as less likable (Verduin & Kendall, 2008). When unsuccessfully treated in childhood, anxiety disorders can be associated with increased substance use over seven years later (Kendall, Safford, Flannery-Schroeder, & Webb, 2004).

When children are asked to answer a question in the classroom, to compete in athletic activities, to be participants in social activities, or to perform in front of friends and relatives, they may become anxious. These reactions are normal. The anxiety disorders of childhood are characterized by more extreme and persistent emotional reactions. It is the severe manifestations of emotional behaviors that require intervention. Another type of emotional disorder, the depressive disorders, are discussed in the next chapter. We are here concerned with the anxiety disorders that are seen in childhood.

Normal emotional development

Before we embark on a discussion of emotional disorders of child-hood, let's begin by asking ourselves a question: Have we ever felt great worry or extreme emotional upset? The answer is most probably "Yes." Everyone has, and alone it is not sufficient to warrant a judgment of abnormality or to contribute to a negative reflection on one's character. Children too experience fears and anxieties—normal emotional challenges—and these fears and anxieties signal psychological disorder only when they are intense, prolonged, and interfering.

Consistently, research findings indicate that fears and anxieties in childhood are numerous and common (McFarlane, Allen, & Honzik, 1954; Muris, Merckelbach, Meesters, & van den Brand, 2002b; Ollendick & King, 1991), with roughly 70% of children reporting that they worry every now and then (Muris, Meesters, Merckelbach, Sermon, & Zwakhalen, 1998). Miller, Barrett, and Hampe (1974) assessed 249 children aged 7 to 12: 25–45% showed no fear, 50–60% showed normal fear, and 4–6% showed excessive fear. It should not be surprising that the vast majority of children (86% of the 568 studied) exposed in 1992 to Hurricane Andrew reported at least mild disaster-related symptoms (Vernberg, LaGreca, Silverman, & Prinstein, 1996), or that following the September 11 terrorist attacks, 85% of proximally exposed children reported that their sense of security had been shaken "somewhat" or "very much" (Comer & Kendall, 2007; Phillips, Prince, & Schiebelhut, 2004). Moreover, experimental work shows that exposure to threat-related news media leads to elevations in anxiety and perceived risks in normal children and adolescents (Comer, Furr, Beidas, Babyar, & Kendall, 2008a; Comer, Furr, Beidas, Weiner, & Kendall, 2008b). Regarding gender, some studies find that girls report more fears than boys (Ollendick & King, 1991), although other studies of clinic cases have found no gender differences (Treadwell, Flannery, & Kendall, 1995) and several studies suggest that both genders report fears associated with the same stimuli (such as getting lost in a strange place, a burglar breaking into the house).

Development is important. There are different fears for different years. Children aged 8 months to 2 years fear separation from the caregiver, though this diminishes between ages 1 and 2. Between ages 2 and 4 new fears appear—such as fears of animals and the dark. Between ages 4 and 6 the child's imagination develops and creates visions of ghosts, half-human/half-animal monsters, and unexplained sounds in the night. After age 6 children are more likely to have fears of injury, death, or natural catastrophes. Both Caucasian and African-American youth reported similar fears (Neal & Knisley, 1995), centering around harm befalling self or others. As adolescence approaches, the child may fear not being an accepted member of the peer group. Importantly, children's fears and worries become more abstract, elaborated, and future-oriented as cognitive abilities develop (Muris, Merckelbach, & Luijten, 2002a; Muris et al., 2002b).

At different points along the life span, the social environment presents different challenges that require the development of new skills, beliefs, or feelings. Fears and anxieties represent such challenges during childhood. Through learning to cope with anxious and fearful situations in childhood, children learn ways to cope with the fears and anxieties of later life. For instance, recognizing a fear, addressing the fear, coping with the fear, and eventually no longer experiencing the fear is a developmental sequence that will bolster the individual's ability to cope with fear and anxiety in the future.

Fears and anxieties are normal developmental challenges facing the maturing individual. During adolescence, autonomy and independence become major developmental challenges and the adolescent must establish a difficult balance between complying with rules and expressing independent competency. Again, it is normal to be involved in the conflicts of emerging independence, but the challenge posed by autonomy can trigger or exacerbate interpersonal problems. Child behaviors that may or may not be signs of psychological disorder must consider the culture (Lambert, Weisz, Knight, Desrosiers, Overly, & Thesiger, 1992; Weisz, Weiss, Suwanlert, & Chaiyasit, 2006) and be judged against the frequency of the same behaviors among nontroubled children. The relative intensity, frequency, and duration of the behaviors must be evaluated, and their role in the course of normal development must be considered.

> Unlike her 12-year-old peers, Marsha doesn't go to school with classmates, choosing instead to walk to school alongside her mother. On many days Marsha refuses to go to school because she does not want to be separated from her mother. Following an interview and discussion, the clinician learned that Marsha preferred not to have friends over to her home because she again feared that she might be away from her mom. The clinician also learned that Marsha worried excessively every night, typically crawling into bed with her parents for security.

Phenomenology and classification

Children can be diagnosed as having any of several anxiety disorders, including but not limited to generalized anxiety disorder (GAD), obsessive-compulsive disorders (OCD), separation anxiety disorder (SAD), social anxiety disorder (SocAD), and posttraumatic stress disorder (PTSD). In general, the symptoms associated with these anxiety disorders in children resemble many found in adults, including physiological, behavioral, and cognitive manifestations. Although the symptoms of anxiety disorders in children may be seen in expressions such as stomach aches, headaches, muscle tension, sweating, jittery behavior, or feelings of suffocation or choking, not all youngsters recognize these bodily reactions as related to anxiety. Cognitively, anxious children worry, often based on misperceptions of the demands in the environment and underestimation of their abilities to cope. A closer look at several of the anxiety disorders will provide more of the details and the distinguishing characteristics.

Generalized anxiety disorder (GAD)

The hallmark of GAD is unrealistic and excessive anxiety and worry that do not present as linked to a specific situation or external stress. According to Strauss (1994), this feature was present in over 95% of children diagnosed with GAD. Children with GAD report worries about future evaluations, social events, family activities, athletics, health issues, and simply what will happen the next day or even the next hour. Although children do not always use these phrases, GAD is also characterized by tension, nervousness, or being on the edge. This chronic persistent anxiety has been referred to as "anxious apprehension" (Barlow, 1988).

GAD involves excessive and unrealistic anxiety that is present more days than not, for a minimum of 6 months. It is experienced as difficult to control, and associated with some physical symptoms (e.g., restlessness, irritability, difficulty concentrating, muscle tension, sleep problems; Kendall & Pimentel, 2003; Strauss, 1994).

Four per cent of the adult population is said to suffer from GAD (Rapee, 1991), and although the number of studies with children are fewer than those with adults, these studies have produced varying estimates that average at about the same rate (see also Beidel, 1991). For example, Costello (1989) studied outpatient clinic participants and reported 4.6%, whereas Anderson, Williams, McGee, and Silva

(1987) studied a large sample of the general population in New Zealand and reported 2.9%.

Obsessive-compulsive disorder (OCD)

OCD involves the presence of recurrent obsessions or compulsions that are time consuming, cause distress, and lead to impairment in the person's functioning. More specifically, obsessions are recurrent intrusive thoughts or images that are perceived as senseless and inappropriate and cause marked anxiety. Compulsions are repetitive behaviors whose primary purpose is to reduce anxiety or distress.

Studies of childhood OCD have identified patterns in the content of the obsessions and compulsions. Common obsessional themes include contamination, dirt, violence, harm, or religious themes. Frequently reported compulsive rituals include cleaning, ordering, or arranging (Bloch, Landeros-Weisenberger, Rosario, Pittenger, & Leckman, 2008; Stewart et al., 2008). In one of the largest prospective studies, Swedo, Rapoport, Leonard, Lenane, and Cheslow (1989) studied 70 consecutive cases of OCD in children. Washing rituals were most often reported (85%), with repeating tasks and checking rituals also occurring frequently (51% and 46%). Dirt and germs were the most often reported obsessions (40%). Rituals were most frequently reported by children with obsessions, whereas the instance of pure obsessions was found to be rare. Do children even experience an obsession without a compulsive ritual? Consider Jim, an 11-year-old boy:

> Jim came to treatment following a phone call from his father. Dad reported that Jim recently disclosed that he was imagining and thinking about his teachers being naked. Jim stated that he couldn't pay attention at school, would occasionally break out into laughter in class, and was distressed even at home in his room when the thoughts would re-enter his mind. Jim reported that the images of naked teachers were "on his mind a lot of the day" and that he couldn't "get them out of his head." Though not a complete explanation, it was discovered that an older sibling's "sex talk" coupled with Jim's having discovered and viewed a "nude video" preceded his obsessional thinking.

OCD in childhood was once considered rare, thought to occur far less than the 2% prevalence seen in adults. Presently, although different studies have reported wide ranges, there is growing acceptance that OCD affects roughly 2–3% of children and adolescents (Henin & Kendall, 1997; Snider & Swedo, 2000). Onset is typically earlier in boys than girls (Snider & Swedo, 2000). Also, it is worth noting that a follow-up of persons with OCD over 40 years after the initial identification of the problem conducted in Sweden (Skoog & Skoog, 1999) revealed that an early age of onset (in youngsters; under age 20) was associated with a worse outcome (less evidence of recovery).

In the absence of overt behavioral compulsions, childhood OCD may be mistaken in clinical practice for GAD, as both disorders present with repetitive thinking about anticipated negative circumstances or feared events that is experienced as uncontrollable (Comer, Kendall, Franklin, Hudson, & Pimentel, 2004). How might OCD and GAD differ? Typically, the intrusive cognitive activity associated with OCD is more rigid, and less reality based, than intrusive cognitive activity associated with GAD. In addition, children with OCD may believe that an intrusive thought—such as imagining that a loved one will get injured in a car accident—could actually make that event more likely to occur (Libby, Reynolds, Derisley, & Clark, 2004). This "thought–action fusion" seen in OCD is rarely found in childhood GAD.

Separation anxiety disorder (SAD)

One anxiety disorder, separation anxiety disorder, is specific to children and remains a distinct category in *DSM-IV* (APA, 1994). Separation anxiety disorder is manifested by obvious distress from and excessive concern about being separated from those to whom the child is attached. Refusing to sleep away from home, staying excessively close to a parent while at home, and separation problems occurring when the child is about to begin school are relatively common. Marsha, described earlier, had been diagnosed with SAD.

What distinguishes SAD from normal behavior is the persistent and unrealistic concern—the child is overly worried about the harm that might befall major attachment figures. The diagnostic criteria appear in Box 6.1. When such symptoms are present and cause clinically significant distress or impairment in social, academic, or other important areas of functioning, a diagnosis of SAD is appropriate.

The contrast between normal and abnormal anxiety, depending on the child's age, is well illustrated by separation anxiety. Anxiety about separation involves a child being distressed in anticipation of or subsequent to being apart from an attachment figure (caregiver).

New parents customarily note that around the ages of 6 to 8 months their child seems extremely "clingy." The child's demands for being in the same room as the adult, being able to see the adult, and being held by the adult are heightened during this time, and the presence of strangers produces more noted discomfort. It is reasonable to conclude, therefore, that at this period in development attachment and separation are major issues for the challenge of growth and competence.

BOX 6.1 Separation anxiety disorder (SAD)

SAD is developmentally inappropriate and excessive anxiety concerning separation from home or from those to whom the child is attached. One of the anxiety disorders specific to young people, this diagnosis is only used for persons younger than 18 years of age. For a diagnosis, the problem must persist for 4 weeks or more and must evidence at least three of the following.

- recurrent excessive distress when separation from home or major attachment figures occurs or is anticipated
- persistent and excessive worry that an untoward event will lead to separation from a major attachment figure
- persistent reluctance or refusal to go to school or elsewhere because of fear of separation
- persistent and excessively fearful or reluctant to be alone or without major attachment figures at home or without significant adults in other settings
- persistent reluctance or refusal to go to sleep without being near a major attachment figure or to sleep away from home
- repeated nightmares involving the theme of separation
- repeated complaints of physical symptoms when separation from major attachment figures occurs or is anticipated
- persistent and excessive worry about losing, or possible harm befalling, major attachment figures.

Reprinted with permission from the *Diagnostic and Statistical Manual of Mental Disorders, Text Revision*, Fourth Edition, (Copyright 2000), American Psychiatric Association.

Infant–adult attachment (Bowlby, 1969) plays an important role in development, and its disruption can have unwanted effects. In early childhood, separation anxiety appears and recedes naturally as part of normal development. In contrast, when separation anxiety occurs in a 12-year-old, it signals anxiety that is beyond the normal developmental timetable, evidences attachment problems, and can reflect maladaptive adjustment (Jones, 1996).

Social anxiety disorder (SocAD)

Social anxiety disorder refers to the presence of pronounced and persistent fears of social or performance situations. Children with SocAD spend a great deal of time worrying that they may embarrass or humiliate themselves, and typically will try to avoid situations that would expose them to unfamiliar people or to the possible scrutiny of others (e.g., meeting new peers, speaking in class, reading in front of others; Puliafico, Comer, & Kendall, 2007). Developmental patterns show SocAD typically onsets in adolescence (Comer & Olfson, in press), with the onset of social fears (~10–13 years) typically preceding the systematic avoidance of social situations (~12–14 years) by about one to two years (Ruscio, Brown, Chiu, Sareen, Stein, & Kessler, 2008). Adolescents with SocAD typically show more pervasive patterns of social dysfunction and impairment than younger children with SocAD (Rao, Beidel, Turner, Ammerman, Crosby, & Sallee, 2007).

Posttraumatic stress disorder (PTSD)

Posttraumatic stress disorder refers to the development of a cluster of symptoms following exposure to an extreme traumatic stress involving actual or perceived threat of serious injury or death. These symptoms are grouped into three clusters: (1) *re-experiencing symptoms*, including distressing and intrusive recollections of the event, a sense that the event is being relived (i.e., flashbacks), intense distress when confronted with memories of the event; (2) *avoidance symptoms*, including efforts to avoid thoughts, feeling, conversations, or activities associated with the trauma; (3) *hyperarousal symptoms*, including increased agitation and irritability, hypervigilence, difficulty concentrating or sleeping, and exaggerated startle response. Children's reactions to traumatic stress are intertwined with key developmental factors and thus posttraumatic stress symptoms may manifest differently in children than in adults (Salmon & Bryant, 2002; Scheeringa, 2008). In children, re-experiencing symptoms may be evident in repetitive play patterns in which aspects or themes of the trauma are expressed—such as seen in the child who continues to crash his toy trucks together following a traumatic car accident. Symptoms of hyperarousal may manifest in the form of excessive temper tantrums.

Assessing anxiety disorders in children

Given our earlier discussion of the methods typically used for the assessment of psychological disorders in children it should not be at all surprising to read that the assessment of anxiety in youngsters is accomplished using self-report measures, structured diagnostic interviewing, and parent and teacher ratings.

There are several self-report scales that measure anxiety in children (Silverman & Ollendick, 2005). The State-Trait Anxiety Inventory for

Children (STAI-C; Spielberger, Gorsuch, & Lushene, 1970) uses 20 items each to measure the state of anxious arousal and the personality characteristic of trait anxiety, but it does not always succeed in terms of divergent validity (Southam-Gerow, Flannery-Schroeder, & Kendall, 2003). The Revised Children's Manifest Anxiety Scale (RCMAS, Reynolds & Paget, 1982; Reynolds & Richmond, 1985) assesses three factors within anxiety: physiological anxiety, worry and oversensitivity, and concentration/fear. A contemporary measure of anxiety in children is the Multidimensional Anxiety Scale for Children (MASC; March & Albano, 1998; March, Parker, Sullivan, Stallings, & Conners, 1997). The MASC consists of 39 items that assess physical symptoms, social anxiety, harm avoidance, and separation concerns. The MASC has demonstrated favorable psychometric properties, including strong reliability, validity, and sensitivity to treatment-related changes (Baldwin & Dadds, 2007; Walkup et al., 2008).

Although self-reports are useful, reaching a diagnosis usually requires a clinician-administered structured interview. As noted in Chapter 3, the ADIS-C is a semi-structured clinical interview for the diagnosis of child disorders such as the anxiety disorders (Silverman & Albano, 1998). Two separate interviews are conducted—one with the child and one with the parent. As with the MASC, solid psychometric data support the use of this interview. The Pediatric Anxiety Rating Scale (PARS), a clinician-rated anxiety assessment instrument is often in conjunction with the ADIS-C (Research Units on Pediatric Psychopharmacology Anxiety Study Group, 2002).

The Child Behavior Checklist (CBCL) contains items that assess emotional distress associated with anxiety. Within the Internalizing side of the CBCL, the anxiety-depression scale provides a parent-rated data base for evaluating children. An advantage of the CBCL is that it has normative data against which the child's ratings are judged. A parent's ratings can produce a score, and the score can be evaluated against the normative data that are provided. This process enables the user to determine the degree to which the child's scores are within or outside the normative range. A teacher rating version of the CBCL, the Teacher Rating Form (TRF), is also available. Anxiety scales for the CBCL and TRF successfully discriminate children with diagnosed anxiety disorders from their nonanxiety-disordered peers, and are sensitive to treatment-related changes (Kendall, Puliafico, Barmish, Choudhury, Henin, & Treadwell, 2007).

Understanding the problem and making a determination of the presence of a disorder benefit from multimethod measurement, including self-reports, interviews, and parent and teacher ratings.

Careful observation of the child's behavior in several settings would also be very valuable.

Who are the children with anxiety disorders?

As noted earlier, when community samples of children are studied, fears and worries are found to be quite common. Roughly 4–8% of children in the general population meet diagnostic criteria for an anxiety disorder (slightly higher in mid-adolescence; Costello et al., 2003; Kashani & Orvaschel, 1988). Substantial rates of anxiety disorders have also been reported in prescohool children (Eggers & Angold, 2006), although such findings should be met with caution given the lack of consensus in distinguishing normal and abnormal preschool behavior, sole reliance on parent report, and absence of data on the predictive validity of early childhood diagnoses.

In terms of meeting diagnostic criteria, boys and girls are relatively comparable in the prevalence of anxiety disorders in childhood, but the ratio changes in adolescence to 1:3. Research examining racial and ethnic differences finds African-American and Caucasian children show similarity in feared situations (Neal, Lilly, & Zakis, 1993) and clinical features of anxiety disorder (Last & Perrin, 1993), although some reports show rates of diagnoses are higher for African-American than for Caucasian children (Kashani & Orvaschel, 1988). Research shows Latino and Hispanic youth may demonstrate higher rates of somatic symptoms (Varela, Sanchez-Sosa, Biggs, & Luis, 2008).

Causal forces

Emotional development is influenced by a variety of factors, including genetic predispositions, parental psychological disorder, early trauma, the child's cognitive and behavioral learning history, and peer and familial interrelationships. Biological, cognitive and behavioral, and family factors offer the greatest promise. These explanations, often offered as explanations of anxiety disorders in adults, apply to disorders in children as well.

Studies of the genetic contribution to the anxiety disorders have indicated significant, though modest, heritability. One adult anxiety disorder—panic disorder—has been found to occur in nearly one-quarter of the close relatives of panic patients compared to 2% among controls (Crow, Noyes, Pauls, & Slymen, 1983). Research using twins (Torgersen, 1983) reported 31% of monozygotic twin pairs, but none of the dizygotic twin pairs, both had panic disorder. Simple phobias also seem to run in families (Fyer et al., 1990). In contrast, research suggests that there is only modest genetic contribution to generalized anxiety disorder (Hettema, Prescott, & Kendler, 2001; Kendler, Neale, Kessler, Heath, & Eaves, 1992). Apparently, not all of the anxiety disorders are alike in terms of the genetic contribution. Twin studies reveal that, among preschoolers, obsessive-compulsive behaviors are more heritable, whereas separation anxiety behaviors are more greatly associated with environmental influences (Eley, Bolton, O'Connor, Perrin, Smith, & Plomin, 2003). Genetic contributions may explain a greater percentage of the variance in male versus female SocAD (Kendler, Jacobson, Myers, & Prescott, 2002).

The basic idea behind the cognitive explanation is that anxiety results from dysfunctional ways of making sense of the world. Cognitive explanations emphasize the role of distorted cognition (Muris & Field, 2008) and self-talk—that is, children's internal dialogues and private self-statements (Sood & Kendall, 2007). Perhaps due to prior experience, or early mistaken interpretations of events, individuals who suffer distressing anxiety process their social world in anxiety-provoking ways. Holding irrational expectations for oneself, for example, can produce anxiety. To be unwilling to participate in a new game for fear that you won't be the best player ever is to hold too grand an expectation. Other cognitive functions are associated with anxiety as well. For example, anxious persons bring a tendency to perceive threat to a variety of situations. Being concerned about evaluation may be rational in a job interview situation, but the anxious person brings evaluative threat to situations that are potentially playful, relaxed, and comfortable. Anxious children report higher rates of negative self-statements, for example, "I thought I was going to do something wrong," "I feel like everybody was looking at me and laughing" (Sood & Kendall, 2007). Interestingly, anxiety-disordered children recognize emotions but do not seem to understand how to think about emotions in order to change them (Southam-Gerow & Kendall, 2000). Anxious youth report negative beliefs about uncertainty and its implications, for example, "Surprise events upset me greatly," "Not knowing what will happen makes me unhappy or sad" (Comer et al., 2009). It has been proposed that a general intolerance of uncertainty is a cognitive vulnerability factor for several anxiety disorders (Koerner & Dugas, 2008).

The behavioral explanation of anxiety disorders was discussed in Chapter 2 when we considered the classical conditioning of fear and we examined the contingencies involved in avoidance learning. As was stated, avoidance responses are responses that are made to prevent an unwanted situation or outcome. The relief of avoiding something unpleasant serves as a positive reward. Consider the child who is being teased by classmates in the playground at school recess. To stop the teasing, the child does not go outdoors during recess. In the future, staying indoors is associated with reduced anxiety. To avoid future anxiety, the child continues to avoid peers and continues to avoid social interactions. Such avoidance responses prevent the unwanted emotions from being experienced. As was also stated, avoidance responses that are not functional—they do not in fact continue to be effective in preventing the unwanted situation—are characteristic of anxious persons. In other words, even though the response (staying inside) is made to prevent a negative condition, the negative condition was not going to occur whether or not the response was made. In our example, the peers had matured, were socially supportive, were favorably interested in the isolated child, and were no longer teasing each other. The avoidance response is maintained, nevertheless, by the person's perception that it has been effective—in fact, the avoidance response was unnecessary.

Other behavioral forces contribute as well. Modeling, for example, plays an important role. A child can acquire dysfunctional behavior by observing a parent's reactions and behavior patterns, and hearing a parent's explanation for social events (Barrett, Rapee, Dadds, & Ryan, 1996b). The child can develop an anxious style without direct experience with anxiety-provoking situations by watching someone else. A child walking with a parent witnesses the parent crossing the street to avoid someone, not entering a store because there are people already inside, or declining an invitation to a social event, and comes to see the presence of other people as threatening. The child can learn to avoid through the vicarious experience.

Considerations of the family system as a contributor to children's anxiety disorders has also received research attention. Initial work suggests that children with an anxiety disorder are more likely to have a parent who is reluctant to grant autonomy and is somewhat controlling and intrusive, particularly in anxious situations (Hudson, Comer, & Kendall, 2008; Siqueland, Kendall, & Steinberg, 1996; Wood, McLeod, Sigman, Hwang, & Chu, 2003). Other work suggests that parents contribute to the child's tendency to avoid by encouraging them to solve problems in ways that are more avoidant than even the initial ideas of the child. That is, the anxious child may be somewhat avoidant, but becomes increasingly so after discussing problems to be solved with the parent (see Rapee, 1997). It appears that parent–child interactions contribute to the development and/or maintainance of children's problems with anxiety.

Treatment

The past 20 years have witnessed an emerging literature that describes the procedures in therapy and documents the efficacy of treatments for childhood anxiety disorders (see Silverman, Pina, & Viswesvaran, 2008). For example, there are treatments for specific phobias (Heimberg, Dodge, Hope, Kennedy, Zollo, & Becker, 1990; Ollendick et al., 2009; Silverman & Rabian, 1994), SocAD (Albano & DiBartolo, 2007; Beidel, Turner, & Young, 2006), and OCD (Leonard, Swedo, Allen, & Rapoport, 1994; March & Mulle, 1998; Piacentini, March, & Franklin, 2006). Given the high comorbidity among the child anxiety disorders, evidence-based treatment programs have been developed to flexibly apply to multiple anxiety disorders (e.g., SAD, SocAD, and/or GAD; Kendall et al., 2008).

The evidence-based psychosocial treatments designed for youngsters with anxiety disorders—typically identified as cognitive-behavioral—often combine skill in the management of unwanted arousal with exposure to the feared or distressing situation (see Kendall & Suveg, 2005). That is, children are first taught about their unwanted emotional, cognitive, and behavioral reactions, and then taught strategies to manage the arousal. The educational component of the treatment helps children identify their anxiety-arousing thoughts, teaches relaxation responses, and provides strategies for use to moderate anxious arousal. These parts are integrated:

F stands for *Feeling Frightened?*
E for *Expecting bad things to happen?*
A is for the *Attitudes and Actions* that you can take
R stands for the *Results and Rewards.*

As an illustration, the *Coping Cat* program (Kendall & Hedtke, 2006) uses the acronym FEAR to put the pieces together and empower children with a plan for mastering anxious distress. Children take the FEAR plan with them into the anxiety-producing situations.

Exposure is critical (Barlow, 1988; Kendall, Robin, Hedtke, Suveg, Flannery-Schroeder, & Gosch, 2005) in treating anxiety. Once the children learn the skills, they practice them in the once-feared context. Investigators on two continents have found that various versions of this approach (Kendall et al., 2008 in the US; Barrett, Dadds, & Rapee, 1996a in Australia) have been an effective means of treating youngsters diagnosed with anxiety disorders such as generalized anxiety disorder, social phobia, and separation anxiety disorder (see also Kendall, Flannery-Schroeder, Panichelli-Mindel, Southam-Gerow, Henin, & Warman, 1997; regarding obsessive-compulsive disorder, see March, 1995). Because anxiety and depressive symptoms often co-occur, the treatment of anxiety can be modified for comorbid depression (Kendall, Kortlander, Chansky, & Brady, 1992).

Studies of the cognitive-behavioral treatment of children who are diagnosed as suffering from an anxiety disorder have produced fairly comparable outcomes. Approximately 65–70% of children show marked improvements. Importantly, efforts are being made to improve the outcomes and recent studies are beginning to include and address parents in the child's treatment (Barmish & Kendall, 2005; Kendall et al., 2008). Over the past 10 years there have also been studies demonstrating the safety and efficacy of selective serotonin reuptake inhibitors for the treatment of the common anxiety disorders (Birmaher, Axelson, Monk, Kalas, & Clark, 2003; March, Entusah, Rynn, Albano, & Tourian, 2007; Research Units on Pediatric Psychopharmacology Anxiety Study Group, 2001; Rynn, Riddle, Yeung, & Kunz, 2007). Antidepressant medications (SSRIs and clomipramine) have also been used to treat obsessive-compulsive disorders in children (e.g., Gellar et al., 2003).

Recent clinical trials have compared cognitive-behavioral treatments to the use of selective serotonin-reuptake inhibitors for the treatment of specific childhood anxiety disorders (e.g., Beidel, Turner, Sallee, Ammerman, Crosby, & Pathak, 2007; POTS Team, 2004). In a recently completed trial (Child/Adolescent Multimodal Treatment Study, CAMS), 488 children with GAD, SAD, and/or SocAD (ages 7–17) presenting to clinics across the United States were randomized to cognitive-behavioral therapy, SSRI medication, a combination of cognitive-behavioral and SSRI treatments, or pill placebo (Walkup et al., 2008). Analyses showed that roughly 80% of children treated with a combination of cognitive-behavioral and SSRI treatments were rated by blind evaluators as "much improved" or "very much improved" at posttreatment, compared to only 24% of placebo-treated children showing comparable improvement. Children treated only with cognitive-behavioral therapy or only with SSRI medication also showed very impressive response rates (i.e., 60% for cognitive-behavioral therapy, 55% for SSRI medication), indicating that families presenting for the treatment of childhood anxiety disorders have three efficacious treatment options from which to choose. In the coming years, analyses of treatment mediators and moderators in the CAMS trial will help inform treatment decision making, identifying what treatment options work best for which children.

Summary

Fears are a normal part of development, but extreme fears can be a part of an anxiety disorder of childhood (e.g., separation anxiety disorder). Children can suffer from generalized anxiety disorder, separation anxiety, and other types of anxiety problems (e.g., specific phobia, obsessive-compulsive disorder). Family influences, learning histories, cognitive processing distortions, and biological predispositions all contribute to the onset of anxiety disorders in childhood. Several studies indicate that cognitive-behavioral procedures, pharmacological approaches, and their combination have been found to alleviate clinical levels of unwanted anxiety.

Depression 7

José was 13 when he was first seen in therapy. His parents made an appointment with a clinical child psychologist at the recommendation of a psychiatrist who had been unable to get José to talk. His parents reported that he stayed in his room, did not play with other kids, and often awoke during the night and very early in the morning. School was said to be uninteresting, sports were out of the question, and even youthful music was unfavored. After several sessions during which the psychologist was very calm and patient, José began to talk. Weeks later, he expressed hatred toward his hypercritical parents, an absence of closeness with any of his siblings, and extreme disappointment with himself. His emotional state was one of depression.

Phenomenology and classification

Believe it or not, depression was once thought to be a disorder limited to adults only! Depressive disorders impair the functioning of numerous adults (see Hammen & Watkins, 2008), but experts now recognize that children can and do experience clinical depression. Early on, childhood depression might have been overlooked simply because no one asked the child about his or her feelings and moods. Children who were brought to clinics for behavior problems might have also suffered from depression, but clinicians did not take notice. Unfortunately, children who were quiet and withdrawn, and perhaps dysphoric or depressed, were often ignored. When researchers began to ask children directly about depressive symptoms, it became apparent that children can and do suffer depression (Harrington, 2002), and childhood depression is associated with a wide range of negative outcomes, including future episodes of depression, impaired social adjustment, academic difficulties, and in some cases an increased risk of suicide.

In the *DSM-IV* diagnostic system (APA, 1994), adult criteria for a depressive episode can be applied to children (see Box 7.1)—although there are some differences in how the disorder is expressed. For instance, younger children might complain of physical symptoms more than adults and might be irritable. Older children might have more subjective symptoms than younger children, such as helplessness and pessimism (Weiss & Garber, 2003). Major depressive disorder (MDD) is the diagnosis when there is evidence of a major depressive episode—an episode that is not better accounted for by the presence of another disorder and there has never been a manic

---

BOX 7.1 Criteria for major depressive episode

A: Five (or more) of the following symptoms during the same 2-week period and representing a change from previous functioning; at least one of the symptoms is either (1) depressed mood or (2) loss of interest or pleasure.

- depressed mood most of the day, nearly every day, as indicated by either subjective report (e.g., feels sad or empty) or observation made by others (e.g., appears tearful).
  Note: In children or adolescents, can be irritable mood.
- markedly diminished interest or pleasure in all, or almost all, activities most of the day, nearly every day (either subjective or observed by others)
- significant weight loss when not dieting or weight gain (more than 5% change in a month), or increase or decrease in appetite nearly every day.
  Note: In children, consider failure to meet expected weight gains.
- insomnia or hypersomnia nearly every day
- psychomotor agitation or retardation nearly every day (observable by others)
- fatigue or loss of energy nearly every day
- feelings of worthlessness or excessive or inappropriate guilt (which may be delusional) nearly every day
- diminished ability to think or concentrate, or indecisiveness, nearly every day
- recurrent thoughts of death (not just fear of dying), recurrent suicidal ideation without a specific plan, or a suicidal attempt or a specific plan for committing suicide.

B: The symptoms do not meet criteria for a mixed episode (i.e., evidence of mania).

C: The symptoms cause clinically significant distress or impairment in social, occupational, or other important areas of functioning.

D: The symptoms are not due to the direct physiological effects of a substance (e.g., drug abuse, medication) or a general medical condition (e.g., hypothyroidism).

E: The symptoms are not better accounted for by a bereavement (i.e., after loss of a loved one), the symptoms persist for longer than 2 months or are characterized by marked functional impairment, morbid preoccupation with worthlessness, suicidal ideation, psychotic symptoms, or psychomotor retardation.

Reprinted with permission from the *Diagnostic and Statistical Manual of Mental Disorders, Text Revision*, Fourth Edition, (Copyright 2000), American Psychiatric Association.

episode. Based on the number of episodes, major depressive disorder is divided into two categories: single episode and recurrent.

Although the symptom picture is similar for youngsters and adults, we know a lot less about childhood and adolescent depression than about adult depression. Nevertheless, there are several facts that are clear. One is that depressive syndromes are relatively rare in early childhood but become more common with increasing age. About 1–2% of preschool children, especially those older than 2 or 3, have been said to have clinically diagnosable depression (Eggers & Angold, 2006; Kashani & Carlson, 1987). In middle childhood (ages 6 to 12), the estimate rises to 2–3%, based on large samples gathered in New Zealand and the US (Anderson et al., 1987; Costello et al., 2003, 2006a). By the time the child reaches adolescence, the rates of depression jump enormously, up to about the same rates as adults—between 4% and 8% if both major depression and dysthymia are combined (Cooper & Goodyear, 1993; Costello, Erkanli, & Angold, 2006a; Roberts, Lewinsohn, & Seeley, 1991). An additional 10% of youth in the general population suffer with symptoms of MDD but do not meet full criteria for diagnosis (AACAP, 2007). Comorbidity adds to the number of youngsters who are depressed. Children who meet the principal criteria for other disorders, such as an anxiety disorder or ADHD, may also meet criteria for a secondary diagnosis of depression.

Gender differences in depression exist, and they evidence a developmental pattern. A 1:1 (male–female) ratio in childhood changes to 1:2 in adolescence (AACAP, 2007). One study reported rates of major depression to be 4.5% for girls and 2.9% for boys (Whitaker et al., 1990). With further development, the ratio reflects an increasing incidence among females (see also Gladstone, Kaslow, Seeley, & Lewinsohn, 1997).

There has been concern in the popular and academic press that the occurrence of depression among youngsters is on the rise. Although we do not have high-quality surveys from previous generations for comparisons, people have pointed to epidemiologic studies of adults suggesting that those born in more recent decades are more likely to meet lifetime criteria for major depression than are their older counterparts (Lewinsohn, Rohde, Seeley, & Fischer, 1993). However, a meta-analysis of epidemiologic studies of children born between 1965 and 1996 showed that when concurrent measurement rather than retrospective recall of depression is assessed, there wasn't evidence of an increase in the prevalence of depression in later born generations (Costello et al., 2006a).

One of the consistent findings with regard to youngsters with depression is the high rate of comorbidity. Epidemiologic research reconfirms an earlier observation that comorbidity is the rule (Brady & Kendall, 1992). Children with a depressive disorder are at almost 30 times increased odds of having a comorbid anxiety disorder. Depressed boys are at 17 times increased odds of also having oppositional defiant disorder, and two times increased odds of having a comorbid ADHD diagnosis (Costello et al., 2003). It is estimated that up to 50% of depressed youth have two or more comorbid diagnoses (AACAP, 2007).

Deliberate self-harm has been found to accompany more severe cases of depression. Non-suicidal self-injury (NSSI) refers to the direct, deliberate destruction of one's own body tissue in the absence of an intent to die (Nock, 2009a). NSSI typically begins in early adolescence, with the most prevalent form of NSSI being cutting (e.g., taking a knife or razor to break the skin of one's arms or legs). Why do some adolescents engage in deliberate self-harm? Only recently have researchers initiated rigorous scientific inquiry into the topic of NSSI, and so much remains to be learned. Current thought is that: (a) NSSI functions as a means both of regulating one's emotional and cognitive experiences; (b) risk for NSSI is increased by genetic factors and the endurance of childhood adversities (e.g., childhood abuse, exposure to family conflict) that contribute to affect regulation problems and interpersonal dysfunction; (c) social learning and modeling likely contributes as well, for example, many self-injurious children report first learning about cutting from friends, movies, songs, the internet, and other forms of media (see also Nock, 2009a).

Suicide constitutes the most serious form of deliberate self-harm, and tragically is the third leading cause of death among youth (Nock, Borges, Bromet, Cha, Kessler, & Lee, 2008). In contrast to NSSI, suicidal behavior is characterized by an intention to die. The search for causal mechanisms in suicidal behavior has been constrained by several factors. As Nock (2009b) noted, well-controlled, prospective, and experimental studies of suicide are not possible due to a host of ethical, legal, and methodological reasons. Consequently, the best work to date in this area has consisted of correlational studies or post-hoc psychological autopsy studies that use retrospective parent interview methods after a child has already taken his or her life (e.g., Gould, Fisher, Parides, Flory, & Shaffer, 1996). Such research has shown that suicidal behavior is more prevalent among females, those with histories of victimization, those with a history of violence, those with a mental or substance use disorder, and those with a family history of mental disorders (Nock, 2009b; Nock et al., 2008).

Assessing depression in children

Measuring depression in children has proven quite complex. There are structured interviews, self-report questionnaires, peer nomination methods, and parent and teacher rating forms, yet the data produced by these various sources show limited cross-informant agreement. Depression as assessed by one method may not be consistent with assessments of children's depression gathered in other ways (e.g., see Comer & Kendall, 2005; Kazdin, Esveldt-Dawson, Unis, & Rancurello, 1983; Klein, Dougherty, & Olino, 2005; Saylor, Finch, Baskin, Furey, & Kelly, 1984a; Wolfe, Finch, Saylor, Blount, Pallmeyer, & Carek, 1987). The dilemma is evident in the following. Peer and staff ratings of depression are not meaningfully related to children's own reports about their level of depression. Self-reports of anxiety are often more highly correlated with depression than are self-reports and teacher ratings of depression (Wolfe et al., 1987), and a mother's depression may influence her report of her child's emotional well-being (e.g., Conrad & Hammen, 1989; Kiss et al., 2007; Kroes, Veerman, & De Bruyn, 2003).

As noted earlier, the emotional disorders of anxiety and depression are highly related (Kendall & Watson, 1989). Further research is needed on the overlap between anxiety and depression and to better understand the differences between self-reports of these disorders and the symptom reports of others. Still, because the child's experience is important, their self-report remains an essential part of the assessment of emotional distress (Finch, Lipovsky, & Casat, 1989; Klein et al., 2005). Indeed, when we need to assess clinical depression in children, researchers recommend that children and their parents be interviewed separately because parents, who can report their observations of some symptoms simply do not know what their children's private experiences might be.

Causal forces

Severe and disturbing levels of depression, in any of its forms, are not caused by a single environmental event or sole biological ingredient. Nevertheless, each of the various factors has been found to contribute to our understanding, and most of the investigations pertain to one or more of the major models discussed in Chapter 2.

Evidence is available on the genetic contribution to depression. Depression runs in families. Having a high genetic risk for depression is the single most predictive factor associated with developing MDD (Nomura, Wickramaratne, Warner, Mufson, & Weissman, 2002; Weissman et al., 2005). Genetics research results, using family history, twin, and adoption studies, support the conclusion that there is a genetic component to clinical depression (AACAP, 2007; Paykel, 1992). Some biological research reports modest associations between polymorphism in serotonin transporter region and depression-related personality traits (Levinson, 2006), but not the same degree of association with MDD itself. Other biological research suggests over-activation of the hypothalamic-pituitary axis may promote the development of depression.

Environmental factors are still important, however, as evident in the fact that the risk for depression among youngsters is increased when the history of the parent's depression includes onset before the age of 20. Experiencing specific parenting behavior has been estimated to explain approximately 8% of the variance in childhood depression (McLeod, Wood, & Weisz, 2007), with parental rejection and parental hostility offering the greatest predictive contributions.

Cognitive models of depression focus on the attributional styles that persons use to explain negative outcomes, and are, in various ways, offshoots of Beck's (1967) model of depression. This view holds that depression is linked to negative views of the self, the world, and the future. A related model (e.g., Abramson, Metalsky, & Alloy, 1989) emphasizes hopelessness and a depressogenic attributional style. When negative outcomes occur, depression-prone children attribute the outcome to stable, internal, and global aspects of the self. Misattributions with regard to loss, separation, and abuse are especially potent. Research with children has documented that negative attributional styles and misperceptions are related to the development of depression and depressive symptoms (Gibb & Alloy, 2006; Gibb, Alloy, Walshaw, Comer, Shen, & Villari, 2006; Kaslow, Brown, & Mees, 1994).

In one study, children (grades 3–6) identified as depressed were found to evaluate themselves more critically than their nondepressed peers (Kendall, Stark, & Adam, 1990a). To determine if the ratings were based in reality, or were a cognitive distortion, teachers also provided ratings of all of the children. The teacher's blind ratings showed no significant difference between the evaluations of the depressed and nondepressed children. The depressed children were showing their bias in harsh self-judgments.

Other data also support an information-processing problem in childhood depression. Judy Garber and her colleagues (Garber, Braafladt, & Zeman, 1991) examined how depressed and nondepressed children addressed negative affective experiences. Nondepressed children were able to identify ways to cope with affective distress, whereas the depressed children were more inclined to choose strategies such as distraction. Depressed children were also less likely to process negative emotions in ways that recognize that negative mood can be modified.

Behavioral explanations of depression (e.g., Lewinsohn, 1974) emphasize problems in the person's response to the environment. Reduced experiences with reinforcement, limited pleasant events, and nonresponsiveness to cues were thought to contribute to the emotional sadness. Interpersonal models emphasize parent–child and peer interactions.

Probably the most accepted model for understanding depression is the diathesis-stress approach. In this instance, biological and genetic predispositions interact with family distress and personal cognitive distortions. Depression runs in families, and it is likely that the early childhood onset of depression represents a genetically transmitted tendency (Holmans et al., 2007; Strober, 1992). However, stress is a contributor as well. Family disruption is a common feature associated with childhood depression. For example, several sources of evidence link negative quality of relationships between parents and children with depression in these youngsters. In depressed adults' reports of their own childhoods, they describe a variety of problems such as rejection by parents, neglect or lack of interest, hostility, or over-controlling behaviors by the parents (Hammen, 1991). One might be skeptical of the accuracy of these results if they were the only information available because depressed people might be biased to report only the negative memories of their childhoods. However, evidence suggests that retrospective reports are not necessarily unreliable or biased (Brewin et al., 1993)—evidence from studies of depressed children and from studies of children of depressed parents has also indicated hostility, arguments, and generally negative quality of interactions (see Hammen, 1991). Apparently, having a poor relationship with one's parents may set the stage for childhood problems. One might speculate that depression is especially likely to occur when the child feels bad about himself- or herself because of feeling unloved, unwanted, or insecure (for example, as a result of a poor early mother–child bond; Cummings & Cicchetti, 1990; Krobak, Cassidy, Lyons-Ruth, & Ziv, 2006).

The course of childhood depression

The median duration of a major depressive episode is roughly 1–2 months in the general population, and up to 8 months in clinic-referred samples (AACAP, 2007). After remission of a major depressive episode in childhood, longitudinal research shows that the probability of recurrence can be as high as 60% by the second post-remission year, and 70% by the fifth post-remission year (Birmaher, Arbalaez, & Brent, 2002; Costello et al., 2002; Kovacs, Feinberg, Crouse-Novak, Paulauskas, & Finkelstein, 1984). Depressed youngsters can show problems with depression as well in adulthood (Garber, Kriss, Koch, & Lindholm, 1988; Hammen, Brennan, Keenan-Miller, & Herr, 2008).

UK researchers recontacted former child patients and found that 60% of those treated for depression in childhood an average of 18 years earlier had experienced at least one recurrence of major depression during adulthood (Harrington, Fudge, Rutter, Pickles, & Hill, 1990). Certainly not all children who are clinically depressed will continue to have depressive episodes, but episodes of depression in childhood do seem to be predictive of future depression (Lewinsohn, Clarke, & Rohde, 1994) and there appears to be continuity in major depressive disorder from adolescence to young adulthood (Lewinsohn, Rohde, Klein, & Seeley, 1999). Youth with depression that onsets by age 15 and who experience a recurrence of a major depressive episode before age 20 seem to represent a particularly high-risk group. In later life, such youth suffer more severe, chronic, suicidal depressions, greater comorbidity, and worse psychosocial functioning (Hammen et al., 2008).

Treatment

Selective serotonin reuptake inhibitors (SSRIs), which have received considerable attention and some support in the treatment of adult depression, have also shown promise in reducing depression in youth. Depressed youth treated with SSRIs generally show a relatively good response rate (~40–70%) (Cheung, Emslie, & Mayes,

2005). However, it is important to note that the placebo response rate is also quite high (30–60%), underscoring the importance of treatment expectations in the remission of depression. Fluoxetine (Prozac) is an SSRI approved by the FDA to treat youth depression, and other SSRIs, such as sertraline, have received research support (Wagner et al., 2003). Depressed adolescents respond better to SSRI intervention than younger children with depression (Bridge et al., 2007).

Research bears out a small but concerning increase in risk of suicidal ideation and suicidal attempts in children treated with SSRIs. The US Food and Drug Administration (2004) concluded that SSRIs are associated with a two-fold increased risk for suicidal behavior and ideation, but not completed suicide, in youth. This finding highlights the importance of conducting a careful benefit-to-risk analysis prior to treating a child with SSRI medication, and the critical need for continued monitoring of SSRI-treated youth. Importantly, along with the widespread use of SSRI medications for youth depression, there has been a decline in adolescent suicide (Olfson, Shaffer, Marcus, & Greenberg, 2003b), although this finding is correlational and cannot afford causal conclusions.

A variety of psychological treatment approaches have received considerable support as well. One approach, interpersonal psychotherapy (IPT), has been used successfully with adults, and has been applied and evaluated with youth. IPT for adolescents (Mufson, Moreau, Weissman, & Klerman, 1993) is a structured psychosocial intervention that emphasizes interpersonal realms of life, including interpersonal disputes, role transitions, grief, and interpersonal deficits. So far, based on a few controlled studies, the gains are promising (Mufson, Moreau, Weissman, Wickramaratne, Martin, & Samoilov, 1994; Mufson, Weissman, Moreau, & Garfinkel, 1999). IPT for adolescents maintains key features of traditional IPT for depressed adults, but also addresses developmental issues most common to adolescents—including peer pressures, autonomy and separation from parents, and the development of romantic interpersonal relationships.

Another psychological treatment approach that has undergone systematic evaluation in the treatment of depression is cognitive-behavioral therapy (CBT). CBT for adolescent depression includes key components of CBT for adults—including mood monitoring, increasing pleasant activities, relaxation training, reducing depressive cognitions, and problem solving. Given developmental factors, depressed youth may lack a sophisticated set of labels for their range of affective experiences (Stark, Hoke, Ballatore, Valdez,

Scammaca, & Griffin, 2005). Accordingly, CBT for youth depression incorporates increased focus on the development of affective awareness and regulation skills in order to equip children with the necessary skills to recognize, identify, and understand emotion. Quality CBT for child depression typically incorporates a parent-training focus as well, in which parents learn to support and manage their child's depression, to reduce family conflict, and to improve relationships. These parent training sessions are often conducted in group formats (see Stark et al., 2005).

Evidence supporting CBT for youth depression is mixed but encouraging. In one controlled outcome evaluation, Stark, Reynolds, and Kaslow (1987) compared a self-control training program, a problem-solving therapy, and a wait-list control condition. The two treatments, each focusing in different ways on the teaching of self-management skills, self-monitoring, and social problem solving, were found to produce meaningful gains in both child self-report and interview measures of depression. Participating youngsters learned to plan and schedule potentially pleasant activities, to be less critical in their self-evaluation, and to view social dilemmas as problems to be solved. The positive gains from such treatment remained evident at an 8-week follow-up. (For examples of a school-based program for pre-adolescents, see Butler, Mietzitiz, Friedman, & Cole, 1980; Stark, 1990.) In a study with depressed adolescents, Lewinsohn and his colleagues (Lewinsohn, Clarke, Hops, & Andrews, 1990) provided and evaluated a treatment that involved a cognitive-behavioral group that taught skills for increasing pleasant activities, controlling depressive thoughts, improving social interactions, and resolving conflict. In a research design that allowed for the examination of the effects of parental involvement, parents of some of the depressed adolescents were told of the program given to their teens and were encouraged to be supportive and reinforcing, especially when the adolescent used the coping skills to address family problems. A look at the overall effects, in terms of self-reported depression and the percentage of patients meeting diagnostic criteria, showed that improvements were achieved. Indeed, the significant reduction in symptoms and diagnoses held up at a 2-year follow-up evaluation.

At the turn of the century, based on a meta-analysis of the reported positive results, Reinecke, Ryan, and DuBois (1998) concluded that CBT was generally found to be useful in reducing dysphoria and depression, and the effects were found to have been maintained at follow-up. Although these outcomes are encouraging (see also Brent et al., 1997), not all of the treated adolescents responded equally favorably to the treatment. Based on a study of 50 depressed adolescents, Jayson and colleagues (Jayson, Wood, Kroll, Fraser, & Harrington, 1998) reported that 60% of adolescents experienced symptom remission, but that adolescents with more severe psychosocial stress and greater symptom severity were less likely to exhibit remission of symptoms.

Meta-analyses including more recent outcome evaluations continue to identify CBT as effective in treating youth depression (e.g., Compton, March, Brent, Albano, Weersing, & Curry, 2004), but recent treatment effect sizes associated with CBT for youth depression are not as high as they were initially (Klein, Jacobs, & Reinecke, 2007). One potential explanation is that the increased methodological rigor characteristic of recent research has afforded more conservative tests of treatment effects. For example, studies can evaluate outcomes; (a) for those who completed the program only or (b) for those who were assigned to the program. Not everyone completes the treatment program. What are called "intent-to-treat evaluations" include and analyze all participants' data, regardless of whether they completed treatment. "Completer" analyses, as you can guess, test to see if the treatment worked for only those who completed the treatment. Treatment-produced gains can be more impressive when examining only those who complete the program. Other methodological factors may contribute as well: for example, evaluations of CBT versus untreated patients suggest larger effects than comparisons of CBT to active supportive comparison treatments.

CBT is an empirically supported treatment, but there are data that inform us about when it may be more or less effective. Recent empirical work shows that CBT is less effective when a parent is depressed as well, or when there is a history of abuse (AACAP, 2007; Barbe, Bridge, Birmaher, Kolko, & Brent, 2004). Weisz and colleagues (e.g., 2006) note some difficulties in the implementation of CBT in community clinics. Whereas therapist training in tightly controlled trials is fairly extensive, community clinicians in underfunded and overburdened mental health facilities rarely have the necessary time to sufficiently learn effective CBT for depression. Clinical trials evaluating CBT for youth depression in community clinics have reported less favorable results than clinical trials conducted in research clinics. For example, Weisz and colleagues (2009) found that CBT delivered by minimally trained community clinicians produced similar response rates to usual care. It is important to note, however, that CBT was shorter and less costly, and associated with a lower need for additional services.

Drawing on the overall separate promise of CBT and medication therapies for youth depression, clinical trials have taken to comparing cognitive-behavioral treatments to the use of SSRIs for the treatment of youth depression. In one such study, the Treatment for Adolescents with Depression Study (TADS), roughly 400 adolescents with major depressive disorder presenting to clinics across the United States were randomized to CBT, SSRI medication, a combination of CBT and medication, or a pill placebo (TADS Study Team, 2003). Analyses revealed the combination of CBT and SSRI treatment to be the superior treatment. This finding was evident at both immediate posttreatment (71% response, compared to 35% for placebo pill) and when participants were re-evaluated 3 years later (86% response) (TADS Study Team, 2004, 2007). Depressed adolescents treated only with SSRI medication also fared well, showing a 61% response rate at posttreatment, and 81% response at 3-year follow-up evaluation. CBT-treated adolescents showed a 43% response rate immediately following treatment. Importantly, although immediate response associated with CBT alone was not as potent as the combination, when these youth were evaluated 3 years later they showed an 81% response rate—a response equivalent to the long-term response of SSRI alone. In addition, adolescents treated with CBT or with a combination of CBT and SSRI medication showed lower rates of suicidal ideation and attempts in the 2 years following treatment. In all, the results of the TADS trial suggest that a combination of CBT and SSRI medication is superior to CBT or medication alone in the treatment of adolescent depression. SSRI medication or a combination of SSRI medication and CBT offer an accelerated treatment response, and the incorporating of CBT in the treatment program enhances safety.

Summary

Children can and do experience depression. With age, more females are found to suffer with the disorder. If children are left untreated, they are at significant risk for depression in adulthood. Family influences, learning histories, cognitive processing distortions, and biological predispositions all contribute to the onset of depressive disorders in childhood. SSRI medication has been shown to be efficacious in the treatment of adolescent depression, but some research suggests caution due to a small increase in the risk of suicidal ideation and behavior in SSRI-treated depressed youth. Research

evaluating cognitive-behavioral therapy has produced mixed but generally positive findings in the treatment of youth depression. A large-scale comparison of medication and cognitive-behavioral approaches to treating youth depression showed that a combination of SSRI medication and cognitive-behavioral therapy may be the optimal approach to safely reducing adolescent depression.

Eating disorders 8

Because eating disorders are characteristically first identified during the pre-adult years, we include them in our consideration of psychological problems of youth. When the problems persist, however, they are troublesome for adults as well (see Wilson & Pike, 2001). Eating disorders often have emotional and behavioral qualities as well as physical consequences. Although many persons with eating disorders do not have other problems, of those who do, they may be comorbid with any of a wide variety of other disorders. The two major disturbances in eating behavior that we discuss are anorexia nervosa and bulimia nervosa. However, before we examine these disorders we will first consider feeding difficulties seen in infancy and early childhood.

Feeding disorder of infancy or early childhood

Feeding is the first task in which the parent and child work together for a common goal. Not surprisingly, many parents show interest in the details of their newborn's eating habits and disturbances in the area of feeding can contribute to parental distress (Budd & Chugh, 1998; Linscheid, Budd, & Rasnake, 2003).

Estimates of the extent of feeding problems vary a great deal—with higher rates reported by studies using more inclusive criteria and lower rates reported by studies with rigorous criteria. Many children may show finicky eating, selective eating, overeating, or some vomiting, but these variations are within normal limits and do not reflect disorder. In fact, over 50% of parents report at least one feeding problem in children below the age of 7 (Nicholls & Bryant-Waugh, 2008). When the stringent criteria are applied, only 1–2% of infants evidence persistent feeding problems.

The central feature of a feeding disorder of infancy is the persistent failure to consume adequate food as evident in a failure to gain weight or significant weight loss over at least one month. For a diagnosis, the child must be under age 6, and must show a problem that is not the result of a general medical condition or gastrointestinal disorder.

As is true for the majority of childhood disorders, a wide variety of etiological models have been proposed (e.g., physical, child temperament, modeling, parent behavior, family factors) to explain variations in eating behavior. For example, maladaptive patterns of parental interaction with the newborn have been implicated in the onset of feeding problems. Nonresponsiveness to the child's needs (Bradley, Casey, & Wortham, 1984) and power struggles over feeding (Chatoor & Egan, 1983) illustrate parental behavior that can contribute to feeding problems. Although the amount of research is limited, the field is increasingly adopting a diathesis-stress model for clinic-referred families in which the interplay of physiological, social, and behavioral factors explain the nature of feeding disorders (Budd et al., 1992). In non-clinic-referred families, parent–child disruptions do not appear to play a role in the development of infant feeding problems (Maldonado-Duran et al., 2008).

Once a feeding problem has been identified, the typical approach to remediate the problem is to work with the parent(s) to alter feeding-related behavior patterns. Parent guidance and education can be useful, as can repeated exposures to models who are responsive to child needs, avoid power struggles, and who are tolerant of individual variability in feeding styles. The infants can also be exposed to various foods, and can receive differential attention for eating increasingly diverse foods. It should be kept in mind that mild feeding difficulties are common in infancy and childhood and they do not require excess attention. However, there are serious eating disorders that emerge during childhood and these often do require professional attention.

Anorexia nervosa

"Nervous loss of appetite" is the exact meaning of the phrase *anorexia nervosa*.

At 15, Alma had been healthy and well-developed, had menstruated at age 12, was 5 feet 6 inches tall, and weighed 172 pounds. At that time her mother urged her to change to a school with higher academic standing, a change she resisted. Her father hounded her to watch her weight, an idea that she took up with great eagerness— and she began a rigid diet. She lost weight rapidly and, surprisingly to her, her menses ceased. She enjoyed becoming thin, as it gave her a sense of pride, power, and accomplishment. She also began a frenetic exercise program, swimming hundreds of laps, running on the treadmill for hours, or doing calisthenics to the point of exhaustion. Whatever low point her weight reached, Alma feared that she might still become "too fat" if she regained as little as an ounce. After several months of the extreme exercise, most of the time her weight was less than 70 pounds, and when she temporarily yielded to others' efforts to make her gain weight, she lost it again almost immediately. There was also a marked change in her character and behavior. Formerly sweet, obedient, and considerate, she became more and more demanding, obstinate, irritable, and arrogant. There was constant arguing, not only about what she should eat but about all other activities as well.

(Adapted and modified from Bruch, 2001)

Phenomenology and classification

Anorexia nervosa was originally applied because theoreticians believed that anorectic patients did not experience pangs of hunger. As it turns out, they do experience hunger pangs, often intensely, so the phrase may be a misnomer. Nevertheless, anorexia nervosa is an eating disorder characterized by an intense fear of becoming obese, a distorted self-perception of body image, refusal to maintain minimal normal body weight (significant weight loss), and, in females, the cessation of menstruation.

Individuals with anorexia are persistent in the desire for additional weight loss. They believe that they are overweight even when others evaluate them as thin or even emaciated. They have a distorted self-perception of body size; they fail to recognize successful weight loss and their need to control their body by weight loss. They may weigh themselves on scales multiple times each day, or continually look in mirrors to reassess their figure. Whereas it is safe to say that the average dieter does not share these characteristics, certain groups (such as ballet dancers and female athletes, male wrestlers) that are quite conscientious about weight may be considered at risk. The exact *DSM-IV* criteria are presented in Box 8.1.

The risk for onset of anorexia is highest between ages 14–18 (Nicholls & Bryant-Waugh, 2008)—the average age of onset is 17 years, although some suggest that the age of onset appears to be at younger ages these days. The estimates of prevalence vary greatly, depending on the manner used to identify persons with anorexia, with one consistency: the disorder is 8 to 11 times more common in females than males (Steinhausen, 1994), but those men with eating disorders are quite similar to their female counterparts (Olivardia & Pope, 1995). Anorexia nervosa is seen in clinical settings as early as 7 years of age (Nicholls & Bryant-Waugh, 2008), but such cases are extremely rare (Van Son, Van Hoeken, Bartelds, Van Furth, & Hoek, 2006). Some early data (Pope, Hudson, & Yurgelun-Tudd, 1984) suggested that 1 in every 200 school-aged girls qualified as anorexic, whereas more conservative estimates have placed the prevalence at 1 in 200,000.

BOX 8.1   DSM criteria for a diagnosis of anorexia nervosa

- Refusal to maintain body weight at or above a minimally normal weight for age and height (e.g., weight loss leading to maintenance of body weight less than 85% of that expected; or failure to make expected weight gain during periods of growth, leading to body weight less than 85% of that expected).
- Intense fear of gaining weight or becoming fat, even though underweight.
- Disturbance in the way in which one's body weight or shape is experienced, undue influence of body weight or shape on self-evaluation, or denial of the seriousness of the current low body weight.
- In postmenarcheal females, amenorrhea, i.e., the absence of at least three consecutive menstrual cycles. (A woman is considered to have amenorrhea if her periods occur only following hormone, e.g., estrogen, administration.)

Reprinted with permission from the *Diagnostic and Statistical Manual of Mental Disorders, Text Revision*, Fourth Edition, (Copyright 2000), American Psychiatric Association.

Anorexia nervosa has been identified worldwide. Incidence rates in the US vary (Jones, Fox, Babigian, & Hutton, 1980; Lucas, Beard, O'Fallon, & Kurland, 1991), but it is generally accepted that anorexia affects less than 1% of the adolescent population (Hoek, 2006). In the US, roughly half of the adolescents suffering with anorexia go undetected in the health care system (Keski-Rahkonen et al., 2007). Anorexia is quite rare in China (Lee, Chiu, & Chen, 1989), but quite common in Japan (Suematsu, Kuboki, & Itoh, 1985). An incidence of 6.3 per 100,000 was reported in a Dutch study (Hoek, 1991). Whereas anorexia is less common among African-Americans in the US (Dolan, 1991), Africa, and the UK, research suggests rates of disorder are on the rise among women of color (Gilbert, 2003). It has been suggested that in the US ethnic differences in clinical presentations may have historically led to underdiagnosis of anorexia in ethnic-minority adolescents (Gilbert, 2003). Of note, African-American and Asian females who present with anorexia are less likely to suffer the body image distortions that are characteristic in Caucasian samples (Holden & Robinson, 1988; Lee et al., 1989).

Is the problem of anorexia on the increase? There are more reported cases of anorexia nervosa now than there were a few years ago, particularly among young women between the ages of 15–19 (Hoek, 2006; Van Son et al., 2006), but does this mean the disorder is on the rise? Some researchers believe that the change reflects increases in the number of young women in the population and an increased awareness of the disorder, however, and not true changes in frequency (Williams & King, 1987).

Unlike many psychological problems, anorexia can lead to serious physical illness and even to death. Estimates vary, but a typical estimate holds that two-thirds of cases are treated successfully and one-third are chronically ill. Less than 5% of anorexics are said to die from the disorder (Steinhausen, 1994). Anorexia nervosa is associated with cardiovascular complications, and can have irreversible effects on physical development, including reduced growth, impaired bone mineral accretion, and structural and functional brain changes (Katzman, 2005).

Causes and course

Eating disorders are most likely to appear in adolescence because of the convergence of physical changes and psychosocial challenges. The increase in body fat, which is most dramatic in adolescent girls, is frequently associated with concerns about increased weight and the need to do something about it. Researchers and theoreticians have amassed considerable data about anorexia nervosa, but no one explanation is accepted by all of the workers in this field.

Psychological factors

Psychodynamic theorizing (such as Bruch, 2001) has argued that because of disturbed mother–child interactions anorexic children failed to develop a body identity and a sense of owning their own bodies. They are said to be overpowered by the body's needs; not eating can provide a false sense of control. The sense of control derived from not eating also appears in explanations based on other theoretical points of view.

Are there personality traits that have been linked to anorexia? Although limited by retrospective reporting that is typical in clinical history taking, a pattern of compliance, perfectionism, and dependence, as well as the absence of school or educational problems, has been described as characteristic of anorexic youngsters (Jordan et al., 2009; Thompson-Brenner, Eddy, Satir, Boisseau, & Westen, 2008). Obsessive-compulsive tendencies and early eating and digestive problems may be present (Manchi & Cohen, 1990).

Minuchin and his colleagues (Minuchin et al., 1978) viewed the family as a system and argued that the symptoms of anorexia cannot be understood outside the system. As noted in Chapter 2, the family of an anorexic child, in this view, is marked by enmeshment. In an enmeshed family, each member lacks a distinct identity. A child in such a family can feel protected by the group, but also fails to develop a personal sense of autonomy or independence. The anorexic individual challenges the family system and wants to break out; failure to eat is the rebellion.

In the view of Minuchin et al. (1978), rigidity and a failure to resolve conflicts are theorized to be a mark of the families of anorexic children. According to Minuchin, the symptoms of the anorexic child regulate the family by keeping parental conflict from getting out of control. The symptoms thus protect the stability of the family. Although these ideas have not received rigorous research evaluations, data are consistent with the view that the families of anorexics have increased parental conflict (Kalucy, Crisp, & Harding, 1977).

Anorexia has also been described as an avoidance response, where excessive anxiety is associated with the avoidance of food. The food avoidance is then reinforced by the attention that it brings to the individual (Leitenberg, Agras, & Thomson, 1968). The anorexic, therefore, is seen as having learned that not eating is a successful way to get attention.

The social pressure to be thin is emphasized in other learning explanations of the disorder. It is easy to imagine how one might learn the expected body size. Evidence of the pressure for thinness is in the photographs and articles in newspapers and magazines and in the advertisements and scripts of television programs and movies. Thinness is often a part of the developing self-concept of teenage girls.

Cultural forces are said to be operative in the eating disorders. In many cultures, the ideal for female beauty has increasingly become a lean woman, and the influence of this ideal is spreading to other cultures (e.g., Eddy, Hennessey, & Thompson-Brenner, 2007). Using a bust-to-waist ratio calculated on female figures in popular magazines, researchers have documented that the cultural ideal of beauty has become increasingly leaner (Williamson, Kahn, Remington, & Anda, 1990). However, the discrepancy between ideal and real has created a widespread desire for "magical" programs that make women healthier, slimmer, and more aesthetically appealing (Brownell, 1991). There are mass-marketed diet aids and stimulant drugs that curb hunger, and many infomercials airing on late-night television. Weight biases and discriminatory practices in society have been well documented (Andreyeva, Puhl, & Brownell, 2008; Brownell, Puhl, Schwartz, & Rudd, 2005). The pressure is on women, and it seems to be internalized in adolescence (Keel, Leon, & Fulkerson, 2001).

Follow-up reports from former anorexics have suggested another explanation. Garner and Bemis-Vitousek (1985) saw a persistent pattern of distorted thinking among anorexic individuals and built the beginnings of a cognitive model of the disorder. They noted that the behavior of anorexic individuals reflects their conviction that they "must" be thin—not just a desire or wish to be thin, but a controlling and demanding must. The striving to lose weight may be a route to alleviate the dysphoria, isolation, low sense of self-worth, and sense of inadequacy often felt by young adolescents. Modern cognitive vulnerability accounts of anorexia emphasize body dissatisfaction, drive for thinness, and other distorted beliefs about weight, shape, and eating (Garner & Magana, 2006). Anorexics also make inaccurate cognitive evaluations: for example, "I must lose more weight since I am not yet thin" and "I must continue to lose weight so I can continue to be in control of my body." While losing weight at alarming and dangerous rates, the anorexic processes the weight loss as success, as evidence of power and control. More is better, so the weight loss continues as the sense of power continues. This aberrant thinking leads to and maintains the eventually self-destructive behavior.

Biological factors

Hormones, genetics, and brain functioning are three areas where biological models have been applied to eating disorders. The hypothalamus has been considered the brain area likely to control eating. Possible biological factors in anorexia, therefore, included malfunctioning of the hypothalamus. For example, researchers found that animals will stop eating, and can literally starve to death, when they are given lesions in one portion of the hypothalamus, or when stimulation is applied to other areas of the hypothalamus. Currently, the hypothalamus is considered important in controlling a variety of motivated behaviors (eating, drinking, temperature, sex). Biological models emphasize the potential role of impaired neurodevelopment, particularly dysregulation of the hypothalamic-pituitary-adrenal (HPA) axis, resulting in persistently elevated corticotrophin releasing hormone (CRH) activity (Connan, Campbell, Katzman, Lightman, & Treasure, 2003). Prolonged CRH release can lead to loss of nutritional homeostasis. A number of obstetrical complications have been empirically linked to the subsequent development of anorexia (e.g., maternal anemia, diabetes mellitus, placental infarction), and it has been suggested that such early experiences may disrupt and impair healthy brain development (Favaro, Tenconi, & Santonastaso, 2006), although the specific mechanisms through which such early experiences may predispose individuals to the development of anorexia remain unclear.

Studies have shown correlations between anorexic behavior and changes in norepinephrine and serotonin (Fava, Copeland, Schweiger, & Herzog, 1989), but the direction of influence is not clear. The extended starvation might cause physiological malfunctioning, just as it is possible that the physiologic dysfunction produces the eating symptoms (Weiner, 1985).

Genetic factors may predispose some people to the onset of anorexia. A review of twin studies remarked that monozygotic twins had a concordance rate that was higher than that for dizygotic twins (Scott, 1986). In one illustrative study (Holland, Sicotte, & Treasure, 1988), 56% of monozygotic twin pairs were concordant for anorexia nervosa and only 5% were concordant among dizygotic twins. Molecular genetic analysis suggests that anorexia may be linked to chromosome 1p34 (Grice et al., 2002). Moreover, many of the personality variables that place youth at risk for the development of eating disorders (e.g., perfectionism, obsessionality) are said to have some genetic links (Collier & Treasure, 2004; Devlin et al., 2002).

The course and outcome of anorexia nervosa is quite varied: some individuals recover after a single episode, whereas others experience patterns of weight gain and successful weight maintenance followed by periods of relapse. Indeed, severe cases of anorexia have required hospitalization. As mentioned earlier—though it occurs in a small percentage—death can result from extreme cases.

Given the evidence to date, the diathesis-stress model has merit in understanding anorexia nervosa (Bemis-Vitousek & Orimoto, 1993; Collier & Treasure, 2004; Keel et al., 2001). Indeed, as is true for many other disorders described in this book, it is the interaction between a biological predisposition and adverse environmental forces that affects the individual.

Bulimia nervosa

The rapid consumption of a large quantity of food in a discrete period of time, and the feeling of a lack of control over the eating, characterizes bulimia.

> Dieting was a common practice for Jenny, with small portions of food at meals and exercise in both the morning and evening being a regular part of every day. Often on weekends when she was home alone, however, Jenny would make eggs, bacon, and pancakes, with whipped cream and syrup, and eat massive quantities of these breakfast foods at one sitting. Soon after the feast, and the cautious and meticulous kitchen cleanup, she would go to the bathroom and self-induce vomiting. During the week, the feast was an entire pizza, again followed by vomiting. For many months, she told no one of her habit. In therapy, however, as her therapist asked the proper questions and her comfort level was sufficient, she disclosed the binge–purge habit.

Phenomenology and classification

Bulimia is characterized by repeated purging to prevent weight gain—whether by self-induced vomiting, use of diuretics, fasting, or vigorous exercise, and a persistent overconcern with body weight and shape. A diagnosis of bulimia requires a minimum of 2 binges per week for at least a 3-month period (see Box 8.2). Bulimia has been referred to as the binge–purge syndrome because typically massive quantities of food are eaten and then actions are taken to rid the body of potentially fat-producing calories. *DSM-IV* (APA, 1994) includes patients with binge–purge episodes in the diagnosis of anorexia nervosa, and not surprisingly there is substantial debate as to whether bulimia is a separate syndrome or merely a manifestation of anorexia nervosa (Eddy, Dorer, Franko, Tahilani, Thompson-Brenner, & Herzog, 2008; Foreyt & Mikhail, 1997).

> **Box 8.2 DSM criteria for a diagnosis of bulimia nervosa**
>
> - Recurrent episodes of binge eating. An episode of binge eating is characterized by both of the following:
>   1. Eating, in a discrete period of time (e.g., within any 2-hour period) an amount of food that is definitely larger than most people would eat during a similar period of time and under similar circumstances.
>   2. A sense of lack of control over eating during the episode (e.g., a feeling that one cannot stop eating or control what or how much one is eating).
> - Recurrent inappropriate compensatory behavior in order to prevent weight gain, such as self-induced vomiting; misuse of laxatives, diuretics, enemas, or other medications; fasting; or excessive exercise.
> - The binge eating and inappropriate compensatory behavior both occur, on average, at least twice a week for 3 months.
> - Self-evaluation is unduly influenced by body shape and weight.
> - The disturbance does not occur exclusively during episodes of anorexia nervosa.
> - DSM specifies purging (regularly engaged in self-induced vomiting or the misuse of laxatives, diuretics, or enemas) and nonpurging types.
>
> Reprinted with permission from the *Diagnostic and Statistical Manual of Mental Disorders, Text Revision*, Fourth Edition, (Copyright 2000), American Psychiatric Association.

Binge eating has been found in roughly 6% of children aged 6 to 13 (Tanofsky-Kraff, Yanovski, Wilfley, Marmarosh, Morgan, & Yanovski, 2004). Fairburn and Beglin (1990) concluded that the prevalence of bulimia among adolescents is about 1%. Although epidemiological data are often based on questionnaires, a number of studies (e.g., Timmerman, Wells, & Chen, 1990) have documented the existence of bulimia in a variety of countries. The majority of studies have focused on North American youngsters, but there are data on binge eating among various racial groups in Zimbabwe (Hopper & Garner, 1986). Given the worldwide occurrence of binge eating, a purely cultural explanation is not likely to be entirely satisfactory.

Bulimia, like anorexia, occurs much more often in females, although the age of onset of bulimia is typically in later adolescence (18.4 years, Fairburn & Cooper, 1984), as opposed to early adolescence for anorexia. Bulimia has often been linked to anorexia—in fact, roughly 50% of anorexic cases show some evidence of bulimia. Longitudinal work shows that adolescent fasting—that is, going without eating for 24 hours to control weight—predicts future binge eating and bulimic pathology (Stice, Davis, Miller, & Marti, 2008). Apparently, a sizable number of persons with anorexia use binge eating and purging as part of their effort to be remarkably thin (Eddy et al., 2008). This practice has unwanted effects, with potentially serious health ramifications such as the acids from vomiting damag-

ing the enamel on your teeth and chemical imbalances in the body—
and it isn't even all that effective in getting rid of the calories!

Causes and course

The etiological models that have been advanced for anorexia are often
applied to bulimia. For example, Humphrey, Apple, and Kirschenbaum (1986) studied the interpersonal behavior of families with a
normal adolescent female and others with an anorexic-bulimic female.
The families interacted around the topic of the daughter's separation
from the family, and trained observers recorded the frequencies of
specific target behaviors. The frequencies of "helping" and "trusting"
behavior on the positive side and "ignoring" and "walling off" on the
negative side differentiated the families. Families with an anorexic-
bulimic daughter displayed more of these negative and fewer of these
positive interactions. Although these observed differences may
possibly be the result of having a family member with an eating
disorder, problematic family interactions are one proposed causal
factor.

Regarding the role of cognitive factors in bulimia, an interesting
series of studies was reported by Polivy and Herman (1985). Normal
eating is generally under the control of appetite; when people feel full,
they stop eating. According to Polivy and Herman, however, people
who watch their weight (restrict their eating) use cognitive strategies
to control their eating. That is, they eat when they believe they
"should" eat, and ignore biological signals of hunger and fullness.
Unfortunately, this pattern is said to set them up for binge eating.
Polivy and Herman identified groups of normal eaters and restrained
eaters (those usually dieting) and had them participate in what they
believed were studies of taste preferences. The participants consumed
high-calorie milkshakes and were then led to a room with unrestricted
access to snacks—they could eat whenever they wanted—while they
awaited the next part of the study. Normal eaters did not eat much;
they were already full. But the restrained eaters ate a lot—as if once
they decided that their diets were broken by the milkshake, they
figured they might as well eat what they wanted. Because they do not
detect the physical cues of satiation, they don't know their bodily cues
for when to stop. Polivy and Herman (1985, 1987) speculated that the
line between this eating pattern in typical dieters and clinical bulimia
may be only a matter of degree.

Recent cognitive theories of bulimia nervosa emphasize attentional
biases and beliefs about the importance of controlling eating, shape,

and weight (Shafran, Lee, Cooper, Palmer, & Fairburn, 2007; Wilson & Pike, 2001). One specific cognitive distortion linked with bulimia nervosa, referred to as *thought-shape fusion* (Shafran & Robinson, 2004), occurs when merely thinking about eating increases the individual's estimate of their shape or weight, and elicits perceptions of moral wrongdoing.

Bulimia usually begins in late adolescence, and binge eating is sometimes associated with an episode of dieting. Until a report by Keel and colleagues (Keel, Mitchell, Miller, Davis, & Crow, 1999), very little was known about the long-term outcome of bulimia. Keel et al. (1999) tracked down 173 women who had been identified as having bulimia nervosa during the years between 1981 and 1987 (average of 11.5 years after the initial presentation). At the point of follow-up, 11% of the sample again met criteria for bulimia. Only 0.6% met criteria for anorexia; yet 18.5% met criteria for an unspeci- fied eating disorder. Of note, 70% of the sample no longer met any criteria. Also of interest, a history of substance-use problems and a longer duration of the disorder at the time of initial presentation was found to be associated with a worse outcome at follow-up. Kotler, Cohen, Davies, Pine, and Walsh (2001) prospectively followed roughly 800 youth across 17 years and found that early adolescent bulimia was associated with a 20-fold increase in risk for adult bulimia nervosa. Although these longitudinal studies contribute to our understanding, some of the patients evaluated had received psychotherapy and medications at some time during their history, and such a situation complicates our understanding of the natural course of bulimia. Despite our limited knowledge, bulimia is often categorized as either chronic or intermittent.

Biological models highlight the loss of control experienced during binge–purge episodes, emphasizing disturbances in neural systems that mediate voluntary self-regulation and control. In normal func- tioning, large regions of the ventral prefrontal cortex (PFC), anterior cingulated cortex (ACC), and basal ganglia are activated during engagement in tasks requiring voluntary self-regulation (Baumeister & Vohs, 2004). During tasks that require individuals to voluntarily overcome prepotent responses and automatic behavioral responses, patients with bulimia nervosa tend to show more impulsivity and less neural activity in specific areas of the PFC and ACC (Marsh et al., 2009). It has also been noted that altered serotonin functioning and dopamine transmission can contribute to loss of inhibitory control and reduced PFC activity, even in healthy individuals. As with anorexia nervosa, a number of obstetrical complications have been linked with the development of bulimia (Favaro et al., 2006), but the specific mechanisms through which such experiences are associated with bulimia remain unclear.

Again, a diathesis-stress model serves as a reasonable integration of what is known about the cause of bulimia. Biological predispositions and environmental forces interact. It is not sufficient to have the predisposition or the environmental conditions—each contribution is needed.

Treatment

Treatments for anorexia nervosa include psychodynamic, behavioral, cognitive, and family systems approaches. Among psychosocial interventions, individual treatments have fared better than group treatments (Thompson-Brenner, Glass, & Westen, 2003). Hospitalization, diet modification, medications, and force feeding have also been tried. Partial hospitalization programs, which have adolescents participate in all-day intensive therapeutic programming but return at night to sleep in their respective homes, have become increasingly common.

Psychodynamic treatments of anorexia and bulimia have reported gains in a small number of controlled trials and pilot studies (Bruch, 1973; Thompson-Brenner, Weingeroff, & Westen, 2009), but research evaluations using more rigorous methods are lacking. Minuchin and colleagues (1978) reported a successful family systems treatment, claiming that 86% of the 53 patients recovered from the anorexia. These results could be considered encouraging, but the evaluation was methodologically lacking.

Well-controlled outcome evaluations have looked at behavioral or cognitive-behavioral treatments for anorexia (Pike, Devlin, & Loeb, 2004; Vitousek & Orimoto, 1993), but research examining these programs specifically in adolescent samples is limited. Cognitive-behavioral programs aim to modify eating patterns, offer specific rewards for eating larger amounts of food, help the client identify faulty beliefs or expectations, and introduce doubt about the beliefs to diminish them.

One study compared cognitive-behavioral, interpersonal psychotherapy, and behavioral therapy for bulimia nervosa (Fairburn, Jones, Peveler, Hope, & O'Connor, 1993). The outcomes (see Figure 8.1) indicated that cognitive-behavioral therapy and interpersonal

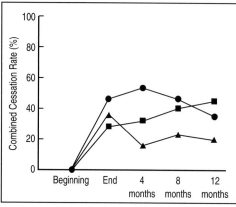

psychotherapy produced comparable beneficial effects. The behavioral treatment was less effective than the other two. Over five-and-a-half years later, Fairburn and colleagues followed up 90% of the treated cases and reported that over 50% of those receiving cognitive-behavioral or interpersonal therapy no longer qualified as having an eating disorder. The figure shows the proportions of the 75 participants who had not only ceased to have binge-eating episodes but who also ceased to vomit and

FIGURE 8.1. Outcomes for different therapies for bulimia nervosa. Cognitive-behavioral (circles), interpersonal (squares), and behavioral (triangles) therapies were compared, with the evidence suggesting that not all treatments for bulimia nervosa are comparably effective. Fairburn et al. (1993, p. 423). Copyright 1993. American Medical Association.

take laxatives. The behavior therapy condition produced half the positive results of the other treatments. As can be seen, the different treatments had differential effects on the target problem. Results such as these indicate that bulimia can be treated with some success. Studies such as this—treatment–outcome research—provide invaluable information about the efficacy and effectiveness of various treatment efforts.

Are individual or family-based programs better for the treatment of adolescent eating disorders? In the case of adolescent bulimia, the reported findings suggest that cognitive-behavioral treatment offers a slight advantage over family therapy, being associated with more rapid reduction of binging, lower cost, and greater adolescent acceptability (Schmidt et al., 2007). In contrast, in the treatment of severe adolescent anorexia, preliminary work suggests that family-based treatment (FBT; Le Grange, Binford, & Loeb, 2005) may fare better than individual adolescent treatments. Developed at the Maudsley Hospital, FBT temporarily places the parents in charge of weight restoration. Whereas other treatments discourage parental involvement and promote sustained autonomy around food, FBT promotes independent adolescent food management only after considerable improvement. FBT has been successfully disseminated to sites beyond the Maudsley Hospital where it was developed, and has been associated with promising outcomes (Loeb et al., 2007).

Although at present there are no medications approved by the US Food and Drug Administration for the treatment of adolescent eating disorders, pharmacological treatments, such as antidepressants used in conjunction with psychosocial treatments, have been used off label to treat adolescent eating disorders and associated comorbid conditions (Craighead & Agras, 1991; Powers & Bruty,

2009; Wilfrey et al., 1993). In the adult literature, antidepressants have been found to reduce binging–purging, but long-term follow-ups are limited. A general conclusion from the adult literature on the treatment of bulimia can be taken from the wide-reaching meta-analytic review of 9 double-blind placebo-controlled medication trials (with 870 participants) and 26 randomized psychosocial studies (with 460 participants) reported by Whittal, Agras, and Gould (1999). These reviewers summarized that, based on binge and purge frequency, depression, and self-monitored eating attitudes, cognitive-behavioral therapy produced significantly larger effects than medications for all treatment outcomes.

Considering the pressure placed on women in most cultures (Cohen, Brownell, & Felix, 1990), it is not surprising that many hold a strong desire to be thin. In excess, however, this desire is abnormal. Present approaches to treating and understanding eating disorders implicate biological processes, family systems, the need for behavior modification, and the relevance of distorted cognitive processing that is in need of reformulation. Multifaceted treatments seem the order of the day.

Summary

Anorexia nervosa is characterized by an intense fear of becoming obese, a distorted self-perception of body image, refusal to maintain minimal body weight, and, in females, a cessation of menses. By far more common among females, anorexia if unchecked can lead to death. Biological processes and family influences have been implicated in anorexia (each family member lacks a distinct identity, and the child fails to develop a personal sense of autonomy and independence). Family treatment and cognitive-behavioral treatments, as well as medications, have been applied with anorexic patients.

Bulimia nervosa is characterized by the rapid consumption of a large quantity of food in a discrete period of time while feeling out of control over the eating. It is also characterized by self-induced vomiting, use of diuretics, fasting, vigorous exercise, and overconcern with body weight.

Mental retardation and learning disorders 9

Unlike earlier chapters that focused on disruptive behavior or disturbances in emotion, the focus of this chapter is on two related themes that both have to do with limitations or difficulties in intellectual and/or academic activities. As we will see in more detail, mental retardation and learning disabilities are childhood disorders that present difficulties for the child in the areas of cognitive functioning. In the UK, both types of problems are listed under the one phrase "learning disabilities," whereas the separate phrase "mental retardation" (or sometimes "intellectual disability") has been maintained in other countries. Like the disorders discussed thus far, children with mental retardation or learning disorders can and do have other childhood disorders as well. It has been estimated that 20–35% of noninstitutionalized children and adults with mental retardation have other diagnoses or behavior problems (Handen & Gilchrist, 2006a).

Mental retardation

Mental retardation is significantly subaverage general intellectual functioning that exists concurrently with deficits in adaptive behavior. Adaptive behavior is the self-care skills and activities of daily living (such as the ability to appropriately dress and groom oneself and hold a simple job) needed to live independently. A person identified as having mental retardation is significantly subaverage in intellectual functioning and is sometimes incapable of self-care or independent living. For a diagnosis of mental retardation, the disorder must be identified before the 18th birthday. Persons older than 18 who, for the first time, display subaverage intellectual functioning and fail to adapt independently are not diagnosed as mentally retarded. Over the years, the term "mental retardation" has acquired a social stigma, and consequently many now prefer the term "intellectual disability" (Matson, Terlonge, & Minshawi, 2008). For consistency with *DSM-IV*, we largely retain the term mental retardation for the present purposes.

Phenomenology and classification

It is important to keep in mind that the identification of mental retardation requires impairment in both intellectual and adaptive functioning (see Box 9.1). Accordingly, no single test can identify who is mentally retarded. Instead, multiple scores and several criteria are combined to make this judgment. For example, mental retardation is not simply a low score on an IQ test. In fact, some practitioners in the field assess levels of IQ only after deficits in adaptive behavior have already been identified.

BOX 9.1   DSM criteria for a diagnosis of mental retardation

- Significantly subaverage intellectual functioning: An IQ of approximately 70 or below on an individually administered IQ test.
- Concurrent deficits or impairments in present adaptive functioning (i.e., the person's effectiveness in meeting the standards expected for his or her age by his or her cultural group) in at least two of the following areas:
  - communication
  - social/interpersonal skills
  - functional academic skills
  - health
  - self-care
  - use of community resources
  - work
  - safety
  - home living
  - self-direction
  - leisure.
- The onset is before age 18 years.

Reprinted with permission from the *Diagnostic and Statistical Manual of Mental Disorders, Text Revision,* Fourth Edition, (Copyright 2000), American Psychiatric Association.

To assess adaptive behaviors, psychologists use inventories such as the Adaptive Behavior Scale (Lambert, Nihira, & Leland, 1993), a measure of independent functioning, language development, responsibility, and economic, domestic, and physical activity (for alternate measures see Handen & Gilchrist, 2006a; Sparrow, Cicchetti, & Balla, 2005). Select examples of the areas of competence that are assessed are provided in Box 9.2. To assess intellectual ability, psychologists use well-standardized and recently normed tests such as revised forms of the Wechsler Intelligence Scale for Children (WISC-IV) or the Stanford-Binet. The Leiter International Performance Scale—Revised and the Test of Nonverbal Intelligence (3rd ed.) are fully nonverbal tests of intellectual and cognitive functioning. As such, they may be suitable for all children regardless of hearing abilities, native language, or developmental delays.

BOX 9.2 Assessing areas of competence

Determinations of mental retardation require assessments of a persons's adaptive functioning. Some of the areas of competence assessed as part of the evaluation of adaptive behavior among the mentally retarded include:

- independent functioning
- physical development
- economic activity
- language development
- numbers and time
- domestic activity
- vocational ability
- self-direction
- responsibility
- socialization.

Who are the children with mental retardation?

Several broad studies have determined the prevalence of mental retardation. Early estimates were quite varied, ranging from 1% to 13%. When the IQ score is used to assess mental retardation, prevalence rates of 3% are typical, whereas when adaptive behavior is the criterion, prevalence rates drop to 1% (McLaren & Bryson, 1987). Taking into account adaptive behavior makes a big difference! Using only an IQ score could "damn" many more people with a limiting label when, in fact, what is important is whether or not you can engage independently in activities of daily living. Based on a review of studies conducted around the world, a range between 1% and 3% is an accepted prevalence estimate (Handen & Gilchrist, 2006a; McDermott, Durkin, Schupf, & Stein, 2007; Scott, 1994; Westerinen, Kaski, Virta, Almqvist, & Iivanainen, 2007).

Are IQ test scores "fair"?

As has been mentioned, one of the criteria for mental retardation is an IQ score—more specifically, an IQ score equal to or greater than two standard deviations below the age-matched general population mean. On the WISC, for example, the average score is 100, with a standard deviation of 15. Thus, a person with a score of 70 or less would meet one of the criteria for a diagnosis of mental retardation. Keep in mind that a change in the criterion—say 1 or 1.5 standard deviations instead of 2—would have a dramatic effect on the identification of mental retardation. What is normal and what is abnormal, in terms of IQ test scores, is based solely on a chosen criterion and the distribution of scores.

The theoretical distribution of IQ scores closely resembles the normal curve (the bell curve). Because only approximately 2% of the distribution earns an IQ score less than 70.2% of the population— about 7.5 million people in the US—meet this criterion. But not all persons who score in this impaired range on IQ tests lack adaptive behavior, and vice versa. For example, in a study by Mastenbrook (1978; cited in Handen & Gilchrist, 2006a), children with IQ scores between 50 and 70 were also assessed for adaptive behavior. Fewer than 35% of these children were classified in the range of mental retardation based on the two-part definition.

Psychologists have argued that intelligence is a culture-bound phenomenon. For example, reasoning and behavior that is considered smart in one culture may be considered ill-advised and foolish in another. The extent to which intelligence and culture can ever fully be disentangled has been questioned (Sternberg, 2007).

One source of controversy regarding tests of intelligence has to do with their "fairness" or "unfairness," especially when used with disadvantaged individuals. To appraise the issue, we must know who the disadvantaged are. Most conceptualizations of disadvantage are relative. The disadvantaged are those, relative to others, who are hindered in leading productive lives in their society. This group may include low-income families, ethnic minorities, very rural families, and in some cases members of bilingual families. If these disadvantaged groups score lower on IQ tests, does it indicate that the tests are unfair? Modern IQ tests use standardized samples that include representatives from all types of backgrounds. By so doing, the test strives to remain fair to all groups. Similarly, the contents of the test— the actual test questions—aspire to be free from cultural bias. On these counts, many agree that the tests have approached fairness. However, the cultural sensitivity of intelligence tests used for such high stakes purposes as academic placement and intellectual classification will always require continued monitoring and reexamination.

Mental retardation occurs in varying degrees of severity (see Box 9.3). Although adaptive behavior and intellectual functioning are dual criteria, IQ test scores are often used to differentiate the levels of mental retardation (see Handen & Gilchrist, 2006a). Nevertheless, different levels of adaptive behavior can be expected for individuals with varying levels of retardation. Box 9.3 provides illustrative examples of the variations in potential outcomes for individuals at different ages. Of the total prevalence of impaired intellectual functioning, approximately 89% are classified in the mild range, 7% in the moderate range, 3% in the severe range, and 1% in the profound range (Madle, 1990).

BOX 9.3 Degrees of mental retardation and school-age (6–21) adaptive behavior

IQ scores are often used to determine degrees of retardation. Within the impaired range, there are associated levels of expected adaptive behavior.

Classification	IQ score	Adaptive Behavior
Very superior	130 and above	
Superior	120–129	
High average	110–119	
Average	90–109	
Low average	80–89	
Borderline	70–79	
Intellectually deficient	69 and below	
Mild retardation	55–70	Learn academic skills of 11-year-old by late teens; typically, cannot learn general high school subjects; need special education.
Moderate	40–55	Can learn functional academic skills of 9-year-old by late teens; special education necessary.
Severe	25–40	Can talk and learn to communicate and can be trained in elementary health habits; cannot learn functional academic skills, but do profit from habit training.
Profound	Less than 25	Some motor development is present, but they do not profit from training in self-help; need total care.

The prevalence of impaired intellectual functioning is affected by factors such as gender, socioeconomic status, and race. Most of the variation takes place within the mild range, whereas there is a more even distribution within the severe range. Somewhat higher prevalence estimates are found among males (2:1), and there is a higher frequency among African-American than Caucasian youth, and among the Aborigines population in Australia (Raghavan & Small, 2004), although the ethnic variations are likely due to cultural and socioeconomic factors associated with race. Socioeconomic status (SES) is regularly linked to variations in the prevalence of mental retardation, with low SES groups accounting for a disproportionate number of cases, especially in the mild range (Crnic, 1988; Scott, 1994).

Those individuals with mental retardation sometimes have other problems as well. Ambulatory problems, fine motor problems, and speech, hearing, and visual impairments are likely to coexist with mental retardation. Some persons have comorbid epilepsy and cerebral palsy.

Other psychological problems have also been identified among those with impaired intellectual functioning (Douma, Dekker, Verhulst, & Koot, 2006; Einfeld & Aman, 1995; Johnson, Lubetsky, & Sacco, 1995). Data gathered in the UK reflect that 22% of young adults with intellectual disabilities have problems with anxiety, and 20% showed conduct disorder or antisocial behavior (Richardson, Katz, Koller, McLaren, & Rubinstein, 1979). In one Dutch sample, 25% of youth with intellectual disabilities met criteria for a comorbid disruptive behavior disorder, 22% met criteria for a comorbid anxiety disorder, and 4% met criteria for a comorbid mood disorder (Dekker & Koot, 2003). Problems also exist with self-injurious behavior (Matson et al., 2008; Myrbakk & von Tetzchner, 2008; Scott, 1994), and other reports have suggested that schizophrenia (Morgan, Leonard, Bourke, & Jablensky, 2008; Romanczyk & Kistner, 1982) can occur among persons with impaired intellectual functioning. Mental health disorders are three to four times more common in children (and adults) with mental retardation than in the general population (Scott, 1994). There is also a relationship between intellectual level and presence of a mental health disorder: The rates of disorder increase with more severe intellectual impairment. How is this explained? One hypothesis is that low intellectual functioning reduces the ability to cope with stress, restricts the environment, and contributes to distress in the family, and that these factors combine to contribute to additional disorder. Indeed, the presence of a child with intellectual disability can place a considerable strain on the family, particularly in the absence of adequate supports (Baker, Bacher, Crnic, & Edelbrock, 2002; Emerson, 2003; Tsai & Wang, 2009). In contrast, it might be that the presence of disorder limits intellectual development. It could also be the case that in some cases cognitive difficulties place limits on one's ability to understand and respond to diagnostic interviews developed for children of average intelligence.

Causes

The influence of genetics on normal as well as abnormal intelligence has been the subject of enormous controversy and a great deal of research. Controversy aside, what do the data tell us? Generally, research has revealed that genes contribute to individual differences in IQ scores (Bartels, Rietveld, Van Baal, & Boomsma, 2002; Sternberg & Grigorenko, 1999)—as the degree of genetic relatedness between two people increases, so too does the correlation between their IQ scores (Neisser et al., 1996). For example, the IQ scores of mono-zygotic (identical) twins are more alike than the scores of dizygotic (fraternal) twins (Plomin, 1989). Similarly, the correlations between IQ scores of adoptees and their biological families are larger than the correlations between scores of adoptees and their adoptive families (Plomin & DeFries, 1980; Scarr & Weinberg, 1976). However, an IQ score is not determined solely by genes—it is influenced by environ-mental factors as well (Neisser et al., 1996). Modern conceptual-izations of intelligence acknowledge heritability in the context of environmental factors that moderate the expression of genetic influences. Twin research supports a diathesis-stress model in the expression of verbal abilities, but less so for nonverbal abilities (Asbury, Wachs, & Plomin, 2005).

In general, mental retardation is considered to be multifaceted, with genetic and environmental factors contributing and interacting. However, some specific conditions that result in intellectual disability can be attributed to biological factors. Prenatal, perinatal, and social environmental forces have also been found to be influential.

Biological factors

Certain biological factors are implicated in specific conditions that are associated with intellectual disability. Chromosomal aberrations, for example, are associated with a specific syndrome implicated in mental retardation that was first described in 1866 by the British physician, Langdon Down. Down syndrome is a condition resulting in impaired intellectual functioning that is caused by the presence of an extra 21st chromosome (Vandenberg & Crowe, 1989). Chromosome 21 emerges as a triplet instead of a pair; all of the other chromosomes are in pairs. Some evidence links this aberration to polymorphisms in genes encoding enzymes of folate metabolism (Hobbs et al., 2000; O'Leary et al., 2002), but other research has not replicated this finding (Hassold & Sherman, 2000; Roizen & Patterson, 2003). The physical characteristics of the Down syndrome child are usually quite apparent: The neck is typically short and broad, there is loose skin on the sides and back, height is below average, the head is small and the back of the head is flat, the eyes slant upward and have folds in the corners, muscle tone is poor (floppy), and hands are often short and square with short fingers. Brain anomalies in persons with Down syndrome include low brain weight, reduced number of cells, and short dendrites (Coyle, Oster-Granite, & Gearhart, 1986). Higher rates of celiac disease and hypothyroidism occur in individuals with Down syndrome, requiring regular screening (Roizen & Patterson, 2003). Individuals with Down syndrome have a significantly shorter life expectancy, although epidemiological work shows that the median age of death for affected individuals grew from 25 in 1983 to 49 in 1997 (Roizen & Patterson, 2003; Yang, Rasmussen, & Friedman, 2002). Individuals with this chromosomal abnormality regularly score in the subaverage range on measures of intellectual ability, although there is considerable variability in terms of intelligence scores and adaptive behavior.

> Lenny had the physical characteristics of most Down syndrome children. His face had a flat nose, his square-shaped ears and his mouth were small, his tongue protruded, and his neck was short and broad. Unfortunately, these characteristics, as well as his mental retardation, were the target for teasing by several children in his neighborhood. Although he rarely voiced complaints, Lenny did feel the rejection.
>
> Now in his middle teens, Lenny was enrolled in a special placement class and had made friends with several other children with Down syndrome in his school. His teacher described him as very likeable, responsive to directions and instructions, and one of the more popular youngsters in his group. One of Lenny's major accomplishments was that he was responsible for his classroom's fish tank—for feeding the fish and cleaning the tank. Prompts were sometimes required, but Lenny was nevertheless very proud of "his tank."

An interesting and important relationship exists between the age of the mother at the time of the child's birth and the incidence of Down syndrome (Hook, 1987; Roizen & Patterson, 2003). Risk increases with increased mother's age. For mothers of age 20, the incidence is 1 in 2000. At 35, the rate of occurrence of Down syndrome has been reported to be 1 in 500 births. At 45, the rate rises to 1 in 20 (Evans & Hammerton, 1985). There has been a report suggesting that the rate of Down syndrome is also related to the father's age, but this is not widely accepted (Hook, Cross, & Regal, 1990; Steen & Steen, 1989). In recent years, the prevalence of Down syndrome births has decreased from about 1 in 700 to 1 in 1000

(Roizen & Patterson, 2003), seemingly due to the availability of prenatal screening and the effect this may have on a woman's decision to continue a pregnancy.

It has been suggested that adults with Down syndrome show a rapid age-related decline in functioning. Although follow-up studies in the US (e.g., Burt, Loveland, Chen, & Chuang, 1995) and the UK (e.g., Shepperdson, 1995) evidenced minimal changes with age, more recent longitudinal work shows that adults with Down syndrome, especially those over the age of 40, show a loss of adaptive behavior skills with age (Callocott & Cooper, 1997). In fact, 75% of individuals with Down syndrome over the age of 60 show clinical signs of Alzheimer's disease, including neuropathological changes, loss of conversational skills, and seizures (Roizen & Patterson, 2003).

Other conditions that result in mental retardation, in addition to Down syndrome, are associated with chromosomal abnormalities. The fragile X syndrome, named for a constricted region at the end of the X chromosome, has associated physical features as well as intellectual deficiencies. Physical features include short stature, prominent forehead, prominent mandible, and large ears, hands, and feet, although these are not reliable indicators of the presence of fragile X syndrome. The fragile X syndrome is more commonly seen in males. Nevertheless, the condition is reported in girls as well (Mazzocco, Kates, Baumgardner, Freund, & Reiss, 1997). Affected individuals manifest neurodevelopmental abnormalities and morphological variations in brain structure—including abnormalities in the hippocampus, cerebellar vermis, and lateral ventricles (Eliez & Reiss, 2000). In one study (Dykens, Hodapp, Ort, & Leckman, 1993), males with fragile X syndrome were found to make positive gains in adaptive behavior over a 2-year period. The participants, especially the older ones, showed strengths in daily living skills. Further changes with development were studied using both longitudinal and cross-sectional approaches, with data coming from six centers. Dykens et al. (1996) reported that boys aged 1 to 10 showed significant gains in adaptive behavior whereas adaptive behavior plateaued and was stable from ages 11 to 20.

Another disorder, phenylketonuria (PKU), is organic and genetically determined. It is a hereditary error of metabolism resulting from an inactive liver enzyme. Infants with PKU are normal at birth but, if untreated, will develop mental retardation during the first year of life. Quite fortunately, research has determined that if identified early and placed on a special diet soon after birth, children with PKU will develop normally.

Carriers of PKU pass on a recessive gene to their children. If these children marry a person who also carries the recessive gene, they may have offspring who are affected (Vandenberg & Crowe, 1989). PKU is rare, occurring only once in approximately 14,000 births (Rubenstein, Lotspeich, & Ciaranello, 1990), and is associated with moderate to profound retardation. This condition is no more prevalent in family members of the affected individual than in the general population, and it occurs equally across the social classes. Unlike many other forces that cause intellectual impairment, the intellectual deficit associated with PKU can be prevented through early detection and dietary modification. In the US, for example, the law requires post-natal blood testing to promote prevention.

Other organic forces, such as infections, poisons, and malnutrition, are also factors in intellectual impairment. Cranial anomalies and head injuries can cause intellectual disability, as well. It is certainly easy to recognize that malformed or dysfunctional portions of the brain, as well as injuries to portions of the brain, can have serious detrimental effects on mental functioning.

Prenatal and perinatal environments

It is widely accepted that unhealthy influences in the prenatal environment can damage the intellectual development of the off-spring. Health problems in the mother have significant effects on the fetus. Maternal conditions and behaviors such as poor nutrition, tobacco smoking and alcohol consumption, infections, drugs, radiation, and a lack of oxygen contribute to subaverage intelligence in the child. These maternal health behaviors can be monitored and changed, and the outcome can affect the fetus (Streissguth, Barr, Sampson, Darby, & Martin, 1989).

Alcohol readily crosses the placenta of the pregnant woman and exposes the developing fetus to a wide range of harmful and irreversible effects. Uniformly, because even small amounts of alcohol may not be safe (Jones, 1988), researchers recommend that pregnant women abstain from alcohol during pregnancy. In the most extreme cases, for 4 to 12 infants per 10,000 births, the mother's drinking during pregnancy causes permanent physical damage to the infant, a condition known as fetal alcohol syndrome (Clarren & Smith, 1978; Jones & Smith, 1973). Fetal alcohol effects include a retardation of physical growth as well as neurological and intellectual impairments (Neisser et al., 1996). Aronson, Hagberg, and Gillberg (1997) reported that children born to mothers who had abused alcohol throughout pregnancy had severe intellectual and behavioral problems that remained at age 11–14 years. Also, there was a correlation between the occurrence and severity of the disorder and the degree of alcohol exposure in utero. The exact amount of maternal alcohol consumption necessary to produce fetal alcohol syndrome is not yet known, but increasingly, concerned, health-conscious pregnant women are discontinuing alcohol consumption during pregnancy. According to O'Leary (2004), prenatal exposure to alcohol is most devastating when occurring during the the first trimester or the final two months of a pregnancy.

A number of obstetric and delivery complications have been found to be associated with impaired intellectual functioning (Taylor & Rogers, 2005). For example, obstetrical histories reveal that mothers of intellectually impaired children have twice the number of hospital admissions prior to delivery than controls (Sussmann, McIntosh, Lawrie, & Johnstone, 2009). Children born preterm are at increased risk of declining intellectual functioning over time, even in the absence of obvious neurological damage (Isaacs, Edmonds, Chong, Lucas, Morley, & Gadian, 2004).

Social environment

Our minds and mental faculties are sparked by the environments to which we are exposed. Environmental factors, such as extreme psychological and social deprivation, are implicated in the cause of impaired intellectual functioning. Because it is unethical to manipulate environments in ways that might restrict intellectual development, consider studies done with animals. Animals reared in deprived environments showed behavioral deficits as well as lighter brains, with less cortical depth and fewer synapses (e.g., Rosenzweig, Bennett, & Diamond, 1972). Lack of contact with people of normal intelligence, limited access to verbal stimulation, and an absence of educational opportunities do impede intellectual development, and it is not difficult to imagine that individuals raised in a culturally deprived environment—one that lacks learning opportunities—are likely to register lower IQ scores. Children reared in institutional settings characterized by extreme deprivation and neglect show pronounced deficits in intellectual functioning (MacLean, 2003). Poverty also hampers intellectual development—economically disadvantaged youngsters are at risk for intellectually deprived lives. Indeed, poverty can have unwanted effects on many features of psychological adjustment—without available resources, the ability to cope with life's difficulties can be hampered. Large family size, poor nutrition, lack of organization in the home, and low expectations for academic achievement can depress intellectual growth. The following case example described by Repp and Deitz (1983) is worth contemplation:

> Steve's parents were migrant workers, so he has moved numerous times. His mother went back to work shortly after he was born, and an older sister took care of him. His sister wanted him to be quiet and nondemanding, and she yelled at him for most behaviors other than sitting quietly. When his parents came home from work, they were tired and wanted to be left alone. He was again urged to keep quiet and out of trouble. The family's living quarters were always sparsely furnished, and Steve had only a few toys, of which he had tired long ago.
>
> When Steve was enrolled in school, his language level was very low for his age. In addition, he did not possess the academic readiness skills that his peers exhibited. Steve was referred for evaluation and, after being given a battery of standardized tests, he was labeled as retarded and placed in a classroom for the retarded.

Not all cases of impaired intellectual functioning are the same, and the causal pathways are equally dissimilar. Biological causes of mental retardation are identified more often in children with severe cognitive delays. Some children's cognitive functioning may simply reflect the low end of the intellectual distribution and these cases may have had a greater environmental influence. For example, McLaren and Bryson (1987) reported that biological causes were more likely (70% vs 50%) in severe intellectual disability than in mild disability.

Services

Wicks-Nelson and Israel (2002) described three types of services for mental retardation: placement, treatment, and education.

Placement

This refers to the living arrangements that must be organized for the person. At one time in history, most persons with mental retardation were placed in public institutions that provided nothing more than custodial care. Since the 1960s, this practice has declined in the US and UK, and the decline can be attributed in part to the criticisms directed at large public institutions. The settings were criticized as being cold and lacking in human interaction, having a shortage of services, and being poorly staffed. Alternative arrangements, such as community centers, provide a more home-like atmosphere and a greater opportunity for the person with intellectual disabilities to interact with people and the local environment. In today's world, children with impaired intellectual functioning often reside at home with their families. In such arrangements, parents often need assistance with daily care, as well as a break from the demands of continuous supervision. A number of intervention programs designed to remediate caregiver stress in parents of children with intellectual disabilities have been developed. Cognitive-behavioral group interventions for caregiver stress have been found to produce positive and promising benefits (Hastings & Beck, 2004).

Treatment

Treatment for children with impaired intellectual functioning refers to interventions aimed at the remediation of the associated emotional and behavioral problems. Research reports have indicated that a substantial number of persons with impaired intellectual functioning also suffer from psychological disorders (Douma et al., 2006; Matson & Barrett, 1982; Matson et al., 2008; Morgan et al., 2008; Myrbakk & von Tetzchner, 2008). A survey of more than 8000 youth with intellectual disabilities (Matson & Barrett, 1982) conducted in New York revealed that 9.8% had significant mental health needs (Jacobson, 1982a, 1982b). The identified problems included cognitive (hallucinations), emotional (depression), and behavioral (aggression, self-injury) disorders. Across levels of intellectual functioning, an average of half of the patients were found to have behavior problems (from 38% to 65%). Not surprisingly, those with dual diagnoses were more likely to have behavior problems. In a sample of Dutch youth, 1 in 4 youth with intellectual disabilities met criteria for a comorbid disruptive behavior disorder, 1 in 5 met criteria for a comorbid anxiety disorder, and 1 in 25 met criteria for a comorbid mood disorder (Dekker & Koot, 2003).

The treatments that are applied for the emotional and behavior problems in children with impaired intellectual functioning resemble the treatments used with the general population, with some adjustments because of the clients' level of conceptual ability. There is a strong tendency for the treatments to follow the behavioral orientation (Baer, Wolf, & Risley, 1968; Birnbauer, 1976; Huguenin,

Weidenman, & Mulick, 1991). Behavioral training programs focus on teaching clients specific skills for more adaptive functioning. These programs emphasize the contingent application of rewards and take many forms. Social reinforcers (such as smiles, verbal praise, or a pat on the back) work well with this population. Behavioral methods have been successfully used, for example, to reduce disruptive behavior (Bagner & Eyberg, 2007; Zimmerman, Zimmerman, & Russell, 1969), control aggressive behavior (Feinfield & Baker, 2004; Mace, Kratochwill, & Fiello, 1983), improve toileting (Giles & Wolf, 1966; Grey & McClean, 2007), and control public masturbation (Barmann & Murray, 1981) among retarded persons. Other applications have been successful with overcoming food refusal (Handen, Mandell, & Russo, 1986) and sleep problems (e.g., Ashbaugh & Peck, 1998; Piazza & Fisher, 1991). Cognitive-behavioral treatments for childhood anxiety disorders (described in Chapter 6) have been flexibly adapted to treat generalized anxiety disorder, selective mutism, and social phobia in cognitively delayed youth (Suveg, Comer, Furr, & Kendall, 2006).

Family members are increasingly involved in treatments for children with impaired intellectual functioning (Baker & Feinfield, 2007; Baker, Landen, & Kashima, 1991; Crnic, Friedrich, & Greenberg, 1983; Crnic & Reid, 1989). Maintaining a behavioral orientation, these treatments focus not only on specific child problems that require change, but also on the goals and feelings of the family and the family's learning and use of behavior modification procedures to rear their special needs child. In one sense, when family members are taught behavioral procedures, there is an increased opportunity for the application of these procedures (both in the home and elsewhere) and a corresponding increase in the potential for beneficial effects.

Treatments for intellectual disability do not cure the cognitive impairments. That is, impaired intellectual functioning is not erased by the interventions. The programs do produce desired gains in the targeted behavior problems, and these gains do contribute to a better life for the recipients.

To achieve that "better life," education is important. In the US, considerable litigation eventually produced laws aimed at guaranteeing education for those with intellectual disabilities (Katz-Garris, 1978). The Education for All Handicapped Children Act of 1975 (Public Law 94–142) requires that all handicapped children receive a free public education designed to meet their specific needs, that the rights of the handicapped be protected, and that the effectiveness of the educational programs be assessed and evaluated. It also stipulates that the education be provided in the least restrictive environment, which means that impaired children should be placed in classrooms with nonimpaired children whenever possible.

Educational interventions

Educational interventions with intellectually impaired youth include using specific teaching strategies to facilitate their learning and programming the learning environment at school and at home to meet their needs. Although the teaching strategies may resemble those used in regular classes, there are adjustments for the pace and level of the learner. Concerns about class size and teacher–student ratios have been addressed in special education classrooms; special education classes have fewer students and a higher teacher–student ratio than regular classes. But special education settings have been criticized for isolating impaired youth and limiting their contact with typically developing children. The movement away from segregated classes to the integration of special needs students with regular students has been called *mainstreaming* and these integrated classrooms are referred to as *inclusive*. Preliminary research suggested that the inclusive classroom may offer moderate benefits for intellectually impaired youth (Haywood, Meyers, & Switzky, 1982). Although communities have been reported to hold mildly positive attitudes about mainstreaming (Eiserman, Shisler, & Healey, 1995), and recommendations for how to facilitate mainstreaming have been offered (Mortimer, 1995), reviews of the research concluded that mainstreaming has not enhanced social competence in special needs children, and there is little convincing evidence that they perform any better academically (Hardiman, Guerin, & Fitzsimons, 2008; MacMillan, Keogh, & Jones, 1986; Wehmeyer & Lee, 2007). What is your opinion about mainstreaming?

Medications

Although drug therapy is used with children with impaired intellectual functioning, it is not intended to improve intellectual abilities. As with other populations, medications are aimed at reducing behavioral and emotional conditions (see Handen & Gilchrist, 2006b). Examples of the conditions likely to improve with medication are disruptive behavior, psychotic symptoms, or attentional problems. Surveys of institutionalized persons have indicated that 40–50% are receiving psychotropic medications (Aman & Singh, 1983). Those most likely to be medicated are older individuals with more severe behavior problems. Perhaps because of their distance from mental health services, the overall medication rate is lower for noninstitutionalized individuals.

As was true for ADHD, stimulant medications are used with intellectually impaired children who evidence attentional problems—estimated to be 9–18%. Double-blind, placebo-controlled trials shows roughly a 45–66% response rate to these medications among youth with impaired intellectual functioning, which is slightly lower than the ~75% response rate associated with these medications when used with youth of average intellectual functioning (Handen & Gilchrist, 2006b). Data hint to a relationship between effectiveness and severity. Stimulants are less useful with severe retardation (Gadow, 1992), but can be safe and effective for some hyperactive children with mild to moderate intellectual impairment (Handen, Breaux, Janosky, McAuliffe, Feldman, & Gosling, 1992; Handen & Gilchrist, 2006b). Antidepressant medications have been used to treat mood and anxiety symptoms in youth with impaired intellectual functioning, and antipsychotic medications and mood stabilizers have been used to treat aggressive, antisocial, and self-injurious behaviors. There is a notable lack of well-designed and properly controlled evaluations of these medications with intellectually impaired youth. The majority of work in this area has consisted of case studies or open trials (Handen & Gilchrist, 2006b). The absence of randomized designs, appropriate control groups, and blind evaluations are a few examples of weaknesses that characterize much of the research in this area (Crnic & Reid, 1989; Handen & Gilchrist, 2006b). Truly determining the effects of these medications is not possible until these methodological problems are corrected.

Learning disorders

Ethan—an attractive and athletic 12-year-old—exhibited normal intellectual functioning, but his mathematics ability was severely restricted. Despite the results of intelligence tests indicating that his IQ score was in the normal range, his performance in math was well below age and grade level. Despite his parents trying to help, Ethan was alone in his struggles with basic subtraction and multiplication. When shopping, for example, Ethan could not determine the total costs of his purchases nor calculate correct change.

Phenomenology and classification

Use of the phrase "learning disability" has become widespread and the number of children identified as learning disabled has increased markedly, with estimates ranging from 5% to 15% (Taylor, 1989). Males are more frequently identified than females, often in a ratio of between 2:1 and 5:1 (Taylor, 1989). Variations in the estimates, however, result from the inconsistency in the definition used to identify children with a learning disability (Fletcher, Francis, Morris, & Lyon, 2005; Lyon, Fletcher, & Barnes, 2003). Of youth in the US who receive special education services, roughly 50% are children with learning disorders (Lyon et al., 2003).

One method defines learning disability as a discrepancy between performance on tests of intellectual functioning (e.g., IQ) and performance on tests of educational achievement, for example, a normal IQ score with below-average achievement in a particular academic topic. This criterion has been recorded as "failing in one or more basic achievement skill areas despite normal intelligence" (Kistner & Torgesen, 1987, p. 289).

Below expected age- and grade-level performance is an alternate definition of learning disability. Recall Ethan, whose mathematics learning disorder was based on below expected grade-level performance. Use of age or grade level as a cutoff creates problems. How discrepant must the scores be? One year? Two years? Although a 1- or 2-year discrepancy is often used, the impact of a grade-level discrepancy changes with increasing age. For example, being 2 years behind is more troublesome for a 10-year-old than for a 13-year-old. Keep in mind that the determination of learning disorders is not without problems. Based on a review of the literature, Morris (1988, p. 793) offered a critical conclusion: "The most commonly used classification systems and definitions of learning disabled children do not meet basic empirical criteria for reliability and validity."

The statutory definition of learning disabilities, in the Individuals with Disabilities Education Act (IDEA, 1990, p. 300), states:

> The term, "specific learning disability" means a disorder in one or more of the basic psychological processes involved in understanding or in using language, spoken or written, which may manifest itself in an imperfect ability to listen, speak, read, write, or spell, or to do mathematical calculations.

DSM-IV (APA, 1994) defines learning disorders (also called academic skills disorders) using a combination of the IQ score-achievement discrepancy approach and the below age- and grade-level approach. *DSM-IV* diagnoses include reading disorder, mathematics disorder, and disorder of written expression, as well as learning disorder not otherwise specified. In each disorder, specific academic achievement, as measured by an individually administered standardized test, is considered below that expected given the person's chronological age, measured intelligence, and age-appropriate education. In addition, the condition must interfere with academic achievement or activities of daily living. According to Lyon et al. (2003), reading disabilities are the most common learning disability, affecting 60–80% of children receiving special education (LD) services (Lerner, 1989).

The need to weigh exclusionary criteria deserves mention. Should a learning disability be independent of emotional or behavioral problems? Research often finds emotional and behavioral complications in children with learning disability (e.g., Goldston et al., 2007; Lahey, Green, & Forehand, 1980). For instance, ADHD is often associated with learning difficulties (Pennington et al., 2009). Estimates vary, but approximately 75% of ADHD boys in a sample from the US were underachieving, and about 33% were performing at least one grade below their expected level (Cantwell, 1987). Estimates of the percentage of ADHD children who have learning disabilities vary widely (Wicks-Nelson & Israel, 2002), with some agreement that about 15% of children with ADHD have a formally defined learning disability (Hinshaw, 1992). Children with learning disorders show poorer psychosocial functioning than children without learning disorders (Gadeyne, Ghesquiere, & Onghena, 2004). Learning-disabled children are also less socially competent than their peers (Toro, Weissberg, Guare, & Liebenstein, 1990), more likely to have internalizing disorders (Goldston et al., 2007; Thompson & Kronenberger, 1990), and more likely to be involved in delinquency (Brier, 1989). Not all learning-disordered children have these or other emotional or behavior problems, but the extent of comorbidity is sufficient to rule out the idea that a learning disorder must be independent of an emotional or behavioral problem. Nevertheless, in the IDEA (1990), there are statements suggesting exclusions:

> Learning disabilities include conditions such as perceptual handicaps, brain injury, and developmental aphasia, but do not include children who have learning difficulties

which are primarily the result of visual, hearing or motor handicaps, or mental retardation or emotional disturbance, or of environmental, cultural, or economic disadvantage.

Although the exact operations used to define the exclusion criteria are not provided, it is clear that the statutory definition is delimiting.

In recent years, researchers have called for learning disorders to be defined not by poor performance on standardized tests, but rather by demonstration of an inability to respond adequately to instruction that is effective with most other students (Gresham, 2002). Proponents of such a definition argue that repeated assessment could evaluate how a child responds to different instructional efforts over time. Multiple assessments are linked to specific attempts to intervene with the child, and learning disorder would be operationalized as nonresponsiveness to instruction. This *response to intervention* (RTI) approach to assessing learning disorders has garnered growing interest and an evidence base in recent years (Fletcher et al., 2005).

Causes

The exact causes of learning disabilities are, at present, unknown. Genetic factors, abnormalities in brain structure and function, and cognitive and motivational influences have all been examined as possible links to learning disorders. We do not yet know, for example, if learning disabilities result from cognitive processing deficits or deficits in motivation or achievement.

Research into genetic causes has been reviewed by Smith, Pennington, Kimberling, and Ing (1990). Children of parents with reading difficulties have a greater chance of reading problems than children of parents who read normally, but these data could be viewed as supporting either a genetic or family environment explanation, or both. A 4-year follow-up study of Latin American children found that 17% of children with reading disabilities had become average readers. Improvements are possible.

Abnormalities in brain structure and function may contribute to learning disorders. According to Taylor (1989), children who have experienced head injury, central nervous system infection, neurological problems, or epilepsy are at higher risk for learning problems than are other children. Not all children with a history of these conditions develop a learning disability, however, and these same conditions can contribute to other emotional and behavioral problems.

Among the learning disorders, neuroanatomical evidence is strongest for the reading disorders (Alarcon, Pennington, Filipek, & DeFries, 2000; Lyon et al., 2003; Pennington, 1999).

Psychological theories have tended to emphasize motivational and cognitive explanations of learning disability. Learning-disabled children may experience an initial degree of failure, come to doubt their abilities, and fail to put forth effort on future tasks. Their expectations for success are lower and, as one study found, they are less likely than nondisabled children to attribute success to their ability, yet more likely to attribute failure to a lack of ability (Tarnowski & Nay, 1989).

Several writers, based on reviews of the literature, have suggested that there is empirical support for differentiating learning-disabled from nondisabled children on the basis of information-processing characteristics (Kistner & Torgesen, 1987; Torgesen, 1986; Wong, 1985). The difficulties in cognitive processing that have been promoted as influential in learning disability have included limited attentional focusing and failure to use effective learning strategies. For example, when learning a list of words, nondisabled readers use memory strategies to enhance recall. Reading-disabled children are less likely to use memory strategies such as rehearsal, clustering, or elaboration.

Treatments

Contemporary treatments for learning disability include *cognitive*, *cognitive-behavioral*, *neuropsychological*, and *constructivist* approaches (Lyon, Fletcher, Fuchs, & Chhabra, 2006). *Cognitive* treatments emphasize information processing, problem solving, and self-instruction. *Cognitive-behavioral* treatments build on cognitive methods and incorporate regular practice and monitoring. For example, one group of learning-disabled children improved their reading comprehension after they were taught to monitor their performance by asking themselves questions while they read (Wong & Jones, 1982). Interestingly, the same strategy was taught to students who were not learning disabled, and their performance was not as enhanced. Perhaps self-questioning helped the learning-disabled children, but not the nondisabled group, because the learning-disabled group initially lacked self-questioning and self-monitoring.

Torgesen (1979) further documented the effectiveness of strategy training. Pictures of objects from four different categories were shown to good and poor readers in the fourth grade. The children were instructed that they would be asked to recall the pictures and that they could do anything they wanted to help them remember the pictures. The children's behavior was observed through a one-way mirror. Compared with the good readers, the poor readers were less likely to organize the pictures into categories, spent more time off-task, and recalled fewer pictures. When these same poor readers were taught to use a categorical clustering strategy, they were able to recall as well as the good readers. Moreover, the time they spent off-task fell to a level that was comparable to that of the good readers. Apparently, various cognitive strategy training approaches have had some beneficial effects with children identified as learning disabled (Hallahan, Kneedler, & Lloyd, 1983; Wong, Harris, & Graham, 1991). Adolescents with learning disabilities have been found to show improved mathematics ability when interventions using strategy instruction, self-monitoring strategies, and cooperative homework assignments have been applied (Maccini & Hughes, 1997). However, it should be kept in mind that not all children in need have the benefit of receiving proper interventions, and, even among those in some form of remedial program, the effects are not always favorable. One report (Shaywitz, Fletcher, & Shaywitz, 1994) indicated that approximately three-quarters of reading disabled 9-year-old children continued to manifest reading difficulties through their high school years.

Neuropsychological models of treatment highlight knowledge about brain regions associated with learning abilities to design instruction methods intended to recruit brain circuits believed to be intact, while bypassing weaker neural systems (Lyon et al., 2006). These approaches have fared less favorably in research evaluations. *Constructivist* models are decidedly nondirective, routed in a notion that child interests, rather than a structured agenda, are better suited to determine what is to be learned and when. These child-centered instructional methods take a more holistic approach and emphasize the quality of the relationship between the student and the teacher. Research evaluations of constructivist treatments have been minimal.

Working with the individual child may not be enough, as evident in a recommendation from the National Agenda for improving services for children with needs. Collaboration with families is one target for the improvement of services (Cheney & Osher, 1997). Families can be involved in the planning and implementation of the services, and family support groups can be provided. The latter influence the families' ability to participate in the former.

Summary

Mental retardation is significantly subaverage general intellectual functioning that exists concurrently with deficits in adaptive behavior. Indeed, adaptive behavior is an important component of the determination of mental retardation. In terms of IQ level, scores that are equal to or greater than two standard deviations below the mean are indicative of impaired intellectual functioning. Estimates have suggested a 1–3% prevalence of mental retardation, with approximately 89% of these in the mildly impaired range. Gender, race, and socioeconomic factors are involved. The causes of impaired intellectual functioning include biological (e.g., genetic) as well as environmental forces. Interventions for individuals with mental retardation strive not to cure the intellectual deficits, but to teach adaptive skills, maximize individual potential, and treat co-occurring mood and behavioral problems.

One definition of learning disability relies on a discrepancy between intellectual ability and achievement. An alternate definition of learning disability is below expected age- and grade-level performance. *DSM-IV* defines learning disorders (academic skills disorders) using a combination of the IQ-achievement discrepancy approach and the below age- and grade-level approach. More recent conceptualizations emphasize a child's inability to respond adequately to instruction that is effective with most other same-aged peers. Biological and environmental factors are said to contribute to learning disorders, but the exact causes are unknown.

Pervasive developmental disorders 10

"Pervasive developmental disorder" is the phrase presently used to refer to severe psychological problems emerging in infancy. Pervasive developmental disorders involve severe upset in the child's cognitive, social, behavioral, and emotional growth that produces widespread complication of the developmental process (Lord & Bailey, 2002; Rutter & Schopler, 1987). *DSM-IV* (APA, 1994) includes several pervasive developmental disorders, including *autism*, *Asperger's disorder*, *Rett's disorder*, and *childhood disintegrative disorder*. Autism has clearly become the dominant pervasive developmental disorder in both the research and clinical realm. Autism affects basic human qualities: interpersonal socialization and complex communication. Children with autism demonstrate severe impairments in social interaction and relationships, interpersonal play, and communication. Volkmar and colleagues (Volkmar, Lord, Bailey, Schultz, & Klin, 2004) noted the dramatic increase in autism research over the past two decades. In the time between the initial descriptions of autism in 1943 until 1989, roughly 2900 research articles were published on the condition. In contrast, from 1990 through 2004, over 3700 articles appeared.

Historically, there were two pervasive developmental disorders: autism and childhood schizophrenia. Because childhood schizophrenia shares many features with adult schizophrenia, the current *DSM* formulation does not include child-onset schizophrenia among the pervasive developmental disorders, but rather allows for child diagnosis within the adult category of "schizophrenia and other psychotic disorders." Childhood-onset schizophrenia is a rare but severe form of adult schizophrenia, associated with particularly poor prognosis (Hollis & Rapoport, 2008). Childhood schizophrenia may resemble the adult disorder in the presence of severe withdrawal and an inability to relate to others, but delusions and hallucinations are less common in children. Age of onset is key in differentiating childhood schizophrenia from autism. Children with schizophrenia have a period of relatively normal adjustment followed by the onset of the severe symptoms of schizophrenia, whereas autism is evident very early in life. Specifically, autism is usually apparent by age 3, whereas childhood-onset schizophrenia typically appears in the seventh year of life (Hollis & Rapoport, 2008). Although these disorders have clear distinctions, roughly 30–50% of cases of the rare childhood-onset schizophrenia are preceded by or comorbid with a diagnosis of pervasive developmental disorder (Rapoport, Chavez, Greenstein, Addington, & Gogtay, 2009). Very few cases of pervasive developmental disorder eventuate into schizophrenia.

Autism

> Nadia, at age 6, produced a drawing of a rooster. The drawing was intricate, complex, and remarkably accurate. Nadia possessed genuine artistic talent, but she did not speak. She preferred to be alone, in a room that she kept in a rigid order, where she would sit unresponsive to the presence of others. Nadia was diagnosed as autistic. A pervasive developmental problem, autistic disorder includes a lack of responsiveness to people and severely delayed language development. The problems begin before the child is 36 months old. It is interesting, if sad, to note that when therapy was effective in promoting Nadia's communication with other people, her artistic talents declined.

Phenomenology and classification

As mentioned earlier, children with autism show severe impairments in interpersonal socialization (relationships, play) and complex communication. Kanner (1943) was the first to describe autism. According to Kanner (p. 242), the outstanding, fundamental feature in autism is "the children's inability to relate themselves in the ordinary way to people and situations from the beginning of life." The severity of the disorder is exemplified by Chuck, a child who had many of the characteristic features of autism:

> Chuck was an attractive 5-year-old of average height and weight, yet he never seemed to hear or respond to other people. His parents had once thought that he was deaf or severely hearing impaired. Adults could come and go from the room, and there would be no indication that Chuck was aware of their movement. When someone

called to him directly by name, there was no answer. Usually, adults had to tap his shoulder before he would show even minimal signs of acknowledgment. Chuck did respond to changes in his environment—when a chair was moved to add a place at the kitchen table, Chuck had a temper outburst. Rearranging living room furniture or adding a new bookcase to a room distressed Chuck, but he was still unlikely to initiate any form of communication. Even in play there was something odd about his behavior. He showed an extreme intensity while playing alone. In one instance, Chuck played with a broken light switch for more than 30 minutes.

Historically, autism assessment drew primarily on parent reports or retrospective review of home movies (Volkmar, Chawarska, & Klin, 2005), typically delaying diagnosis until the age of 4. With the advent of structured behavioral observation systems that evaluate early communication, social interaction, and play, autism can now be reliably diagnosed by experts by the second year of life (Moore & Goodson, 2003; Volkmar et al., 2004). Some of the early symptoms of autistic disorder were outlined by Borden and Ollendick (1992). In the newborn, the baby seems different from other babies, seems not to need the mother, is indifferent to being held, has flaccid muscle tone, and cries infrequently but may be intensely irritable. In the first 6 months, the baby fails to notice the mother; is undemanding; has delayed or absent smiling, babbling, or anticipatory responses; and lacks interest in toys. In the second 6 months, the child shows minimal interest in social games, is unaffectionate, demonstrates deficits in verbal and nonverbal communication, and is underreactive or overreactive to stimulation. Can autism be diagnosed in children by 8 months of age? Data (Baird et al., 2000) indicate that with the current screening tools, a diagnosis of autism can be reliably ruled out by 18 months with 98% accuracy, but that only 40% of true cases can be detected at this age.

Often, parents of autistic children are the first to have noticed that the children are unresponsive socially. The severely autistic child's imperviousness to the social and physical environment does not lie on a continuum with normal behavior (Wenar, Ruttenberg, Kalish-Weiss, & Wolf, 1986). According to Wenar (1982), the autistic child approaches the world as intrinsically noxious. Descriptions of autistic children often mention their lack of cuddling in the early months of life, an obsessive desire for sameness in the environment, self-stimulatory behaviors (such as rocking, spinning, and arm flapping), self-destructive behaviors (such as head banging, arm banging, and self-biting), lack of eye contact (gaze avoidance) with other people, and fascination with inanimate objects (see also Newsom & Hovanitz, 1997). A research study found that children with autism engaged in more ritualized behavior and initiated interactions with peers much less frequently than intellectually disabled youth (Hauck, Fein, Waterhouse, & Feinstein, 1995). Lack of responsiveness to people is a characteristic of autistic children—a characteristic that contributes meaningfully to parental frustration when caregiving.

From the wide array of unusual behavior seen in autism, *DSM-IV* identifies three key features: (1) qualitative impairment in social interaction, (2) severe impairments in communication, and (3) restricted, repetitive, and stereotyped patterns of behavior. Onset occurs before age 3. According to Volkmar (1996), this definition is consistent with the *ICD-10* (WHO, 1992). The details of the diagnostic criteria are presented in Box 10.1. Most cases are characterized by a

---

BOX 10.1   Criteria for a diagnosis of autism

A child reaches the diagnostic criteria for autism if the child evidences at least 6 items from the categories provided below, with at least 2 from the first category and 1 from each of the second and third categories. The child must evidence onset before the age of 3.

First category: Qualitative impairment in social interaction

- marked impairment in the use of multiple nonverbal behaviors such as eye-to-eye gaze, facial expression, body posture, and gestures to regulate social interaction
- failure to develop peer relationships appropriate to developmental level
- lack of spontaneous seeking to share enjoyment, interests, or achievements with other people
- lack of social or emotional reciprocity.

Second category: Qualitative impairments in communication

- delay in, or total lack of, the development of spoken language in individuals with adequate speech
- in individuals with adequate speech, marked impairments in the ability to initiate or sustain a conversation with others
- stereotyped and repetitive use of language or idiosyncratic language
- lack of varied spontaneous make-believe play or social imitative play appropriate to developmental level.

Third category: Restrictive, repetitive, and stereotyped patterns of behavior, interests, and activities

- encompassing preoccupation with one or more stereotyped and restricted patterns of interest that is abnormal either in intensity or focus
- apparently compulsive adherence to specific, nonfunctional routines or rituals
- stereotypes and repetitive motor mannerisms (e.g., hand- or finger-flapping, complex whole body movements)
- persistent preoccupation with parts of objects.

Reprinted with permission from the *Diagnostic and Statistical Manual of Mental Disorders, Text Revision*, Fourth Edition, (Copyright 2000), American Psychiatric Association.

failure to acquire developmentally appropriate language and social skills, although roughly 20–40% of cases are characterized by developmental regression—that is, a gradual or rapid loss of previously acquired skills (Volkmar et al., 2005).

Echolalia is one striking example of the communication difficulties typical of autistic children. Echolalia is the repetition or echoing back of speech, as in the following example:

Therapist: Can you point to Chuck's shoe?
Chuck: Can you point to Chuck's shoe?
Therapist: Use this finger [touches finger] and point like this to your shoe [directs finger pointing].
Chuck: Point like this to your shoe.

Because communication problems like this occur very early in life, they probably reflect an inherent cognitive defect (Rutter, 1978).

What could this defect be? Much recent research has focused on perceptual and cognitive difficulties that might underlie echolalia and other symptoms of autism (Donnellan, 1985; Litrownik & McInnis, 1986; Prior, 1984). For example, many studies have examined autistic children's tendency to display stimulus overselectivity—responding to only select aspects of stimulus materials (see Lovaas, Koegal, & Schreibman, 1979). For instance, let us suppose that a therapist who is trying to teach language skills shows a picture of a shoe to an autistic child, says the word "shoe," and emphasizes the movements of the mouth to make the sounds. The autistic child might look at the picture, but fail to attend to the sounds. Autistic children seem unable to pay attention to multiple cues (stimulus feature) at a time. What may make matters worse is that they may pay attention to idiosyncratic and often irrelevant stimuli. For example, touching the paper on which the picture is printed, but not attending to the picture or to the sounds. This pattern of attention hinders their ability to functionally communicate and to interact with the social and physical environment.

Processing and integrating information also present as difficulties for autistic children. For example, they do not use the meaning of words to assist in the recall of information, nor do they reorganize incoming information to reduce redundancy (Hermelin, 1976). Children with autism often have difficulty transforming or manipulating information in their minds (Shulman, Yirmiya, & Greenbaum, 1995). Autism can be described as a disorder of multiple primary deficits (Goodman, 1989).

Recent thinking has suggested that children with autism have a deficit in their understanding of their own and others' mental states. "Theory of mind" has been described as the ability to consider people in terms of internal mental states, such as beliefs, intentions, and emotions, and an understanding of the social environment and the ability to engage in socially competent behavior has been said to be linked to a person's having a "theory of mind." To make sense of the social world, one needs to recognize that people's behaviors are products of their internal states. Many studies have examined theory of mind in children with autism (e.g., Baron-Cohen, Leslie, & Frith, 1985; Bauminger & Kasari, 1999), and most studies have indicated that these children do have limited abilities. It is worth noting that the data do not suggest that a limited understanding of others' mental states is the cause of autism. However, it does appear that a limited theory of mind is a descriptive feature of childood autism, and the severity of this impairment may offer clues into the long-term prognosis of a child's social functioning.

Some children with autism achieve IQ scores in the normal range, and some display some remarkable mental abilities (5–10% of autistic persons; O'Connor & Hermelin, 1988), over half of persons with autism show intellectual deficits that fall into the range of mental retardation (Bristol et al., 1996; Rutter & Schopler, 1987; Volkmar et al., 2004). Because the lower IQ scores are related both to more severe communication problems and a poorer prognosis, researchers have suggested that children with autistic disorder be divided into high- and low-functioning groups. High-functioning autistic children typically have a better prognosis (Howlin, 2000; Newsom, 1998; Tsatsanis, 2003), but not all studies find meaningful differences between high- and low-functioning cases (Myles, Simpson, & Johnson, 1995).

Perhaps you were wondering about the "remarkable mental abilities" mentioned earlier. With regard to these rare but quite interesting people, recall the character portrayed by Dustin Hoffman in the movie *Rain Man*. The character, whose pattern was that of someone with an autistic disorder, could perform remarkable calendar calculations, determining the day of the week of a date several years in the future. Equally impressive, if not equally puzzling, Nadia's drawing of a rooster, mentioned earlier in this chapter, illustrated remarkable special talents that are seen in a small percentage of autistic children.

Structured approaches to diagnosing autism (e.g., interviews) have shown international applicability (Lord et al., 1997). Diagnoses can be reached using parent reports of current behavior, but the accuracy is enhanced if a behavioral history is taken into account (Lord et al., 1997). It is important to keep in mind that, although the field has made substantial progress in assessing and classifying autism (e.g., Cohen, Paul, & Volkmar, 1986), there are still sources of uncertainty as well as advocates for other approaches. For example, the classification and study of children with autistic disorder has sometimes followed an approach referred to as "autistic spectrum" (Wing & Attwood, 1987). That is, to learn about the disorder, children with varying degrees of symptoms would be studied. The continuum is one of pervasiveness and severity. At the pervasive end of the continuum fall those children who are profoundly retarded, multiply handicapped, and with profound impairments across intellectual, adaptive, social, language, and motor functioning. At the least pervasive end of the continuum are children with relatively mild impairment in one domain.

Who are the autistic children?

Autistic disorder is relatively rare, occurring in only 5–13 births per 10,000 (Bristol et al., 1996; Lord & Bailey, 2002; Volkmar et al., 2004). Strikingly, the documented prevalence of autism in community samples has risen over the past 15 years. Wazana, Bresnahan, and Kline (2007) concluded that there has been an 11-fold increase in the number of autism cases identified since 1994. Reviewing the results of 30 epidemiological studies, Volkmar and colleagues (2004) noted that research conducted prior to 1991 found a mean prevalence of roughly 4 cases per 10,000 individuals, whereas research conducted since 1992 has found a mean prevalence of roughly 13 cases per 10,000. What could account for such a dramatic increase? Could there be, as the popular press has reported, an autism epidemic? Many in the academic community have suggested that this changing prevalence may simply reflect a number of methodological artifacts, including the improving detection of autism in very young children and the broadening definition of autism characteristic of more recent diagnostic formulations (e.g., Costello, Foley, & Angold, 2006b; Rutter, 2005; Wazana et al., 2007). Some have suggested changes in the environment (e.g., mercury levels) are responsible for the rising prevalence, but to date empirical evidence to support such theories is lacking.

Autism is seen in both genders, but at a frequency that is three to four times higher in boys than in girls (Bryson, 1996). One study of gender differences among higher functioning persons with autistic disorder reported that males were rated to be more severely autistic than females in terms of early social development but not on stereo-typic behaviors (McLennan, Lord, & Schopler, 1993). The higher rate of autism among males has led some to some speculations, such as the prenatal exposure to testosterone places the fetus at increased risk for the development of autism (Auyeung & Baron-Cohen, 2008; Knickmeyer & Baron-Cohen, 2006).

Autism has been found in families throughout the world and in all social classes (Gilberg, 1990; Gillberg, Cederlund, Lamberg, & Zeijlon, 2006; Sponheim & Skjeldal, 1998). Some data, however, suggest different prevalence rates in certain countries. In China, for instance, Kuo-Tai (1987) reported only 5 cases from among 1190 childhood psychiatric clients over a 26-year period. What about the rate of autism relative to all births? Kuo-Tai (1987) set the population of Nanjing, a city in China, at 4.5 million; only two cases of autism came from the entire population of Nanjing. At the other end of the distribution is Japan, where the prevalence rates for autism have been estimated to be higher than elsewhere in the world. One study reported a prevalence of 0.16% (Tanoue, Oda, Asano, & Kawashima, 1988). Another, which examined 12,263 Japanese children, reported a minimum prevalence of 0.13% (Sugiyama & Abe, 1989). What might be an explanation for these differences?

At present there is no apparent explanation for the varying prevalence rates. Perhaps, a failure to identify all of the true cases of autism could explain the very low frequency in China. Other possi-bilities include methodological dissimilarities (for example, studies of population-based samples versus studies of clinic samples) and diagnostic differences (such as use of different diagnostic criteria). It is also possible that the differences reflect true differences in the number of cases, and research is needed to test hypotheses to help explain them. For example, are birthing practices, nutritional vari-ations, or genetic factors contributing to different prevalence rates?

Causes

What could conceivably cause this extremely serious disorder called autism? A historically relevant theory proposed by Bettelheim (1967) was influential for well over a decade. During the 1950s and 1960s, psychoanalytic theory was prevalent, and Bettelheim's notions were in this tradition. He argued that when a child faces an unresponsive world that is frustrating and destructive, the child withdraws from it and from people. Thus, the theory blamed autism on the actions of the caregiver (mother): the cold and unloving "refrigerator" parent. But Bettelheim's theory is no longer viable and has not maintained its prominence. Both an increased interest in behavioral and biological theories, and the lack of scientific evidence needed to support the theory, contributed to its being largely abandoned—although not before tragically stigmatizing countless parents already coping with the hardships of raising a child with autism. A contrasting explanation was proposed by Ferster (1961). He attempted to untangle autistic behavior using an analysis of each child's reinforcement history. This behavioral theory, too, failed to receive empirical support (Schreibman, 1988), although the behavioral approach has had a favorable impact on the treatment of autistic disorder.

Based on the data it is clear that autistic disorder is not caused by a cold, disinterested, or in some other way pathological parent. Children with autism are not the product of being reared by unemotional and ineffectual mothers, and they do not seem to have experienced more instances of undue stress in the early years of their lives. Moreover, studies of the parents of autistic children have generally failed to find any characteristic pattern of maladjustment in them (McAdoo & DeMeyer, 1978).

Other explanations for autism must be explored. Do these children suffer from a genetically transmitted abnormality? Although early work (see Hansen & Gottesman, 1976) suggested that no strong evidence existed implicating genetics in the development of autism, the dominant view in the field now is that genetic factors do play a role (Fombonne, 1998, p. 349). Early support for a genetic contribution to autism came from a study of 21 pairs of same-sex twins in which one twin met stringent criteria for autism (Folstein & Rutter, 1977). Of the identical twins, 36% were concordant for autism, as compared to none of the fraternal twins. When criteria for autism are loosened (as is done for considering youth on the autistic spectrum), and concordance is sought in cognitive and linguistic problems, not just in the diagnostic criteria for autistic disorder, 82% of the identical twins and only 10% of the fraternal twins are considered concordant (see also Bailey, Palferman, Heavey, & Le Couteur, 1998). It is both interesting and important to keep in mind that research in molecular genetics does not support a simple, single-gene inheritance pattern in the conferred vulnerability for autism. Rather, multiple susceptibility genes are said to increase vulnerability. An explanation for the inheritance for autism involves the interaction of more than 15 genes, with each contributing only a small risk (Happe, Ronald, & Plomin, 2006; State et al., 2000).

Of course, it is possible that there are other biological factors contributing to the autistic disorder. One such biological component to autism has been suggested using a wide range of new technologies. Research finds the brains of persons with autism to be slightly larger and heavier, enlarged by as much as 10% in volume (Courchesne et al., 2001; Minshew, 1996; Sparks et al., 2002). Up to one in four children with autism suffers from a co-occurring seizure disorder, and an even larger proportion show abnormal EEGs, further implicating neurobiological underpinnings. High-resolution neuroimaging studies conducted over the past decade have implicated a diverse and widely distributed set of neural systems (Volkmar et al., 2004), including the cerebellum and limbic circuitry which play central roles in sensory integration, emotion regulation, and learning (Schultz & Klin, 2002). Other studies have reported gray matter abnormalities in language-related brain regions (Herbert et al., 2002; Rojas, Bawn, Benkers, Reite, & Rogers, 2002), as well as reduced white matter in various cortical regions. Autism has also been linked to abnormalities in the fusiform gyrus, which is used in facial recognition (Schultz et al., 2003).

A small portion of autistic cases have been said to arise from diseases as diverse as congenital rubella, tuberous sclerosis, and neuro-fibromatosis. Children with congenital rubella (measles existing at birth), for example, are affected with the rubella virus early in prenatal development and, as a result of the infection, are born with a variety of malformations and resulting deafness, blindness, and central nervous system abnormalities, as well as seizures and mental retardation. In the 1970s, studies reported that 8–13% of children with rubella were diagnosed as autistic (see Chess, 1977). Recent studies, however have not supported an association between congenital rubella and autism, leading some to question the accuracy of diagnosis in the earlier reports (Volkmar et al., 2004). Moreover, extensive reports in the popular press have attempted to link autism to immunizations for measles and rubella. Importantly, research has not provided any causal support for this hypothesis (Hondo, Shimizu, & Rutter, 2005), although sadly in the wake of this extensive media coverage, rates of measles vaccinations have fallen, accompanied by a rise in the incidence of measles in the general population (Ramsay, 2001).

Despite advances in neuroimaging, there is no compelling evidence to fully explain the social and communication deficits that characterize autism. The consensus among scholars of autism is that the disorder is largely a cognitive and social one that has multiple

biological causes that initiate sometime between conception and birth. According to Rutter and Schopler (1987), the vast majority of cases of autism have no identifiable medical cause, and it has been estimated that a definite cause can be identified in only 5–10% of cases (Rutter, Bailey, Bolton, & Le Couteur, 1994). Nevertheless, children with autism do seem to enter the world biologically different. Environmental factors, however, do affect the development of the disorder and the prognosis for later adjustment. For example, children with autism themselves contribute to the production of an interpersonal environment that is suboptimal, but specially designed educational settings and supportive homes can improve their chances of acquiring skills.

Course

Although some individuals with autistic disorder show improvements, most autistic children continue into adulthood severely handicapped and unable to take full care of themselves (Howlin, Goode, Hutton, & Rutter, 2004). In the absence of early and intensive intervention, only 1–2% of autistic individuals develop to the point that there is no difference between them and children never diagnosed. An estimated 10% achieve adequate functioning in language and social areas but maintain peculiarities, whereas 20% make some school and social progress in spite of a significant handicap such as impoverished speech. About 70% evidence limited progress and evidence continuing major handicaps (Newsom, 1998).

What predicts who will and who will not show some improvement? Language skills and IQ scores are often the best prognostic indicators: Early language development and IQ above 70 suggest a better prognosis (Howlin et al., 2004; Lord & Bailey, 2002).

Useful speech develops in only about 50% of persons with autism. During adolescence, behavior and emotional problems often emerge: Aggression, oppositional behavior, and tantrums may occur and are quite distressing to parents. Roughly two out of every three adolescents with autism meet diagnostic criteria for a co-occurring mental disorder (Simonoff, Pickles, Charman, Chandler, Loucas, & Baird, 2008). Estimates have suggested that approximately 75% of autistic children fall in the moderate range of mental retardation and that 25% develop seizure disorders by adulthood (Crnic & Reid, 1989).

The social deficits in children with autism persist into adulthood. How do these deficits affect the sexual lives of adults with autism? Although this topic has only recently been studied, the data suggest that masturbation was the most common sexual behavior. In one study, one-third of the adults with autism engaged in person-oriented behavior such as touching and holding with some kissing. Known attempts at sexual intercourse are rare (Van Bourgondien, Reichle, & Palmer, 1997).

Programs

Without treatment, the long-term prognosis for persons with autistic disorder is guarded. Generally, persons with autism do not form strong interpersonal relationships, nor do they develop repertoires of social interaction considered "normal." Persons with autistic disorder achieve, however, different levels of functioning. Children who, early in life, have at least some language ability and score near the average range on nonverbal tests of intelligence have a much better long-term prognosis than children who do not show either of these qualities. In some instances, programs for children with autism teach learning readiness skills (sitting in a chair, attending to the teacher, looking at task materials) to help prepare the child for other programs. But, as noted, even optimistic estimates have suggested that at least two-thirds of children with autism remain severely handicapped and dependent into adulthood. Only a small proportion of affected children live largely independent lives without any signs of the disorder. Despite these prognostications, early and intensive interventions give children with autism their best shot at maximizing their potential. The care of the child with autism can include intervention programs for parents (Schreibman & Koegal, 1996), and programs designed to improve communication (Koegal & Koegal, 1995), reduce disruptive behavior, and enhance socialization (e.g., peer-mediated programs; Strain, Kohler, & Goldstein, 1996).

Over the years, a wide variety of treatments for autism have been employed. When the psychoanalytic explanation of autism was dominant, the treatment followed from the theory. That is, if the disorder is the result of faulty or failed parenting, then the child must be taken from the parents and placed in an environment where the milieu will allow the child to return to more normal development. Reviews of evaluations of such treatment programs find this therapy to be ineffective with children with autism (Levitt, 1963; Rimland, 1974).

Are there medications that benefit autistic children? The use of medications to reduce symptoms and help the child profit from behavioral and educational interventions is fairly widespread, although the number of well-controlled research trials evaluating their efficacy is limited (Volkmar, 2001; Volkmar et al., 2004). Most studied in children with autism have been the newer classes of antipsychotic medications used to treat aggressive, stereotyped, self-injurious, and/or other problematic behaviors. These medications have a clinical effect on problematic behaviors, but are also associated with unfavorable weight gain and drowsiness (RUPP Autism Network, 2002; Williams et al., 2006). Antidepressants are commonly used in children with autism to treat compulsive behavior and difficulties with transitions and change, but rigorous research on these agents in autistic samples is lacking. Stimulants are commonly prescribed to target hyperactivity, inattentive, and impulsive behavior (Nickels, Katusic, Colligan, Weaver, Voigt, & Barbaresi, 2008), but these agents have also received inadequate research attention in autistic samples. One study (Quintana et al., 1995) found that stimulants improved the hyperactivity of autistic children but did not alter the autistic symptoms.

At the present time, the majority of psychological programs for autism are based on research evaluations and emphasize the application of behavior modification procedures and parent training. The evidence supports the continued use of these programs (see Newsom, 1998). However, this raises the question: "If autism is a cognitive and social disorder produced by biological causes, why is the treatment a behavioral and parent training program?" As one of many possible answers, consider the case of Helen Keller (after Rimland, 1974). Helen Keller, who was blind and deaf from birth, learned to speak and write, not through treatments for blindness and deafness, but as a result of training like that used in behavioral programs. The cause of a problem need not be behavioral for a behavioral treatment to be useful.

Educational opportunities for youth with autism are a source of debate: Should children with autism be mainstreamed to receive full inclusion—be educated in the same settings as their normally developing peers? Or, are special education classrooms or specialized schools the most appropriate (see Zigmond & Baker, 1995)? According to Mesibov and Shea (1996), advocates of full inclusion mention increased expectations by teachers, modeling of normal development by peers, increased learning, and potentially improved self-esteem as supportive reasons. However, Mesibov and Shea reviewed the literature and also concluded that autistic children benefit from smaller and highly structured environments—situations more likely in the specialized environments created for them.

Autistic children can receive treatment while in a residential setting. However, the trend for children with autism has definitely shifted from institutionalization to providing appropriate treatment in home and regular school settings (Schopler & Hennike, 1990). The trend for adults with autism has shifted toward group homes in the community, thus helping adolescents and adults move toward independence from their families (Van Bourgondien & Schopler, 1990).

The dominant approach to treatment for autism involves behavioral programs that seek to treat behavioral deficits or excesses by applying reinforcements on a contingent basis. Targets may be learning readiness skills, social behavior, or communication skills. Because children with autism are not as social as their typically developing peers, they do not respond in the same way to smiles, verbal praise, or peer social events. Consequently, more concrete and sensory rewards are employed, as illustrated in the case of Dicky (see Wolf, Risley, & Mees, 1964):

> Dicky received a behaviorally based treatment beginning at age 3. To overcome his refusal to wear his spectacles, a shaping procedure was used. He was rewarded for touching and holding his glass frames, for trying them on, and eventually for wearing them. To control his tantrum behaviors, he was removed from the pleasant environment whenever a tantrum occurred (that is, time out). Similarly, his food plate was removed whenever he ate with his fingers, and he was physically removed for throwing food or taking the food of others. His lack of communication was addressed by a consistent program of showing Dicky a picture, labeling the object, prompting Dicky to repeat the label, and eventually rewarding him (for example, with apple sauce) for identifying the object in the picture without the therapist's prompting.

Language development is the focus of many behavioral programs. The shaping process is evident in the sequence of the training. First, the child is rewarded for any verbalizations. Second, the reward is provided only when the verbalization follows a prompt by the therapist. Next, the rewards are given only when the child makes closer and closer approximations to the verbalizations of the therapist. Once the child has acquired the word, the therapist provides reward only when the child follows the correct prompt, in spite of the therapist's introducing other sounds. Through this shaping sequence, using modeling and reward, the child gradually learns language skills. The improvements are noteworthy, when judged against initial levels, but the process is painstaking and the end result is not the achievement of "normal" communication. A great deal of time and effort is required for autistic children to respond verbally and to generate sentences.

An example of an intensive and extensive intervention was provided by Lovaas and his colleagues at the University of California at Los Angeles. Lovaas initiated an intensive behavior modification program in which very young children with autism receive full-time day treatment (see Lovaas & Smith, 2003). The children were diagnosed as autistic, younger than 3 years 10 months of age, and evidenced a minimum level of mental ability. Three groups of children were compared: children who received intensive training, children who received minimal training, and another group received no training at all. The intensive treatment lasted two or more years and involved more than 40 hours of one-to-one treatment per week. Minimal treatment was similar, but with 10 hours of one-to-one treatment per week.

There were several goals for the treatment. In the first year, therapists sought to achieve compliance to verbal commands, imitation, and appropriate play. To reduce self-stimulation or aggression, the therapist ignored these undesirable behaviors. Therapists also used a loud "no" or a light slap on the thigh as a last resort. Language growth was emphasized in the second year, and preacademic skills and emotional expression were goals in the third year. An overarching goal of the entire program was the placement of the children into regular school settings.

Lovaas (1987) reported the results, including that the children in the intensive treatment achieved significantly higher educational placements than the other two groups of children. Specifically, 47% of those in the intensive treatment condition completed the first year of regular elementary school, as compared to 0% and 5% for the other groups. A further study (Lovaas, Smith, & McEachin, 1989) of the intensively treated children at age 13 reported that, in terms of clinical interviews and measures of adaptive behavior, 8 of the original 19 were "indistinguishable" (p. 166) from an age-matched control group of typically developing children.

Although these results are very encouraging they should be viewed with some caution. Other treatments, though less intense, have not had as great a success rate, and the present study does require replication. Given that a minimum mental age was required for inclusion in the study, these children were probably from the high-functioning end of the autism continuum, thus limiting generalization to all children with autism. Similarly, the sample was quite a young group. The dramatic effect reported by Lovaas (1987), however, caused others to take notice. Schopler, Short, and Mesibov (1989) offered a more conservative conclusion. Due to methodological factors (such as apparent absence of random assignment to treatment and control groups), it is not possible to truly determine the effects of the intervention. Others (e.g., Gresham & MacMillan, 1997) have identified methodological shortcomings and suggest that the limitations (e.g., school placement as an outcome measure) should give reason for concern. Nevertheless, the study adds to the evidence of the benefits of behavior programs for the child with autism and suggests that early, intensive, and extensive treatments may be necessary to have a meaningful effect on such a pervasive disorder as autism. Recently, Smith, Groen, and Wynn (2000) reported the results of a fully randomized and controlled trial with a lower functioning sample of children with autism. The outcomes were consistent with those reported by Lovaas. The Smith et al. report supported the Lovaas findings, although treatment effects were noticeably smaller.

Summarizing the years of applying behavior modification to children with autism, the data provide evidence of measurable progress, though progress is often slow. Not all interventions with children with autism produce dramatic success, and, indeed, the prognosis for most affected children is not optimistic. The highest successes are based on very intensive intervention (40 hours per week) with very young and select patients. However, at least one study has suggested that when parents are trained in the behavioral program and take over as therapists, the results remain stable (see Lovaas, Koegal, Simmons, & Long, 1973). At least one point of current emphasis is on early introduction (Mesibov, 1997), with many professionals agreeing that intervention in the preschool years is critical.

Training parents

The training that was originally provided for parents of children with autism focused on their disruptive and sometimes dangerous behaviors that were evident in the home. More recently, to facilitate generalization to settings outside of the treatment context, parents have become involved in language training as well. Lastly, though no less important, parents can suffer emotional problems linked to parenting a child with autism, and these needs, too, can and should become goals for parent training interventions.

As is true for parent training in general, programs include a variety of procedures, such as lectures and readings, demonstrations and role playing, home visits and telephone contacts. The main focus is training in the behavior modification principles used in treatments of autism: shaping, reinforcement, ignoring, and generalization. Parent groups provide opportunities for discussion of difficulties as well as social support (Koegal & Koegal, 1995; Koegal, Koegal, & Brookman, 2003).

With regard to the shaping of communication skills, a parent would be taught to first reward eye contact as a step toward increased communicativeness. For example, a parent would be told, "When Joanne makes eye contact with you, immediately provide a reward, no matter how busy you might be at the time." Later on, parents can become involved in teaching specific words—saying the word "toy" when pointing to Joanne's toy—and concepts of ownership—pointing to Joanne when saying "your toy" and pointing to oneself when saying "my toy."

Some of the benefits of parent training are illustrated by the work of Koegal and colleagues (Koegal, Schreibman, Britten, Burke, & O'Neill, 1982). Their project compared 25–50 hours of parent training in behavior modification procedures with outpatient clinic treatment (4–5 hours a week for a year). Both treatments improved the social behavior, play, and speech, and decreased tantrums and echolalia. Relative to the parent-trained group, the clinic-trained children did not show generalization of their improvements during an assessment in the home. The parent training condition resulted in observable gains in the home environment. In a more recent report, parent training procedures improved the pattern of parent–child interactions—children were happier and parents were more interested and less stressed (Koegal, Bimbela, & Schreibman, 1996).

A program in the UK also produced some illuminating findings. Howlin (1981) and Howlin and Rutter (1987) reported on a home-based parent training program where 16 families with a high-functioning autistic boy (average age 6 years) received treatment over an 18-month period. Comparison groups received outpatient treatment. Mothers in parent training were individually trained to use behavioral procedures and to teach language and manage behavior problems. Psychologists visited the parents in their home for 2 to 3 hours weekly or biweekly for 6 months and monthly for the final 12 months. There were also instances of counseling regarding other matters and the occasional inclusion of some other services.

The outcomes were favorable, but mixed. For example, the boys with autism whose parents received training showed significantly more social responsiveness to parents, but no more interactive play with peers. There were fewer tantrums and instances of aggression, but no changes in stereotypic behavior or hyperactivity. Based on an examination of audiotapes, the children with trained parents showed improved quantity and communicativeness of speech yet no significant differences in IQ scores. Many of the outcomes were favorable and, where differences were observed, they favored the parent training approach. As Howlin and Rutter (1987) concluded, the results were sufficiently positive to be encouraging, but not so overwhelming as to preclude the need for more intensive intervention. Indeed, their recommendation—for a more comprehensive parent-training intervention—is consistent with the recommendations of others as well (see also Agosta & Melda, 1996).

Bibby, Eikeseth, Martin, Mudford, and Reeves (2001) reported that parent-managed intensive interventions that draw heavily on the use of paraprofessionals offer less favorable outcomes than clinic-directed programs, likely due to the reduced structure and quality control of these programs. Indeed, the data suggest that parent-managed programs are best when used in conjunction with intensive clinic-directed interventions. Regrettably, the need far outweighs the supply for such high-quality clinic-directed interventions (Lovaas & Smith, 2003).

Parents of children with autistic disorder have their own needs and concerns. Living with a child with a pervasive developmental disorder creates problems in addition to those of interacting with the child. Not the least of these problems is simply facing the life-long task of managing a severely handicapped child. Sandra Harris (1983), of Rutgers University, provided a set of recommendations that include pragmatic issues (dealing with a community that may not have resources), emotional issues (personal distress), and interpersonal problems (withdrawal of the extended family). Parents must address their responsibilities toward the autistic child and recognize their own work and recreational needs as well. Siblings must face the challenge of being a responsible member of the helping family while also maintaining their independent existence. In families in which these issues are met with less than adequate adjustment, depression, guilt, anger, and a sense of inadequacy can become a source for concern. Interventions for parents may not have a direct effect on the behavior of the autistic child, but they are nevertheless valued as they improve the home and general family environment and may prevent parental burnout and distress.

What can be done about self-injury?

The topic of self-injury will be discussed here, but it should not be taken as an indication that children with autism are the only ones who self-injure, or that self-injury is solely characteristic of autism. Although it is true that one of the distressing features commonly associated with autism is self-injurious behavior (Luiselli, 2009; Newsom & Hovanitz, 1997), a variety of severely handicapped and psychologically disturbed children sometimes engage in self-injurious behavior. Examples of self-injury include head-banging, hair-pulling, self-biting, and eating nonedible substances. At times, the self-injurious behavior is so extreme that it actually poses a threat to the life of the child. Perhaps you recall from Chapter 1 the brief description of Ginger, who engaged in pin-sticking. Pins or needles can travel in the bloodstream! Also, other behavior, such as forceful head-banging, can result in serious brain damage. What should be done when a child with disabilities engages in uncompromising self-injurious actions?

The use of physical restraints is one approach that is proffered by some: put the self-injurious child in a restraint and prevent the actions that are harmful. Others recommend medications (Hammock, Schroeder, & Levine, 1995) to restrain the child from self-harm. As in adults, risperidone, an antipsychotic medication, has been reported to reduce aggression and self-injury in youth with autism, although there have only been a few placebo-controlled trials (Arnold et al., 2003; Parikh, Kolevzon, & Hollander, 2008). Unfortunately, both physical and chemical restraints, although helpful options for some patients, can prevent in others the ability to fully participate in therapeutic, social, and educational programs. What follows next is a discussion of psychosocial approaches to treatment that have been found to be effective. We later note and discuss a relevant controversy about the use of certain procedures.

In 1982 a monograph on the treatment of self-injurious behavior was prepared by a special task force, and Favell and colleagues commented that self-injurious behavior is repetitious and chronic, and that the incidence and severity of self-injurious behavior is greatest among persons with intellectual impairments, autism, and severe disabilities. The task force consisted of 14 preeminent clinicians and researchers who reviewed the research literature and provided recommendations.

Favell and associates (1982) were clear in recommending that whatever intervention is to be used it should be evaluated in terms of its ability to reduce the self-injurious behavior by a clinically significant amount. That is, reduce its frequency and intensity to the extent that the individual refrains from self-injury and is capable of participation in therapeutic activities. Although the need for evaluation may seem obvious, evaluation of treatments for self-injurious behavior is especially important because of the controversy that exists among practitioners and parents about the use of aversive procedures.

Behavioral procedures, such as the removal of reinforcement for self-injury, punishing self-injury, and reinforcing more desirable behavior, have been evaluated as methods to produce clinically significant changes in self-injurious behavior (see Baumeister & Rollings, 1976; Favell & Green, 1981; Russo, Carr, & Lovaas, 1980). One behavioral procedure, differential reinforcement of other behavior (DRO), involves providing reinforcement after periods of time when no self-injury occurs. With DRO, an increase in self-injurious behavior may occur at first, though it is followed by a meaningful reduction of the unwanted behavior. Another procedure, extinction, involves withholding previously given reinforcement after episodes of self-injury. Time out consists of taking the self-injuring child away from the opportunity to receive reinforcement for self-injury. Each of these procedures has been used both singly and in combination with other approaches to try to reduce self-injury. There are documented cases where the procedures have been successful, but there are also cases where reinforcements are difficult to identify or manipulate, and other cases where the procedures were less than fully effective.

What about the use of aversive procedures, such as mild electric stimulation, to reduce self-injurious behavior? What does the research say about its effectiveness? And, if it is effective, would you consider using the procedures? According to the Favell task force report: "Aversive electrical stimulation (informally termed shock) is the most widely researched and, within the parameters of shock employed in the research literature, the most generally effective method of initially suppressing self-injury" (Favell et al., 1982, p. 540). Despite this conclusion, such methods have only been evaluated in small samples (e.g., Salvy, Mulick, Butter, Bartlett, & Linscheid, 2004), and remain highly controversial. Accordingly, it is considered appropriate only in extreme cases of medical necessity when applied in carefully controlled situations by experienced and trained professionals. When electrical stimulation is used for treating self-injury, the stimulation is physically harmless but subjectively noxious and is applied for a brief duration immediately after each occurrence of self-injury. Case reports document its potential utility—clinically significant reductions in self-injury—but there is controversy around its use (Mudford, 1995), which has fallen out of favor. In addition to supporting evidence, it is apparent that politics and personal beliefs are also factored into decisions about the treatments to be employed when treating self-injurious behavior.

Other pervasive developmental disorders

Although much less common than autism, there are other pervasive developmental disorders. Rett's disorder, Asperger's disorder, and childhood disintegrative disorder are included in *DSM-IV* among the pervasive developmental disorders. We review these briefly here.

Rett's disorder

There is the development of multiple specific deficits, but the deficits appear after a period of normal motor development (e.g., first 5 months of life). Head size is normal at birth, but head growth decelerates between 5 months and 4 years of age. Noteworthy, too, is the loss of previously purposeful hand movements between 5 months and two-and-a-half years of age. Interest in social activities diminishes, language development is impaired, and there is the appearance of poorly coordinated gait or trunk movements. Rett's disorder, which occurs almost exclusively in females, is usually accompanied by severe intellectual impairment and persists throughout life.

Asperger's disorder

The essential features of Asperger's disorder are severe and sustained impairment in social interaction and the development of repetitive patterns of behavior and activities. These features cause clinically meaningful impairment in functioning, yet there are no clinically meaningful delays in cognitive development of age-appropriate self-help skills. Although similar to autism, cases with Asperger's disorder less frequently exhibit deviance in language and communication than children with autism. More common in males, the majority of cases of the disorder are lifelong (see also Volkmar, Klin, & Pauls, 1998; Klin, McPartland, & Volkmar, 2005).

Childhood disintegrative disorder

When a child shows 2 years of normal development in communication, social relationships, play, and adaptive behavior followed by a clinically meaningful loss of previously acquired skills before age 10, it may be the very rare childhood disintegrative disorder (recall also the discussion earlier in the chapter about childhood schizophrenia). The essential feature of childhood disintegrative disorder is the marked deterioration of functioning following at least 2 years of apparently normal development. The social and communicative deficits seen in autism, as well as severe retardation, are also seen in childhood disintegrative disorder. Somewhat more common in males, this disorder is relatively constant throughout life.

Much work has been completed since the initial description of autism and the disorder is now better understood and treated. With continued effort, the future is likely to bring a clearer understanding of and treatment for the other pervasive developmental disorders.

Summary

Pervasive developmental disorders involve severe upset in the child's cognitive, social, behavioral, and emotional growth, producing widespread impact on the process of development. One such disorder, autism, affects the basic human qualities of interpersonal socialization and complex communication. Autism is relatively rare, although it does occur worldwide and with no pattern linked to social class or educational background. It is not thought to be caused by the actions of the caregiver, nor can it be explained by behavioral learning principles. Data have suggested a biological and potential genetic component.

Programs for autistic persons do not expect to cure the disorder, but are designed and provided to maximize personal adjustment. Programs based on psychodynamic thinking have not provided effective leads. Medications are used to treat problematic behaviors that interfere with functioning. Intensive behavior modification interventions have shown promising results. Increasingly, interventions also focus on the family, providing parent training to address child problems and parent counseling to address the difficulties associated with rearing a child with autism.

Tics and elimination disorders 11

Our coverage of behavioral, emotional, eating, and pervasive developmental disorders of childhood closes with contemplation of tic disorders and disorders associated with elimination (enuresis and encopresis). Some children with tic or elimination disorders also display other diagnosable conditions, whereas some cases occur in otherwise normal children.

Tic disorders

Tics are involuntary, rapid, recurrent, and stereotyped motor movements or vocalizations. Tics are sudden and nonrhythmic. Usually of brief duration, individual tics rarely last more than a second, but many tics tend to occur in bouts with a brief inter-tic interval (Leckman & Cohen, 2002). The tics occur many times a day, nearly every day or intermittently. In *DSM-IV* (APA, 1994), both motor and verbal tics may be classified as either chronic or transient, depending on the duration. As would be expected, chronic tics have a history of lasting for a period of more than 1 year, whereas the transient tic has been seen for less than 12 consecutive months. Transient tic disorders, which are almost invariably disorders of childhood, wax and wane over periods of weeks or months (Leckman & Cohen, 2002).

Some common motor tics include neck jerking and facial grimacing, and common verbal tics include grunting and throat-clearing. Some tics can be more complex, such as self-biting, smelling objects, and repeating sounds made by others. Tic behaviors may be exacerbated by stress, diminished during absorbing activities (such as reading), and reduced during sleep.

Of the several tic disorders, Tourette's is perhaps the best known and the most complex. In 1885, Gilles de la Tourette described nine cases of tic disorder characterized by motor incoordinations (or tics) and inarticulate shouts. Known today as Tourette's disorder, this tic disorder involves both multiple motor and one or more verbal tics. The tics can be simultaneous or occur at different times; they may occur daily or intermittently; the location, frequency, and intensity of the tics may change over time. The tics usually involve the head, although complex tics involving other parts of the body are often present. The *DSM* diagnostic criteria for Tourette's are presented in Box 11.1.

BOX 11.1   DSM criteria for a diagnosis of Tourette's disorder

- Both multiple motor and one or more vocal tics have been present at some time during the illness, although not necessarily concurrently.
- The tics occur many times a day, nearly every day, intermittently throughout a period of more than one year, and during this period there was never a tic-free period of more than three consecutive months.
- The disturbance causes marked distress or significant impairment in social, occupational, or other important areas of functioning.
- The onset is before 18 years of age.
- The disturbance is not due to the direct physiological effects of a substance (e.g., stimulants) or a general medical condition (e.g., Huntington's disease or postviral encephalitis).

Reprinted with permission from the *Diagnostic and Statistical Manual of Mental Disorders*, *Text Revision*, Fourth Edition, (Copyright 2000), American Psychiatric Association.

One of the unusual tics is coprolalia. Coprolalia, in which the individual utters, calls, or screams obscenities, is apparent in only about one-third of all patients with Tourette's disorder. Simple swearing when angry is not coprolalia.

Motor tics typically onset in childhood between the ages of 3 and 8, years before the onset of vocal tics (Swain, Scahill, Lombroso, King, & Leckman, 2007). The initial symptoms are often rapid eye-blinking, facial grimacing, and throat-clearing (Comings & Comings, 1985). Interestingly, although tics in children suffering from Tourette's are markedly reduced during sleep, they do not disappear completely (Janovic & Rohaidy, 1987). Many young children are oblivious to their tics, and experience them as entirely involuntary. By the age of 10, most children with tics are aware of any signals or urges that come before the tic (Leckman, Walker, & Cohen, 1993). Tic severity typically reaches its peak in mid-adolescence, declining considerably by the end of adolescence (Coffey et al., 2004; Pappert, Goetz, Louis, Blasucci, & Leurgans, 2003). Only 20% of childhood Tourette's cases persist into adulthood with functional impairment (Bloch et al., 2006; Swain et al., 2007).

Children with Tourette's disorder have difficulty maintaining age-appropriate social skills (Stokes, Bawden, Camfield, Ackman, & Dooley, 1991). One of the recurring themes emerging from interviews of the families of persons with Tourette's disorder is the presence of discipline problems (Budman, Bruun, Park, Lesser, & Olson, 2000; Comings & Comings, 1985). Parents report that the discipline problems are greater than routine and more severe than for nonaffected siblings. "Overreactive" and "explosive" were typical descriptions used by parents. Of the behavioral and emotional problems that frequently complicate Tourette's, impulsive, disinhibited, and immature behavior and compulsive touching and sniffing are common. At present, there are no clear dividing lines between these disruptive behaviors and complex tics on the one hand and comorbid conditions of ADHD and obsessive-compulsive disorder (OCD) on the other (Leckman & Cohen, 2002). Within the current diagnostic system, roughly 60–70% of youth with a tic disorder are found to meet criteria for a co-morbid diagnosis of ADHD (Eapen, Fox-Hiley, Banerjee, & Robertson, 2004; Swain et al., 2007).

Tourette's is certainly unusual. What is thought to be the cause of Tourette's? Because there is an increased incidence of Tourette's disorder in the first-degree relatives of people with the disorder, and mutual occurrence is higher in monozygotic twins than dizygotic twins (Swain et al., 2007), a genetic factor has been implicated in the etiology. Some researchers believe that it is an inherited disorder (e.g., Comings, Comings, Devor, & Cloninger, 1984; Pauls, 2003), and others have noted an increased frequency among Jewish people (Shapiro, Shapiro, Brunn, & Sweet, 1978). However, the high frequency of Jews reported in earlier studies may simply reflect the high percentage of Jews in the community (New York) where the research was carried out (Nee, Caine, & Polinsky, 1980). One study found that first-degree relatives of patients with Tourette's disorder were at substantially higher risk for developing Tourette's disorder, chronic motor tic disorder, and obsessive-compulsive disorder than were unrelated individuals. Interestingly, risk was gender related. The risk to male first-degree relatives for any tic disorder was 50% (18% for Tourette's disorder, 31% for chronic motor tics, and 7% for OCD) and only 31% for females (5% for Tourette's disorder, 9% for chronic motor tics, and 7% for OCD) (Pauls, Raymond, Stevenson, & Leckman, 1991). As with most childhood disorders, multiple vulnerability genes are likely to play a partial role in the development of tic disorders (Leckman et al., 2003; Zhang, Leckman, Tsai, Kidd, & Rosario Campos, 2002). Brain structures and neural circuits that underlie habit formation, procedural learning, and motor control have also been implicated (Leckman, 2002; Mink, 2006; Peterson et al., 2003). In the context of biological vulnerability, exposure to heat, stress, fatigue, and even infection have also been known to increase the likelihood of tic behaviors (Swain et al., 2007).

Medications historically prescribed to treat high blood pressure such as clonidine and guanfacine, have been used and reported to be helpful in treating childhood tics (Scahill et al., 2001). Antipsychotic medications, such as risperidone, haloperidol, or pimozide, have also been prescribed for Tourette's disorder, as they appear to decrease dopamine input to the basal ganglia (Swain et al., 2007); 70–80% of patients show some degree of benefit. Because of unwanted side effects, only 20–30% of those to whom the medication is prescribed take the drug for extended periods. In lower doses, however, patients may experience a remission of symptoms and few adverse reactions (Leckman & Cohen, 2002). As in any other psychopharmacological intervention for youth, careful monitoring of side effects is necessary and critical to ensure child safety.

You might wonder what it would be like to have Tourette's—to engage in nonsensical movements or blurt out verbalizations in an involuntary fashion. Bliss (1980) provided a rare self-description of the experience of Tourette's disorder. In his published account he described his 35-year attention to events that preceded, accompanied, and followed his motor and verbal tics. According to Bliss, the tics are actions taken to satisfy unfulfilled sensations and urges. By paying close attention, he claimed to be able to identify when his sensations would be overwhelming and when he needed to substitute a socially appropriate action. Bliss's self-description is not a scientific study, but recent empirical work supports some of Bliss's personal account. Indeed, many tics are under some degree of voluntary control, providing the foundation for treatments that rely on behavioral management procedures to address and reduce Tourette's and other tic disorders. Individuals with tic disorders consistently report experiencing a *premonitory urge*—a sensory experience of inner tension that signals the upcoming tic—immediately prior to tic engagement, and a feeling of relief immediately following the tic (Banaschewski et al., 2003b; Kwak, Vuong, & Jankovic, 2003; Swain et al., 2007; Woods, Piacentini, Himle, & Chang, 2005). Habit reversal training is a behavioral therapy approach for tic disorders. Habit reversal training assists youth to self-monitor and become more aware of premonitory urges, and then trains them to immediately engage in a competing response (i.e., a response that is physically incompatible with the tic).

A growing body of controlled evaluations supports the efficacy of habit reversal training for the treatment of tic disorders (Himle, Woods, Piacentini, & Walkup, 2006; Verdellen, Keijsers, Cath, & Hoogduin, 2004; Wilhelm et al., 2003), providing a promising non-pharmacological treatment option for families of affected youth.

Enuresis and encopresis

Elimination disorders are typically identified during childhood. Enuresis, the occurrence of wetting in the absence of a urologic or neurologic pathology, can be a source of concern to parents whose child is 3 to 5 years of age or older (*DSM* criteria are presented in Box 11.2). Some sources estimate that as many as 20% of all 5-year-olds wet their beds a sufficient number of times to qualify as enuretic (Doleys, 1983). Fortunately, the problem is much less frequent among older children—it occurs in less than 2% of 12- to 14-year-olds. There are some gender differences. Bed-wetting is equally common for boys and girls until age 5, but by 11 boys are twice as likely to be wet as girls (Shaffer, 1994).

BOX 11.2   DSM criteria for a diagnosis of enuresis

- Repeated voiding of urine into bed or clothes (whether involuntary or intentional).
- The behavior is clinically significant as manifested by either the frequency of twice a week for at least three consecutive months or the presence of clinically significant distress or impairment in social, academic (occupational), or other important areas of functioning.
- Chronological age is at least five years (or equivalent developmental level).
- The behavior is not due exclusively to the direct physiological effect of a substance (e.g., a diuretic) or a general medical condition (e.g., diabetes, spina bifida, a seizure disorder).

Reprinted with permission from the *Diagnostic and Statistical Manual of Mental Disorders, Text Revision*, Fourth Edition, (Copyright 2000), American Psychiatric Association.

Encopresis, the fecal parallel to enuresis, is reported in approximately 2–3% of 3- to 5-year-olds with a 3:1 male–female ratio (Hersov, 1994). The *DSM* diagnostic criteria for encopresis are listed in Box 11.3. By ages 10–12, 1% or fewer children are encopretic.

Research on the elimination disorders has focused mainly on enuresis; encopresis has not been studied extensively. Potential explanations of the cause of enuresis include genetic inheritance, a response to arousal during sleep, the expression of underlying emotional conflicts, smaller bladder capacity, and the failure to learn an adaptive response to the sensation of a full bladder. The research

- Repeated passage of feces into inappropriate places (e.g., clothing or floor) whether involuntary or intentional.
- At least one such event a month for at least three months.
- Chronological age is at least 5 years (or equivalent developmental level).
- The behavior is not due exclusively to the direct physiological effects of a substance (e.g., laxatives) or a general medical condition except through a mechanism involving constipation.

Reprinted with permission from the *Diagnostic and Statistical Manual of Mental Disorders*, *Text Revision*, Fourth Edition, (Copyright 2000), American Psychiatric Association.

evidence is nonexistent for some of these explanations and equivocal for others, leaving the field to be uncertain of the etiology but to assume that there are potentially multiple causes for the problem.

Although the cause of the problem remains a puzzle, there are well-studied, effective methods for bladder control training. The clear majority of the programs that have been demonstrated to be effective apply behavioral procedures. Medications such as imipramine (a medication used to treat depression in adults) increase bladder control in a reported 85% of patients (Shaffer, 1977), although total continence is achieved in only 30% of the patients. Unfortunately, up to 95% of these children relapse after the medication is withdrawn (Doleys, 1983). Based on a meta-analytic review of several studies, the customary psychological treatment was reported to be superior to medications (Houts, Berman, & Abramson, 1994).

Perhaps the most often used treatment for enuresis is the urine alarm system sometimes called the "bell and pad," which has been used in some form or another for over 100 years (Mikkelsen, 2001). The bell and pad system is based on classical conditioning. A urine-sensing device rests between the child and the mattress during sleep hours. Urine that passes on to the device triggers an audible alarm. Once awake, the child urinates in the toilet and can then return to bed. Doleys (1977), summarizing results over 15 years, concluded that 75% of the more than 600 children treated with the urine alarm showed remission. The average length of treatment with the urine alarm is 5–12 weeks. Relapse remains a problem, however, as 41% of the treated children were unable to maintain the dry state after treatment discontinued. Newer alarm-based programs use an ultra-sonic monitor mounted to an elastic abdominal belt to replace the liquid-sensitive "pad." In this modality, the alarm goes off when the monitor identifies that the bladder has reached capacity (Mikkelsen, 2001). Initial outcome data are promising (Pretlow, 1999).

Two modifications to the urine alarm approach help reduce the relapse rate (Doleys, 1983; Finley, Wansley, & Blenkarn, 1977; Jehu,

Morgan, Turner, & Jones, 1977). First, because responses are more persistent under conditions of partial reinforcement, the alarm is set to go off 50–75% of the time that the pad is wet. Second, the child sometimes consumes liquids before bed and after dryness days have been achieved. By so doing, the child learns bladder control when the bladder is full as well as when it is not as full.

Dry-bed training combines other behavioral procedures with the urine alarm (Azrin, Sheed, & Foxx, 1974), including opportunities for positive practice, nighttime awakening, practice in retention control, and full cleanliness training. In research reported by Fincham and Spettell (1984), parents who were actually involved in the treatment of enuretic children viewed the urine alarm as more acceptable than the dry-bed training.

Summary

Tics are involuntary, rapid, recurrent, and stereotyped movements or verbalizations. Tics may be motor or verbal, simple or complex, and transient or chronic. Tourette's disorder involves both multiple motor and one or more verbal tics. Coprolalia occurs when an individual utters, calls, or screams obscenities.

Enuresis, wetting in the absence of urologic or neurologic disorder, is common among 3- to 5-year-olds but becomes a source of concern as age progresses. Treatment with the bell and pad has been reported to be quite successful. Encopresis, the fecal parallel to enuresis, occurs less frequently and is much less studied.

Questions for your consideration 12

The psychological disorders of youth are diverse and multifaceted. There is no one single causal agent to explain the disorders and, likewise, although some treatments are more effective than others, there is no one therapeutic approach that is universally effective. Add to the presence of diverse disorders the fact that there are many social pressures facing both nondisturbed and the less well adjusted children and it is apparent that progressing through development is not an easy task for today's youngsters.

Should psychologists take an active stance with regard to the challenges of childhood? Consider that some children are not unaware or unexperienced about the stresses and dangers of life. Numerous examples have been brought to our attention by media exposure of children who are involved in crime, victims of violence and abuse, abandoned and assaulted, and suffering from poverty and hunger. Consider also that research suggests that many problems of childhood do not naturally go away, and that the research data support the benefits of early intervention. All the information combines to alert us to the need, be it with individuals, families, or communities, for action and intervention.

Owing to society's increased awareness of the challenges facing child adjustment, there has been and will continue to be a broadening of the research scope and a flourishing of the research literature that addresses the causes and treatments for the psychological disorders of childhood. In addition, the more we learn about the challenges that face children as a part of their normal development, and about how well-adjusted children cope and adjust, the more we will advance our understanding and be able to enhance our interventions.

That childhood experiences influence adult behavior patterns is a principal theme in several theories of psychopathology. For example, both cognitive and learning approaches accent the important role of early acquired patterns of behavior. The outlook for the future contains continued emphasis on the importance of early experiences, but with greater specificity—advances in theory and treatment address the precise role of (a) child experiences, (b) the nature of cognitive processing, and (c) behavioral pattern of childhood with specific disorders.

The family matters, and research on topics within family psychology has come of age. No longer are family approaches criticized as cult-like, nor are they burdened by sole reliance on nonempirical theories. The increasingly evidence-based focus on parent–child interactions, parenting styles, and parent and family interventions combines to promote an evolving and expanding knowledge base about the contribution of family forces to child adjustment and maladjustment. The past 20 years have been witness to this emerging focus.

A trend in the treatment of mental retardation and pervasive disorders specifically, and childhood disorders in general, is an increased involvement of the family. In particular, the trend is away from custodial care, with a corresponding increase in community centers and family programs. Progress in the treatment of behavior problems in individuals with the disorder has been significant, and these advances are now being coordinated with interventions for the family. For example, there is widespread recognition that the family of a child with intellectual impairment or autism is a part of the system that influences the child's behavior and adjustment.

The appeal of biological models is likely to continue. Advances in genetic research methods will have application to the study of the childhood disorders. Developments in noninvasive neuroimaging technology provide windows into the living brain in ways previously unimagined (Gerber & Peterson, 2008), and with such advances will come continued research into the neurobiological underpinnings of childhood disorders. With reference to treatments, randomized clinical trials evaluating cognitive-behavioral and pharmacological approaches, and their combinations, will likely dominate future intervention research efforts. Finally, as evidence-based treatments are preferred but not readily available to a considerable number of youth, dissemination efforts are needed to expand access to first-rate interventions. As a glimpse into the future, efforts are already under way to implement and evaluate computer software and internet-delivered treatments for the delivery of evidence-based mental health services for childhood disorders.

What would you do?

In the following specific situations, questions are raised pertaining to child adjustment, the psychological disorders of childhood, parenting practices, and societal decisions. The seven situations will be described with some details and descriptive information, but they could occur in any of a variety of contexts. The answers, too, are not black and white—there are many debatable points and a great deal of room for the influence of personal beliefs and opinions. Nevertheless, all of the situations are relevant to how we, as members of society, address the psychological issues and challenges of childhood.

It is suggested that you read and weigh each situation separately—one at a time—and engage in a discussion or self-reflection about the issues and your responses to them. Space is provided for you to list your ideas and arguments and to make related notes and suggestions.

Situation 1: The educated parent

No matter how old you are at the present time, skip either ahead or back to the time in your life soon after you first choose/chose to become a parent. To help set the situation, think about where you might be (were) living at this time and your likely (usual) friends and activities at the time. Think about your aspirations for your child.

Now, move ahead several years and suppose that your 6-year-old son, André, has been described by his teacher as wiggly and full of excess energy. You know from your time with him that there are occasions when André can be very difficult to manage, but you really didn't expect his teacher to suggest to you and your spouse that he is more active than the other children, that he appears hyperactive, and that he may have ADHD.

What do you think about these comments about André? Do you blame the school or the classroom teacher? Do you blame yourselves? Independent of the possible causes, you and your spouse have to consider whether or not to have André seen by a psychologist and tested and, if he is diagnosed, whether or not to seek treatment and possibly use medications? Given what you have learned in this book, can you anticipate the issues to weigh? What data sources would you want the diagnostician to consider?

Use the space below to list (a) the issues and (b) the data sources to be considered.

_____	_____
_____	_____
_____	_____
_____	_____

Situation 2: Should the pharmaceutical industry be allowed to advertise psychotropic medications directly to consumers?

If you have watched television in the United States in recent years, you have probably encountered advertisements for a range of medications intended to target mental and physical conditions. These advertisements often include an actor playing the part of an attractive doctor who emphasizes the benefits of a particular trademarked drug and the promise of a better quality of life. You may have also noticed how well-crafted and effective these advertisements can be, and you might easily see how individuals could be persuaded to ask their doctor about a particular drug as recommended by the "doctor" in the commercial. Indeed, in the context of such "direct-to-consumer" (DTC) advertising from the pharmaceutical industry, it is not uncommon for US doctors to report that their patients often arrive requesting to be treated with a particular medication for a self-diagnosed condition. Data support the efficacy of DTC advertising—the more money a pharmaceutical company spends on marketing a particular drug directly to consumers, the more that drug is subsequently prescribed by doctors. At present, the United States is one of the only governments to permit DTC advertising from the pharmaceutical industry, although other governments may follow suit in the coming years.

Document your thinking about the pros and cons of DTC advertising for psychotropic medications. First, imagine you support DTC advertising for psychotropic medication and list all of the potential benefits you can think of for pharmaceutical companies to be able to directly inform families of pharmaceutical options to treat their emotional maladies. Second, assume that you support a ban on DTC advertising practices by the pharmaceutical industry and list the reasons to justify this position.

Pro: _____

_____

_____

_____

Con: _____

_____

_____

_____

Situation 3: Do we legislate the right to reproduce?

You spent most of your childhood in a medium-sized town with many but not all of the niceties of life. Your school was safe, there were playgrounds and parks near your home, and the local recreational facilities included outdoor activities and several regional sports. Suppose also that a neighbor—someone about the same age as yourself—was someone with an intellectual disability. And suppose further that, as a young adult, he now goes daily to a sheltered workshop where he has met a young woman. Both have cognitive impairments, but are in otherwise good physical health. They fall in love.

Often held as a basic human right, many adults marry and start a family. But, with regard to persons with intellectual disabilities, we know of their limitations in self-care and social functioning, and of the increased risk (both genetic and environmental) of impaired intellectual functioning among their offspring. Can society impose rules and regulations to govern reproduction among those with intellectual disabilities? Who is to say whether or not a cognitively impaired couple can marry and reproduce? Should the couple be given sex education (Shepperdson, 1995)? To what extent should they be counseled about the risks and rewards associated with their particular reproduction situation?

All of these questions and possible answers become especially difficult when one considers the criteria for making decisions about whether or not impaired intellect is present: Who would decide? Would a panel of experts decide? The courts? Would an IQ test and IQ score be involved and, if so, what test score would be used? Even more difficult would be a situation in which a person had an IQ that was just one point above or below the cutoff score? Would exceptions be made, and on what basis?

As is apparent, questions of an individual's personal freedoms can be legally complicated and philosophically troublesome—but let's now turn to another complicated dilemma. Although not a frequent problem, how best to address sexual acting out among persons with impaired intellectual functioning? Are they to be held responsible?

Document your thinking about both sides of these issues. For one list, assume that you support the position that persons deemed intellectually impaired should be restrained from reproducing and list the criteria that you would propose for determining the presence and absence of mental retardation. For the second list, assume that you are against regulating the reproductive rights of those with intellectual impairments and list the reasons to justify this position.

Pro: _____

_____

_____

_____

Con: _____

_____

_____

_____

Situation 4: To use prebirth information?
With scientific investigation comes increased knowledge. For example, there are modern screening tests that can provide early identification of yet to be born children with

Down syndrome. Such early identification also unearths a potential predicament. First, it is clear that there are inordinate benefits to be gained by early identification. In PKU, for example, early identification leads to treatment that prevents the disorder. However, with early identification also come both personal and professional challenges to ethics. How will the parents of these offspring address prebirth decisions? Advances in science can stimulate social debates, provoke personal challenges, and create new dilemmas as yet unknown to future parents. The real and potential gains associated with early identification merit continued investigation, but there are issues to consider.

Describe and justify your position with regard to the following question. How would you use prebirth information about the nature of your unborn child's health?

_____

_____

_____

_____

_____

_____

Situation 5: Educational tracking?

For this next situation, again suppose that you are a parent. In this case your daughter is an exceptionally bright 9-year-old student who has come home on several occasions complaining that she is totally bored at school. On this particular day you ask a few questions and quickly learn something that you consider a major source of concern—the teacher is spending much of her class time repeating the lessons for some of the students in the classroom showing learning difficulties. As you consider this scenario, ask yourself the following questions. Should your daughter be separated from the students in the class showing learning difficulties? Should the bright students, in general, be separated and given more advanced work?

Is it an optimal educational strategy to mainstream the students with developmental delays into classrooms with typically developing youth, or should they be selected out for special education opportunities? Do you see benefits in having a variety of educational levels represented in one class? Are there benefits to classrooms that are stratified by ability levels?

List the pro and con arguments. What problems can you identify for each side of the debate? After you consider the arguments, make a choice for yourself. Then, specify how the benefits of your decision would outweigh the related problems?

Pro: _____

_____

Con: _____

_____

Cost/benefit: _____

_____

_____

Situation 6: How best to improve the availability of expert mental health care for youth?

Imagine you are flying on an airplane and have started a conversation with the woman seated next to you. You learn that she lives with her husband and 10-year-old child in a bucolic town located roughly 3 hours from the nearest city. She tells you that in almost every way they enjoy living far from the noise and stress of city living, but as you continue to chat you learn that her child also suffers from a very severe and debilitating case of OCD that has profoundly interfered with his academic performance, the functioning of the family, and the general quality of life for all three of them. You learn that living in such a remote town has been problematic for the child's condition, as there are no mental health professionals in her area, let alone professionals sufficiently trained in cognitive-behavioral therapy. The child's condition has gotten progressively worse over the past year, and you learn that she and her husband are now reluctantly forced to consider moving closer to the city, far away from their extended family and dear friends, solely to be closer to expert care for their child's OCD.

The above situation is not as uncommon as you might guess. Although there has been progress in the development of programs with substantial empirical support for childhood disorders, a sizable gap exists between what has been found effective in research and what is actually implemented and/or received in remote communities. Inadequate numbers of mental health professionals trained in evidence-based programs impinge on the availability of effective care for many youth.

Use the space below to list innovative methods that might be used to overcome traditional geographic barriers to children's mental health care for children living in remote communities. In particular, focus on ways in which new media, such as the internet, may be useful in this endeavor.

_____

_____

_____

_____

_____

_____

Situation 7: Allocating funding

Our knowledge and awareness of autism has mushroomed. Despite this, its exact cause remains unknown and most interventions are of circumscribed success. How should society respond? Although it is severe and quite troubling, it is not as common as other childhood disorders. Do we need to spend more time and money on research, and place greater focus on treating autism? With regard to services, should parents be prepared to be the primary providers for youth with autism, or should care be provided by society? Attitudes in the US have changed from segregating people with pervasive disabilities and considered to be a burden to others to the modern prevailing view that such individuals have equal rights, can make positive contributions to society, and deserve full inclusion. Although attitudes change and answers are not always readily available, mental health professionals and citizens are nevertheless faced with perplexing issues such as these.

Assume that you have a vote in the control of the national budget that was designated for the treatment of childhood disorders. One of your tasks is to assign portions of the money to different problems. How would you distribute the funds? What percentage of the total would be allocated for autism? Given your knowledge of childhood disorders, here are two tasks. First, assign percentages of the total to each of the disorders we have addressed, and describe your rationale for the allocations that you made. Second, provide an argument for allocating all of the money to one topic—what topic would it be and why?

1 Conduct disorder _____

2 ADHD _____

3 Anxiety disorder _____

4 Depression _____

5 Eating disorder _____

6 Mental retardation and learning disorders _____

7 Pervasive developmental disorders _____

8 Tics and elimination _____

Which topic deserves special allocation and why? _____

_____

_____

_____

Summary

Our journey through the disorders of childhood has exposed us to the diverse psychological problems affecting children, to the fact that there are manifold causal ingredients that can lead to psychological distress, and to the assorted interventions that have been developed, evaluated, and provided for children in need. Importantly, however, we also discovered that there is much yet to be learned. For example, we do not have a full appreciation of the biological forces operating in autism, the familial factors that contribute to conduct disorder, or the parenting styles that unwittingly foster anxiety disorders. Similarly, we do not yet have a sufficient grasp of exactly how best to treat specific disorders or how, in the ideal, to prevent them from developing. Moreover, although we have gained a greater appreciation of the steps that need to be taken to further advance our knowledge, we are still faced with many grave and penetrating questions that require careful and serious consideration. It is hoped that the applications of our knowledge about childhood disorders will result in a series of reasoned and well-balanced decisions—decisions that should, in the end, benefit our overall society as well as the specific affected children.

Suggested readings

There are now several contemporary and advanced edited books that address the nature and treatment of childhood disorders. Although the interested reader can pursue topics by going to the references to specific studies, the following select readings offer collections of chapters, reviews of literatures, and some conceptual and theoretical advances.

Cicchetti, D., & Cohen, D.J. (Eds.) (2006). *Developmental psychopathology, Volume 1: Theory and Method* (2nd ed.). New York: Wiley.

Cicchetti, D., & Cohen, D.J. (Eds.) (2006). *Developmental psychopathology, Volume 2: Developmental neuroscience* (2nd ed.). New York: Wiley.

Cicchetti, D., & Cohen, D.J. (Eds.) (2006). *Developmental psychopathology, Volume 3: Risk, disorder, and adaptation* (2nd ed.). New York: Wiley.

Hammen, C. (1991). *Depression runs in families: The social context of risk and resilience in children of depressed mothers.* New York: Springer-Verlag.

Hammen, C., & Watkins, E. (2008). *Depression.* London: Psychology Press/ Taylor & Francis.

Hibbs, E., & Jensen, P. (Eds.) (2004). *Psychosocial treatments for child and adolescent disorders: Empirically based strategies for clinical practice* (2nd ed.). Washington, DC: American Psychological Association.

Kazdin, A.E., & Weisz, J.R. (Eds.) (2003). *Evidence-based psychotherapies for children and adolescents.* New York: Guilford Press.

Kendall, P.C. (Ed.) (2005). *Child and adolescent therapy: Cognitive-behavioral procedures* (3rd ed.). New York: Guilford Press.

Kendall, P.C., & MacDonald, J.P. (1993). Cognition in the psychopathology of youth, and implications for treatment. In K.S. Dobson & P.C. Kendall (Eds.), *Psychopathology and cognition* (pp. 387–432). San Diego, CA: Academic Press.

Mash, E., & Barkley, R. (Eds.) (2006). *Child psychopathology* (3rd ed.). New York: Guilford Press.

Mash, E., & Terdal, L. (Eds.) (2007). *Assessment of childhood disorders* (4th ed.). New York: Guilford Press.

Patterson, G.R. (1982). *Coercive family process.* Eugene, OR: Castalia.

Prinstein, M.J., & Dodge, K.A. (Eds.) (2008). *Understanding peer influence in children and adolescents.* New York: Guilford Press.

Rutter, M., Bishop, D., Pine, D., Scott, S., Stevenson, J., Taylor, E., et al. (Eds.) (2008). *Rutter's child and adolescent psychiatry* (5th ed.). Oxford: Wiley-Blackwell.

References

AACAP (2007). Practice parameters for the assessment and treatment of children and adolescents with depressive disorders. *Journal of the American Academy of Child and Adolescent Psychiatry, 46,* 1503–1526.

AACAP Work Group on Quality Issues (2007). Practice parameter for the assessment and treatment of children and adolescents with attention-deficit/hyperactivity disorder. *Journal of the American Academy of Child and Adolescent Psychiatry, 46,* 894–921.

Abela, J.R.Z., & Hankin, B.L. (2008). Cognitive vulnerability to depression in children and adolescents: A developmental psychopathology perspective. In J.R.Z. Abela & B.L. Hankin (Eds.), *Handbook of depression in children and adolescents* (pp. 35–78). New York: Guilford Press.

Abikoff, H. (1985). Efficacy of cognitive training interventions in hyperactive children: A critical review. *Clinical Psychology Review, 5,* 479–512.

Abikoff, H. (1991). Cognitive training in ADHD children: Less to it than meets the eye. *Journal of Learning Disabilities, 24,* 205–209.

Abikoff, H., & Hechtman, L. (1996). Multimodal therapy and stimulants in the treatment of children with ADHD. In E. Hibbs & P. Jensen (Eds.), *Psychosocial treatments for child and adolescent disorders: Empirically based strategies for clinical practice* (pp. 341–370). Washington, DC: American Psychological Association.

Abramson, L., Metalsky, G., & Alloy, L.B. (1989). Hopelessness depression: A theory-based subtype of depression. *Psychological Review, 96,* 358–372.

Achenbach, T.M. (1990). Conceptualization of developmental psychopathology. In M. Lewis & S. M. Miller (Eds.), *Handbook of developmental psychopathology.* New York: Plenum Press.

Achenbach, T.M. (1991). *Manual for the child behavior checklist: 4–18 and 1991 profile.* Burlington, VT: University of Vermont.

Achenbach, T.M., & Edelbrock, C. (1978). The classification of child psychopathology: A review and analysis of empirical efforts. *Psychological Bulletin, 85,* 1275–1301.

Achenbach, T.M., & Rescorla, L.A. (2001). *Manual for ASEBA school-age forms and profiles.* Burlington, VT: University of Vermont.

Achenbach, T.M., & Rescorla, L.A. (2006). Developmental issues in assessment, taxonomy, and diagnosis of psychopathology: Life span and multicultural perspectives. In D. Cicchetti & D.J. Cohen (Eds.), *Development and psychopathology, Vol 1: Theory and method* (2nd ed., pp. 139–180). Hoboken, NJ: Wiley.

Agosta, J., & Melda, K. (1996). Supporting families who provide care at home for children with disabilities. *Exceptional Children, 62,* 271–282.

Alarcon, M., Pennington, B.F., Filipek, P.A., & DeFries, J.C. (2000). Etiology of neuroanatomical correlates of reading disability. *Developmental Neuropsychology, 17,* 339–360.

Albano, A.M., & DiBartolo, P.M. (2007). *Cognitive-behavioral therapy for social phobia in adolescents: Stand up, speak out.* New York: Oxford University Press.

Albano, A.M., & Silverman, W. (1996). *Anxiety Disorders Interview Schedule for DSM-IV: Child version.* San Antonio, TX: Psychological Corporation.

Alessandri, S.M. (1992). Attention, play, and social behavior in ADHD preschoolers. *Journal of Abnormal Child Psychology, 20,* 289–302.

Alford, B.A., & Norcross, J.C. (1991). Cognitive therapy as integrative therapy. *Journal of Psychotherapy Integration, 1,* 175–190.

Alloy, L., Abramson, L., Murray, L., Whitehouse, W., & Hogan, M. (1997). Self-referrant information processing in individuals at high and low risk for depression. *Cognition and Emotion, 11,* 539–568.

Alloy, L.B., Abramson, L.Y., Walshaw, P.D., & Neeren, A.M. (2006). Cognitive vulnerability to unipolar and bipolar mood disorders. *Journal of Social and Clinical Psychology, 25,* 726–754.

Aman, M.G., & Singh, N.N. (1983). Pharmacological intervention. In L. Matson & F. Andrasik (Eds.), *Treatment issues and innovations in mental retardation* (pp. 347–372). New York: Plenum Press.

Amato, P.R. (2001). Children of divorce in the 1990's: An update of the Amato and Keith (1991) meta-analysis. *Journal of Family Psychology, 15,* 355–370.

American Psychiatric Association (APA, 1952). *Diagnostic and statistical manual of mental disorders.* Washington, DC: American Psychiatric Association.

American Psychiatric Association (APA, 1994). *Diagnostic and statistical manual of mental disorders* (4th ed.). Washington, DC: American Psychiatric Association.

American Psychologist (1992). Reflections on B.F. Skinner and psychology [Special Issue], 47(11).

Anastopoulos, A.D. (1996). Facilitating parental understanding and management of attention deficit and hyperactivity disorder. In M.A. Reinecke, F.M. Dattilio, & A. Freeman (Eds.), *Cognitive therapy with children and adolescents: A casebook for clinical practice* (pp. 327–343). New York: Guilford Press.

Anastopoulos, A.D., & Farley, S.E. (2003). A cognitive-behavioral training program for parents of children with attention-deficit/hyperactivity disorder. In A.E. Kazdin & J.R. Weisz (Eds.), *Evidence-based psychotherapies for children and adolescents.* New York: Guilford Press.

Anastopoulos, A.D., Shelton, T., & Barkley, R.A. (2005). Family based treatment: Psychosocial intervention for children and adolescents with attention deficit hyperactivity disorder. In E. Hibbs & P. Jensen (Eds.), *Psychosocial treatments for child and adolescent disorders: Empirically based strategies for clinical practice* (2nd ed., pp. 327–350). Washington, DC: American Psychological Association.

Anastopoulos, A.D., Shelton, T., DuPaul, G.J., & Gouvremont, D.C. (1993). Parent training for attention-deficit hyperactivity disorder: Its impact on parent functioning. *Journal of Abnormal Child Psychology, 21,* 581–596.

Anderson, J.C., Williams, S., McGee, R., & Silva, P.A. (1987). DSM-III disorders in preadolescent children: Prevalence in a large sample from the general population. *Archives of General Psychiatry, 44,* 69–76.

Andreyeva, T., Puhl, R.M., & Brownell, K.D. (2008). Changes in perceived weight discrimination among Americans, 1995–1996 through 2004–2006. *Obesity, 16,* 1129–1134.

Arnold, L.E., Vitiello, B., McDougle, C.J., Scahill, L., Shah, B., Gonzalez, N.M., et al. (2003). Patient-defined target symptoms respond to risperidone in

RUPP Autism Study: Customer approach to clinical trials. *Journal of the American Academy of Child and Adolescent Psychiatry, 42,* 1443–1450.

Arnsten, A.F.T. (2006). Stimulants: Therapeutic actions in ADHD. *Neuropsychopharmacology, 31,* 2376–2383.

Aronson, M., Hagberg, B., & Gillberg, C. (1997). Attention deficits and autistic spectrum problems in children exposed to alcohol during gestation: A follow-up study. *Developmental Medicine and Child Neurology, 39,* 583–587.

Asbury, K., Wachs, T.D., & Plomin, R. (2005). Environmental moderators of genetic influence on verbal and nonverbal abilities in early childhood. *Intelligence, 33,* 643–661.

Ashbaugh, R., & Peck, S. (1998). Treatment of sleep problems in a toddler: A replication of the faded bedtime with response cost protocol. *Journal of Applied Behavior Analysis, 31,* 127–129.

Askew, C., & Field, A.P. (2008). The vicarious learning pathway to fear 40 years on. *Clinical Psychology Review, 28,* 1249–1265.

August, G.J. (1987). Production deficiencies in free recall: A comparison of hyperactivity learning-disabled and normal children. *Journal of Abnormal Child Psychology, 15,* 429–440.

Auyeung, B., & Baron-Cohen, S. (2008). A role for fetal testosterone in human sex differences: Implications for understanding autism. In A.W. Zimmerman (Ed.), *Autism: Current theories and evidence* (pp. 185–208). Totowa, NJ: Humana Press.

Azrin, N.H., Sheed, T.J., & Foxx, R.M. (1974). Dry bed: Rapid elimination of childhood enuresis. *Behavior Research and Therapy, 12,* 147–156.

Baer, D., Wolf, M., & Risley, T. (1968). Some current dimensions of applied behavior analysis. *Journal of Applied Behavior Analysis, 1,* 91–97.

Bagner, D.M., & Eyberg, S.M. (2007). Parent–child interaction therapy for disruptive behavior in children with mental retardation: A randomized controlled trial. *Journal of Clinical Child and Adolescent Psychology, 36,* 418–429.

Bailey, A., Palferman, S., Heavey, L.M., & Le Couteur, A. (1998). Genetics of autism: Overview and new directions. *Journal of Autism and Developmental Disabilities, 28,* 351–368.

Baird, G., Charman, T., Baron-Cohen, S., Cox, A., Swettenham, J., Wheelwright, S., et al. (2000). A screening instrument for autism at 18 months of age: A 6-year follow-up study. *Journal of the American Academy of Child and Adolescent Psychiatry, 39,* 694–702.

Baker, B.L., Bacher, J., Crnic, K.A., & Edelbrock, C. (2002). Behavior problems and parenting stress in families of three-year-old children with and without developmental delays. *American Journal on Mental Retardation, 107,* 433–444.

Baker, B.L., & Feinfield, K.A. (2007). Early intervention and parent education. In A. Carr, G. O'Reilly, P.N. Walsh, & J. McEvoy (Eds.), *The handbook of intellectual disability and clinical psychology practice* (pp. 336–370). New York: Routledge/Taylor & Francis.

Baker, B.L., Landen, S.J., & Kashima, K.J. (1991). Effects of parent training on families of children with mental retardation: Increased burden or generalized benefit? *American Journal on Mental Retardation, 96,* 127–136.

Baldwin, J.S., & Dadds, M.R. (2007). Reliability and validity of parent and child versions of the Multidimensional Anxiety Scale for Children in community samples. *Journal of the American Academy of Child and Adolescent Psychiatry, 46,* 252–260.

Banaschewski, T., Brandeis, D., Heinrich, H., Albrecht, B., Brunner, E., & Rothenberg, A. (2003a). Association of

ADHD and conduct disorder—brain electrical evidence for the existence of a distinct subtype. *Journal of Child Psychology and Psychiatry*, 44, 356–376.

Banaschewski, T., Hollis, C., Oosterlaan, J., Roeyers, H., Rubia, K., Willcutt, E., et al. (2005). Towards an understanding of unique and shared pathways in the psychopathophysiology of ADHD. *Developmental Science*, 8, 132–140.

Banaschewski, T., Woerner, W., & Rothenberger, A. (2003b). Premonitory sensory phenomena and suppressibility of tics in Tourette syndrome: Developmental aspects in children and adolescents. *Developmental Medicine and Child Neorology*, 45, 700–703.

Bandura, A. (1969). *Principles of behavior modification*. New York: Holt, Rinehart & Winston.

Bandura, A. (1986). *Social learning theory*. Englewood Cliffs, NJ: Prentice-Hall.

Banerjee, T.D., Middleton, F., & Faraone, S.V. (2007). Environmental risk factors for attention-deficit hyperactivity disorder. *Acta Paediatrica*, 96, 1269–1274.

Barbe, R.P., Bridge, J., Birmaher, B., Kolko, D.J., & Brent, D.A. (2004). Lifetime history of sexual abuse, clinical presentation, and outcome in a clinical trial for adolescent depression. *Journal of Clinical Psychiatry*, 65, 77–83.

Barclay, M., & Hoffman, J. (1990). Conduct disorders. In M. Lewis & S. Miller (Eds.), *Handbook of developmental psychopathology*. New York: Plenum Press.

Barkley, R.A. (1997). Behavioral inhibition, sustained attention, and executive functions: Constructing a unifying theory of ADHD. *Psychological Bulletin*, 121, 65–94.

Barkley, R.A. (2006a). *Attention deficit hyperactivity disorder: A handbook for diagnosis and treatment, Third Edition*. New York: Guilford Press.

Barkley, R.A. (2006b). Attention-deficit/ hyperactivity disorder. In E.J. Mash & R.A. Barkley (Eds.), *Child psychopathology* (pp. 63–112). New York: Guilford Press.

Barkley, R.A., Anastopoulos, A. Guevremont, D., & Fletcher, K. (1992a). Adolescents with ADHD: Mother–adolescent interactions, family beliefs and conflicts, and maternal psychopathology. *Journal of Abnormal Child Psychology*, 20, 263–288.

Barkley, R.A., Fischer, M., Edelbrock, C., & Smallish, L. (1991). The adolescent outcome of hyperactive children diagnosed by research criteria-III: Mother–child interactions, family conflicts and maternal psychopathology. *Journal of Child Psychology and Psychiatry*, 32, 233–255.

Barkley, R.A., Guevremont, D.C., Anastopoulos, A.D., DuPaul, G.J., & Shelton, T.L. (1993). Driving-related risks and outcomes of attention-deficit hyperactivity disorder in adolescents and young adults: 3- to 5-year follow-up survey. *Pediatrics*, 92, 212–218.

Barkley, R.A., Guevremont, D.C. Anastopoulos, A.D., & Fletcher, K.E. (1992b). A comparison of three family conflicts in adolescents with attention deficit hyperactivity disorder. *Journal of Consulting and Clinical Psychology*, 60, 450–462.

Barkley, R.A., Karlsson, J., Pollard, S., & Murphy, J.U. (1985). Developmental changes in the mother–child interactions of hyperactive boys: Effects of two dose levels of Ritalin. *Journal of Child Psychology and Psychiatry*, 26, 705–715.

Barkley, R.A., McMurray, M.B., Edelbrock, C., & Robbins, K. (1990). Side effects of methylphenidate in children with attention-deficit hyperactivity disorder: A systematic, placebo-controlled evaluation. *Pediatrics*, 86, 184–192.

Barlow, D.H. (1988). *Anxiety and its disorders*. New York: Guilford Press.

Barmann, B.C., & Murray, W.J. (1981). Suppression of inappropriate sexual behavior by facial screening. *Behavior Therapy, 12*, 730–735.

Barmish, A.J., & Kendall, P.C. (2005). Should parents be co-clients in cognitive-behavioral therapy for anxious youth? *Journal of Clinical Child and Adolescent Psychology, 34*, 569–581.

Baron-Cohen, S., Leslie, A., & Frith, U. (1985). Does the autistic child have a "theory of mind"? *Cognition, 21*, 37–46.

Barrett, P.M., Dadds, M., & Rapee, R.M. (1996a). Family treatment of childhood anxiety: A controlled trial. *Journal of Consulting and Clinical Psychology, 64*, 333–342.

Barrett, P.M., Rapee, R.M., Dadds, M., & Ryan, S.M. (1996b). Family enhancement of cognitive style in anxious and aggressive children. *Journal of Abnormal Child Psychology, 24*, 187–203.

Barry, T., Lyman, R.D., & Klinger, L.G. (2002). Academic underachievement and attention-deficit/hyperactivity disorder: The negative impact of symptom severity on school performance. *Journal of School Psychology, 40*, 259–283.

Bartels, M., Rietveld, M.J., Van Baal, G.C., & Boomsma, D.I. (2002). Genetic and environmental influences on the development of intelligence. *Behavioral Genetics, 32*, 237–249.

Baumeister, A.A., & Rollings, J.P. (1976). Self-injurious behavior. In N.R. Ellis (Ed.), *International review of research in mental retardation* (Vol. 8, pp. 87–112). New York: Academic Press.

Baumeister, R.F., & Vohs, K.D. (2004). *Handbook of self-regulation*. New York: Guilford Press.

Bauminger, N., & Kasari, C. (1999). Theory of mind in high-functioning children with autism. *Journal of Autism and Developmental Disabilities, 29*, 81–87.

Beaver, K.M., Wright, J.P., DeLisi, M., Walsh, A., Vaughn, M.G., Boisvert, D., et al. (2007). A gene X gene interaction between DRD2 and DRD4 is associated with conduct disorder and antisocial behavior in males. *Behavioral and Brain Functions, 3*, 1–8.

Beck, A.T. (1967). *Depression: Clinical, experimental, and theoretical aspects*. New York: Harper & Row.

Beck, A.T. (1976). *Cognitive theory and the emotional disorders*. New York: International Universities Press.

Beck, A.T. (1987). Cognitive models of depression. *Journal of Cognitive Psychotherapy, 1*, 5–38.

Beck, A.T., & Emery, G. (1985). *Anxiety disorders and phobias: A cognitive perspective*. New York: Basic Books.

Beidel, D. (1991). Social phobia and overanxious disorder in school-aged children. *Journal of the American Academy of Child and Adolescent Psychiatry, 30*, 545–552.

Beidel, D.C., Turner, S.M., Sallee, F.R., Ammerman, R.T., Crosby, L.A., & Pathak, S. (2007). SET-C versus fluoxetine in the treatment of childhood social phobia. *Journal of the American Academy of Child and Adolescent Psychiatry, 46*, 1622–1632.

Beidel, D.C., Turner, S.M., & Young, B.J. (2006). Social effectiveness therapy for children: Five years later. *Behavior Therapy, 37*, 416–425.

Bemis-Vitousek, K., & Orimoto, L. (1993). Cognitive-behavioral models of anorexia nervosa, bulimia nervosa, and obesity. In K.S. Dobson & P.C. Kendall (Eds.), *Psychopathology and cognition* (pp. 193–245). San Diego: Academic Press.

Bettelheim, B. (1967). *The empty fortress*. New York: Free Press.

Bibby, P., Eikeseth, S., Martin, N.T., Mudford, O.C., & Reeves, D. (2001). Progress and outcomes for children with autism receiving parent-managed intensive interventions. *Research in Developmental Disabilities, 22,* 425–447.

Bickett, L., & Milich, R. (1990). First impressions formed of boys with learning disabilities and attention deficit disorder. *Journal of Learning Disabilities, 23,* 253–259.

Biederman, J., Faraone, S.V., & Monuteaux, M.C. (2002). Differential effect of environmental adversity by gender: Rutter's index of adversity in a sample of boys and girls with and without ADHD. *American Journal of Psychiatry, 159,* 1556–1562.

Biederman, J., Milberger, S., Faraone, S.V., Kiely, K., Guite J., Mick, E., Ablon, S., Warburton, R., et al. (1995). Family-environment risk factors for attention-deficit hyperactivity disorder. *Archives of General Psychiatry, 52,* 464–470.

Bijttebier, P., Vasey, M.W., & Braet, C. (2003). The information-processing paradigm: A valuable framework for clinical child and adolescent psychology. *Journal of Clinical Child and Adolescent Psychology, 32,* 2–9.

Birmaher, B., Arbalaez, C., & Brent, D. (2002). Course and outcome of child and adolescent major depressive disorder. *Child and Adolescent Psychiatric Clinics of North America, 11,* 619–637.

Birmaher, B., Axelson, D.A., Monk, K., Kalas, C., Clark, D.B., & Ehmann, M., et al. (2003). Fluxetine for the treatment of childhood anxiety disorders. *Journal of the American Academy of Child and Adolescent Psychiatry, 42,* 415–423.

Birnbauer, J.S. (1976). Mental retardation. In H. Leitenberg (Ed.), *Handbook of behavior modification and behavior therapy* (pp. 227–249). Englewood Cliffs, NJ: Prentice-Hall.

Bliss, J. (1980). Sensory experiences of Gilles de la Tourette syndrome. *Archives of General Psychiatry, 37,* 1343–1347.

Bloch, M.H., Landeros-Weisenberger, A., Rosario, M.C., Pittenger, C., & Leckman, J.F. (2008). Meta-analysis of the symptom structure of obsessive-compulsive disorder. *American Journal of Psychiatry, 165,* 1532–1542.

Bloch, M.H., Peterson, B.S., Scahill, L., Otka, J., Katsovich, L., Zhang, H., et al. (2006). Adulthood outcome of tic and obsessive-compulsive symptom severity in children with Tourette syndrome. *Archives of Pediatrics and Adolescent Medicine, 160,* 65–69.

Bloomquist, M.L. (1996). *Skills training for children with behavior disorders.* New York: Guilford Press.

Bocella, K. (1995, September 24). Use of Ritalin for children is on the rise. *Philadelphia Inquirer,* pp. B1–B4.

Borden, M.C., & Ollendick, T.H. (1992). The development and differentiation of social subtypes in autism. In B. Lahey & A.E. Kazdin (Eds.), *Advances in clinical child psychology* (Vol. 14, pp. 61–106). New York: Plenum Press.

Borsari, B., & Carey, K.B. (2001). Peer influences on college drinking: A review of the research. *Journal of Substance Abuse, 13,* 391–424.

Bouchard, T.J., Lykken, D.T., McGue, M., Segal, N.L., & Tellegen, A. (1990). Sources of human psychological differences: The Minnesota study of twins reared apart. *Science, 250,* 223–250.

Bower, G.H., & Sivers, H. (1998). Cognitive impact of traumatic events. *Development and Psychopathology, 10,* 625–654.

Bowlby, J. (1969). *Attention and loss: Attachment.* New York: Basic Books.

Bradley, R., Casey, P., & Wortham, B. (1984). Home environments of low SES nonorganic failure to thrive infants. *Merrill Palmer Quarterly, 30,* 393–402.

Brady, E.U., & Kendall, P.C. (1992). Comorbidity of anxiety and depression in children and adolescents. *Psychological Bulletin, 111,* 244–255.

Bramlett, M.D., & Mosher, W.D. (2002). *Cohabitation, marriage, divorce, and remarriage in the United States.* Washington, DC: National Center for Health Statistics.

Braswell, L. (1991). Involving parents in cognitive-behavioral therapy with children and adolescents. In P.C. Kendall (Ed.), *Child and adolescent therapy: Cognitive-behavioral procedures* (pp. 316–351). New York: Guilford Press.

Braswell, L., August, G., Bloomquist, M.L., Realmuto, G.M., Skare, S., & Crosby, R. (1997). School-based secondary prevention for children with disruptive behavior: Initial outcomes. *Journal of Abnormal Child Psychology, 25,* 197–208.

Braswell, L., & Bloomquist, M.L. (1991). *Cognitive-behavioral therapy with ADHD children: Child, family, and school interventions.* New York: Guilford Press.

Breedlove, S.M., Rosenzweig, M.R., & Watson, N.V. (2007). *Biological psychology: An introduction to behavioral, cognitive, and clinical neuroscience* (5th ed.). Sunderland, MA: Sinauer Associates.

Brennan, C. (1955). *An elementary textbook of psychoanalysis.* New York: International Universities Press.

Brent, D.A., Holder, D., Kolko, D., Birmaher, B., Baugher, M., Roth, C., et al. (1997). A clinical psychotherapy trial for adolescent depression comparing cognitive, family, and supporting therapy. *Archives of General Psychiatry, 54,* 877–885.

Brewin, C.R. (1997). Psychological defenses and the distortion of meaning. In M. Power & C.R. Brewin (Eds.), *The transformation of meaning in psychological therapies* (pp. 107–123). Chichester: Wiley.

Brewin, C.R., Andrews, B., & Gotlib, I.H. (1993). Psychopathology and early experience: A reappraisal of retrospective reports. *Psychological Bulletin, 113,* 82–98.

Bridge, J.A., Iyengar, S., Salary, C.B., Barbe, R., Birmaher, B., Pincus, H.A., et al. (2007). Clinical response and risk for reported suicidal ideation and suicide attempts in pediatric antidepressant treatment: A meta-analysis of randomized controlled trials. *Journal of the American Medical Association, 297,* 1683–1696.

Brier, N. (1989). The relationship between learning disability and delinquency: A review and reappraisal. *Journal of Learning Disabilities, 22,* 546–553.

Brinkmeyer, M., & Eyberg, S.M. (2003). Parent–child interaction therapy for oppositional children. In A.E. Kazdin & J.R. Weisz (Eds.), *Evidence-based psychotherapies for children and adolescents* (pp. 204–223). New York: Guilford Press.

Bristol, M.M., Cohen, D.J., Costello, E.J., Denckla, M., Eckberg, T.J., Kallen, R., et al. (1996). State of the science in autism: Report to the national institutes of health. *Journal of Autism and Developmental Disorders, 26,* 121–153.

Brownell, K.D. (1991). Dieting and the search for the perfect body: Where physiology and culture collide. *Behavior Therapy, 22,* 1–12.

Brownell, K.D., Puhl, R.M., Schwartz, M.B., & Rudd, L. (2005). *Weight bias: Nature, consequences, and remedies.* New York: Guilford Press.

Bruch, H. (1973). *Eating disorders: Obesity, anorexia nervosa, and the person within.* New York: Basic Books.

Bruch, H. (2001). *The golden cage: The enigma of anorexia nervosa.* Cambridge, MA: Harvard University Press.

Bryson, S.E. (1996). Brief report: Epidemiology of autism. *Journal of Autism and Developmental Disorders, 26,* 165–167.

Budd, K.S., & Chugh, C. (1998). Common feeding problems in young children. In

T. Ollendick & R. Prinz (Eds.), *Advances in clinical child psychology* (Vol. 20, pp. 183–212). New York: Plenum Press.

Budd, K.S., McGraw, T., Farbisz, R., Murphy, T., Hawkins, D., Heilman, N., et al. (1992). Psychosocial concomitants of children's feeding disorders. *Journal of Pediatric Psychology, 17,* 81–94.

Budman, C.L., Bruun, R.D., Park, K.S., Lesser, M., & Olson, M. (2000). Explosive outbursts in children with Tourette's disorder. *Journal of the American Academy of Child and Adolescent Psychiatry, 39,* 1270–1276.

Buka, S.L., Cannon, T.D., Torrey, E.F., & Yolken, R.H. (2008). Maternal exposure to herpes simplex virus and risk of psychosis among adult offspring. *Biological Psychiatry, 63,* 809–815.

Burt, D.B., Loveland, K., Chen, Y., & Chuang, A. (1995). Aging in adults with Down syndrome: Report from a longitudinal study. *American Journal on Mental Retardation, 100,* 262–270.

Butler, L., Mietzitiz, S., Friedman, R., & Cole, E. (1980). The effects of two school-based intervention programs on depressive symptoms in preadolescents. *American Educational Research Journal, 17,* 111–119.

Callocott, R., & Cooper, S. (1997). The five year follow-up study of adaptive behavior in adults with Down syndrome. *Journal of Intellectual and Developmental Disability, 22,* 187–197.

Camara, K.A., & Resnick, G. (1988). Interparental conflict and cooperation: Factors moderating children's post-divorce adjustment. In E.M. Hetherington & J.D. Arasteh (Eds.), *Impact of divorce, single parenting, and stepparenting on children* (pp. 169–195). Hillsdale, NJ: Lawrence Erlbaum Associates, Inc.

Campbell, S.M. (1986). Developmental issues. In R. Gittelman (Ed.), *Anxiety disorders of childhood* (pp. 24–57). New York: Guilford Press.

Cantwell, D.P. (1987, June). *Assessment and invention.* Paper presented at the conference "The nature of ADHD." Minneapolis, MN.

Caplan, M., Weissberg, R.P., Grober, J.S., Sivo, P.J., Grady, K., & Jacoby, C. (1992). Social competence promotion with inner-city and suburban young adolescents: Effects on social adjustment and alcohol use. *Journal of Consulting and Clinical Psychology, 60,* 56–63.

Carter, J.F. (1993). Self-management: Education's ultimate goal. *Teaching Exceptional Children, 25,* 28–33.

Cascio, C.J., Gerig, G., & Piven, J. (2007). Diffusion tensor imaging: Application to the study of the developing brain. *Journal of the American Academy of Child and Adolescent Psychiatry, 46,* 213–223.

Castellanos, F.X., Lee, P.P., Sharp, W., Jeffries, N.O., Greenstein, D.K., Clasen, L.S., et al. (2002). Developmental trajectories of brain volume abnormalities in children and adolescents with attention-deficit/hyperactivity disorder. *Journal of the American Medical Association, 288,* 1740–1748.

Chambless, D.L., & Ollendick, T.H. (2001). Empirically supported psychological interventions: Controversies and evidence. *Annual Review of Psychology, 52,* 685–716.

Champion, L.A., Goodall, G., & Rutter, M. (1995). Behavior problems in childhood and stressors in early adult life: A 20 year follow-up of London school children. *Psychological Medicine, 25,* 231–246.

Chatoor, I., & Egan, J. (1983). Nonorganic failure to thrive and dwarfism due to food refusal: A separation disorder. *Journal of the American Academy of Child and Adolescent Psychiatry, 22,* 294–301.

Cheney, D., & Osher, T. (1997). Collaborate with families. *Journal of Emotional and Behavioral Disorders, 5,* 36–44.

Cherlin, A.J., Furstenberg, F.F., Chase-Lansdale, P.L., Kiernan, K., Robins, P., Morrison, D., et al. (1991). Longitudinal studies of effects of divorce on children in Great Britain and the United States. *Science, 252*, 1368–1389.

Chess, S. (1977). Report on autism in congenital rubella. *Journal of Autism and Childhood Schizophrenia, 7*, 68–81.

Cheung, A.H., Emslie, G.J., & Mayes, T.L. (2005). Review of the efficacy and safety of antidepressants in youth depression. *Journal of Child Psychology and Psychiatry, 46*, 735–754.

Chodorow, N. (1978). *The reproduction of mothering: Psychoanalysis and the sociology of gender.* Berkeley, CA: University of California Press.

Cicchetti, D. (1993). Developmental psychopathology: Reactions, reflections, projections. *Developmental Review, 13*, 471–502.

Cicchetti, D. (2006). Development and psychopathology. In D. Cicchetti & D.J. Cohen (Eds.), *Development and psychopathology, Vol 1: Theory and method* (2nd ed., pp. 1–23). Hoboken, NJ: Wiley.

Cicchetti, D. (2007). Gene-environment interaction. *Development and Psychopathology, 19*, 957–959.

Clarren, S., & Smith, D.W. (1978). The fetal alcohol syndrome. *New England Journal of Medicine, 298*, 1063–1068.

Coffey, B.J., Biederman, J., Geller, D., Frazier, J., Spencer, T., Doyle, R., et al. (2004). Reexamining tic persistence and tic-associated impairment in Tourette's disorder: Findings from a naturalistic follow-up study. *Journal of Nervous and Mental Disorders, 192*, 776–780.

Cohen, D., Paul, R., & Volkmar, F. (1986). Issues in the classification of pervasive and other developmental disorders: Toward DSM-IV. *Journal of the American Academy of Child Psychiatry, 25*, 213–220.

Cohen, R.Y., Brownell, K., & Felix, M.R.J. (1990). Age and sex differences in health habits of school children. *Health Psychology, 9*, 208–224.

Collier, D.A., & Treasure, J.L. (2004). The aetiology of eating disorders. *British Journal of Psychiatry, 185*, 363–365.

Comer, J.S., Furr, J.M., Beidas, R.S., Babyar, H.M., & Kendall, P.C. (2008a). Media use and children's perceptions of societal threat and personal vulnerability. *Journal of Clinical Child and Adolescent Psychology, 37*, 622–630.

Comer, J.S., Furr, J.M., Beidas, R.S., Weiner, C.L., & Kendall, P.C. (2008b). Children and terrorism-related news: Training parents in coping and media literacy. *Journal of Consulting and Clinical Psychology, 77*, 517–525.

Comer, J.S., & Kendall, P.C. (2004). A symptom-level examination of parent–child agreement in the diagnosis of anxious youths. *Journal of the American Academy of Child and Adolescent Psychiatry, 43*, 878–886.

Comer, J.S., & Kendall, P.C. (2005). High-end specificity of the Children's Depression Inventory (CDI) in a sample of anxiety-disordered youth. *Depression and Anxiety, 22*, 11–19.

Comer, J.S., & Kendall, P.C. (2007). Terrorism: The psychological impact on youth. *Clinical Psychology: Science and Practice, 14*, 179–212.

Comer, J.S., Kendall, P.C., Franklin, M.E., Hudson, J.L., & Pimentel, S.S. (2004). Obsessing/worrying about the overlap between obsessive-compulsive disorder and generalized anxiety disorder in youth. *Clinical Psychology Review, 24*, 663–683.

Comer, J.S., & Olfson, M. (in press). The epidemiology of anxiety disorders. In H.B. Simpson, F. Schneier, Y. Neria, & R. Lewis-Fernandez (Eds.), *Anxiety Didorders: Theory, Research, and Clinical Perspectives.* New York: Cambridge University Press.

Comer, J.S., Roy, A.K., Furr, J.M., Gotimer,

K., Beidas, R.S., Dugas, M., et al. (2009). The Intolerance of Uncertainty Scale for Children: A psychometric evaluation. *Psychological Assessment, 21*, 402–411.

Comings, D.E., & Comings, B.G. (1985). Tourette syndrome: Clinical and psychological aspects of 250 cases. *American Journal of Human Genetics, 37*, 435–450.

Comings, D.E., Comings, B.G., Devor, E.J., & Cloninger, C.R. (1984). Detection of a major gene for Gilles de la Tourette syndrome. *American Journal of Human Genetics, 37*, 435–450.

Compas, B. (1997). Depression in children and adolescents. In E. Mash & L. Terdal (Eds.), *Assessment of childhood disorders* (3rd ed., pp. 197–229). New York: Guilford Press.

Compton, S.N., March, J.S., Brent, D., Albano, A.M., Weersing, V.R., & Curry, J. (2004). Cognitive behavioral psychotherapy for anxiety and depressive disorders in children and adolescents: An evidence based medicine review. *Journal of the American Academy of Child and Adolescent Psychiatry, 43*, 930–959.

Connan, F., Campbell, I.C., Katzman, M., Lightman, S.L., & Treasure, J. (2003). A neurodevelopmental model for anorexia nervosa. *Physiology and Behavior, 79*, 13–24.

Conners, C.K. (1980). *Food additives and hyperactive children.* New York: Plenum Press.

Conners, C.K. (1990). *The Conners rating scales.* North Tonawanda, NY: Multi-Health Systems.

Conners, C.K., Sitarenios, G., Parker, J.D., & Epstein, J. (1998a). The Revised Conners Parent Rating Scale (CPRS-R): Factor structure, reliability, and criterion validity. *Journal of Abnormal Child Psychology, 26*, 257–268.

Conners, C.K., Sitarenios, G., Parker, J.D., & Epstein, J. (1998b). Revision and standardization of the Conners Teacher Rating Scale (CTRS-R): Factor structure, reliability, and criterion validity. *Journal of Abnormal Child Psychology, 26*, 279–292.

Conrad, M., & Hammen, C. (1989). Role of maternal depression in perceptions of child maladjustment. *Journal of Consulting and Clinical Psychology, 57*, 663–667.

Cook, E.H., Stein, M.A., Krasowski, M.D., Cox, N.J., Olkon, D.M., Kieffer, J., et al. (1995). Association of attention deficit disorder and the dopamine transporter gene. *American Journal of Human Genetics, 56*, 993–998.

Cooper, P.J., & Goodyear, I. (1993). A community study of depression in adolescent girls: Estimates of symptom and syndrome prevalence. *British Journal of Psychiatry, 163*, 369–374.

Costello, E.J. (1989). Child psychiatric disorders and their correlates: A primary care pediatric sample. *Journal of the American Academy of Child and Adolescent Psychiatry, 28*, 851–855.

Costello, E.J., Egger, H., & Angold, A. (2005). 10-year research update review: The epidemiology of child and adolescent psychiatric disorders: 1. Methods and public health burden. *Journal of the American Academy of Child and Adolescent Psychiatry, 44*, 972–986.

Costello, E.J., Erkanli, A., & Angold, A. (2006a). Is there an epidemic of child or adolescent depression? *Journal of Child Psychology and Psychiatry, 47*, 1263–1271.

Costello, E.J., Foley, D.L., & Angold, A. (2006b). 10-year research update review. The epidemiology of child and adolescent psychiatric disorders: II. Developmental epidemiology. *Journal of the American Academy of Child and Adolescent Psychiatry, 45*, 8–25.

Costello, E.J., Mustillo, S., Erkanli, A., Keeler, G., & Angold, A. (2003). Prevalence and development of psychiatric disorders in childhood and adolescence. *Archives of General Psychiatry, 60,* 837–844.

Costello, E.J., Pine, D.S., Hammen, C., March, J.S., Plotsky, P.M., Weissman, M.M., et al. (2002). Development and natural history of mood disorders. *Biological Psychiatry, 52,* 529–542.

Courchesne, E., Karns, C.M., Davis, H.R., Ziccardi, R., Carper, R.A., Tigue, Z.D., et al. (2001). Unusual brain growth patterns in early life in patients with autistic disorder. An MRI study. *Neurology, 57,* 245–254.

Coyle, J.T., Oster-Granite, D., & Gearhart, L. (1986). The neurobiological consequences of Down's syndrome. *Brain Research Bulletin, 16,* 773–787.

Coyne, J.C. (1982). A critique of cognition as causal entities with particular reference to depression. *Cognitive Therapy and Research, 6,* 3–13.

Craighead, L., & Agras, S. (1991). Mechanisms of action in cognitive-behavioral and pharmacological interventions for obesity and bulimia nervosa. *Journal of Consulting and Clinical Psychology, 59,* 115–125.

Craighead, W.E., Meyers, A.W., & Craighead, L.W. (1985). A conceptual model for cognitive-behavior therapy with children. *Journal of Abnormal Child Psychology, 13,* 331–342.

Crick, N.R. (1996). The role of overt aggression, relational aggression, and prosocial behavior in the prediction of children's future social adjustment. *Child Development, 67,* 2317–2327.

Crick, N.R., Casas, J.F., & Ku, H.C. (1999). Relational and physical forms of peer victimization in preschool. *Developmental Psychology, 35,* 276–285.

Crick, N.R., Ostrov, J.M., Burr, J.E., Cullerton-Sen, C., Jansen-Yeh, E., & Ralston, P. (2006). A longitudinal study of relational and physical aggression in preschool. *Applied Developmental Psychology, 27,* 254–268.

Crnic, K.A. (1988). Mental retardation. In E.J. Mash & L. Terdal (Eds.), *Behavioral assessment of childhood disorders* (2nd ed., pp. 317–354). New York: Guilford Press.

Crnic, K.A., Friedrich, W.N., & Greenberg, M.T. (1983). Adaptation of families with mentally retarded children: A model of stress, coping, and family ecology. *American Journal of Mental Deficiency, 88,* 125–138.

Crnic, K.A., & Reid, M. (1989). Mental retardation. In E. Mash & R. Barkley (Eds.), *Treatment of childhood disorders* (pp. 379–420). New York: Guilford Press.

Crow, R.R., Noyes, R., Pauls, D.L., & Slymen, D.J. (1983). A family study of panic disorder. *Archives of General Psychiatry, 40,* 1065–1069.

Cummings, E.M., & Cicchetti, D. (1990). Attachment, depression, and the transmission of depression. In M.T. Greenberg, D. Cicchetti, & E.M. Cummings (Eds.), *Attachment during the preschool years*. Chicago: University of Chicago Press.

Dalenberg, C., Loewenstein, R., Spiegel, D., Brewin, C., Lanius, R., Frankel, S., et al. (2007). Scientific study of the dissociative disorders. *Psychotherapy and Psychosomatics, 76,* 400–401.

Dalgleish, T., & Brewin, C.R. (2007). Autobiographical memory and emotional disorder: A special issue of Memory. *Memory, 15,* 225–226.

Dalgleish, T., & Watts, F.N. (1990). Biases of attention and memory in disorders of anxiety and depression. *Clinical Psychology Review, 10,* 589–604.

DeBellis, M.D., Keshavan, M.S., Clark, D.B., Casey, B.J., Giedd, J.N., Boring, A.M., et al. (1999). Developmental traumatology. II: Brain development. *Biological Psychiatry, 45,* 1271–1284.

Dekker, M.C., & Koot, H.M. (2003). DSM-IV disorders in children with borderline to moderate intellectual disability. I: Prevalence and impact. *Journal of the*

American Academy of Child and Adolescent Psychiatry, 42, 915–922.

De Los Reyes, A., & Kazdin, A.E. (2005). Informant discrepancies in the assessment of childhood psychopathology: A critical review, theoretical framework, and recommendations for further study. *Psychological Bulletin, 131*, 483–509.

DeRicco, D.A., & Niemann, J.E. (1980). In vivo effects of peer modeling on drinking rate. *Journal of Applied Behavior Analysis, 13*, 149–152.

Deutsch, K. (1987). Genetic factors in attention deficit disorder. Paper presented at symposium on Disorders of Brain and Development and Cognition, Boston, MA. As cited in Barkley, R., & Anastopoulos, A. (1988). Biological factors in attention-deficit hyperactivity disorder. *The Behaviour Therapist, 11*, 47–53.

Devlin, B., Bacanu, S.A., Klump, K.L., Bulik, C.M., Fichter, M.M., Halmi, K.A., et al. (2002). Linkage analysis of anorexia nervosa incorporating behavioral covariates. *Human Molecular Genetics, 11*, 689–696.

Dishion, T., French, D., & Patterson, G. (1995). The development and ecology of antisocial behavior. In D. Cicchetti & D. Cohen (Eds.), *Developmental psychopathology: Risk, disorder, and adaptation* (Vol. 2, pp. 421–471). New York: Wiley.

Dobson, K.S., & Kendall, P.C. (Eds.) (1993). *Psychopathology and cognition.* San Diego: Academic Press.

Dodge, K.A. (1985). Attributional bias in aggressive children. In P.C. Kendall (Ed.), *Advances in cognitive-behavioral research and therapy* (Vol. 4, pp. 75–111). New York: Academic Press.

Dodge, K.A. (2006). Translational science in action: Hostile attributional style and the development of aggressive behavior problems. *Development and Psychopathology, 18*, 791–814.

Dodge, K.A., Pettit, G.S., Bates, J.E. & Valente, E. (1995). Social information-processing patterns partially mediate the effect of early physical abuse on later conduct problems. *Journal of Abnormal Psychology, 104*, 632–643.

Dolan, B. (1991). Cross-cultural aspects of anorexia nervosa and bulimia: A review. *International Journal of Eating Disorders, 10*, 67–79.

Doleys, D.M. (1977). Behavioral treatments for nocturnal enuresis in children: A review of the recent literature. *Psychological Bulletin, 84*, 30–54.

Doleys, D.M. (1983). Enuresis and encopresis. In T.H. Ollendick & M. Hersen (Eds.), *Handbook of child psychopathology* (pp. 291–316). New York: Plenum Press.

Dollard, J., & Miller, N.E. (1950). *Personality and psychotherapy.* New York: McGraw-Hill.

Donnellan, A.M. (Ed.) (1985). *Classic readings in autism.* New York: Teachers College Press.

Douglas, V.I. (1983). Attention and cognitive problems. In M. Rutter (Ed.), *Developmental neuropsychiatry* (pp. 280–329). New York: Guilford Press.

Douma, J.C.H., Dekker, M.C., Verhulst, F.C., & Koot, H.M. (2006). Self-reports on mental health problems of youth with moderate to borderline intellectual disabilities. *Journal of the American Academy of Child and Adolescent Psychiatry, 45*, 1224–1231.

Drabick, D. (2009). Can a developmental psychopathology perspective facilitate a paradigm shift toward a mixed categorical-dimensional classification system? *Clinical Psychology: Science and Practice, 16*, 41–49.

Dumas, J.E. (1989). Treating antisocial behavior in children: Child and family approaches. *Clinical Psychology Review, 9*, 197–222.

DuPaul, G.J., Barkley, R.A., & McMurray, M.B. (1994). Response of children with

ADHD to methylphenidate: Interaction with internalizing symptoms. *Journal of the American Academy of Child and Adolescent Psychiatry, 33*, 894–903.

DuPaul, G.J., McGoey, K.E., Eckert, T.L., & Vanbrakle, J. (2001). Preschool children with attention-deficit/hyperactivity disorder: Impairments in behavioral, social, and school functioning. *Journal of the American Academy of Child and Adolescent Psychiatry, 40*, 508–515.

Durston, S., Hulshoff Pol, H.E., Schnack, H.G., Buitelaar, J.K., Steenhuis, M.P., Minderaa, R.B., et al. (2004). Magnetic resonance imaging of boys with attention-deficit/hyperactivity disorder and their unaffected siblings. *Journal of the American Academy of Child and Adolescent Psychiatry, 43*, 332–340.

Dwyer, D.M. (2003). Learning about cues in their absence: Evidence from flavour preferences and aversions. *Quarterly Journal of Experiemental Psychology (Section B): Comparative and Physiological Psychology, 56*, 56–67.

Dykens, E., Hodapp, R.M., Ort, S., & Leckman, J.F. (1993). Trajectory of adaptive behavior in males with fragile X syndrome. *Journal of Autism and Developmental Disorders, 26*, 287–301.

Dykens, E., Ort, S., Cohen, I., Spiridigliozzi, G., Lachiewicz, A., Reiss, A., et al. (1996). Trajectories and profiles of adaptive behavior in males with fragile X syndrome: Multicenter studies. *Journal of Autism and Developmental Disorders, 26*, 287–301.

Eapen, V., Fox-Hiley, P., Banerjee, S., & Robertson, M. (2004). Clinical features and associated psychopathology in a Tourette syndrome cohort. *Acta Neurologica Scandinavica, 109*, 255–260.

Earls, F., & Mezzacappa, E. (2002). Oppositional-defiant and conduct disorders. In M. Rutter & E. Taylor (Eds.), *Child and adolescent psychiatry*, (4th ed., pp. 419–437). Oxford: Blackwell.

Eddy, K.T., Dorer, D.J., Franko, D.L., Tahilani, K., Thompson-Brenner, H., & Herzog, D.B. (2008). Diagnostic crossover in anorexia nervosa and bulimia nervosa: Implications for DSM-V. *American Journal of Psychiatry, 165*, 245–250.

Eddy, K.T., Hennessey, M., & Thompson-Brenner, H. (2007). Eating pathology in East African women: The role of media exposure and globalization. *Journal of Nervous and Mental Disease, 195*, 196–202.

Edelbrock, C., & Costello, A.J. (1988). Structured psychiatric interviews for children. In M. Rutter, A.H. Tuma, & I.S. Lann (Eds.), *Assessment and diagnosis in child psychopathology*. New York: Guilford Press.

Eggers, H.L., & Angold, A. (2006). Common emotional and behavioral disorders in preschool children: Presentation, nosology, and epidemiology. *Journal of Child Psychology and Psychiatry, 47*, 313–337.

Einfeld, S.L., & Aman, M. (1995). Issues in the taxonomy of psychopathology in mental retardation. *Journal of Autism and Developmental Disorders, 25*, 143–167.

Eiserman, W.D., Shisler, L., & Healey, S. (1995). A community assessment of preschool providers' attitudes toward inclusion. *Journal of Early Intervention, 19*, 149–167.

Eley, T.C., Bolton, D., O'Connor, T.G., Perrin, S., Smith, P., & Plomin, R. (2003). A twin study of anxiety-related behaviours in pre-school children. *Journal of Child Psychology and Psychiatry, 44*, 945–960.

Eliez, S., & Reiss, A.L. (2000). Genetics of childhood disorders: XI. Fragile X syndrome. *Journal of the American Academy of Child and Adolescent Psychiatry, 39*, 262–266.

Ellis, A., & Harper, R. (1975). *A new guide to rational living*. New York: Wilshire Books.

Eme, R.F., & Kavanaugh, L. (1995). Sex differences in conduct disorder. *Journal of Consulting and Clinical Psychology, 24,* 406–426.

Emerson, E. (2003). Mothers of children and adolescents with intellectual disability: Social and economic situation, mental health status, and the self-assessed social and psychological impact of the children's difficulties. *Journal of Intellectual Disability Research, 47,* 385–399.

Emery, R.E., Laumann-Billings, L., Waldron, M.C., Sbarra, D.A., & Dillon, P. (2001). Child custody mediation and litigation: Custody, contact, and coparenting 12 years after initial dispute resolution. *Journal of Consulting and Clinical Psychology, 69,* 323–332.

Erdelyi, M.H. (1985). *Psychoanalysis: Freud's cognitive psychology*. New York: Freeman.

Erhardt, D., & Hinshaw, S.P. (1994). Initial sociometric impressions of ADHD and comparison boys: Predictions from social behaviors and from nonbehavioral variables. *Journal of Consulting and Clinical Psychology, 62,* 833–842.

Eron, L.D., & Huesmann, L.R. (1990). The stability of aggressive behavior—even unto the third generation. In M. Lewis & S.M. Miller (Eds.), *Handbook of developmental psychopathology* (pp. 110–136). New York: Plenum Press.

Eurostat (2001). *Annuaire Eurostat 2001: De A comme agriculture a Z comme zone euro. L'Europe de annees 1990 vue a travers les chiffres* [Annual statistics of European countries in the 1990s]. Luxembourge: Office Statistique des Communautes Europeenes.

Evans, J.A., & Hammerton, J.L. (1985). Chromosomal anomalies. In A.M. Clarke, A.D. Clark, & J.M. Berg (Eds.), *Mental deficiency: The changing outlook* (pp. 74–92). New York: Free Press.

Eyberg, S. (1988). Parent–child interaction therapy: Integration of traditional and behavioral concerns. *Child and Family Behaviour Therapy, 10,* 33–46.

Eyberg, S.M., Nelson, M.M., & Boggs, S.R. (2008). Evidence-based psychosocial treatments for children and adolescents with disruptive behavior. *Journal of Clinical Child and Adolescent Psychology, 37,* 215–237.

Fairburn, C.G., & Beglin, S.J. (1990). Studies of the epidemiology of bulimia nervosa. *American Journal of Psychiatry, 147,* 401–408.

Fairburn, C.G., & Cooper, P.J. (1984). The clinical features of bulimia nervosa. *British Journal of Psychiatry, 144,* 238–246.

Fairburn, C.G., Jones, R., Peveler, R.C., Hope, R.A., & O'Connor, M. (1993). Psychotherapy and bulimia nervosa: Longer-term effects of interpersonal psychotherapy, behavior therapy, and cognitive-behavior therapy. *Archives of General Psychiatry, 50,* 419–428.

Faraone, S.V., Biederman, J., & Mick, E. (2006). The age-dependent decline of attention deficit hyperactivity disorder: A meta-analysis of follow-up studies. *Psychological Medicine, 36,* 159–165.

Faraone, S.V., Biederman, J., Monuteaux, M., & Spencer, T. (2005a). Long-term effects of extended-release mixed amphetamine salts treatment of attention-deficit/hyperactivity disorder on growth. *Journal of Child and Adolescent Psychopharmacology, 15,* 191–202.

Faraone, S.V., Biederman, J., Morley, C.P., & Spencer, T.J. (2008). Effect of stimulants on height and weight: A review of the literature. *Journal of the American Academy of Child and Adolescent Psychiatry, 47,* 994–1009.

Faraone, S.V., Perlis, R.H., Doyle, A.E.,

Smoller, J.W., Goralnick, J.J., Holmgren, M.A., et al. (2005b). Molecular genetics of attention-deficit/hyperactivity disorder. *Biological Psychiatry, 57,* 1313–1323.

Fauber, R., & Kendall, P.C. (1992). Children and families: Integrating the focus of interventions. *Journal of Psychotherapy Integration, 2,* 107–124.

Fava, M., Copeland, P., Schweiger, U., & Herzog, D.B. (1989). Neurochemical abnormalities of anorexia nervosa and bulimia nervosa. *American Journal of Psychiatry, 146,* 963–971.

Favaro, A., Tenconi, E., & Santonastaso, P. (2006). Perinatal factors and the risk of developing anorexia nervosa and bulimia nervosa. *Archives of General Psychiatry, 63,* 82–88.

Favell, J.E., Azrin, N.H., Baumeister, A.A., Carr, E.G., Dorsey, M.F., Forehand, R., et al. (1982). The treatment of self-injurious behavior. *Behavior Therapy, 13,* 529–554.

Favell, J.E., & Green, J.W. (1981). *How to treat self-injurious behavior.* Lawrence, KS: H & H Enterprises.

Feinfield, K.A., & Baker, B.L. (2004). Empirical support for a treatment program for families of young children with externalizing problems. *Journal of Clinical Child and Adolescent Psychology, 33,* 182–195.

Feingold, B.F. (1975). *Why your child is hyperactive.* New York: Random House.

Fergusson, D., Lynskey, M., & Horwood, L. (1997). Attentional difficulties in middle childhood and psychosocial outcomes in young adulthood. *Journal of Child Psychology and Psychiatry, 38,* 633–644.

Ferster, C.B. (1961). Positive reinforcement and behavioral deficits in autistic children. *Child Development, 32,* 437–456.

Field, A.P. (2006). Is conditioning a useful framework for understanding the development and treatment of phobias? *Clinical Psychology Review, 26,* 857–875.

Finch, A.J., Lipovsky, J., & Casat, C. (1989). Anxiety and depression in children and adolescents: Negative affectivity or separate constructs. In P.C. Kendall & D. Watson (Eds.), *Anxiety and depression: Distinctive and overlapping features* (pp. 171–204). New York: Academic Press.

Fincham, F., & Spettell, C. (1984). The acceptability of dry bed training and urine alarm training as treatments of nocturnal enuresis. *Behavior Therapy, 15,* 388–394.

Finley, W.W., Wansley, R.A., & Blenkarn, M.M. (1977). Conditioning treatment of enuresis using a 70% intermittent reinforcement schedule. *Behaviour Research and Therapy, 15,* 419–427.

Fischer, M., Barkley, R.A., Edelbrock, C.S., & Smallish, L. (1990). The adolescent outcome of hyperactive children diagnosed by research criteria: Academic, attentional, and neuropsychological status. *Journal of Consulting and Clinical Psychology, 58,* 580–588.

Fischler, G., & Kendall, P.C. (1988). Social cognitive problem-solving and childhood adjustment: Qualitative and topological analyses. *Cognitive Therapy and Research, 12,* 133–154.

Fletcher, J.M., Francis, D.J., Morris, R.D., Lyon, G.R. (2005). Evidence-based assessment of learning disabilities in children and adolescents. *Journal of Clinical Child and Adolescent Psychology, 34,* 506–522.

Folstein, S., & Rutter, M. (1977). Autism: Familial aggregation and genetic implications. *Journal of Autism and Developmental Disorders, 18,* 3–30.

Fombonne, E. (1998). Preface to the special issue on the genetics of autism. *Journal of Autism and Developmental Disabilities, 28,* 349–451.

Foote, R., Eyberg, S., & Schuhmann, E. (1998). Parent–child interaction approaches to the treatment of child behavior problems. In T. Ollendick & R. Prinz (Eds.), *Advances in clinical child psychology* (Vol. 20). New York: Plenum Press.

Foreyt, J.P., & Mikhail, C. (1997). Anorexia nervosa and bulimia nervosa. In E. Mash & L. Terdal (Eds.), *Assessment of childhood disorders* (3rd ed., pp. 683–716). New York: Guilford Press.

Frankel, F., & Feinberg, D. (2002). Social problems associated with ADHD vs. ODD in children referred for friendship problems. *Child Psychiatry and Human Development, 33*, 125–146.

Frazier, T.W., Demaree, H.A., & Youngstrom, E.A. (2004). Meta-analysis of intellectual and neuropsychological test performance in attention-deficit/ hyperactivity disorder. *Neuropsychology, 18*, 543–555.

Freud, S. (1914). *Psychopathology of everyday life*. London: Fischer Unwin.

Freud, S. (1943). *A general introduction to psychoanalysis*. Garden City, NY. (Original work published 1917 in German)

Freud, S. (1984). *The Pelican Freud Library: Vol 11. A note on the unconscious in psychoanalysis*. Harmondsworth: Penguin. (Original work published 1912)

Freud, S. (1984). *The Pelican Freud Library: Vol 11. The unconscious*. Harmondsworth: Penguin. (Original work published 1915)

Frick, P.J., Bodin, S.D., & Barry, C.T. (2000). Psychopathic traits and conduct problems in community and clinic-referred samples of children: Further development of the Psychopathy Screening Device. *Psychological Assessment, 12*, 382–393.

Frick, P.J., Cornell, A.H., Bodin, S.D., Dane, H.E., Barry, C.E., & Loney, B.R. (2003). Callous-unemotional traits and developmental pathways to severe conduct problems. *Developmental Psychology, 39*, 246–260.

Frick, P.J., & Dantagnan, A.L. (2005). Predicting the stability of conduct problems in children with and without callous-unemotional traits. *Journal of Child and Family Studies, 14*, 469–485.

Frick, P.J., & Loney, B.R. (2002). Understanding the association between parent and child antisocial behavior. In R.J. McMahon & R. DeV. Peters (Eds.), *The effects of parental dysfunction on children* (pp. 105–126). New York: Kluwer Academic/Plenum.

Frick, P.J., Stickle, T.R., Dandreaux, D.M., Farrell, J.M., & Kimonis, E.R. (2005). Callous-unemotional traits in predicting the severity and stability of conduct problems and delinquency. *Journal of Abnormal Child Psychology, 33*, 471–487.

Furstenberg, F.K., & Kiernan, K.E. (2001). Delayed parental divorce: How much do children benefit? *Journal of Marriage and Family, 63*, 446–457.

Fyer, A.J., Mannuzza, S., Gallops, M.S., Martin, L.Y, Aaronson, C., Gorman, J.M., et al. (1990). Familial transmission of simple phobias and fears. *Archives of General Psychiatry, 47*, 252–256.

Gadeyne, E., Ghesquiere, P., & Onghena, P. (2004). Psychosocial functioning of young children with learning problems. *Journal of Child Psychology and Psychiatry, 45*, 510–521.

Gadow, K.D. (1992). Pediatric psychopharmacology: A review of recent research. *Journal of Child Psychology and Psychiatry, 33*, 153–195.

Gadow, K.D., Sverd, J., Sprafkin, J., Nolan, E.E., & Ezor, S.N. (1995). Efficacy of methylphenidate for attention-deficit hyperactivity disorder in children with tic disorder. *Archives of General Psychiatry 52*, 444–455.

Garber, J., Braafladt, N., & Zeman, J. (1991). The regulation of sad affect: An information processing perspective. In

J. Garber & K. Dodge (Eds.), *The development of emotion regulation and dysregulation* (pp. 208–240). New York: Cambridge University Press.

Garber, J., Kriss, M.R., Koch, M., & Lindholm, L. (1988). Recurrent depression in adolescents: A follow-up study. *Journal of the American Academy of Child and Adolescent Psychiatry, 27,* 49–54.

Garner, D.M., & Bemis-Vitousek, K.M. (1985). Cognitive therapy for anorexia nervosa. In D.M. Garner & P.E. Garfinkel (Eds.), *Handbook of psychotherapy for anorexia nervosa and bulimia* (pp. 107–146). New York: Guilford Press.

Garner, D.M., & Magana, C. (2006). Cognitive vulnerability to anorexia nervosa. In L.B. Alloy & J.H. Riskind (Ed.), *Cognitive vulnerability to emotional disorders* (pp. 365–403). Mahwah, NJ: Lawrence Erlbaum Associates, Inc.

Gelhorn, H., Stallings, M.C., Young, S.E., Corley, R.P., Rhee, S.H., & Hewitt, J.K. (2005). Genetic and environmental influences on conduct disorder: Symptom, domain, and full-scale analyses. *Journal of Child Psychology and Psychiatry, 46,* 580–591.

Gelhorn, H., Stallings, M., Young, S., Corley, R., Rhee, S.H., Hopfer, C., et al. (2006). Common and specific genetic influences on aggressive and nonaggressive conduct disorder domains. *Journal of the American Academy of Child and Adolescent Psychiatry, 45,* 570–577.

Gellar, D.A., Biederman, J., Stewart, S.E., Mullin, B., Martin, A., Spencer, T., et al. (2003). Which SSRI? A meta-analysis of pharmacotherapy trials in pediatric obsessive-compulsive disorder. *American Journal of Psychiatry, 160,* 1919–1928.

Gerber, A.J., & Peterson, B.S. (2008). What is an image? *Journal of the American Academy of Child and Adolescent Psychiatry, 47,* 245–248.

Gershon, J. (2002). A meta-analytic review of gender differences in ADHD. *Journal of Attention Disorders, 5,* 143–154.

Gerull, F.C., & Rapee, R.M. (2002). Mother knows best: The effects of maternal modelling on the acquisition of fear and avoidance behaviour in toddlers. *Behaviour Research and Therapy, 40,* 279–287.

Gewirtz, J.L., & Peláez-Nogueras, M. (1992). B.F. Skinner's legacy to human infant behavior and development. *American Psychologist, 47,* 1411–1422.

Gibb, B.E., & Alloy, L.B. (2006). A prospective test of the hopelessness theory of depression in children. *Journal of Clinical Child and Adolescent Psychology, 35,* 264–274.

Gibb, B.E., Alloy, L.B., Walshaw, P.D., Comer, J.S., Shen, G.H.C., & Villari, A.G. (2006). Predictors of attributional style change in children. *Journal of Abnormal Child Psychology, 34,* 425–439.

Gilberg, C. (1990). Autism and pervasive developmental disorders. *Journal of Child Psychology and Psychiatry, 31,* 99–119.

Gilberg, C., Cederlund, M., Lamberg, K., & Zeijlon, L. (2006). "The autism epidemic." The registered prevalence of autism in a Swedish urban area. *Journal of Autism and Developmental Disorders, 36,* 429–439.

Gilbert, S.C. (2003). Eating disorders in women of color. *Clinical Psychology: Science and Practice, 10,* 444–455.

Giles, D.K., & Wolf, M.W. (1966). Toilet training institutionalized, severe retardates: An application of operant behavior modification techniques. *American Journal of Mental Deficiency, 70,* 766–780.

Gilger, J.W., Pennington, B.F., & DeFries, J.C. (1992). A twin study of the etiology of comorbidity: Attention-deficit hyperactivity disorder and dyslexia.

Journal of the American Academy of Child and Adolescent Psychiatry, 31, 343–348.

Gill, M., Daly, G., Heron, S., Hawi, Z., & Fitzgerald, M. (1997). Confirmation of an association between attention deficit disorder hyperactivity disorder and a dopamine transporter polymorphism. *Molecular Psychiatry, 2*, 311–313.

Gittelman, R., Mannuzza, S., Shenker, R., & Bonagura, N. (1985). Hyperactive boys almost grown up. *Archives of General Psychiatry, 42*, 937–947.

Gladstone, T.R.G., Kaslow, N.J., Seeley, J.R., & Lewinsohn, P.M. (1997). Sex differences, attributional style, and depressive symptoms among adolescents. *Journal of Abnormal Child Psychology, 25*, 297–305.

Goldstein, S., & Goldstein, M. (1998). *Managing attention deficit hyperactivity disorder in children: A guide for practitioners.* New York: Wiley.

Goldston, D.B., Walsh, A., Mayfield Arnold, E., Reboussin, B., Sergeant Daniel, S., Erkanli, A., et al. (2007). Reading problems, psychiatric disorders, and functional impairment from mid- to late adolescence. *Journal of the American Academy of Child and Adolescent Psychiatry, 46*, 25–32.

Goodman, R. (1989). Infantile autism: A syndrome of multiple primary deficits? *Journal of Autism and Developmental Disorders, 19*, 409–429.

Gottesman, I.I., & Erlenmeyer-Kimling, L. (2001). Family and twin strategies as a head start in defining prodromes and endophenotypes for hypothetical early-interventions in schizophrenia. *Schizophrenia Research, 51*, 93–102.

Gottesman, I.I., McGuffin, P., & Farmer, A.E. (1987). Clinical genetics as clues to the "real" genetics of schizophrenia. *Schizophrenia Bulletin, 13*, 23–47.

Gottesman, I.I., & Shields, J. (1972). *Schizophrenia and genetics: A twin study vantage point.* New York: Academic Press.

Gould, M.S., Fisher, P., Parides, M., Flory, M., & Shaffer, D. (1996). Psychosocial risk factors of child and adolescent completed suicide. *Archives of General Psychiatry, 53*, 1155–1162.

Greene, R., Biederman, J., Faraone, S., Sienna, M., & Garcia-Jetton, J. (1997). Adolescent outcome of boys with ADHD and social disability: Results from a 4-year longitudinal follow-up study. *Journal of Consulting and Clinical Psychology, 65*, 758–767.

Greene, S.M., Anderson, E., Hetherington, E.M., Forgatch, M.S., & DeGarmo, D.S. (2002). Risk and resilience after divorce. In F. Walsh (Ed.), *Normal family processes* (3rd ed., pp. 86–108). New York: Guilford Press.

Greenhill, L., Kollins, S., Abikoff, H., McCracken, J., Riddle, M., Swanson, J., et al. (2006). Efficacy and safety of immediate-release methylphenidate treatment for preschoolers with ADHD. *Journal of the American Academy of Child and Adolescent Psychiatry, 45*, 1284–1293.

Greenhill, L.L. (2002). Stimulant medication treatment of children with attention deficit hyperactivity disorder. In P.S. Jensen & J.R. Cooper (Eds.), *Attention deficit hyperactivity disorder: State of science. Best practices* (pp. 9.1–9.27). Kingston, NJ: Civic Research Institute.

Greenwald, A.G., McGhee, D.E., & Schwartz, J.L.K. (2008). Measuring individual differences in implicit cognition: The Implicit Association Test. In R.H. Fazio & R.E. Petty (Eds.), *Attitudes: Their structure, function, and consequences* (pp. 109–131). New York: Psychology Press.

Gresham, F., & MacMillan, D. (1997). Denial and defensiveness in the place of fact and reason: Rejoinder to Smith and Lovaas. *Behavioral Disorders, 22*, 219–230.

Gresham, F.M. (2002). Responsiveness to intervention: An alternative approach to the identification of learning disabilities. In R. Bradley, L. Danielson, & D.P. Hallahan (Eds.), *Identification of learning disabilities: Research to practice* (pp. 467–564). Mahwah, NJ: Lawrence Erlbaum Associates, Inc.

Grey, I., & McClean, B. (2007). Toileting problems. In A. Carr, G. O'Reilly, P.N. Walsh, & J. McEvoy (Eds.), *The handbook of intellectual disability and clinical psychology practice* (pp. 422–446). New York: Routledge/Taylor & Francis.

Grice, D.E., Halmi, K.A., Fichter, M.M., Strober, M., Woodside, D.B., Kaplan, A.S., et al. (2002). Evidence for a susceptibility gene for anorexia nervosa on chromosome 1. *American Journal of Human Genetics, 70,* 787–792.

Hagan, J.W., & Hale, G.H. (1973). The development of attention in children. In A. Pick (Ed.), *Minnesota Symposium on Child Psychology* (Vol. 7). Minneapolis, MN: University of Minnesota Press.

Hallahan, D.P., Kneedler, R.D., & Lloyd, J.W. (1983). Cognitive behavior modification techniques for learning disabled children. In J.D. McKinney & L. Feagans (Eds.), *Current topics in learning disabilities* (Vol. 1). New York: Ablex.

Hammen, C. (1991). *Depression runs in families: The social context of risk and resilience in children of depressed mothers.* New York: Springer-Verlag.

Hammen, C., Brennan, P.A., Keenan-Miller, D., & Herr, N.R. (2008). Early onset recurrent subtype of adolescent depression: Clinical and psychosocial correlates. *Journal of Child Psychology and Psychiatry, 49,* 433–440.

Hammen, C., & Watkins, E. (2008). *Depression.* London: Psychology Press/Taylor & Francis.

Hammock, R.G., Schroeder, S.R., & Levine, W.R. (1995). The effect of clozapine on self-injurious behavior. *Journal of Autism and Developmental Disorders, 25,* 611–626.

Handen, B., & Gilchrist, R.H. (2006a). Mental retardation. In E. Mash & R. Barkley (Eds.), *Treatment of childhood disorders* (3rd ed., pp. 411–454). New York: Guilford Press.

Handen, B., & Gilchrist, R.H. (2006b). Practitioner review: Psychopharmacology in children and adolescents with mental retardation. *Journal of Child Psychology and Psychiatry, 47,* 871–882.

Handen, B., Mandell, F., & Russo, D. (1986). Feeding induction in children who refuse to eat. *American Journal of Diseases of Children, 140,* 52–54.

Handen, B.L., Breaux, A.M., Janosky, J., McAuliffe, S., Feldman, S., & Gosling, A. (1992). Effects and noneffects of methylphenidate in children with mental retardation and ADHD. *Journal of the American Academy of Child and Adolescent Psychiatry, 31,* 455–461.

Hansen, C., Weiss, D., & Last, C. (1999). ADHD boys in young adulthood: Psychosocial adjustment. *Journal of the American Academy of Child and Adolescent Psychiatry, 38,* 165–171.

Hansen, D.R., & Gottesman, I.I. (1976). The genetics, if any, of infantile autism and childhood schizophrenia. *Journal of Autism and Childhood Schizophrenia, 6,* 209–234.

Happe, F., Ronald, A., & Plomin, R. (2006). Time to give up on a single explanation for autism. *Nature Neuroscience, 9,* 1218–1220.

Hardiman, S., Guerin, S., & Fitzsimons, E. (2008). A comparison of the social competence of children with moderate intellectual disability in inclusive versus segregated school settings. *Research in Developmental Disabilities, 30,* 397–407.

Hardt, J., & Rutter, M. (2004). Validity of adult retrospective reports of adverse childhood experiences: Review of the evidence. *Journal of Child Psychology and Psychiatry, 45,* 260–273.

Harrington, R.C. (2002). Affective disorders. In M. Rutter & E. Taylor (Eds.), *Child and adolescent psychiatry: A modern approach.* Oxford, UK: Blackwell Scientific Publications.

Harrington, R.C., Fudge, H., Rutter, M., Pickles, A., & Hill, J. (1990). Adult outcomes of childhood and adolescent depression: I. Psychiatric status. *Archives of General Psychiatry, 47,* 465–473.

Harris, S.L. (1983). *Families of the developmentally disabled: A guide to behavioral intervention.* New York: Pergamon Press.

Hassold, T., & Sherman, S. (2000). Down syndrome: Genetic recombination and the origin of the extra chromosome 21. *Clinical Genetics, 57,* 95–100.

Hastings, R.P., & Beck, A. (2004). Practitioner review: Stress intervention for parents of children with intellectual disabilities. *Journal of Child Psychology and Psychiatry, 45,* 1338–1349.

Hauck, M., Fein, D., Waterhouse, L., & Feinstein, C. (1995). Social initiations by autistic children to adults and other children. *Journal of Autism and Developmental Disorders, 25,* 579–595.

Hawkins, J.D., Arthur, M., & Olson, J. (1997). Community interventions to reduce risks and enhance protection against antisocial behavior. In D. Stoff, J. Breiling, & J. Maser (Eds.), *Handbook of antisocial behavior* (pp. 365–374). New York: Wiley.

Haywood, H.C., Meyers, C.E., & Switzky, H.N. (1982). Mental retardation. In M. Rosenzweig & L. Porter (Eds.), *Annual review of psychology.* Palo Alto, CA: Annual Reviews.

Heimberg, R.G., Dodge, C.S., Hope, D.A., Kennedy, C.R., Zollo, L.J., & Becker, R.J. (1990). Cognitive behavioral group treatment for social phobia: Comparison with a credible placebo control. *Cognitive Therapy and Research, 14,* 1–23.

Henggeler, S., & Borduin, C. (1990). *Family therapy and beyond: A multisystemic approach to treating the behavior problems of children and adolescents.* Pacific Grove, CA: Brooks/Cole.

Henggeler, S., Melton, G., Brondino, M., Scherer, D., & Hanley, J. (1997). Multisystemic therapy with violent and chronic juvenile offenders and their families: The role of treatment fidelity in successful dissemination. *Journal of Consulting and Clinical Psychology, 65,* 821–833.

Henggeler, S.W., Sheidow, A.J., & Lee, T. (2007). Multisystemic treatment of serious clinical problems in youths and their families. In D.W. Springer & A.R. Roberts (Eds.), *Handbook of forensic mental health with victims and offenders: Assessment, treatment, and research* (pp. 315–345). New York: Springer.

Henin, A., & Kendall, P.C. (1997). Obsessive-compulsive disorder in childhood and adolescence. In T. Ollendick & R. Prinz (Eds.), *Advances in clinical child psychology* (Vol. 19, pp. 75–132), New York: Plenum Press.

Herbert, M.R., Harris, G.J., Adrien, K.T., Ziegler, D.A., Makris, N., Kennedy, D.N., et al. (2002). Abnormal symmetry in language association cortex in autism. *Annals of Neurology, 52,* 588–596.

Herjanic, B., & Reich, W. (1982). Development of a structured psychiatric interview for children: Agreement between child and parent on individual symptoms. *Journal of Abnormal Child Psychology, 10,* 307–324.

Hermelin, B. (1976). Coding and the sense modalities. In L. Wing (Ed.), *Early childhood autism* (2nd ed.). Oxford: Pergamon Press.

Hersov, L. (1994). Fecal soiling. In M. Rutter, E. Taylor, & L. Hersov (Eds.), *Child and adolescent psychiatry* (pp. 520–528). Oxford: Blackwell.

Hetherington, E.M. (1987). Family

relations six years after divorce. In K. Pasley & M. Ihinger-Tallman (Eds.), *Remarriage and stepparenting: Current research and theory*. New York: Guilford Press.

Hettema, J.M., Prescott, C.A., & Kendler, K.S. (2001). A population-based twin study of generalized anxiety disorder in men and women. *Journal of Nervous and Mental Disease, 189,* 413–420.

Hibbs, E., & Jensen, P. (Eds.) (2005). *Psychosocial treatments for child and adolescent disorders: Empirically based strategies for clinical practice.* (2nd ed). Washington, DC: American Psychological Association.

Himle, M.B., Woods, D.W., Piacentini, J.C., & Walkup, J.T. (2006). Brief review of habit reversal training for Tourette syndrome. *Journal of Child Neurology, 21,* 719–725.

Hinshaw, S.P. (1987). On the distinction between attentional deficits/ hyperactivity and conduct problems/ aggression in child psychopathology. *Psychological Bulletin, 101,* 443–463.

Hinshaw, S.P. (1992). Externalizing behavior problems and academic underachievement in children and adolescence: Causal relationships and underlying mechanisms. *Psychological Bulletin, 111,* 127–155.

Hinshaw, S.P. (2005a). Enhancing social competence: Integrating self-management strategies with behavioral procedures for children with ADHD. In E. Hibbs & P. Jensen (Eds.), *Psychosocial treatments for child and adolescent disorders: Empirically based strategies for clinical practice* (2nd ed., pp. 285–310). Washington, DC: American Psychological Association.

Hinshaw, S.P. (2005b). Attention-deficit hyperactivity disorder. In P.C. Kendall (Ed.), *Child and adolescent therapy: Cognitive-behavioral procedures* (3rd ed., pp. 82–113). New York: Guilford Press.

Hinshaw, S.P., Henker, B., & Whalen, C.K. (1984a). Cognitive-behavioral and pharmacologic interventions for hyperactive boys: Comparative and combined effects. *Journal of Consulting and Clinical Psychology, 52,* 739–749.

Hinshaw, S.P., Henker, B., & Whalen, C.K. (1984b). Self-control in hyperactive boys in anger-inducing situations: Effects of cognitive-behavioral training and of methylphenidate. *Journal of Abnormal Child Psychology, 12,* 55–77.

Hinshaw, S.P., & Zupan, B. (1997). Assessment of antisocial behavior in children and adolescents. In D. Stoff, J. Breiling, & J. Maser (Eds.), *Handbook of antisocial behavior* (pp. 36–50). New York: Wiley.

Hinshaw, S.P., Owens, E.B., Sami, N., & Fargeon, S. (2006). Prospective follow-up of girls with attention-deficit/ hyperactivity disorder into adolescence: Evidence for continuing cross-domain impairment. *Journal of Consulting and Clinical Psychology, 74,* 489–499.

Hobbs, C.A., Sherman, S.L., Yi, P., Hopkins, S.E., Torfs, C.P., Hine, R.J., et al. (2000). Polymorphisms in genes involved in folate metabolism as maternal risk factors for Down syndrome. *American Journal of Human Genetics, 67,* 623–630.

Hodgens, J.B., Cole, J., & Boldizar, J. (2000). Peer-based differences among boys with ADHD. *Journal of Clinical Child Psychology, 29,* 443–452.

Hoek, H.W. (1991). The incidence and prevalence of anorexia nervosa and bulimia nervosa in primary care. *Psychological Medicine, 21,* 455–460.

Hoek, H.W. (2006). Incidence, prevalences and mortality of anorexia nervosa and other eating disorders. *Current Opinion in Psychiatry, 19,* 389–894.

Holden, N.L., & Robinson, P.H. (1988). Anorexia nervosa and bulimia nervosa in British blacks. *British Journal of Psychiatry, 152,* 544–549.

Holland, A.J., Sicotte, N., & Treasure, J. (1988). Anorexia nervosa—evidence for a genetic basis. *Journal of Psychosomatic Research, 32,* 561–572.

Hollis, C., & Rapoport, J. (2008). Child and adolescent schizophrenia. In D. Weinberger & P. Harrison (Eds.), *Schizophrenia* (3rd ed.). London: Blackwell.

Holmans, P., Weissman, M.M., Zubenko, G.S., Scheftner, W.A., Crowe, R.R., DePaulo, J.R., et al. (2007). Genetics of recurrent early-onset major depression (GenRED): Final genome scan report. *American Journal of Psychiatry, 164,* 248–258.

Homatidis, S., & Konstantareas, M.M. (1981). Assessment of hyperactivity: Isolating measures of high discriminant validity. *Journal of Consulting and Clinical Psychology, 49,* 533–541.

Hondo, H., Shimizu, Y., & Rutter, M. (2005). No effect of MMR withdrawal on the incidence of autism: A total population study. *Journal of Child Psychology and Psychiatry, 46,* 572–579.

Hook, E.B. (1987). Issues in analysis of data on parental age: Implications for genetic counseling for Down's syndrome. *Human Genetics, 77,* 303–306.

Hook, E.B., Cross, P.K., & Regal, R.R. (1990). Factual, statistical and logical issues in the search for a paternal age effect for Down syndrome. *Human Genetics, 85,* 387–388.

Hopper, M., & Garner, D. (1986). Applications of the eating disorder inventory to a sample of black, white, and mixed-race schoolgirls in Zimbabwe. *International Journal of Eating Disorders, 5,* 161–168.

Houts, A.C., Berman, J.S., & Abramson, H. (1994). The effectiveness of psychological and pharmacologic treatments for nocturnal enuresis. *Journal of Consulting and Clinical Psychology, 62,* 737–745.

Howlin, P. (2000). Outcome in adult life for more able individuals with autism or Asperger syndrome. *Autism, 4,* 63–83.

Howlin, P., Goode, S., Hutton, J., & Rutter, M. (2004). Adult outcome for children with autism. *Journal of Child Psychology and Psychiatry, 45,* 212–229.

Howlin, P.A. (1981). The effectiveness of operant language training with autistic children. *Journal of Autism and Developmental Disorders, 11,* 89–105.

Howlin, P.A., & Rutter, M. (1987). *Treatment of autistic children.* New York: Wiley.

Hoza, B., Mrug, S., Gerdes, A.C., Hinshaw, S.P., Bukowski, W.M., Gold, J.A., et al. (2005). What aspects of peer relationships are impaired in children with ADHD? *Journal of Consulting and Clinical Psychology, 73,* 411–423.

Hudson, J.L., Comer, J.S., & Kendall, P.C. (2008). Parental responses to positive and negative emotions in anxious and nonanxious children. *Journal of Clinical Child and Adolescent Psychology, 37,* 303–313.

Hughes, A.A., Lourea-Waddell, B., & Kendall, P.C. (2008). Somatic complaints in children with anxiety disorders and their unique prediction of poorer academic performance. *Child Psychiatry and Human Development, 39,* 211–220.

Huguenin, N., Weidenman, L., & Mulick, J. (1991). Programmed instruction. In J. Matson & J. Mulick (Eds.), *Handbook of mental retardation* (2nd ed., pp. 250–277). New York: Pergamon Press.

Humphrey, L.L., Apple, R.F., & Kirschenbaum, D.S. (1986). Differentiating bulimic-anorexic from normal families using interpersonal and behavioral observational systems. *Journal of Consulting and Clinical Psychology, 54,* 190–195.

Iaboni, F., Douglas, V.I., & Baker, A.G. (1995). Effects of reward and response costs on inhibition in ADHD children.

Journal of Abnormal Psychology, 104, 232–240.

Individuals with Disabilities Education Act (IDEA) (1990). Public Law No. 101–476, 20, U.S.C. 1400.

Ingram, R.E. (Ed.) (1986). *Information processing approaches to clinical psychology.* New York: Academic Press.

Ingram, R.E. (2003). Origins of cognitive vulnerability to depression. *Cognitive Therapy and Research, 27,* 77–88.

Ingram, R.E., Miranda, J., & Segal, Z.V. (2006). Cognitive vulnerability to depression. In L.B. Alloy & J.H. Riskind (Eds.), *Cognitive vulnerability to emotional disorders.* Mahwah, NJ: Lawrence Erlbaum Associates, Inc.

Isaacs, E.B., Edmonds, C.J., Chong, W.K., Lucas, A., Morley, R., & Gadian, D.G. (2004). Brain morphometry and IQ measurements in preterm children. *Brain, 127,* 2595–2607.

Jacobson, J.W. (1982a). Problem behavior and psychiatric impairment within a developmentally disabled population: I. Behavior frequency. *Applied Research in Mental Retardation, 3,* 369–381.

Jacobson, J.W. (1982b). Problem behavior and psychiatric impairment within a developmentally disabled population: II. Behavior severity. *Applied Research in Mental Retardation, 3,* 369–381.

Janovic, J., & Rohaidy, H. (1987). Motor, behavioral and pharmacologic findings in Tourette's syndrome. *Canadian Journal of Neurological Science, 14,* 541–546.

Jayson, D., Wood, A., Kroll, L., Fraser, J., & Harrington, R. (1998). Which depressed patients respond to cognitive-behavioral treatment? *Journal of the American Academy of Child and Adolescent Psychiatry, 37,* 35–39.

Jehu, D., Morgan, R.T.T., Turner, R.K., & Jones, A. (1977). A controlled trial of the treatment of nocturnal enuresis in residential homes for children. *Behavior Research and Therapy, 15,* 1–16.

Jennings, J., Van der Molen, M., Pelham, W., Brock, K., & Hoza, B. (1997). Psychophysiology of inhibition in boys with attention deficit disorder. *Developmental Psychology, 33,* 308–318.

Jensen, P.S., Arnold, L.E., Swanson, J.M., Vitiello, B., Abikoff, H.B., Greenhill, L.L., et al. (2007). 3-year follow-up of the NIMH MTA study. *Journal of the American Academy of Child and Adolescent Psychiatry, 46,* 989–1002.

Jerome, L., & Segal, A. (1997). ADHD and dangerous driving. *Journal of the American Academy of Child and Adolescent Psychiatry, 36,* 13–25.

Johnson, C.R., Lubetsky, M.J., & Sacco, K.A. (1995). Psychiatric and behavioral disorders in hospitalized preschoolers with developmental disabilities. *Journal of Autism and Developmental Disorders, 25,* 169–182.

Jones, D.J., Fox, M.M., Babigian, H., & Hutton, H. (1980). Epidemiology of anorexia nervosa in Monroe County, New York: 1960–1976. *Psychosomatic Medicine, 42,* 551–558.

Jones, K.L. (1988). *Smith's recognizable patterns of human malformation* (4th ed.). Philadelphia: Saunders.

Jones, K.L., & Smith, B.W. (1973). Recognition of the fetal alcohol syndrome in early infancy. *Lancet, 2,* 999–1001.

Jones, R.L. (1996, August 21). Sharp rise reported in teenagers' drug use. *Philadelphia Inquirer,* pp. A1–A15.

Jordan, J., Joyce, P.R., Carter, F.A., McIntosh, V.V.W., Luty, S.E., McKenzie, J.M., et al. (2009). The Yale-Brown-Cornell Eating Disorder Scale in women with anorexia nervosa: What is it measuring? *International Journal of Eating Disorders, 42,* 267–274.

Jouriles, E.N., Bourg, W.J., & Farris, A.M. (1991). Marital adjustment and child conduct problems: A comparison of the correlation across subsamples. *Journal of*

Consulting and Clinical Psychology, 59, 354–357.

Jouriles, E.N., McDonald, R., Norwood, W., Ware, H., Spiller, L., & Swank, P. (1998). Knives, guns, and interparental violence: Relations with child behavioral problems. Journal of Family Psychology, 12, 178–194.

Kalat, J.W. (2007). Biological psychology (9th ed.). Belmont, CA: Thomson Wadsworth.

Kalucy, R.S., Crisp, A.H., & Harding, B. (1977). A study of 56 families with anorexia nervosa. British Journal of Medical Psychology, 50, 381–395.

Kanner, L. (1943). Autistic disturbances of affective contact. Nervous Child, 21, 217–250.

Kashani, J.H., & Carlson, G.A. (1987). Seriously depressed preschoolers. American Journal of Psychiatry, 144, 348–350.

Kashani, J.H., & Orvaschel, H. (1988). Anxiety disorders in midadolescence: A community sample. American Journal of Psychiatry, 145, 960–964.

Kaslow, N., Brown, R., & Mees, L. (1994). Cognitive and behavioral correlates of childhood depression: A developmental perspective. In W.M. Reynolds & H. Johnston (Eds.), Handbook of depression in children and adolescents (pp. 97–122). New York: Plenum Press.

Kaslow, N., & Thompson, M. (1998). Applying the criteria for empirically supported treatments to studies of psychosocial interventions for child and adolescent depression. Journal of Clinical Child Psychology, 27, 146–155.

Katz-Garris, L. (1978). The right to education. In J. Wortis (Ed.), Mental retardation and developmental disabilities (Vol. 10). New York: Bruner/Mazel.

Katzman, D.K. (2005). Medical complications in adolescents with anorexia nervosa: A review of the literature. International Journal of Eating Disorders, 37, S52–59.

Kazdin, A.E. (2005). Child, parent, and family-based treatment of aggressive and antisocial behavior. In E. Hibbs & P. Jensen (Eds.), Psychosocial treatments for child and adolescent disorders: Empirically based strategies for clinical practice (2nd ed., pp. 445–476). Washington, DC: American Psychological Association.

Kazdin, A.E., Esveldt-Dawson, K., Unis, A.S., & Rancurello, M.D. (1983). Child and parent evaluations of depression and aggression in psychiatric inpatient children. Journal of Abnormal Child Psychology, 11, 401–413.

Kazdin, A.E., & Kendall P.C. (1998). Current progress and future plans for developing effective treatments: Comments and perspectives. Journal of Clinical Child Psychology, 27, 217–226.

Kazdin, A.E., Siegel, T.C., & Bass, D. (1992). Cognitive-behavioural problem-solving skills training and parent management training in the treatment of antisocial child behavior. Journal of Consulting and Clinical Psychology, 60, 733–747.

Kazdin, A.E., & Weisz, J.R. (Eds.) (2006). Evidence-based psychotherapies for children and adolescents. New York: Guilford Press.

Keel, P.K., Mitchell, J., Miller, K., Davis, T., & Crow, S. (1999). Long-term outcome of bulimia nervosa. Archives of General Psychiatry, 56, 63–69.

Keel, P.L., Leon, G.R., & Fulkerson, J.A. (2001). Vulnerability to eating disorders in childhood and adolescence. In R.E. Ingram & J.M. Price (Eds.), Vulnerability to psychopathology: Risk across the lifespan (pp. 389–411). New York: Guilford Press.

Keller, M.B., Lavori, P., Wunder, J., Beardslee, W.R., Schwartz, C.E., & Roth, J. (1992). Chronic cause of anxiety disorders in children and adolescents. *Journal of the American Academy of Child and Adolescent Psychiatry, 31,* 595–599.

Kendall, P.C. (1993). Cognitive-behavioral therapies with youth: Guiding theory current status, and emerging developments. *Journal of Consulting and Clinical Psychology, 61,* 235–247.

Kendall, P.C. (Ed.) (2006). *Child and adolescent therapy: Cognitive-behavioral procedures* (3rd ed.). New York: Guilford Press.

Kendall, P.C., & Braswell, L. (1993). *Cognitive behavioral therapy for impulsive children* (2nd ed.). New York: Guilford Press.

Kendall, P.C., Cantwell, D., & Kazdin, A.E. (1989). Depression in children and adolescents: Assessment issues and recommendations. *Cognitive Therapy and Research, 13,* 109–146.

Kendall, P.C., Flannery-Schroeder, E., Panichelli-Mindel, S.M., Southam-Gerow, M., Henin, A., & Warman, M.J. (1997). Therapy for youth with anxiety disorders: A second randomized clinical trial. *Journal of Consulting and Clinical Psychology, 65,* 366–380.

Kendall, P.C., & Hedtke, K. (2006). *Coping Cat Workbook* (2nd ed.). Ardmore, PA: Workbook Publishing.

Kendall, P.C., & Hollon, S.D. (Eds.) (1979). *Cognitive-behavioral interventions: Theory, research and procedures.* New York: Academic Press.

Kendall, P.C., Hudson, J.L., Gosch, E., Flannery-Schroeder, E., & Suveg, C. (2008). Cognitive-behavioral therapy for anxiety disordered youth: A randomized clinical trial evaluating child and family modalities. *Journal of Consulting and Clinical Psychology, 76,* 282–297.

Kendall, P.C., Kortlander, E., Chansky, T.E., & Brady, E.U. (1992). Comorbidity of anxiety and depression in youth: Treatment implications. *Journal of Consulting and Clinical Psychology, 60,* 869–880.

Kendall, P.C., & MacDonald, J.P. (1993). Cognition in the psychopathology of youth, and implications for treatment. In K.S. Dobson & P.C. Kendall (Eds.), *Psychopathology and cognition* (pp. 387–432). San Diego: Academic Press.

Kendall, P.C., & Pimentel, S.S. (2003). On the physiological symptom constellation in youth with generalized anxiety disorder (GAD). *Journal of Anxiety Disorders, 17,* 211–221.

Kendall, P.C., Puliafico, A.C., Barmish, A.J., Choudhury, M.S., Henin, A., & Treadwell, K.S. (2007). Assessing anxiety with the Child Behavior Checklist and the Teacher Report Form. *Journal of Anxiety Disorders, 21,* 1004–1015.

Kendall, P.C., Reber, M., McLeer, S., Epps, J., & Ronan, K.R. (1990b). Cognitive-behavioral treatment of conduct-disordered children. *Cognitive Therapy and Research, 14,* 279–197.

Kendall, P.C., Robin, J.A., Hedtke, K.A., Suveg, C., Flannery-Schroeder, E., & Gosch, E. (2005). Considering CBT with anxious youth? Think exposures. *Cognitive and Behavioral Practice, 12,* 136–150.

Kendall, P.C., Safford, S., Flannery-Schroeder, E., & Webb, A. (2004). Child anxiety treatment: Outcomes in adolescence and impact on substance use and depression at 7.4-year follow-up. *Journal of Consulting and Clinical Psychology, 72,* 276–287.

Kendall, P.C., Stark, K.D., & Adam, T. (1990a). Cognitive deficit or cognitive distortion in childhood depression. *Journal of Abnormal Child Psychology, 18,* 255–270.

Kendall, P.C., & Suveg, C. (2005). Treating anxiety disorders in youth. In P.C. Kendall (Ed.), *Child and adolescent therapy: Cognitive-behavioral procedures* (3rd ed.). New York: Guilford Press.

Kendall, P.C., & Watson, D. (Eds.) (1989). *Anxiety and depression: Distinctive and overlapping features.* New York: Academic Press.

Kendler, K.S., Jacobson, K.C., Myers, J., & Prescott, C.A. (2002). Sex differences in genetic and environmental risk factors for irrational fears and phobias. *Psychological Medicine, 32,* 209–217.

Kendler, K.S., Neale, M.C., Kessler, R.C., Heath, A.C., & Eaves, L.J. (1992). Generalized anxiety disorder in women: A population-based twin study. *Archives of General Psychiatry, 49,* 267–272.

Kerig, P. (1998). Moderators and mediators of the effects of interparental conflict on children's adjustment. *Journal of Abnormal Child Psychology, 26,* 199–212.

Kernberg, O.F. (1976). *Object relations theory and clinical psycho-analysis.* New York: Jason Aronson.

Keski-Rahkonen, A., Hoek, H.W., Susser, E.S., Linna, M.S., Sihvola, E., Raevuori, A., et al. (2007). Epidemiology and course of anorexia nervosa in the community. *American Journal of Psychiatry, 164,* 1259–1265.

Kessler, R.C., Adler, L.A., Barkley, R., Biederman, J., Conners, C.K., Faraone, S.V., et al. (2005a). Patterns and predictors of attention-deficit/hyperactivity disorder persistence into adulthood: Results from the National Comorbidity Survey Replication. *Biological Psychiatry, 57,* 1442–1451.

Kessler, R.C., Berglund, P., Demler, O., Jin, R., Koretz, D., Merikangas, K.R., et al. (2003). The epidemiology of major depressive disorder: Results from the National Comorbidity Survey Replication (NCS-R). *Journal of the American Medical Association, 289,* 3095–3105.

Kessler, R.C., Berglund, P., Demler, O., Jin, R., Merikangas, K.R., & Walters, E.E. (2005b). Lifetime prevalence and age-of-onset distributions of DSM-IV disorders in the National Comorbidity Survey Replication. *Archives of General Psychiatry, 62,* 593–602.

Kessler, R.C., Lane, M., Stang, P.E., & Van Brunt, D.L. (2009). The prevalence and workplace costs of adult attention deficit hyperactivity disorder in a large manufacturing firm. *Psychological Medicine, 39,* 137–147.

Kihlstrom, J.F. (1987). The cognitive unconscious. *Science, 237,* 1445–1452.

Kiss, E., Gentzler, A.M., George, C., Kapornai, K., Tamas, Z., Kovacs, M., et al. (2007). Factors influencing mother–child reports of depressive symptoms and agreement among clinically referred depressed youngsters in Hungary. *Journal of Affective Disorders, 100,* 143–151.

Kistner, J.A., & Torgesen, J.K. (1987). Motivational and cognitive aspects of learning disabilities. In B. Lahey & A.E. Kazdin (Eds.), *Advances in clinical child psychology* (Vol. 10). New York: Plenum Press.

Kitzmann, K.M., & Emery, R.E. (1994). Child and family coping one year after mediated and litigated child custody disputes. *Journal of Family Psychology, 8,* 150–157.

Klein, D.N., Dougherty, L.R., & Olino, T.M. (2005). Toward guidelines for evidence-based assessment of depression in children and adolescents. *Journal of Clinical Child and Adolescent Psychology, 34,* 412–432.

Klein, J.B., Jacobs, R.H., & Reinecke, M.A. (2007). Cognitive-behavioral therapy for adolescent depression: A meta-analytic investigation of changes in effect-size estimates. *Journal of the American Academy of Child and Adolescent Psychiatry, 46,* 1403–1413.

Klin, A., McPartland, J., & Volkmar, F.R. (2005). Asperger syndrome. In R. Paul, A. Klin, & D. Cohen (Eds.), *Handbook of autism and pervasive developmental disorders, Vol 1: Diagnosis, development, neurobiology, and behavior* (3rd ed.). Hoboken, NJ: Wiley.

Klorman, R., Brumaghim, J.T., Fitzpatrick, P.A., Borgstedt, A.D., & Strauss, J. (1994). Clinical and cognitive effects of methylphenidate on children with attention deficit disorder as a function of aggression/oppositionality and age. *Journal of Abnormal Psychology, 103*, 206–221.

Knickmeyer, R.C., & Baron-Cohen, S. (2006). Fetal testosterone and sex differences in typical social development in autism. *Journal of Child Neurology, 21*, 825–845.

Knouse, L.E., Mitchell, J.T., Brown, L.H., Silvia, P.J., Kane, M.J., Myin-Gereys, I., et al. (2008). The expression of adult ADHD symptoms in daily life: An application of experience sampling methodology. *Journal of Attention Disorders, 11*, 652–663.

Koegal, R.L., Bimbela, A., & Schreibman, L. (1996). Collateral effects of parent training on family interactions. *Journal of Autism and Developmental Disorders, 26*, 347–359.

Koegal, R.L., & Koegal, L. (Eds.) (1995). *Teaching children with autism: Strategies for initiating positive interactions and improving learning opportunities.* Baltimore: Paul H. Brooks.

Koegal, R.L., Koegal, L.K., & Brookman, L.I. (2003). Empirically supported pivotal response interventions for children with autism. In A.E. Kazdin & J.R. Weisz (Eds.), *Evidence-based psychotherapies for children and adolescents* (pp. 341–357). New York: Guilford Press.

Koegal, R.L., Schreibman, L., Britten, K.R., Burke, J., & O'Neill, R.E. (1982). A comparison of parent training to direct child treatment. In R.L. Koegel, A. Rincover, & A.L. Egel (Eds.), *Educating and understanding autistic children* (pp. 86–109). San Diego, CA: College Hill Press.

Koerner, N., & Dugas, M.J. (2008). An investigation of appraisals in individuals vulnerable to excessive worry: The role of intolerance of uncertainty. *Cognitive Therapy and Research, 32*, 619–638.

Kohut, H. (1977). *The restoration of the self.* New York: International Universities Press.

Kokko, K., & Pulkkinen, L. (2005). Stability of aggressive behavior from childhood to middle age in women and men. *Aggressive Behavior, 31*, 485–497.

Kolb, B., & Whishaw, I.Q. (2008). *Fundamentals of human neuropsychology.* New York, NY: Worth Publishers.

Kotler, L.A., Cohen, P., Davies, M., Pine, D.S., & Walsh, B.T. (2001). Longitudinal relationships between childhood, adolescent, and adult eating disorders. *Journal of the American Academy of Child and Adolescent Psychiatry, 40*, 1434–1440.

Kovacs, M. (1981). Rating scales to assess depression in school aged children. *Acta Paedopsychiatrica, 46*, 305–315.

Kovacs, M. (1991). *The children's depression inventory (CDI).* North Tonawanda, NY: Multi-health Systems.

Kovacs, M., Feinberg, T.L., Crouse-Novak, M.A., Paulauskas, S.L., & Finkelstein, R. (1984). Depressive disorders in childhood: I. A longitudinal prospective study of characteristics and recovery. *Archives of General Psychiatry, 41*, 229–237.

Krain, A.L., & Castellanos, F.X. (2006). Brain development and ADHD. *Clinical Psychology Review, 26*, 433–444.

Krobak, R., Cassidy, J., Lyons-Ruth, K., & Ziv, Y. (2006). Attachment, stress, and psychopathology: A developmental pathways model. In D. Cicchetti & D.J. Cohen (Eds.), *Developmental psychopathology, Volume 1: Theory and Method* (3rd ed.). Hoboken, NJ: Wiley.

Kroes, G.K., Veerman, J.W., & De Bruyn, E.J. (2003). Maternal psychopathology and the reporting of problem behavior in clinic-referred children. *European Journal of Psychological Assesssment, 19,* 195–203.

Kuo-Tai, T. (1987). Infantile autism in China. *Journal of Autism and Developmental Disorders, 17,* 289–296.

Kwak, C., Vuong, K.D., & Jankovic, J. (2003). Premonitory sensory phenomenon in Tourette's syndrome. *Movement Disorders, 18,* 1530–1533.

Lahey, B.B., Green, K., & Forehand, R. (1980). On the independence of ratings of hyperactivity, conduct problems, and attention deficits in children: A multiple regression analysis. *Journal of Consulting and Clinical Psychology, 48,* 566–574.

Lahey, B.B., Loeber, R., Hart, E.L., Frick, P.J., Applegate, B., Zhang, Q., et al. (1995). Four-year longitudinal study of conduct disorder in boys: Patterns and predictors of persistence. *Journal of Abnormal Psychology, 104,* 83–93.

Lambert, E.W., Wahler, R.G., Andrade, A.R., & Bickman, L. (2001). Looking for the disorder in conduct disorder. *Journal of Abnormal Psychology, 110,* 110–123.

Lambert, M.C., Weisz, J.R., Knight, F., Desrosiers, M., Overly, K., & Thesiger, C. (1992). Jamaican and American adult perspectives on child psychopathology: Further exploration of the threshold model. *Journal of Consulting and Clinical Psychology, 60,* 146–149.

Lambert, N., Nihira, K., & Leland, O. (1993). *Manual for the adaptive behavior scale—school* (2nd ed.) Austin, TX: Pro-Ed.

Lansford, J.E., Dodge, K.A., Pettit, G.S., Bates, J.E., Crozier, J., & Kaplow, J. (2002). Long-term effects of early child physical maltreatment on psychological, behavioral, and academic problems in adolescence: A 12-year prospective study. *Archives of Pediatrics and Adolescent Medicine, 156,* 824–830.

Lara, C., Fayyad, J., de Graaf, R., Kessler, R.C., Aguilar-Gaxiola, S., Angermeyer, M., et al. (2009). Childhood predictors of adult attention-deficit/hyperactivity disorder: Results from the World Health Organization Mental Health Survey Initiative. *Biological Psychology, 65,* 46–54.

Last, C.G., Hersen, M., Kazdin, A., Francis, G., & Grubb, H. (1987). Psychiatric illness in mothers of anxious children. *American Journal of Psychiatry, 144,* 1580–1583.

Last, C.G., & Perrin, S. (1993). Anxiety disorders in African-American and white children. *Journal of Abnormal Child Psychology, 21,* 153–164.

Leckman, J.F. (2002). Tourette's syndrome. *Lancet, 360,* 1577–1586.

Leckman, J.F., & Cohen, D.J. (2002). Tic disorders. In M. Rutter & E. Taylor (Eds.), *Child and adolescent psychiatry* (4th ed., pp. 593–611). Oxford: Blackwell.

Leckman, J.F., Pauls, D.L., Zhang, H., Rosario-Campos, M.C., Katsovich, L., Kidd, K.K., et al. (2003). Obsessive-compulsive symptom dimensions in affected sibling pairs diagnosed with Gilles de la Tourette syndrome. *American Journal of Medical Genetics. Part B, Neuropsychiatric Genetics, 116,* 60–68.

Leckman, J.F., Walker, D.E., & Cohen, D.J. (1993). Premonitory urges in Tourette's syndrome. *American Journal of Psychiatry, 150,* 98–102.

Lee, S., Chiu, H.F.K., & Chen, C.N. (1989). Anorexia nervosa in Hong Kong: Why not more in Chinese? *British Journal of Psychiatry, 154,* 683–688.

Le Grange, D., Binford, R., & Loeb, K.L. (2005). Manualized family-based treatment for anorexia nervosa: A case series. *Journal of the American Academy of Child and Adolescent Psychiatry, 44,* 41–46.

Leitenberg, H., Agras, W.S., & Thomson, L.E. (1968). A sequential analysis of the effect of selective positive reinforcement in modifying anorexia nervosa. *Behaviour Research and Therapy, 6,* 211–218.

Leonard, H., Swedo, S., Allen, A., & Rapoport, J. (1994). Obsessive-compulsive disorder. In T. Ollendick, N. King, & W. Yule (Eds.), *International handbook of phobic and anxiety disorders in children and adolescents* (pp. 207–222). New York: Plenum Press.

Lerner, J. (1989). Educational interventions in learning disabilities. *Journal of the American Academy of Child and Adolescent Psychiatry, 28,* 326–331.

Lerner, R.M., Hess, L.E., & Nitz, K. (1990). A developmental perspective on psychopathology. In M. Hersen & C. Last (Eds.), *Handbook of child and adult psychopathology: A longitudinal perspective* (pp. 9–32). New York: Pergamon Press.

Leung, P.W.L., Hung, S.F., Ho, T.P., Lee, C.C., Liu, W.S., Tang, C.P., et al. (2008). Prevalence of DSM-IV disorders in Chinese adolescents and the effects of an impairment criterion: A pilot community study in Hong Kong. *European Child and Adolescent Psychiatry, 17,* 452–461.

Leung, P.W.L., & Wong, M.M.T. (1998). Can cognitive distortions differentiate between internalising and externalising problems? *Journal of Child Psychology and Psychiatry, 39,* 263–269.

Levinson, D.F. (2006). The genetics of depression: A review. *Biological Psychiatry, 60,* 84–92.

Levitt, E.E. (1963). Psychotherapy with children: A further evaluation. *Behaviour Research and Therapy, 21,* 326–329.

Lewinsohn, P.M. (1974). A behavioral approach to depression. In R.J. Friedman & M.M. Katz (Eds.), *The psychology of depression: Contemporary theory and research* (pp. 157–184). Washington, DC: Winston-Wiley.

Lewinsohn, P.M., Clarke, G.N., Hops, H., & Andrews, J. (1990). Cognitive-behavioral group treatment of depression in adolescents. *Behavior Therapy, 21,* 385–401.

Lewinsohn, P.M., Clark, G.N., & Rohde, P. (1994). Psychological approaches to the treatment of depression in adolescents. In W.M. Reynolds & H.F. Johnston (Eds.), *Handbook of depression in children and adolescents* (pp. 309–344). New York: Plenum Press.

Lewinsohn, P.M., Rohde, P., Klein, D., & Seeley, J. (1999). Natural course of adolescent major depressive disorder: I. Continuity into young adulthood. *Journal of the American Academy of Child and Adolescent Psychiatry, 38,* 56–63.

Lewinsohn, P.M., Rohde, P., Seeley, J.R., & Fischer, S.A. (1993). Age-cohort changes in the lifetime occurrence of depression and other mental disorders. *Journal of Abnormal Psychology, 102,* 110–120.

Libby, S., Reynolds, S., Derisley, J., & Clark, S. (2004). Cognitive appraisals in young people with obsessive-compulsive disorder. *Journal of Child Psychology and Psychiatry, 45,* 1076–1084.

Linscheid, T.R., Budd, K.S., & Rasnake, L.K. (2003). Pediatric feeding problems. In M.C. Roberts (Ed.), *Handbook of pediatric psychology.* New York: Guilford Press.

Lips, H.M. (1988). *Sex and gender.* Mountain View, CA: Mayfield.

Litrownik, A.J., & McInnis, E.T. (1986). Information processing and autism. In R.E. Ingram (Ed.), *Information processing approaches to clinical psychology.* New York: Academic Press.

Lochman, J.E. (1992). Cognitive-behavioral intervention with aggressive boys: Three-year follow-up and preventive effects. *Journal of Consulting and Clinical Psychology, 60,* 426–434.

Lochman, J.E., Powell, N.R., Whidby, J.M., & Fitzgerald, D.P. (2006). Aggressive children: Cognitive-behavioral assessment and treatment. In P.C. Kendall (Ed.), *Child and adolescent therapy: Cognitive-behavioral procedures* (3rd ed., pp. 33–81). New York: Guilford Press.

Loeb, K.L., Walsh, B.T., Lock, J., Le Grange, D., Jones, J., Marcus, S., et al. (2007). Open trial of family-based treatment for full and partial anorexia nervosa in adolescence: Evidence of successful dissemination. *Journal of the American Academy of Child and Adolescent Psychiatry, 46*, 792–800.

Loeber, M., Van Kammen, W.B., & Maughan, B. (1993). Developmental pathways in disruptive child behavior. *Development and Psychopathology, 5*, 103–133.

Loeber, R. (1990). Development and risk factors of juvenile antisocial behavior and delinquency. *Clinical Psychology Review, 10*, 1–41.

Loeber, R., & Farrington, D.P. (2000). Young children who commit crime: Epidemiology, developmental origins, risk factors, early interventions, and policy implications. *Development and Psychopathology, 12*, 737–762.

Loeber, R., & Keenen, K. (1994). Interaction between conduct disorder and its comorbid conditions: Effects of age and gender. *Clinical Psychology Review, 14*, 497–523.

Lonigan, C., Elbert, J., & Johnson, S.B. (1998). Empirically supported psychosocial interventions for children: An overview. *Journal of Clinical Child Psychology, 27*, 138–145.

Lord, C., & Bailey, A. (2002). Autism spectrum disorders. In M. Rutter & E. Taylor (Eds.), *Child and adolescent psychiatry* (4th ed., pp. 636–663). Oxford: Blackwell.

Lord, C., Pickles, A., McLennan, J., Rutter, M., Bregman, J., Folstein, S., et al. (1997). Diagnosing autism: Analyses of data from the autism diagnostic interview. *Journal of Autism and Developmental Disorders, 27*, 501–518.

Lovaas, O.I. (1987). Behavioral treatment and normal educational and intellectual functioning in young autistic children. *Journal of Consulting and Clinical Psychology, 55*, 3–9.

Lovaas, O.I., Koegal, R.L., & Schreibman, L. (1979). Stimulus overselectivity in autism: A review of research. *Psychological Bulletin, 86*, 1236–1254.

Lovaas, O.I., Koegal, R.L., Simmons, J.Q., & Long, J.S. (1973). Some generalization and follow-up measures on autistic children in behavior therapy. *Journal of Consulting and Clinical Psychology, 55*, 3–9.

Lovaas, O.I., & Smith, T. (2003). Early and intensive behavioral intervention in autism. In A.E. Kazdin & J.R. Weisz (Eds.), *Evidence-based psychotherapies for children and adolescents* (pp. 325–340). New York: Guilford Press.

Lovaas, O.I., Smith, T., & McEachin, J.J. (1989). Clarifying comments on the Young autism study: Reply to Schopler, Short, and Mesibov. *Journal of Consulting and Clinical Psychology, 57*, 165–167.

Lucas, A.R., Beard, C.M., O'Fallon, W., & Kurland, L. (1991). Fifty year trends in the incidence of anorexia nervosa in Rochester, Minnesota: A population-based study. *American Journal of Psychiatry, 148*, 917–922.

Luiselli, J.K. (2009). Nonsuicidal self-injury among people with developmental disabilities. In M.K. Nock (Ed.), *Understanding nonsuicidal self-injury: Origins, assessment, and treatment* (pp. 157–179). Washington, DC: American Psychological Association.

Luk, S., & Leung, P.W. (1989). Conners' teachers' rating scale: A validity study in Hong Kong. *Journal of Child Psychology and Psychiatry, 30*, 785–794.

Lyon, G.R., Fletcher, J.M., & Barnes, M.C. (2003). Learning disabilities. In E.J.

Mash & R.A. Barkley (Eds.), *Child psychopathology* (2nd ed., pp. 520–586). New York: Guilford Press.

Lyon, G.R., Fletcher, J.M., Fuchs, L.S., & Chhabra, V. (2006). Learning disabilities. In E.J. Mash & R.A. Barkley (Eds.), *Treatment of childhood disorders* (3rd ed., pp. 512–594). New York: Guilford Press.

Maccini, P., & Hughes, C. (1997). Mathematics interventions for adolescents with learning disabilities. *Learning Disabilities Research and Practice, 12,* 168–176.

Mace, F., Kratochwill, T.R., & Fiello, R.A. (1983). Positive treatment of aggressive behavior in a mentally retarded adult: A case study. *Behavior Therapy, 14,* 689–696.

Macfie, J., Cicchetti, D., & Toth, S.L. (2001). The development of dissociation in maltreated preschool-aged children. *Development and Psychopathology, 13,* 233–254.

MacLean, K. (2003). The impact of institutionalization on child development. *Development and Psychopathology, 15,* 853–884.

MacMillan, D.L., Keogh, B., & Jones, R.L. (1986). Special education research on mildly handicapped learners. In M.C. Wittrock (Ed.), *Handbook of research on teaching* (pp. 90–111), New York: Macmillan.

Madle, R. (1990). Mental retardation in adulthood. In M. Hersen & C. Last (Eds.), *Handbook of child and adult psychopathology: A longitudinal perspective.* New York: Pergamon Press.

Mahoney, M.J. (1977). Reflections in the cognitive-learning trend in psychotherapy. *American Psychologist, 32,* 5–18.

Mahoney, M.J. (1993). Theoretical developments in the cognitive psychotherapies. *Journal of Consulting and Clinical Psychology, 61,* 187–193.

Maldonado-Duran, J.M., Fonagy, P.,

Helmig, L., Millhuff, C., Moody, C., Rosen, L., et al. (2008). In-depth mental health evaluation of a community sample of nonreferred infants with feeding difficulties. *International Journal of Eating Disorders, 41,* 513–519.

Manchi, M., & Cohen, P. (1990). Early childhood eating behaviour and adolescent eating disorders. *Journal of the American Academy of Child and Adolescent Psychiatry, 29,* 112–117.

Mann, B.J., & MacKenzie, E.P. (1996). Pathways among marital functioning, parental behaviors, and child behavior problems in school-age boys. *Journal of Consulting and Clinical Psychology, 25,* 183–191.

March, J. (1995). Behavioral psychotherapy for children and adolescents with obsessive-compulsive disorder: A review of the literature and recommendation for treatment. *Journal of the American Academy of Child and Adolescent Psychiatry, 34,* 7–18.

March, J., & Albano, A.M. (1998). New developments in assessing pediatric anxiety disorders. In T. Ollendick & R. Prinz (Eds.), *Advances in clinical child psychology* (Vol. 20, pp. 213–242). New York: Plenum Press.

March, J., & Mulle, K. (1998). *OCD in children and adolescents: A cognitive-behavioral treatment manual.* New York: Guilford Press.

March, J., Parker, J., Sullivan, K., Stallings, P., & Conners, C. (1997). The Multidimensional Anxiety Scale for Children (MASC): Factor structure, reliability and validity. *Journal of the American Academy of Child and Adolescent Psychiatry, 36,* 554–565.

March, J.S., Entusah, A.R., Rynn, M., Albano, A.M., & Tourian, K.A. (2007). A randomized controlled trial of venlafaxine ER versus placebo in pediatric social anxiety disorder. *Biological Psychiatry, 62,* 1149–1154.

Marmorstein, N.R., & Iacono, W.G. (2005).

Longitudinal follow-up of adolescents with late-onset antisocial behavior: A pathological yet overlooked group. *Journal of the American Academy of Child and Adolescent Psychiatry, 44,* 1284–1291.

Marsh, R., Gerber, A.J., & Peterson, B.S. (2008). Neuroimaging studies of normal brain development and their relevance for understanding childhood neuropsychiatric disorders. *Journal of the American Academy of Child and Adolescent Psychiatry, 47,* 1233–1251.

Marsh, R., Steinglass, J.E., Gerber, A.J., O'Leary, K.G., Wang, Z., Murphy, D., et al. (2009). Deficient activity in the neural systems that mediate self-regulatory control in bulimia nervosa. *Archives of General Psychiatry, 66,* 51–63.

Martin, B., & Hoffman, J.A. (1990). Conduct disorders. In M. Lewis & S.M. Miller (Eds.), *Handbook of developmental psychopathology.* New York: Plenum Press.

Mash, E., & Terdal, L. (1997). Assessment of child and family disturbance: A behavioral-systems approach. In E. Mash & L. Terdal (Eds.), *Assessment of childhood disorders* (3rd ed., pp. 3–70). New York: Guilford Press.

Mash, E.J. (2006). Treatment of child and family disturbance: A cognitive-behavioral systems perspective. In E.J. Mash & R.A. Barkley (Eds.), *Treatment of childhood disorders* (3rd ed.). New York: Guilford Press.

Mash, E.J., Terdal, L.G., & Anderson, K. (1973). The response-class matrix: A procedure for recording parent–child interactions. *Journal of Consulting and Clinical Psychology, 40,* 163–164.

Massetti, G.M., Lahey, B.B., Pelham, W.E., Loney, J., Ehrhardt, A., Lee, S.S., et al. (2008). Academic achievement over 8 years among children who met modified criteria for attention-deficit/hyperactivity disorder at 4–6 years of age. *Journal of Abnormal Child Psychology, 36,* 399–410.

Mastenbrook, J. (1978). Future directions in adaptive behavior assessment: Environmental adaptation measures. In A.T. Fisher (Chair), *Impact of adaptive behavior: ABIC and the environmental adaptation measure.* Symposium conducted at the meeting of the American Psychological Association, Toronto.

Masters, J., Burish, T., Hollon, S.D., & Rimm, D. (1987). *Behavior therapy: Techniques and empirical findings.* San Diego, CA: Harcourt Brace Jovanovich.

Matson, J., & Barrett, R. (Eds.) (1982). *Psychopathology in the mentally retarded.* New York: Grune & Stratton.

Matson, J.L., Terlonge, C., & Minshawi, N.F. (2008). Children with intellectual disabilities. In R.J. Morris & T.R. Kratochwill (Eds.), *The practice of child therapy* (4th ed., pp. 337–361). Mahwah, NJ: Lawrence Erlbaum Associates, Inc.

Maughan, B., & Rutter, M. (1998). Continuities and discontinuities in antisocial behavior from childhood to adult life. In T. Ollendick & R. Prinz (Eds.), *Advances in clinical child psychology* (Vol. 20, pp. 1–47). New York: Plenum Press.

Maughan B., & Rutter, M. (2001). Antisocial children grown up. In J. Hill & B. Maughan (Eds.), *Conduct disorders in childhood and adolescence* (pp. 507–552). New York: Cambridge University Press.

Mayron, L.M., Ott, J.N., Nations, R., & Mayron, E.L. (1974). Light, radiation, and academic behavior: Initial studies on the effects of full-spectrum lighting and radiation shielding on behavior and academic performance of school children. *Academic Therapy, 10,* 33–47.

Mazur, E., Wolchik, S.A., & Sandler, I. (1992). Negative cognitive errors and positive illusions for negative divorce events: Predictors of children's psychological adjustment. *Journal of Abnormal Child Psychology, 20,* 523–542.

Mazzocco, M., Kates, W., Baumgardner, T., Freund, L., & Reiss, A. (1997). Autistic behaviors among girls with fragile X syndrome. *Journal of Autism and Developmental Disabilities, 27,* 415–435.

McAdoo, W.G., & DeMeyer, M.K. (1978). Personality characteristics of parents. In M. Rutter & E. Schopler (Eds.), *Autism: A reappraisal of concepts and treatment.* New York: Plenum Press.

McDermott, S., Durkin, M.S., Schupf, N., & Stein, Z.A. (2007). Epidemiology and etiology of mental retardation. In J.W. Jacobson, J.A. Mulick, & J. Rojahn (Eds.), *Handbook of intellectual and developmental disabilities* (pp. 3–40). New York: Springer.

McFarlane, J.W., Allen, L., & Honzik, M.P. (1954). *A developmental study of the behavior problems of normal children between 21 months and 14 years.* Berkeley, CA: University of California Press.

McGee, R., Silva, P.A., & Williams, S. (1984). Behavior problems in a population of seven-year-old children: Prevalence, stability, and types of disorder—a research report. *Journal of Child Psychology and Psychiatry, 25,* 251–259.

McLaren, J., & Bryson, S.E. (1987). Review of recent epidemiological studies of mental retardation: Prevalence, associated disorders, and etiology. *American Journal of Mental Retardation, 92,* 243–254.

McLennan, J.M., Lord, C., & Schopler, E. (1993). Sex differences in higher functioning people with autism. *Journal of Autism and Developmental Disorders, 23,* 217–228.

McLeod, B.D., Wood, J.J., & Weisz, J.R. (2007). Examining the association between parenting and childhood anxiety: A meta-analysis. *Clinical Psychology Review, 27,* 155–172.

McMahon, R.C. (1980). Genetic etiology in the hyperactive child syndrome: A critical review. *American Journal of Orthopsychiatry, 50,* 145–150.

McMahon, R.J., Forehand, R.L., & Foster, S.L. (2005). *Helping the noncompliant child: Family-based treatment for oppositional behavior* (2nd ed.). New York: Guilford Press.

McMahon, R.J., & Frick, P.J. (2007). Conduct and oppositional disorders. In E.J. Mash and R.A. Barkley (Eds.), *Assessment of childhood disorders* 4th ed., pp. 132–183). New York: Guilford Press.

Meehl, P. (1962). Schizotaxia, schizotypy, schizophrenia. *American Psychologist, 17,* 827–838.

Meichenbaum, D. (1977). *Cognitive behavior modification: An integrative approach.* New York: Plenum Press.

Meichenbaum, D. (1985). *Stress inoculation training.* New York: Pergamon Press.

Meichenbaum, D. (1993). Changing conceptions of cognitive behavior modification: Retrospect and prospect. *Journal of Consulting and Clinical Psychology, 61,* 202–205.

Mendlowicz, M.V., & Stein, M.B. (2000). Quality of life in individuals with anxiety disorders. *American Journal of Psychiatry, 157,* 669–682.

Mesibov, G.B. (1997). Preschool issues in autism: Introduction. *Journal of Autism and Developmental Disorders, 27,* 637–640.

Mesibov, G.B., & Shea, V. (1996). Full inclusion and students with autism. *Journal of Autism and Developmental Disorders, 26,* 337–346.

Mikkelsen, E. (2001). Enuresis and encopresis: Ten years of progress. *Journal of the American Academy of Child and Adolescent Psychiatry, 40,* 1146–1158.

Miletic, M.P. (2002). The introduction of a feminine psychology to psychoanalysis: Karen Horney's legacy. *Contemporary Psychoanalysis, 38,* 287–299.

Milich, R., Loney, J., & Landau, S. (1982).

The independent dimensions of hyperactivity and aggression: A validation with playroom observation data. *Journal of Abnormal Psychology, 91,* 183–198.

Milich, R., Loney, J., & Roberts, M. (1986). Playroom observations of activity level and sustained attention: Two-year stability. *Journal of Consulting and Clinical Psychology, 54,* 272–274.

Miller, L.C., Barrett, C.L., & Hampe, E. (1974). Phobias of childhood in a prescientific era. In S. David (Ed.), *Child personality and psychopathology* (pp. 89–134). New York: Wiley.

Mink, J.W. (2006). Neurobiology of basal ganglia and Tourette syndrome: Basal ganglia circuits and thalamocortical outputs. *Advances in Neurology, 99,* 89–98.

Minshew, N.J. (1996). Brief report: Brain mechanisms in autism—functional and structural abnormalities. *Journal of Autism and Developmental Disorders, 26,* 205–209.

Minuchin, S., Roseman, B.L., & Baker, L. (1978). *Psychosomatic families: Anorexia nervosa in context.* Cambridge, MA: Harvard University Press.

Mitchell, S.A. (1988). *Relational concepts in psychoanalysis.* Cambridge, MA: Harvard University Press.

Moffitt, T.E. (2006). Life-course-persistent versus adolescence-limited antisocial behavior. In D. Cicchetti & D.J. Cohen (Eds.), *Developmental psychopathology, Vol 3: Risk, disorder, and adaptation* (2nd ed., pp. 570–598). Hoboken, NJ: Wiley.

Molina, B.S.G., Hinshaw, S.P., Swanson, J.M., Arnold, L.E., Vitiello, B., Jensen, P.S., et al. (2009). MTA at 8 years: Prospective follow-up of children treated for combined-type ADHD in a multisite study. *Journal of the American Academy of Child and Adolescent Psychiatry, 48,* 484–500.

Moore, V., & Goodson, S. (2003). How well does early diagnosis of autism stand the test of time? Follow-up study of children assessed for autism at age 2 and development of an early diagnostic service. *Autism, 7,* 47–63.

Moreno, C., Laje, G., Blanco, C., Jiang, H., Scmidt, A.B., & Olfson, M. (2007). National trends in the outpatient diagnosis and treatment of bipolar disorder in youth. *Archives of General Psychiatry, 64,* 1032–1039.

Morgan, V.A., Leonard, H., Bourke, J., & Jablensky, A. (2008). Intellectual disability co-occurring with schizophrenia and other psychiatric illness: Population-based study. *British Journal of Psychiatry, 193,* 364–372.

Morris, R.D. (1988). Classification of learning disabilities: Old problems and new approaches. *Journal of Consulting and Clinical Psychology, 56,* 789–794.

Mortimer, H. (1995). Welcoming young children with special needs into mainstream education. *Support for Learning, 10,* 87–99.

MTA Cooperative Group (1999). A 14-month randomized clinical trial of treatment strategies for attention-deficit/hyperactivity disorder. *Archives of General Psychiatry, 56,* 1073–1086.

MTA Cooperative Group (2004a). National Institute of Mental Health Multimodal Treatment Study of ADHD follow-up: 24 month outcomes of treatment strategies for attention-deficit/hyperactivity disorder. *Pediatrics, 113,* 754–761.

MTA Cooperative Group (2004b). National Institute of Mental Health Multimodal Treatment Study of ADHD follow-up: Changes in effectiveness and growth after the end of treatment. *Pediatrics, 113,* 762–769.

Mudford, O.C. (1995). An intrusive and restrictive alternative to contingent shock. *Behavioral Interventions, 10,* 87–99.

Mufson, L., Moreau, D., Weissman, M.M., & Klerman, G.L. (1993). *Interpersonal* psychotherapy for depressed adolescents. New York: Guilford Press.

Mufson, L., Moreau, D., Weissman, M.M., Wickramaratne, P., Martin, J., & Samoilov, A. (1994). The modification of interpersonal psychotherapy with depressed adolescents (IPT-A): Phase I and II studies. *Journal of the American Academy of Child and Adolescent Psychiatry, 33*, 695–705.

Mufson, L., Weissman, M.M., Moreau, D., & Garfinkel, R. (1999). The efficacy of interpersonal psychotherapy for depressed adolescents. *Archives of General Psychiatry, 56*, 573–579.

Muris, P., & Field, A.P. (2008). Distorted cognition and pathological anxiety in children and adolescents. *Cognition and Emotion, 22*, 395–421.

Muris, P., Meesters, C., Merckelbach, H., Sermon, A., & Zwakhalen, S. (1998). Worry in normal children. *Journal of the American Academy of Child and Adolescent Psychiatry, 37*, 703–710.

Muris, P., Merckelbach, H., & Luijten, M. (2002a). The connection between cognitive development and specific fears and worries in normal children and children with below-average intellectual abilities: A preliminary study. *Behaviour Research and Therapy, 40*, 37–56.

Muris, P., Merckelbach, H., Meesters, C., & van den Brand, K. (2002b). Cognitive development and worry in normal children. *Cognitive Therapy and Research, 26*, 775–785.

Murray-Close, D., Ostrov, J.M., & Crick, N.R. (2007). A short-term longitudinal study of growth of relational aggression during middle childhood: Associations with gender, friendship intimacy, and internalizing problems. *Development and Psychopathology, 19*, 187–203.

Myles, B.S., Simpson, R.L., & Johnson, S. (1995). Students with higher functioning autistic disorder: Do we know who they are? *Focus on Autistic Behavior, 9*, 1–12.

Myrbakk, E., & von Tetzchner, S. (2008). Psychiatric disorders and behavior problems in people with intellectual disability. *Research in Developmental Disabilities, 29*, 316–332.

Neal, A.M., & Knisley, H. (1995). What are African American children afraid of? II. A twelve-month follow-up. *Journal of Anxiety Disorders, 9*, 151–161.

Neal, A.M., Lilly, R.S., & Zakis, S. (1993). What are African American children afraid of: A preliminary study. *Journal of Anxiety Disorders, 7*, 129–139.

Nee, L.E., Caine, E.D., & Polinsky, R.J. (1980). Gilles de la Tourette syndrome: Clinical and family study in 50 cases. *Annals of Neurology, 7*, 41–49.

Neisser, U., Boodoo, G., Bouchard, T.J., Boykin, A.W., Brody, N., Ceci, S.J., et al. (1996). Intelligence: Knowns and unknowns. *American Psychologist, 51*, 77–101.

Nelson, C.A., & Bloom, F.E. (1997). Child development and neuroscience. *Child Development, 68*, 970–987.

Nelson, W.M., & Finch, A.J. (1996). *"Keeping your cool": The anger management workbook.* Ardmore, PA: Workbook Publishing.

Newsom, C. (1998). Autistic disorder. In E. Mash & R. Barkley (Eds.), *Treatment of childhood disorders* (2nd ed., pp. 416–467). New York: Guilford Press.

Newsom, C., & Hovanitz, C. (1997). Autistic disorder. In E. Mash & L. Terdal (Eds.), *Assessment of childhood disorders* (3rd ed.). New York: Guilford Press.

Nicholls, D., & Bryant-Waugh, R. (2008). Eating disorders of infancy and childhood: Definition, symptomatology, epidemiology and comorbidity. *Child and Adolescent Psychiatric Clinics of North America, 18*, 17–30.

Nichols, M.P., & Schwartz, R.C. (2007).

Family therapy: Concepts and Methods (8th ed.). Needham Heights, MA: Allyn & Bacon.

Nickels, K.C., Katusic, S.K., Colligan, R.C., Weaver, A.L., Voigt, R.G., & Barbaresi, W.J. (2008). Stimulant medication treatment of target behaviors in children with autism: A population-based study. *Journal of Developmental and Behavioral Pediatrics, 29*, 75–81.

Nigg, J.T. (2001). Is ADHD a disinhibitory disorder? *Psychological Bulletin, 127*, 571–598.

Nijmeijer, J.S., Minderaa, R.B., Buitelaar, J.K., Mulligan, A., Hartman, C.A., & Hoekstra, P.J. (2008). Attention-deficit/hyperactivity disorder and social dysfunction. *Clinical Psychology Review, 28*, 692–708.

Nock, M.J. (2009b). Suicidal behavior among adolescents: Correlates, confounds, and (the search for) causal mechanisms. *Journal of the American Academy of Child and Adolescent Psychiatry, 48*, 237–239.

Nock, M.K. (2009a). Why do people hurt themselves: New insights into the nature and functions of self-injury. *Current Directions in Psychological Science, 18*, 78–83.

Nock, M.K., Borges, G., Bromet, E.J., Cha, C.B., Kessler, R.C., & Lee, S. (2008). Suicide and suicidal behavior. *Epidemiologic Reviews, 30*, 133–154.

Nock, M.K., Kazdin, A.E., Hiripi, E., & Kessler, R.C. (2006). Prevalence, subtypes, and correlates of DSM-IV conduct disorder in the National Comorbidity Survey Replication. *Psychological Medicine, 36*, 699–710.

Nock, M.K., Kazdin, A.E., Hiripi, E., & Kessler, R.C. (2007). Lifetime prevalence, correlates, and persistence of oppositional defiant disorder: Results from the National Comorbidity Survey Replication. *Journal of Child Psychology and Psychiatry, 48*, 703–713.

Nomura, Y., Wickramaratne, P.J., Warner, V., Mufson, L., & Weissman, M.M. (2002). Family discord, parental depression, and psychopathology in offspring: Ten-year follow-up. *Journal of the American Academy of Child and Adolescent Psychiatry, 41*, 402–409.

Obel, C., Henriksen, T.B., Dalsgaard, S., Linnet, K.M., Skajaa, E. Thomsen, P.H., et al. (2004). Does children's watching of television cause attention problems? Retesting the hypothesis in a Danish cohort. *Pediatrics, 114*, 1372–1373.

O'Connor, N., & Hermelin, B. (1988). Annotation: Low intelligence and special abilities. *Journal of Child Psychology and Psychiatry, 29*, 391–396.

Offord, D.R., Boyle, M.C., & Racine, Y. (1991). The epidemiology of antisocial behavior in childhood and adolescence. In D. Pepler & K.H. Rubin (Eds.), *The development and treatment of childhood aggression*. Hillsdale, NJ: Lawrence Erlbaum Associates, Inc.

Ogren, M.P., & Lombroso, P.J. (2003). Epigenetics: Behavioral influences on gene function, Part 1. Maternal behavior permanently affects adult behavior in offspring. *Journal of the American Academy of Child and Adolescent Psychiatry, 47*, 240–244.

O'Leary, C.M. (2004). Fetal alcohol syndrome: Diagnosis, epidemiology, and developmental outcomes. *Journal of Paediatric Child Health, 40*, 2–7.

O'Leary, K.D. (1980). Pills or skills for hyperactive children. *Journal of Applied Behavior Analysis, 13*, 191–204.

O'Leary, K.D., Pelham, W.E., Rosenbaum, A., & Price, G.H. (1976). Behavioral treatment of hyperkinetic children: An experimental evaluation of its usefulness. *Clinical Pediatrics, 15*, 510–515.

O'Leary, K.D., Rosenbaum, A., & Hughes, P.C. (1978). Fluorescent lighting: A purported source of hyperactive behavior. *Journal of Abnormal Child Psychology, 6*, 285–289.

O'Leary, K.D., & Wilson, G.T. (1987). *Behavior therapy: Application and outcome* (2nd ed.). Englewood Cliffs, NJ: Prentice-Hall.

O'Leary, V.B., Parle-McDermott, A., Molloy, A.M., Kirke, P.N., Johnson, Z., Conley, M., et al. (2002). MTRR and MTHFR polymorphism: Link to Down syndrome? *American Journal of Medical Genetics, 107*, 151–155.

Olfson, M., Gameroff, M.J., Marcus, S.C., & Jensen, P.S. (2003a). National trends in the treatment of attention deficit hyperactivity disorder. *American Journal of Psychiatry, 160*, 1071–1077.

Olfson, M., Shaffer, D., Marcus, S.C., & Greenberg, T. (2003b). Relationship between antidepressant medication treatment and suicide in adolescents. *Archives of General Psychiatry, 60*, 978–982.

Olivardia, R., & Pope, H.G. (1995). Eating disorders in college men. *American Journal of Psychiatry, 152*, 1279–1285.

Ollendick, T.H., & Davis, T.E. (2006). Empirically supported treatments for children and adolescents: Where to from here? *Clinical Psychology: Science and Practice, 11*, 289–294.

Ollendick, T.H., & King, N. (1991). Origins of childhood fears. *Behavior Research and Therapy, 29*, 117–123.

Ollendick, T.H., King, N., & Chorpita, B.F. (2006). Empirically supported treatments for children and adolescents. In P.C. Kendall (Ed.), *Child and adolescent therapy: Cognitive-behavioral procedures* (3rd ed., pp. 492–520). New York: Guilford Press.

Ollendick, T.H., Ost, L.G., Reuterskiold, L., Costa, N., Cederlund, R., Sirbu, C., et al. (2009). One-session treatment of specific phobias in youth: A randomized clinical trial in the United States and Sweeden. *Journal of Consulting and Clinical Psychology, 77*, 504–516.

Owens, E. B., Hinshaw, S. P., Lee, S. S., & Lahey, B. B. (2009). Few girls with childhood attention-deficit/hyperactivity disorder show positive adjustment during adolescence. *Journal of Clinical Child and Adolescent Psychology, 38*, 1–12.

Ozmert, E., Toyran, M., & Yurdakok, K. (2002). Behavioral correlates of television viewing in primary school children evaluated by the child behavior checklist. *Archives of Pediatrics and Adolescent Medicine, 156*, 910–914.

Pappert, E.J., Goetz, C.G., Louis, E.D., Blasucci, L., & Leurgans, S. (2003). Objective assessments of longitudinal outcome in Gilles de la Tourette's syndrome. *Neurology, 61*, 936–940.

Parikh, M.S., Kolevzon, A., & Hollander, E. (2008). Psychopharmacology of aggression in children and adolescents with autism: A critical review of efficacy and tolerability. *Journal of Child and Adolescent Psychopharmacology, 18*, 157–178.

Patterson, G.R. (1974). Interventions for boys with conduct problems: Multiple settings, treatments, and criteria. *Journal of Consulting and Clinical Psychology, 42*, 471–481.

Patterson, G.R., & Bank, L. (1989). Some amplifying mechanisms for pathologic processes in families. In M. Gunnar & E. Thelen (Eds.), *Minnesota symposium on child psychology: Systems and development* (pp. 167–209). Hillsdale, NJ: Lawrence Erlbaum Associates Inc.

Patterson, G.R., Chamberlain, P., & Reid, J.B. (1982). A comparative evaluation of a parent-training program. *Behavior Therapy, 13*, 638–650.

Pauls, D.L. (2003). An update on the genetics of Gilles de la Tourette syndrome. *Journal of Pyschosomatic Research, 55*, 7–12.

Pauls, D.L, Raymond, C.L., Stevenson, J.F., & Leckman, J.F. (1991). A family study of Gilles de la Tourette. *American Journal of Human Genetics, 48,* 154–163.

Pavlov, I.P. (1928). *Lectures on conditioned reflexes.* New York: Liveright.

Paykel, E. (Ed.) (1992). *Handbook of affective disorders.* New York: Guilford Press.

Pediatric OCD Treatment Study (POTS) Team (2004). Cognitive-behavior therapy, sertraline, and their combination for children and adolescents with obsessive-compulsive disorder: The Pediatric OCD Treatment Study (POTS) randomized controlled trial. *Journal of the American Medical Association, 292,* 1969–1976.

Pelham, W., Fabiano, G.A., Gnagy, E.M., Greiner, A.R., & Hoza, B. (2005). The role of summer treatment programs in the context of comprehensive treatment for attention-deficit/hyperactivity disorder. In E. Hibbs & P. Jensen (Eds.), *Psychosocial treatments for child and adolescent disorders: Empirically based strategies for clinical practice* (2nd ed., pp. 377–409). Washington, DC: American Psychological Association.

Pelham, W., & Sams, S. (1992). Behavior modification. *Child and Adolescent Psychiatric Clinics of North America, 1*(2), 505–518.

Pelham, W.E., & Fabiano, G.A. (2008). Evidence-based psychosocial treatments for attention-deficit/ hyperactivity disorder. *Journal of Clinical Child and Adolescent Psychology, 37,* 184–214.

Pennington, B.F. (1999). Dyslexia as a neurodevelopmental disorder. In H. Tager-Flusberg (Ed.), *Neurodevelopmetnal disorders* (pp. 307–330). Cambridge, MA: MIT Press.

Pennington, B.F., McGrath, L.M., Rosenberg, J., Barnard, H., Smith, S.D., Willcutt, E.G., et al. (2009). Gene x environment interactions in reading disability and attention-deficit/ hyperactivity disorder. *Developmental Psychology, 45,* 77–89.

Peris, T.S., & Emery, R.E. (2004). A prospective study of the consequences of marital disruption for adolescents: Predisruption family dynamics and postdisruption adolescent adjustment. *Journal of Clinical Child and Adolescent Psychology, 33,* 694–704.

Peterson, B.S. (2003). Conceptual, methodological, and statistical challenges in brain imaging studies of developmentally based psychopathologies. *Development and Psychopathololgy, 15,* 811–832.

Peterson, B.S., Thomas, P., Kane, M.J., Scahill, H., Zhang, R., Bronen, R.A., et al. (2003). Basal ganglia volumes in patients with Gilles de la Tourette syndrome. *Archives of General Psychiatry, 60,* 415–424.

Phillips, D., Prince, S., & Schiebelhut, L. (2004). Elementary school children's responses 3 months after the September 11 terrorist attacks: A study in Washington, DC. *American Journal of Orthopsychiatry, 74,* 509–528.

Piacentini, J.C., March, J.S., & Franklin, M.E. (2006). Cognitive-behavioral therapy for youth with obsessive-compulsive disorder. In P.C. Kendall (Ed.), *Child and adolescent therapy: Cognitive-behavioral procedures.* New York: Guilford Press.

Piazza, C., & Fisher, W. (1991). A faded bedtime with response cost protocol for treatment of multiple sleep problems in children. *Journal of Applied Behavior Analysis, 24,* 129–140.

Pike, K.M., Devlin, M.J., & Loeb, K.L. (2004). Cognitive-behavioral therapy in the treatment of anorexia nervosa, bulimia nervosa, and binge eating disorder. In K.J. Thompson (Ed.), *Handbook of eating disorders and obesity* (pp. 130–162). Hoboken, NJ: Wiley.

Plomin, R. (1989). Environment and genes: Determinants of behavior. *American Psychologist, 42,* 105–111.

Plomin, R., & DeFries, J. (1980). Genetics and intelligence: Recent data. *Intelligence, 4*, 15–24.

Polanczyk, G., de Limas, M.S., Horta, B.L., Biederman, J., & Rohde, L.A. (2007). The worldwide prevalence of ADHD: A systematic review and metaregression analysis. *American Journal of Psychiatry, 164*, 942–948.

Polivy, J., & Herman, C. (1985). Dieting and binging. *American Psychologist, 40*, 193–210.

Polivy, J., & Herman, C. (1987). Diagnosis and treatment of normal eating. *Journal of Consulting and Clinical Psychology, 55*, 635–644.

Pollock, V., Schneider, L., Gabrielli, W., & Goodwin, D. (1986). Sex of parent and offspring in the transmission of alcoholism: A meta-analysis. *Journal of Nervous and Mental Disease, 175*, 668–673.

Pope, H.G., Jr., Hudson, J.I., & Yurgelun-Tudd, D. (1984). Anorexia nervosa and bulimia among 300 suburban women shoppers. *American Journal of Psychiatry, 141*, 292–294.

Power, M., & Brewin, C. (1991). From Freud to cognitive science: A contemporary account of the unconscious. *British Journal of Clinical Psychology, 30*, 289–310.

Powers, P.S., & Bruty, H. (2009). Pharmacotherapy for eating disorders and obesity. *Child and Adolescent Psychiatric Clinics of North America, 18*, 175–187.

Pretlow, R.A. (1999). Treatment of nocturnal enuresis with an ultrasound bladder volume controlled alarm device. *Journal of Urology, 162*, 1224–1228.

Prior, M. (1984). Developing concepts of childhood autism: The influence of experimental cognitive research. *Journal of Consulting and Clinical Psychology, 52*, 4–16.

Puliafico, A.C., Comer, J.S., & Kendall, P.C. (2007). Social phobia in youth: The diagnostic utility of feared social situations. *Psychological Assessment, 19*, 152–158.

Quay, H.C. (1986). Conduct disorders. In H.C. Quay & J.S. Wherry (Eds.), *Psychopathological disorders of childhood*. New York: Wiley.

Quintana, H., Birmaher, B., Stedge, D., Lennon, S., Freed, J., Bridge, J., et al. (1995). Use of methylphenidate in the treatment of children with autistic disorder. *Journal of Autism and Developmental Disorders, 25*, 283–294.

Rachman, S. (1998). *Anxiety*. Hove, UK: Psychology Press.

Raghavan, R., & Small, N. (2004). Cultural diversity and intellectual disability. *Current Opinion in Psychiatry, 17*, 371–375.

Ramsay, S. (2001). UK starts campaign to reassure parents about MMR-vaccine safety. *Lancet, 357*, 290.

Rao, P.A., Beidel, D.C., Turner, S.M., Ammerman, R.T., Crosby, L.E., & Sallee, F.R. (2007). Social anxiety disorder in childhood and adolescence: Descriptive psychopathology. *Behaviour Research and Therapy, 45*, 1181–1191.

Rapaport, M.H., Clary, C., Fayyad, R., & Endicott, J. (2005). Quality-of-life impairment in depressive and anxiety disorders. *American Journal of Psychiatry, 162*, 1171–1178.

Rapee, R. (1991). Generalized anxiety disorder: A review of clinical features and theoretical concepts. *Clinical Psychology Review, 11*, 419–440.

Rapee, R. (1997). The potential role of childrearing practices in the development of anxiety and depression. *Clinical Psychology Review, 17*, 47–67.

Rapee, R., Barrett, P., Dadds, M., & Evans, L. (1994). Reliability of the DSM-III-R childhood anxiety disorders using structured interviews: Interrater and parent–child agreement. *Journal of the*

American Academy of Child and Adolescent Psychiatry, 33, 984–992.

Rapoport, J., Chavez, A., Greenstein, D., Addington, A., & Gogtay, N. (2009). Autism spectrum disorders and childhood-onset schizophrenia: Clinical and biological contributions to a relation revisited. Journal of the American Academy of Child and Adolescent Psychiatry, 48, 10–18.

Rapoport, J.L., Buchsbaum, M.S., Zahn, T.P., Weingartner, H., Ludlow, C., & Mikkelsen, E.J. (1978). Dextroamphetamine: Cognitive and behavioral effect in normal prepubertal boys. Science, 199, 560–563.

Reinecke, M.A., Ryan, N., & DuBois, D. (1998). Cognitive-behavioral therapy of depression and depressive symptoms during adolescence: A review and meta-analysis. Journal of the American Academy of Child and Adolescent Psychiatry, 37, 26–34.

Reiss, D., Hetherington, E.M., Plomin, R., Howe, G.W., Simmens, S.J., Henderson, S.H., et al. (1995). Genetic questions for environmental studies. Archives of General Psychiatry, 52, 925–936.

Repp, A.C., & Deitz, D.E.D. (1983). Mental retardation. In T. Ollendick & M. Hersen (Eds.), Handbook of child psychopathology. New York: Plenum Press.

Rescorla, L., Achenbach, T., Ivanova, M.Y., Dumenci, L., Almqvist, F., Bilenberg, N., et al. (2007). Behavioral and emotional problems reported by parents of children ages 6 to 16 in 31 societies. Journal of Emotional and Behavioral Disorders, 15, 130–142.

Research Units on Pediatric Psychopharmacology Anxiety Study Group (2001). Fluoxetine for the treatment of anxiety disorders in children and adolescents. New England Journal of Medicine, 344, 1279–1285.

Research Units on Pediatric Psychopharmacology Anxiety Study Group (2002). The Pediatric Anxiety Rating Scale (PARS): Development and psychometric properties. Journal of the American Academy of Child and Adolescent Psychiatry, 41, 1061–1069.

Reynolds, C.R., & Paget, K.D. (1982, March). National normative and reliability data for Revised Children's Manifest Anxiety Scale. Paper presented at the meeting of the National Association of School Psychologists, Toronto, Ontario, Canada.

Reynolds, C.R., & Richmond, B.O. (1985). Revised children's manifest anxiety scale (RCMAS): Manual (pp. 6–9). Los Angeles: Western Psychological Services.

Reynolds, W.M. (1992). The study of internalizing disorders in children and adolescents. In W.M. Reynolds (Ed.), Internalizing disorders in children and adolescents. New York: Wiley.

Rhee, S.H., & Waldman, I.D. (2002). Genetic and environmental influences on antisocial behavior: A meta-analysis of twin and adoption studies. Psychological Bulletin, 128, 490–529.

Rhule, D.M., McMahon, R.J., & Spieker, S.J. (2004). Relation of adolescent mothers' history of antisocial behavior to child conduct problems and social competence. Journal of Clinical Child and Adolescent Psychology, 33, 524–535.

Richardson, S.A., Katz, M., Koller, H., McLaren, L., & Rubinstein, B. (1979). Some characteristics of a population of mentally retarded young adults in a British city: A basis for estimating service needs. Journal of Mental Deficiency Research, 23, 275–283.

Rimland, B. (1974). Infantile autism: Status and research. In A. Davids (Ed.), Child personality and psychopathology: Current topics (pp. 137–168). New York: Wiley.

Riskind, J.H., & Alloy, L.B. (2006). Cognitive vulnerability to emotional disorders. Mahwah, NJ: Lawrence Erlbaum Associates, Inc.

Roberts, R.E., Lewinsohn, P.M., & Seeley, J.R. (1991). Screening for adolescent depression: A comparison of depression scales. *Journal of the American Academy of Child and Adolescent Psychiatry*, 30, 58–66.

Robins, L.N. (1966). *Deviant children grown up*. Baltimore: Williams & Wilkins.

Robins, L.N. (1978). Sturdy childhood predictors of antisocial behavior: Replications from longitudinal studies. *Psychological Medicine*, 8, 611–622.

Robins, L.N., & Price, R.K. (1991). Adult disorders predicted by childhood conduct problems. Results from the NIMH Epidemiologic Catchment Area project. *Psychiatry*, 54, 116–132.

Roizen, N.J., & Patterson, D. (2003). Down's syndrome. *Lancet*, 361, 1281–1289.

Rojas, D.C., Bawn, S.D., Benkers, T.L., Reite, M.L., & Rogers, S.J. (2002). Smaller left hemisphere planum temporale in adults with autistic disorder. *Neuroscience Letters*, 328, 237–240.

Romanczyk, R., & Kistner, J. (1982). Psychosis and mental retardation: Issues of coexistence. In J. Matson & R. Barrett (Eds.), *Psychopathology in the mentally retarded* (pp. 147–194). New York: Grune & Stratton.

Rosenzweig, M.R., Bennett, E.L., & Diamond, M.C. (1972). Brain changes in response to experience. *Scientific American*, 226, 22–29.

Rosler, M., Fischer, R., Ammer, R., Ose, C., & Retz, W. (2008). A randomised, placebo-controlled, 24-week, study of low-dose extended-release methylphenidate in adults with attention-deficit/hyperactivity disorder. *European Archives of Psychiatry and Clinical Neuroscience*, 259, 120–129.

Rothbaum, F., Rosen, K., Ujie, T., & Uchida, N. (2002). Family systems theory, attachment theory, and culture. *Family Process*, 41, 328–350.

Rubenstein, J.L.R., Lotspeich, L., & Ciaranello, R.D. (1990). The neurobiology of developmental disorders. In B. Lahey & A.E. Kazdin (Eds.), *Advances in clinical child psychology* (Vol. 13, pp. 1–52). New York: Plenum Press.

RUPP Autism Network (2002). Risperidone in children with autism and serious behavioral problems. *New England Journal of Medicine*, 347, 314–321.

Ruscio, A.M., Brown, T.A., Chiu, W.T., Sareen, J., Stein, M.B., & Kessler, R.C. (2008). Social fears and social phobia in the USA: Results from the National Comorbidity Survey Replication. *Psychological Medicine*, 38, 15–28.

Russo, D.C., Carr, E.G., & Lovaas, O.I. (1980). Self-injury in pediatric populations. In J. Ferguson & C.B. Taylor (Eds.), *Comprehensive handbook of behavioral medicine*. New York: Spectrum.

Rutter, M. (1977). Brain damage syndromes in childhood: Concepts and findings. *Journal of Child Psychology and Psychiatry*, 139, 21–33.

Rutter, M. (1978). Language disorder and infantile autism. In M. Rutter & E. Schopler (Eds.), *Autism: A reappraisal of concepts and treatment*. New York: Plenum Press.

Rutter, M. (2005). Incidence of autism spectrum disorders: Changes over time and their meaning. *Acta Paediatrica*, 94, 2–15.

Rutter, M., Bailey, A., Bolton, P., & Le Couteur, A. (1994). Autism and known medical conditions: Myth and substance. *Journal of Child Psychology and Psychiatry*, 35, 311–322.

Rutter, M., & Quinton, D. (1984). Parental psychiatric disorder: Effects on children. *Psychological Medicine*, 14, 853–880.

Rutter, M., & Schopler, E. (1987). Autism and pervasive developmental disorders: Concepts and diagnostic issues. *Journal of Autism and Developmental Disabilities, 17,* 159–186.

Rutter, M., Silberg, J., O'Connor, T., & Simonoff, E. (1999). Genetics and child psychiatry: II. Empirical research findings. *Journal of Child Psychology and Psychiatry, 40,* 19–55.

Rutter, M., Tizard, J., Yule, W., Graham, P., & Whitmore, K. (1976). Research report: Isle of Wight studies, 1964–1974. *Psychological Medicine, 6,* 313–332.

Rynn, M.A., Riddle, M.A., Yeung, P.P., & Kunz, N.R. (2007). Efficacy and safety of extended-release venlafaxine in the treatment of generalized anxiety disorder in children and adolescents: Two placebo-controlled trials. *American Journal of Psychiatry, 164,* 290–300.

Safer, D.J., & Krager, J.M. (1988). A survey of medication treatment for hyperactive/inattentive students. *Journal of the American Medical Association, 260,* 2256–2259.

Safren, S.A., Heimberg, R.G., Lerner, J., Henin, A., Warman, M., & Kendall, P.C. (2000). Differentiating anxious and depressive self-statements: Combined factor structure of the Anxious Self-Statements Questionnaire and the Automatic Thoughts Questionnaire-Revised. *Cognitive Therapy and Research, 24,* 327–344.

Saldana, L., & Henggeler, S.W. (2006). Multisystemic therapy in the treatment of adolescent conduct disorder. In W.M. Nelson, A.J. Finch, & K.J. Hart (Eds.), *Conduct disorders: A practitioner's guide to comparative treatments.* New York: Springer.

Salmon, K., & Bryant, R.A. (2002). Posttraumatic stress disorder in children: The influence of developmental factors. *Clinical Psychology Review, 22,* 163–188.

Salvy, S.J., Mulick, J.A., Butter, E., Bartlett, R.K., & Linscheid, T.R. (2004). Contingent electric shock (SIBIS) and a conditioned punisher eliminate severe head banging in a preschool child. *Behavioral Intervention, 19,* 59–72.

Sanders, A.R., Duan, J., & Gejman, P.V. (2004). Complexities in psychiatric genetics. *International Review of Psychiatry, 16,* 284–293.

Saylor, C.F., Finch, A.J., J.Jr., Baskin, C.H., Furey, W., & Kelly, M.M. (1984a). Construct validity for measures of childhood depression: Application of multitrait-multimethod methodology. *Journal of Consulting and Clinical Psychology, 52,* 977–985.

Saylor, C.F., Finch, A.J., J.Jr., Spirito, A., & Bennett, B. (1984b). The Children's Depression Inventory: A systematic evaluation of psychometric properties. *Journal of Consulting and Clinical Psychology, 52,* 955–967.

Scahill, L., Chappell, P.B., Kim, Y.S., Schultz, R.T., Katsovich, L., Shepherd, E., et al. (2001). A placebo-controlled study of guanficine in the treatment of children with tic disorders and attention deficit hyperactivity disorder. *American Journal of Psychiatry, 158,* 1067–1074.

Scarr, S., & Weinberg, R.A. (1976). The IQ performance of black children adopted by white families. *American Psychologist, 31,* 726–739.

Schachar, R., Tannock, R., Marriott, M., & Logan, G. (1995). Deficient inhibitory control in ADHD. *Journal of Abnormal Child Psychology, 23,* 411–437.

Scheeringa, M.S. (2008). Developmental considerations for diagnosing PTSD and acute stress disorder in preschool and school-age children. *American Journal of Psychiatry, 165,* 1237–1239.

Schmidt, U., Lee, S., Beecham, J., Perkins, S., Treasure, J., Yi, I., et al. (2007). A randomized controlled trial of family therapy and cognitive behavior therapy guided self care for adolescents with bulimia nervosa and related disorders.

American Journal of Psychiatry, 164, 591–598.

Schopler, E., & Hennike, J.M. (1990). Past and present trends in residential treatment. Journal of Autism and Developmental Disorders, 20, 291–298.

Schopler, E., Short, A., & Mesibov, G. (1989). Relation of behavioral treatment to "normal functioning": Comment on Lovaas. Journal of Consulting and Clinical Psychology, 57, 162–164.

Schreibman, L. (1988). Autism. Newbury Park, CA: Sage.

Schreibman, L., & Koegal, R. (1996). Fostering self-management: Parent delivered pivotal response training for children with autistic disorder. In E. Hibbs & P. Jensen (Eds.), Psychosocial treatments for child and adolescent disorders: Empirically based strategies for clinical practice (pp. 525–554). Washington, DC: American Psychological Association.

Schultz, R.T., Grelotti, D.J., Klin, A., Kleinman, J., Van der Gaag, C., Marois, R., et al. (2003). The role of the fusiform gace area in social cognition: Implications for the pathobiology of autism. In U. Frith & E. Hill (Eds.), Autism: Mind and brain (pp. 267–293). New York: Oxford University Press.

Schultz, R.T., & Klin, A. (2002). Genetics of childhood disorders: XLIII Autism, part 2: Neural foundations. Journal of the American Academy of Child and Adolescent Psychiatry, 41, 1259–1262.

Scott, D.W. (1986). Anorexia nervosa: A review of possible genetic factors. International Journal of Eating Disorders, 5, 1–20.

Scott, S. (1994). Mental retardation. In M. Rutter, E. Taylor, & L. Hersov (Eds.), Child and adolescent psychiatry (pp. 616–646). Oxford: Blackwell.

Seguin, J.R., Pihl, R.O., Harden, P.W., Tremblay, R.E., & Boulerice, B. (1995). Cognitive and neuropsychological characteristics of physically aggressive boys. Journal of Abnormal Psychology, 104, 614–624.

Sejnowski, T.J., Koch, C., & Churchland, P.S. (1988). Computational neuroscience. Science, 99, 1299–1306.

Sergeant, J.A., Geurts, H., & Oosterlaan, J. (2002). How specific is a deficit of executive functioning for attention-deficit/hyperactivity disorder? Behavioural Brain Research, 130, 3–28.

Sexton, T.L., Alexander, J.F., & Mease, A.L. (2003). Levels of evidence for the models and mechanisms of therapeutic change in family and couple therapy. In M.J. Lambert (Ed.), Bergin and Garfield's handbook of psychotherapy and behavior change (5th ed., pp. 590–646). New York: Wiley.

Shaffer, D. (1977). Enuresis. In M. Rutter & L. Herzov (Eds.), Child psychiatry: Modern approaches. Philadelphia: Blackwell.

Shaffer, D. (1994). Enuresis. In M. Rutter, E. Taylor, & L. Hersov (Eds.), Child and adolescent psychiatry. Oxford: Blackwell.

Shaffer, D., Fisher, P., Lucas, C.P., Dulcan, M.K., & Schwab-Stone, M.E. (2000). NIMH Diagnostic Interview Schedule for Children Version IV (NIMH DISC-IV): Description, differences from previous versions, and reliability of some common diagnoses. Journal of the American Academy of Child and Adolescent Psychiatry, 39, 28–38.

Shafran, R., Lee, M., Cooper, Z., Palmer, R.L., & Fairburn, C.G. (2007). Attentional bias in eating disorders. International Journal of Eating Disorders, 40, 369–380.

Shafran, R., & Robinson, P. (2004). Thought-shape fusion in eating disorders. British Journal of Clinical Psychology, 43, 399–407.

Shapiro, A.K., Shapiro, E.S., Brunn, R.D., & Sweet, R.D. (1978). Gilles de la Tourette syndrome. New York: Raven Press.

Shaw, P., Exkstrand, K., Sharp, W., Blumenthal, J., Lerch, J.P., Greenstein,

D., et al. (2007). Attention-deficit/
hyperactivity disorder is characterized
by a delay in cortical maturation.
*Proceedings of the National Academy of
Sciences of the United States of America,
104,* 19649–19654.

Shaywitz, B.A., Shaywitz, S.E., Byrne, T.,
Cohen, D.J., & Rothman, S. (1983).
Attention deficit disorder: Quantitative
analysis of CT. *Neurology, 33,*
1500–1503.

Shaywitz, S., Fletcher, J., & Shaywitz, B.
(1994). Issues in the definition and
classification of attention deficit
disorder. *Topics in Language Disorders,
14,* 1–25.

Shepperdson, B. (1995). The control of
sexuality in young people with Down's
syndrome. *Child Care, Health and
Development, 21,* 333–349.

Sheridan, M.A., Hinshaw, S., &
D'Esposito, D. (2007). Efficacy of the
prefrontal cortex during working
memory in attention-deficit/
hyperactivity disorder. *Journal of the
American Academy of Child and
Adolescent Psychiatry, 46,* 1357–1366.

Shirk, S.R., & Russell, R. (1996). *Change
processes in child psychotherapy:
Revitalizing treatment and research.* New
York: Guilford Press.

Shulman, C., Yirmiya, N., & Greenbaum,
C.W. (1995). From categorization to
classification: A comparison among
individuals with autism, mental
retardation, and normal development.
Journal of Abnormal Psychology, 104,
601–609.

Sikstrom, S., & Soderlund, G. (2007).
Stimulus-dependent dopamine release
in attention-deficit/hyperactivity
disorder. *Psychological Review, 114,*
1047–1075.

Silverman, W.K., & Albano, A.M. (1998).
*Anxiety Disorders Interview Schedule for
Children (ADIS-C).* San Antonio, TX:
Psychological Corporation.

Silverman, W.K., & Hinshaw, S.P. (2008).
The second special issue on evidence-
based psychosocial treatments for
children and adolescents: A 10-year
update. *Journal of Clinical Child and
Adolescent Psychology, 37,* 1–7.

Silverman, W.K., & Nelles, W.B. (1988).
The Anxiety Disorders Interview
Schedule for Children. *Journal of the
American Academy of Child and
Adolescent Psychiatry, 27,* 772–778.

Silverman, W.K., & Ollendick, T.H. (2005).
Evidence-based assessment of anxiety
and its disorders in children and
adolescents. *Journal of Clinical Child and
Adolescent Psychology, 34,* 380–411.

Silverman, W.K., Pina, A.A., &
Viswesvaran, C. (2008). Evidence-based
psychosocial treatments for phobic and
anxiety disorders in children and
adolescents. *Journal of Clinical Child and
Adolescent Psychology, 37,* 105–130.

Silverman, W.K., & Rabian, B. (1994).
Specific phobias. In T. Ollendick, N.
King, & W. Yule (Eds.), *International
handbook of phobic and anxiety disorders in
children and adolescents* (pp. 87–109).
New York: Plenum Press.

Silverman, W.K., & Rabian, B. (1995). Test–
retest reliability of DSM-III-R childhood
anxiety disorders and symptoms using
the anxiety disorders interview
schedule for children. *Journal of Anxiety
Disorders, 9,* 139–150.

Simonoff, E., Pickles, A., Charman, T.,
Chandler, S., Loucas, T., & Baird, G.
(2008). Psychiatric disorders in children
with autism spectrum disorders:
Prevalence, comorbidity, and
associated factors in a population-
derived sample. *Journal of the American
Academy of Child and Adolescent
Psychiatry, 47,* 921–929.

Siqueland, L., Kendall, P.C., & Steinberg,
L. (1996). Anxiety in children: Perceived
family environments and observed
family interaction style. *Journal of
Clinical Child Psychology, 25,* 225–237.

Skinner, B.F. (1953). *Science and human behavior*. New York: Macmillan.

Skoog, G., & Skoog, I. (1999). A 40-year follow-up of patients with obsessive-compulsive disorder. *Archives of General Psychiatry, 56*, 121–127.

Slutske, W.S., Heath, A.C., Dinwiddie, S.H., Madden, P.A.F., Bucholz, K.K., Dunne, M.P., et al (1997). Modeling genetic and environmental influences in the etiology of conduct disorder: A study of 2,682 adult twin pairs. *Journal of Abnormal Psychology, 106*, 266–279.

Smith, A., Taylor, E., Rogers, J.W., Newman, S., & Rubia, K. (2002). Evidence for a pure time perception deficit in children with ADHD. *Journal of Child Psychology and Psychiatry, 43*, 529–542.

Smith, B.H., Barkley, R.A., & Shapiro, C.J. (2007). Attention-deficit/hyperactivity disorder. In E. Mash & L. Terdal (Eds.), *Assessment of childhood disorders* (4th ed., pp. 53–131). New York: Guilford Press.

Smith, S.D., Pennington, B.F., Kimberling, W.J., & Ing, P. (1990). Familial dyslexia: Use of genetic linkage data to define subtypes. *Journal of the American Academy of Child and Adolescent Psychiatry, 29*, 204–213.

Smith, T., Groen, A., & Wynn, J.W. (2000). Randomized trial of intensive early intervention for children with pervasive developmental disorder. *American Journal on Mental Retardation, 4*, 269–285.

Smith, T.W., & Allred, K.D. (1986). Rationality revisited: A reassessment of the empirical support for the rational-emotive model. In P.C. Kendall (Ed.), *Advances in cognitive-behavioral research and therapy* (Vol. 5, pp. 63–88). New York: Academic Press.

Smucker, M., Craighead, W.E., Craighead, L., & Green, B.J. (1986). Normative and reliability data for the children's depression inventory. *Journal of Abnormal Child Psychology, 14*, 25–39.

Snider, L.A., & Swedo, S.E. (2000). Pediatric obsessive-compulsive disorder. *Journal of the American Medical Association, 284*, 3104–3106.

Solanto, M.V. (2002). Dopamine dysfunction in AD/HD: Integrating clinical and basic neuroscience research. *Behavioural Brain Research, 130*, 65–71.

Sonuga-Barke, E.J. (1998). Categorical models of childhood disorder: A conceptual and empirical analysis. *Journal of Child Psychology and Psychiatry, 39*, 115–123.

Sonuga-Barke, E.J.S., Daley, D., Thompson, M., Laver-Bradbury, C., & Weeks, A. (2001). Parent-based therapies for preschool attention-deficit/hyperactivity disorder: A randomized, controlled trial with a community sample. *Journal of the American Academy of Child and Adolescent Psychiatry, 40*, 402–408.

Sood, E.D., & Kendall, P.C. (2007). Assessing anxious self-talk in youth: The Negative Affectivity Self-Statement Questionnaire—Anxiety Scale. *Cognitive Therapy and Research, 31*, 603–618.

Southam-Gerow, M.A., Flannery-Schroeder, E.C., & Kendall, P.C. (2003). A psychometric evaluation of the parent report form of the State-Trait Anxiety Inventory for Children-Trait Version. *Journal of Anxiety Disorders, 17*, 427–446.

Southam-Gerow, M.A., & Kendall, P.C. (1997). Parent-focused and cognitive-behavioral treatments of antisocial youth. In D. Stoff, J. Breiling, & J.D. Maser (Eds.), *Handbook of antisocial behavior*. New York: Wiley.

Southam-Gerow, M.A., & Kendall, P.C. (2000). Emotion understanding in youth referred for treatment for anxiety disorders. *Journal of Clinical Child Psychology. 29*, 319–327.

Sowell, E.R., Thompson, P.M., Welcome,

S.E., Henkenius, A.L., Toga, A.W., & Peterson, B.S. (2003). Cortical abnormalities in children and adolescents with attention-deficit hyperactivity disorder. *Lancet, 362,* 1699–1707.

Sparks, B.F., Friedman, S.D., Shaw, D.W., Aylward, E.H., Echelard, D., Artru, A.A., et al. (2002). Brain structural abnormalities in young children with autism spectrum disorders. *Neurology, 59,* 184–192.

Sparrow, S.S., Cicchetti, D.V., & Balla, D.A. (2005). *Vineland Adpative Behavior Scales, Second Edition (Vineland-II).* Minneapolis, MN: NCS Pearson.

Spencer, T., Biederman, J., Wilens, T., Doyle, R., Surman, C., Prince, J., et al. (2005). A large, double-blind, randomized clinical trial of methylphenidate in the treatment of adults with attention-deficit/ hyperactivity disorder. *Biological Psychiatry, 57,* 456–463.

Spencer, T., Biederman, J., Wilens, T., Harding, M., O'Donnell, D., & Griffin, S. (1996). Pharmacotherapy of attention-deficit hyperactivity disorder across the life cycle. *Journal of the American Academy of Child and Adolescent Psychiatry, 35,* 409–432.

Spencer, T., Faraone, S.V., Biederman, J., Lerner, M., Cooper, K., & Zimmerman, B. (2006). Does prolonged stimulant therapy suppress growth in children with ADHD? Analysis of data from 21 months of therapy with once-daily OROS MPH. *Journal of the American Academy of Child and Adolescent Psychiatry, 45,* 527–537.

Spielberger, C., Gorsuch, R., & Lushene, R. (1970). *STAI manual.* Palo Alto, CA: Consulting Psychologists Press.

Sponheim, E., & Skjeldal, O. (1998). Autism and related disorders: Epidemiological findings in a Norwegian study using ICD-10 diagnostic criteria. *Journal of Autism and Developmental Disabilities, 28,* 217–228.

Sroufe, A., & Rutter, M. (1984). The domain of developmental psychopathology. *Child Development, 55,* 17–29.

Stark, K.D. (1990). *The treatment of depression during childhood: A school-based program.* New York: Guilford Press.

Stark, K.D., Hoke, J., Ballatore, M., Valdez, C., Scammaca, N., & Griffin, J. (2005). Treatment of child and adolescent depressive disorders. In E. Hibbs & P. Jensen (Eds.), *Psychosocial treatments for child and adolescent disorders: Empirically based strategies for clinical practice* (2nd ed., pp. 239–265). Washington, DC: American Psychological Association.

Stark, K.D., Reynolds, W.M., & Kaslow, N. (1987). A comparison of the relative efficacy of self-control therapy and behavioral problem-solving therapy for depression in children. *Journal of Abnormal Child Psychology, 15,* 91–113.

State, M.W., Lombroso, P.J., Pauls, D.L., & Leckman, J.F. (2000). The genetics of childhood psychiatric disorders: A decade of progress. *Journal of the American Academy of Child and Adolescent Psychiatry, 39,* 946–962.

Stattin, H., & Magnusson, D. (1998). Onset of official delinquency. *British Journal of Criminology, 35,* 417–449.

Steen, E., & Steen, J. (1989). Controversy concerning parental age effect in Down's syndrome. *Human Genetics, 81,* 300–301.

Steinhausen, H.C. (1994). Anorexia and bulimia nervosa. In M. Rutter, E. Taylor, & I. Hersov (Eds.), *Child and adolescent psychiatry* (pp. 425–440). Oxford, UK: Blackwell Scientific Publications.

Sternberg, R.J. (2007). Intelligence and culture. In S. Kitayama & D. Cohen (Eds.), *Handbook of cultural psychology* (pp. 547–568). New York: Guilford Press.

Sternberg, R.J., & Grigorenko, E. (1999). Genetics of childhood disorders: I. Genetics and intelligence. *Journal of the American Academy of Child and Adolescent Psychiatry, 38,* 486–488.

Stewart, S.E., Rosario, M.C., Baer, L., Carter, A.S., Brown, T.A., Scharf, J.M., et al. (2008). Four-factor structure of obsessive-compulsive disorder symptoms in children, adolescents, and adults. *Journal of the American Academy of Child and Adolescent Psychiatry, 47,* 763–772.

Stice, E., Davis, K., Miller, N.P., & Marti, C.N. (2008). Fasting increases risk for onset of binge eating and bulimic pathology: A 5-year prospective study. *Journal of Abnormal Psychology, 117,* 941–946.

Stokes, A., Bawden, H., Camfield, P., Ackman, J., & Dooley, J. (1991). Peer problems in Tourette's disorder. *Pediatrics, 87,* 936–942.

Strain, P., Kohler, F., & Goldstein, H. (1996). Learning experiences . . . an alternative program: Peer-mediated interventions for young children with autism. In E. Hibbs & P. Jensen (Eds.), *Psychosocial treatments for child and adolescent disorders: Empirically based strategies for clinical practice* (pp. 573–590). Washington, DC: American Psychological Association.

Strauss, C. (1994). Overanxious disorder. In T. Ollendick, N. King, & W. Yule (Eds.), *International handbook of phobic and anxiety disorders in children and adolescents* (pp. 80–97). New York: Plenum Press.

Streissguth, A.P., Barr, H.M., Sampson, P.D., Darby, B.L., & Martin, D. (1989). IQ at age 4 in relation to maternal alcohol use and smoking during pregnancy. *Developmental Psychology, 25,* 3–11.

Strober, M. (1992). Relevance of early age-of-onset in genetic studies of affective disorder. *Journal of the American Academy of Child and Adolescent Psychiatry, 31,* 505–510.

Suematsu, H., Kuboki, T., & Itoh, T. (1985). Statistical studies on the prognosis of anorexia nervosa. *Psychosomatics, 43,* 104–112.

Sugiyama, T., & Abe, T. (1989). The prevalence of autism in Nagoya, Japan: A total population study. *Journal of Autism and Developmental Disorders, 19,* 87–96.

Summers, P., Forehand, R., Armistead, L., & Tannenbaum, L. (1998). The role of family process variables in predicting the long-term consequences for early adult psychosocial adjustment. *Journal of Consulting and Clinical Psychology, 66,* 327–336.

Sussmann, J.E., McIntosh, A.M., Lawrie, S.M., & Johnstone, E.C. (2009). Obstetric complications and mild to moderate intellectual disability. *British Journal of Psychiatry, 194,* 224–228.

Suveg, C., Comer, J.S., Furr, J.M., & Kendall, P.C. (2006). Adapting manualized CBT for a cognitively delayed child with multiple anxiety disorders. *Clinical Case Studies, 5,* 488–510.

Suveg, C., & Zeman, J. (2004). Emotion regulation in children with anxiety disorders. *Journal of Clinical Child and Adolescent Psychology, 33,* 750–759.

Swain, J.E., Scahill, L., Lombroso, P.J., King, R.A., & Leckman, J.F. (2007). Tourette syndrome and tic disorders: A decade of progress. *Journal of the American Academy of Child and Adolescent Psychiatry, 46,* 947–968.

Swanson, J., & Kinsbourne, M. (1980). Artificial color and hyperactive children. In R.M. Knights & D.J. Bakker (Eds.), *Treatment of hyperactive and learning disabled children.* Baltimore: University Park Press.

Swanson, J.M., Elliott, G.R., Greenhill, L.L.,

Wigal, T., Arnold, L.E., Vitiello, B., et al. (2007). Effects of stimulant medication on growth rates across 3 years in the MTA follow-up. *Journal of the American Academy of Child and Adolescent Psychiatry, 46,* 1015–1027.

Swedo, S., Rapoport, J., Leonard, J., Lenane, M., & Cheslow, D. (1989). Obsessive-compulsive disorder in children and adolescents: Clinical phenomenology of 70 consecutive cases. *Archives of General Psychiatry, 46,* 335–341.

Szatmari, P., Offord, D.R., & Boyle, M.H. (1989). Ontario child health study: Prevalence of attention deficit disorder with hyperactivity. *Journal of Child Psychology and Psychiatry, 30,* 219–230.

TADS Study Team (2003). Treatment for Adolescents with Depression Study (TADS): Rationale, design, and methods. *Journal of the American Academy of Child and Adolescent Psychiatry, 42,* 531–542.

TADS Study Team (2004). Fluoxetine, cognitive-behavioral therapy, and their combination for adolescents with depression: Treatment for Adolescents with Depression Study (TADS) Randomized Controlled Trial. *Journal of the American Medical Association, 292,* 807–820.

TADS Study Team (2007). The Treatment for Adolescents with Depression Study (TADS). Long-term effectiveness and safety outcomes. *Archives of General Psychiatry, 64,* 1132–1144.

Tanofsky-Kraff, M., Yanovski, S.Z., Wilfley, D.E., Marmarosh, C., Morgan, C.M., & Yanovski, J.A. (2004). Eating-disordered behaviors, body fat, and psychopathology in overweight and normal-weight children. *Journal of Consulting and Clinical Psychology, 2004, 72,* 53–61.

Tanoue, Y., Oda, S., Asano, F., & Kawashima, K. (1988). Epidemiology of infantile autism in Southern Ibaraki, Japan: Differences in prevalence rates in birth cohorts. *Journal of Autism and Developmental Disorders, 18,* 155–166.

Target, M., & Fonagy, P. (1994). Efficacy of psychoanalysis for children with emotional disorder. *Journal of the American Academy of Child and Adolescent Psychiatry, 33,* 361–371.

Tarnowski, K.J., & Nay, S.M. (1989). Locus of control in children with learning disabilities and hyperactivity: A subgroup analysis. *Journal of Learning Disabilities, 22,* 381–383.

Taylor, E. (1994). Syndromes of attention deficit and overactivity. In M. Rutter, E. Taylor, & L. Hersov (Eds.), *Child and adolescent psychiatry* (pp. 285–307). Oxford: Blackwell.

Taylor, E., & Rogers, J.W. (2005). Practitioner review: Early adversity and developmental disorders. *Journal of Child Psychology and Psychiatry, 46,* 451–467.

Taylor, H.G. (1989). Learning disabilities. In E.J. Mash & R.A. Barkley (Eds.), *Treatment of childhood disorders.* New York: Guilford Press.

Thapar, A., Holmes, J., Poulton, K., & Harrington, R. (1999). Genetic basis of attention deficit and hyperactivity. *British Journal of Psychiatry, 174,* 105–111.

Thompson, R.J., & Kronenberger, W. (1990). Behavior problems in children with learning problems. In H.L. Swanson & B. Keogh (Eds.), *Learning disabilities: Theoretical and research issues.* Hillsdale, NJ: Lawrence Erlbaum Associates, Inc.

Thompson-Brenner, H., Eddy, K.T., Satir, D.A., Boisseau, C.L., & Westen, D. (2008). Personality subtypes in adolescents with eating disorders: Validation of a classification approach. *Journal of Child Psychology and Psychiatry, 49,* 170–180.

Thompson-Brenner, H., Glass, S., &

Westen, D. (2003). A multidimensional meta-analysis of psychotherapy for bulimia nervosa. *Clinical Psychology: Science and Practice, 10*, 269–287.

Thompson-Brenner, H., Weingeroff, J., & Westen, D. (2009). Empirical support for psychodynamic psychotherapy for eating disorders. In R.A. Levy & S.J. Ablon (Eds.), *Handbook of evidence-based psychodynamic psychotherapy: Bridging the gap between science and practice* (pp. 67–92). Totowa, NJ: Humana Press.

Thorndike, E. L. (1898). *Animal intelligence: An experimental study of the associative processes in animals.* New York: Macmillan.

Timbremont, B., Braet, & Dressen, L. (2004). Assessing depression in youth: Relation between the Children's Depression Inventory and a structured interview. *Journal of Clinical Child and Adolescent Psychology, 33*, 149–157.

Timmerman, M.G., Wells, L.A., & Chen, S. (1990). Bulimia nervosa and associated alcohol abuse among secondary school students. *Journal of the American Academy of Child and Adolescent Psychiatry, 29*, 118–222.

Torgersen, S. (1983). Genetic factors in anxiety disorders. *Archives of General Psychiatry, 40*, 1085–1089.

Torgesen, J.K. (1979). What shall we do with psychological processes? *Journal of Learning Disabilities, 12*, 6–23.

Torgesen, J.K. (1986). Learning disabilities theory: Its current state and future prospects. *Journal of Learning Disabilities, 19*, 399–407.

Toro, P.A., Weissberg, R.P., Guare, J., & Liebenstein, N.L. (1990). A comparison of children with and without learning disabilities on social cognitive-problem solving skills, social behavior, and family background. *Journal of Learning Disabilities, 23*, 115–120.

Treadwell, K., Flannery, E., & Kendall, P.C. (1995). Ethnicity and gender in relation to adaptive functioning, diagnostic status, and treatment outcome in children from an anxiety clinic. *Journal of Anxiety Disorders, 9*, 373–384.

Tremblay, R.E., McCord, J., Boileau, H., LeBlanc, M., Gagnon, C., Charlesbois, P., et al. (1990). *The Montreal experiment: School adjustment and self-reported delinquency after three-years of follow-up.* Paper presented at the annual meeting of the American Society of Criminology, Baltimore.

Tsai, S.M., & Wang, H.H. (2009). The relationship between caregiver's strain and social support among mothers with intellectually disabled children. *Journal of Clinical Nursing, 18*, 539–548.

Tsatsanis, K.D. (2003). Outcome research in Asperger syndrome and autism. *Child and Adolescent Psychiatric Clinics of North America, 12*, 47–63.

Tuma, J.M. (1989). Mental health services for children: The state of the art. *American Psychologist, 44*, 188–199.

US Food and Drug Administration (2004). *Relationship between psychotropic drugs and pediatric suicidality: Review and evaluation of clinical data.* Washington, DC: US Food and Drug Administration.

Van Bourgondien, M.E., Reichle, N., & Palmer, A. (1997). Sexual behavior in adults with autism. *Journal of Autism and Developmental Disabilities, 27*, 113–125.

Van Bourgondien, M.E., & Schopler, E. (1990). Critical disuses in the residential care of people with autism. *Journal of Autism and Developmental Disorders, 20*, 291–298.

Vandenberg, S.G., & Crowe, L. (1989). Genetic factors in childhood psychopathology. In B. Lahey & A.E. Kazdin (Eds.), *Advances in clinical child psychology* (Vol. 12, pp. 139–179). New York: Plenum Press.

Van der Kolk, B.A., van der Hart, O.V., & Marmar, C.R. (1996). Dissociation and information processing in posttraumatic stress disorder. In B.A. van der Kolk, A.C. McFarlane, & L. Weisaeth (Eds.), *Traumatic stress: The effects of overwhelming experience on mind, body, and society* (pp. 303–327). New York: Guilford Press.

Van Son, G.E. Van Hoeken, D., Bartelds, A.I., Van Furth, E.F., & Hoek, H.W. (2006). Time trends in the incidence of eating disorders: A primary care study in the Netherlands. *International Journal of Eating Disorders, 39*, 565–569.

Varela, R.E., Sanchez-Sosa, J.J., Biggs, B.K., & Luis, T.M. (2008). Anxiety symptoms and fears in Hispanic and European American children: Cross-cultural measurement equivalence. *Journal of Psychopathology and Behavioral Assessment, 30*, 132–145.

Vasey, M.W., & MacLeod, C. (2001). Information-processing factors in childhood anxiety: A review and developmental perspective. In M.W. Vasey & M.R. Dadds (Eds.), *The developmental psychopathology of anxiety* (pp. 253–277). Oxford: Oxford University Press.

Verdellen, C.W.J., Keijsers, G.P.J., Cath, D.C., & Hoogduin, C. (2004). Exposure with response prevention versus habit reversal in Tourette's syndrome: A controlled study. *Behaviour Research and Therapy, 42*, 501–511.

Verduin, T.L., & Kendall, P.C. (2008). Peer perceptions and liking of children with anxiety disorders. *Journal of Abnormal Child Psychology, 36*, 459–469.

Vernberg, E.M., LaGreca, A.M., Silverman, W., & Prinstein, M. (1996). Prediction of post-traumatic stress symptoms in children after hurricane Andrew. *Journal of Abnormal Psychology, 105*, 237–248.

Vitousek, K.B., & Orimoto, L. (1993). Cognitive-behavioral models of anorexia nervosa, bulimia nervosa, and obesity. In K.S. Dobson & P.C. Kendall (Eds.), *Psychopathology and cognition* (pp. 193–245). Orlando, FL: Academic Press.

Volkmar, F., Chawarska, K., & Klin, A. (2005). Autism in infancy and early childhood. *Annual Review of Psychology, 56*, 315–336.

Volkmar, F.R. (1996). Brief report: Diagnostic issues in autism: Results of the DSM-IV field trial. *Journal of Autism and Developmental Disorders, 26*, 155–157.

Volkmar, F.R. (2001). Pharmacological interventions in autism: Theoretical and practical issues. *Journal of Clinical Child Psychology, 30*, 80–87.

Volkmar, F.R., Klin, A., & Pauls, D. (1998). Autism: The phenotype in relatives. *Journal of Autism and Developmental Disabilities, 28*, 457–463.

Volkmar, F.R., Lord, C., Bailey, A., Schultz, R.T., & Klin, A. (2004). Autism and pervasive developmental disorders. *Journal of Child Psychology and Psychiatry, 45*, 135–170.

Wagner, K.D., Ambrosini, P., Rynn, M., Wohlberg, C., Yang, R., Greenbaum, M.S., et al. (2003). Efficacy of sertraline in the treatment of children and adolescents with major depressive disorders. *Journal of the American Medical Association, 290*, 1033–1041.

Wahler, R.G., & Dumas, J.E. (1989). Attentional problems in dysfunctional mother–child interactions. *Psychological Bulletin, 105*, 116–130.

Waldman, I.D., Rowe, D.C., Abramowitz, A., Kozel, S., Mohr, J., Sherman, S., et al. (1998). Association and linkage of the dopamine transporter gene and attention-deficit hyperactivity disorder in children: Heterogeneity owing to diagnostic subtype and severity. *American Journal of Human Genetics, 63*, 1767–1776.

Walkup, J.T., Albano, A.M., Piacentini, J., Birmaher, B., Compton, S.N., Sherrill, J.T., et al. (2008). Cognitive behavioral therapy, sertraline, or a combination in childhood anxiety, *New England Journal of Medicine, 359*, 2753–2766.

Wallerstein, J.S., & Blakeslee, S. (1989). *Second chances*. New York: Ticknor & Fields.

Wallerstein, J.S., Corbin, S.B., & Lewis, J.M. (1988). Children of divorce: A 10-year study. In E.M. Hetherington & J.D. Arasteh (Eds.), *Impact of divorce, single parenting, and stepparenting on children*. Hillsdale, NJ: Lawrence Erlbaum Associates, Inc.

Wang, P.S., Berglund, P., Olfson, M., Pincus, H.A., Wells, K.B., & Kessler, R.C. (2005). Failure and delay in initial treatment contact after first onset of mental disorders in the National Comorbidity Survey Replication. *Archives of General Psychiatry, 62*, 603–613.

Wazana, A., Bresnahan, M., & Kline, J. (2007). The autism epidemic: Fact of artifact. *Journal of the American Academy of Child and Adolescent Psychiatry, 46*, 721–730.

Webster-Stratton, C. (2005). The Incredible Years: A training series for the prevention and treatment of conduct problems in young children. In E. Hibbs & P. Jensen (Eds.), *Psychosocial treatments for child and adolescent disorders: Empirically based strategies for clinical practice* (2nd ed., pp. 507–556). Washington, DC: American Psychological Association.

Webster-Stratton, C., & Hammond, M. (1999). Marital conflict management skills, parenting style, and early-onset conduct problems: Process and pathways. *Journal of Child Psychology and Psychiatry, 40*, 917–927.

Webster-Stratton, C., Reid, M.J., & Stoolmiller, M. (2008). Preventing conduct problems and improving school readiness: Evaluation of the Incredible Years teacher and child training programs in high-risk schools.

Journal of Child Psychology and Psychiatry, 49, 471–488.

Weems, C.F., Costa, N.M., Watts, S.E., Taylor, L.K., & Cannon, M.F. (2007). Cognitive errors, anxiety sensitivity, and anxiety control beliefs: Their unique and specific associations with childhood anxiety symptoms. *Behavior Modification, 31*, 174–201.

Wehmeyer, M.L., & Lee, S.H. (2007). Educating children with intellectual disability. In A. Carr, G. O'Reilly, P. Noonan-Walsh, & J. McEvoy (Eds.), *The handbook of intellectual disability and clinical psychology practice* (pp. 559–605). New York: Routledge/Taylor & Francis.

Weiner, H. (1985). The physiology of eating disorders. *International Journal of Eating Disorders, 4*, 347–388.

Weingartner, H., Rapaport, J., Buchsbaum, M., Bunney, W., Ebert, M., Mikkelsen, E., et al. (1980). Cognitive processes in normal and hyperactive children and their responses to amphetamine treatment. *Journal of Abnormal Psychology, 89*, 25–37.

Weiss, B., & Garber, G. (2003). Developmental differences in the phenomenology of depression. *Development and Psychopathology, 15*, 403–430.

Weiss, B., & Weisz, J. (1995). Relative effectiveness of behavioral versus nonbehavioral child psychotherapy. *Journal of Consulting and Clinical Psychology 63*, 317–320.

Weiss, G., & Hechtman, L. (1986). *Hyperactive children grown up*. New York: Guilford Press.

Weiss, R.S. (1979). Growing up a little faster: The experience of growing up in a single parent household. *Journal of Social Issues, 35*, 97–111.

Weissman, M.M., Wickramaratne, P., Nomura, Y., Warner, V., Verdeli, H., & Pilowsky, D.J. (2005). Families at high and low risk for depression: A 3-

generation study. *Archives of General Psychiatry, 62,* 29–36.

Weisz, J., Weiss, B., Hans, S., Granger, D., & Morton, T. (1995). Effects of psychotherapy with children and adolescents revisited: A meta-analysis of treatment outcome studies. *Psychological Bulletin, 117,* 450–468.

Weisz, J., Weiss, B., Suwanlert, S., & Chaiyasit, W. (2006). Culture and youth psychopathology: Testing the syndromal sensitivity model in Thai and American adolescents. *Journal of Consulting and Clinical Psychology, 74,* 1098–1107.

Weisz, J.R., Southam-Gerow, M.A., Gordis, E.B., Connor-Smith, J.K., Chu, B.C., Langer, D.A., et al. (2009). Cognitive-behavioral therapy versus usual clinical care for youth depression: An initial test of transportability to community clinics and clinicians. *Journal of Consulting and Clinical Psychology, 77,* 383–396.

Wells, K.C., & Forehand, R. (1985). Conduct and oppositional disorders. In P.H. Bornstein & A.E. Kazdin (Eds.), *Handbook of clinical behavior therapy with children* (pp. 190–209). Homewood, IL: Dorsey.

Wenar, C. (1982). *Psychopathology from infancy through adolescence: A developmental approach.* New York: Random House.

Wenar, C., Ruttenberg, B.A., Kalish-Weiss, B., & Wolf, E.G. (1986). The development of normal and autistic children: A comparative study. *Journal of Autism and Developmental Disorders, 16,* 317–323.

Werry, J. (1997). Severe conduct disorder: Some key issues. *Canadian Journal of Psychiatry, 42,* 577–583.

West, D.J. (1982). *Delinquency: Its roots, careers, and prospects.* Cambridge, MA: Harvard University Press.

Westen, D., & Shedler, J. (2007). Personality diagnosis with the Shedler-Westen Assessment Procedure (SWAP):

Integrating clinical and statistical measurement and prediction. *Journal of Abnormal Psychology, 116,* 810–822.

Westerinen, H., Kaski, M., Virta, L., Almqvist, F., & Iivanainen, M. (2007). Prevalence of intellectual disability: A comprehensive study based on national registers. *Journal of Intellectual Disability Research, 51,* 715–725.

Whalen, C.K., & Henker, B. (1991). Therapies for hyperactive children: Comparisons, combinations, and compromises. *Journal of Consulting and Clinical Psychology, 59,* 126–137.

Whitaker, A., Johnson, J., Shaffer, D., Rapoport, J.L., Kalikow, K., Walsh, B.T., et al. (1990). Uncommon troubles in young people: Prevalence estimates of selected psychiatric disorders in a nonreferred adolescent population. *Archives of General Psychiatry, 47,* 487–496.

Whittal, M., Agras, S., & Gould, R. (1999). Bulimia nervosa: A meta-analysis of psychosocial and pharmacological treatments. *Behavior Therapy, 30,* 117–136.

Wicks-Nelson, R., & Israel, A.C. (2002). *Behavior disorders of childhood* (5th ed.). Englewood Cliffs, NJ: Prentice-Hall.

Widom, C.S. (1997). Child abuse, neglect, and witnessing violence. In D. Stoff, J. Breiling, & J. Maser (Eds.), *Handbook of antisocial behaviour* (pp. 159–179). New York: Wiley.

Wilfrey, D., Agras, S., Telch, C., Rossiter, E., Schneider, J., Cole, A., et al. (1993). Group cognitive-behavioral therapy and group interpersonal psychotherapy for the nonpurging bulimic individual: A controlled comparison. *Journal of Consulting and Clinical Psychology, 61,* 296–305.

Wilhelm, S., Deckersbach, T., Coffey, B.J., Bohne, A., Peterson, A.L., & Baer, L. (2003). Habit reversal versus supportive psychotherapy for Tourette's disorder:

A randomized controlled trial. *American Journal of Psychiatry, 160,* 1175–1177.

Willcutt, E.G., Doyle, A.E., Nigg, J.T., Faraone, S.V., & Pennington, B.F. (2005). Validity of the executive function theory of attention-deficit/hyperactivity disorder: A meta-analytic review. *Biological Psychiatry, 57,* 1336–1346.

Williams, P., & King, M. (1987). The "epidemic" of anorexia nervosa: Another medical myth? *Lancet* (January), 205–208.

Williams, S.K., Scahill, L., Vitiello, B., Aman, M.G., Arnold, L.A., McDougle, C.J., et al. (2006). Risperidone and adaptive behavior in children with autism. *Journal of the American Academy of Child and Adolescent Psychiatry, 45,* 431–439.

Williamson, D.F., Kahn, H.S., Remington, P.I., & Anda, R.F. (1990). The 10-year incidence of overweight and major weight gain in US adults. *Archives of Internal Medicine, 150,* 665–672.

Wilson, T., & Pike, K.M. (2001). *Eating disorders.* In D. H. Barlow (Ed.), *Clinical handbook of psychological disorders* (3rd ed.). New York: Guilford Press.

Wing, L., & Attwood, A. (1987). Syndromes of autism and atypical development. In D.J. Cohen & A.M. Donnellan (Eds.), *Handbook of pervasive development disorders.* New York: Wiley.

Wolf, M.M., Risley, T., & Mees, H. (1964). Application of operant conditioning procedures to the behavior problems of an autistic child. *Behavioral Research and Therapy, 1,* 305–312.

Wolfe, V.V., Finch, A.J., Saylor, C.F., Blount, R.L., Pallmeyer, T.P., & Carek, D.J. (1987). Negative affectivity in children: A multitrait-multimethod investigation. *Journal of Consulting and Clinical Psychology, 55,* 245–250.

Wong, B.Y.I. (1985). Issues in cognitive-behavioral interventions in academic skill areas. *Journal of Abnormal Child Psychology, 13,* 425–442.

Wong, B.Y.I., Harris, K., & Graham, S. (1991). Academic applications of cognitive-behavioral programs with learning disabled students. In P.C. Kendall (Ed.), *Child and adolescent therapy: Cognitive-behavioral procedures* (pp. 245–275). New York: Guilford Press.

Wong, B.Y.I., & Jones, W. (1982). Increasing metacomprehension in learning disabled and normally achieving students through self questioning training. *Learning Disabilities Quarterly, 5,* 228–240.

Wood, J.J., McLeod, B.D., Sigman, M., Hwang, W.-C., & Chu, B.C. (2003). Parenting and childhood anxiety: Theory, empirical findings, and future directions. *Journal of Child Psychology and Psychiatry, 44,* 134–151.

Woods, D.W., Piacentini, J., Himle, M.B., & Chang, S. (2005). Initial psychometric results and examination of the premonitory urge phenomenon in youths with tic disorders. *Journal of Development and Behavior Pediatrics, 26,* 397–403.

World Health Organization (WHO, 1992). *International classification of diseases* (10th ed.). Geneva: World Health Organization.

Yang, Q., Rasmussen, S.A., & Friedman, J.M. (2002). Mortality associated with Down's syndrome in the USA from 1983 to 1997: A population-based study. *Lancet, 359,* 1019–1025.

Zahn-Waxler, C., Shirtcliff, E.A., & Marceau, K. (2008). Disorders of childhood and adolescence: Gender and psychopathology. *Annual Review of Clinical Psychology, 4,* 275–303.

Zametkin, A.J., Liebenauer, L.L., Fitzgerald, G.A., King, A.C., Minkunas, D.V., Herscovitch, P., et al. (1993). Brain metabolism in teenagers with attention-deficit hyperactivity disorder. *Archives of General Psychiatry, 50*, 333–340.

Zhang, H., Leckman, J.F., Tsai, C.P., Kidd, K.K., & Rosario Campos, M.C. (2002). The Tourette Syndrome Association International Consortium for Genetics. Genome wide scan of hoarding in sibling pairs both diagnosed with Gilles de la Tourette syndrome. *American Journal of Human Genetics, 70*, 896–904.

Zigmond, N., & Baker, J.M. (1995). Concluding comments: Current and future practices in inclusive schooling. *Journal of Special Education, 29*, 245–250.

Zill, N. (1988). Behavior, achievement, and health problems among children in stepfamilies: Findings from a national survey of child health. In M. Heatherington & J. Arasteh (Eds.), *Impact of divorce, single parenting, and stepparenting on children* (pp. 325–368). Hillsdale, NJ: Lawrence Erlbaum Associates, Inc.

Zimmerman, E.H., Zimmerman, J., & Russell, C.D. (1969). Differential effects of token reinforcement in instruction-following behavior in retarded students instructed in a group. *Journal of Applied Behavior Analysis, 2*, 101–112.

Zoccolillo, M. (1993). Gender and the development of conduct disorder. *Development and Psychopathology, 5*, 65–78.

Author index

Note: Page references in **bold** indicate boxes, figures and tables.

Brown, L.H., 90
Brown, R., 120
Brown, T.A., 103, 106
Brownell, K., 135, 143
Bruch, H., 130–131, 133, 141
Brumaghim, J.T., 91
Brunn, R.D., 193
Brunner, E., 85
Bruty, H., 142
Bruun, R.D., 193
Bryant, R.A., 106
Bryant-Waugh, R., 129, 132
Bryson, S.E., 147, 156, 173
Bucholz, K.K., 68
Buchsbaum, M., 92
Budd, K.S., 129, 130
Budman, C.L., 193
Buitelaar, J.K., 79, 84
Buka, S.L., 15
Bukowski, W.M., 79
Bulik, C.M., 136
Bunney, W., 92
Burish, T., 18
Burke, J., 183
Burr, J.E., 64
Burt, D.B., 153
Butler, L., 124
Butter, E., 186
Byrne, T., 84

Caine, E.D., 193
Callocott, R., 153
Camara, K.A., 45
Camfield, P., 193
Campbell, I.C., 136
Campbell, S.M., 42
Cannon, M.F., 25
Cannon, T.D., 15
Cantwell, D.P., 49, 88, 162
Caplan, M., 73
Carek, D.J., 119
Carey, K.B., 23
Carlson, G.A., 117
Carper, R.A., 176
Carr, E.G., 185–186
Carter, A.S., 103

Carter, F.A., 134
Carter, J.F., 93
Casas, J.F., 64
Casat, C., 119
Cascio C.J., 14
Casey, B.J., 15
Casey, P., 130
Castellanos, F.X., 84
Cath, D.C., 195
Ceci, S.J., 151, 154
Cederlund, M., 56, 174
Cederlund, R., 111
Cha, C.B., 118, 119
Chaiyasit, W., 101, 125
Chamberlain, P., 70, 73
Chambless, D.L., 27
Champion, L.A., 39
Chandler, S., 177
Chang, S., 194
Chansky T.E., 112
Chappell, P.B., 194
Charlesbois, P., 75–76
Charman, T., 169, 177
Chase-Lansdale, P.L., 45
Chatoor, I., 130
Chavez, A., 168
Chawarska, K., 169, 171
Chen, C.N., 132, 133
Chen, S., 138
Chen, Y., 153
Cheney, D., 165
Cherlin, A.J., 45
Cheslow, D., 103
Chess, S., 176
Cheung, A.H., 122
Chhabra, V., 164, 165
Chiu, H.F.K., 132, 133
Chiu, W.T., 106
Chodorow, N., 33
Chong, W.K., 155
Chorpita, B.F., 12, 57
Choudhury, M.S., 107
Chu, B.C., 110, 125
Chuang A., 153
Chugh, C., 129
Churchland, P.S., 15
Ciaranello, R.D., 154

Cicchetti, D., 35, 40, 41, 42, 146
Clark, D.B., 15, 112
Clark, S., 104
Clarke, G.N., 122, 124
Clarren, S., 154
Clary, C., 99
Clasen, L.S., 84
Cloninger, C.R., 193
Coffey, B.J., 192, 195
Cohen, D.J., 84, 172, 173, 191, 192, 193, 194
Cohen, I., 153
Cohen, P., 134, 140
Cohen, R.Y., 143
Cole, A., 143
Cole, E., 124
Cole, J., 79
Collier, D.A., 136
Colligan, R.C., 179
Comer, J.S., 1, 49, 52, 99, 100, 104, 106, 109, 110, 119, 120, 158
Comings, B.G., 192, 193
Comings, D.E., 192, 193
Compas, B., 48, 49
Compton, S.N., 59, 107, 112, 125
Conley, M., 151
Connan, F., 136
Conners, C.K., 80, 85, 90, 107
Connor-Smith, J.K., 125
Conrad, M., 119
Cook, E.H., 84
Cooper, K., 92
Cooper, P.J., 117, 138
Cooper, S., 153
Cooper, Z., 140
Copeland, P., 136
Corbin, S.B., 44
Corley, R., 68–69
Cornell, A.H., 68
Costa, N., 25, 111
Costello, A.J., 152
Costello, E.J., 39, 40, 55, 56, 65, 80, 99, 102, 117, 118, 122, 172, 173

Shields, J., 16
Shimizu, Y., 76
Shirk, S.R., 57
Shirtcliff, E.A., 65
Shisler, L., 159
Short, A., 182
Shulman, C., 171
Sicotte, N., 136
Siegel, T.C., **75**
Sienna, M., 88
Sigman, M., 110
Sihvola, E., 132
Sikstrom, S., 84
Silberg, J., 35
Silva, P.A., 66, 102–103, 117
Silverman, W., 27, 48, 52, 57, 100, 106, 107, 111
Silvia, P.J., 90
Simmens, S.J., 71
Simmons, J.Q., 182
Simonoff, E., 35, 177
Simpson, R.L., 172
Singh, N.N., 159
Siqueland, L., 110
Sirbu, C., 111
Sitarenios, G., 80
Sivers, H., 42
Sivo, P.J., 73
Skajaa, E, 86
Skare, S., 73
Skinner, B.F., 20
Skjeldal, O., 174
Skoog, G., 104
Skoog, I., 104
Slutske, W.S., 68
Slymen, D.J., 109
Small, N., 149
Smallish, L., 80, 88, 89
Smith, A., 85
Smith, B.H., 77, 80
Smith, B.W., 154
Smith, D.W., 154
Smith, P., 109
Smith, S.D., 162, 163
Smith, T., 181, 182, 184
Smith, T.W., 26
Smoller, J.W., 83, 92

Smucker, M., 49
Snider, L.A., 104
Soderlund, G., 84
Solanto, M.V., 84
Sonuga-Barke, E.J., 13, 53, 93
Sood, E.D., 25, 109
Southam-Gerow, M.A., 72, 99, 107, 109, 112, 125
Sowell, E.R., 84
Sparks, B.F., 176
Sparrow, S.S., 146
Spencer, T., 59, 91, 92, 112, 192
Spettell, C., 197
Spiegel, D., 42
Spieker, S.J., 69
Spielberger, C., 107
Spiller, L., 70
Spiridigliozzi, G., 153
Spirito, A., 49
Sponheim, E., 174
Sprafkin, J., 92
Sroufe, A., 41
Stallings, M.C., 68–69
Stallings, P., 107
Stang, P.E., 90
Stark, K.D., 120, 123–124
State, M.W., 16, 18, 175
Stattin, H., 72
Stedge, D., 179
Steen, E., 152
Steen, J., 152
Steenhuis, M.P., 84
Stein, M.A., 84
Stein, M.B., 99, 106
Stein, Z.A., 147
Steinberg, L., 110
Steinglass, J.E., 140
Steinhausen, H.C., 132, 133
Sternberg, R.J., 148, 151
Stevenson, J.F., 193
Stewart, S.E., 103, 112
Stice, E., 138
Stickle, T.R., 68
Stokes, A., 193
Stoolmiller, M., 76

Strain, P., 178
Strauss, C., 102
Strauss, J., 91
Streissguth, A.P., 154
Strober, M., 121, 136
Suematsu, H., 132
Sugiyama, T., 174
Sullivan, K., 107
Summers, P., 44
Surman, C., 91
Susser, E.S., 132
Sussman, J.E., 155
Suveg, C., 52, 99, 111, 112, 158
Suwanlert, S., 101, 125
Sverd, J., 92
Swain, J.E., 192, 193, 194
Swank, P., 70
Swanson, J., 85, 91, 92, 96
Swedo, S., 103, 104, 111
Sweet, R.D., 193
Swettenham, J., 169
Switzky, H.N., 159
Szatmari, P., 80

TADS Study Team 03, 125
Tahilani, K., 137, 138
Tamas, Z., 119
Tang, C.P., 77
Tannenbaum, L., 44
Tannock, R., 79
Tanofsky-Kraff, M., 138
Tanoue, Y., 174
Target, M., 57
Tarnowski, K.J., 164
Taylor, E., 81, 85, 155
Taylor, H.G., 161, 163
Taylor, L.K., 25
Telch, C., 143
Tellegen, A., 16
Tenconi, E., 136, 141
Terdal, L., 48, 51
Terlonge, C., 146, 150, 157
Thapar, A., 83
Thesiger, C., 101
Thomas, P., 194
Thompson, M., 57, 93
Thompson, P.M., 84

WHO (World Health Organization), 52, 170
Wickramaratne, P., 120, 123
Wicks-Nelson, R., 156, 162
Widom, C.S., 70
Wigal, T., 92
Wilens, T., 91
Wilfley, D.E., 138
Wilfrey, D., 143
Wilhelm, S., 195
Willcutt, E., 83, 84, 85, 162
Williams, P., 133
Williams, S., 66, 102–103, 117
Williams, S.K., 179
Williamson, D.F., 135
Wilson, G.T., 18
Wilson, T., 129, 140
Wing, L., 173
Woerner, W., 194
Wohlberg, C., 123
Wolchik, S.A., 45
Wolf, E.G., 169
Wolf, M., 157
Wolf, M.M., 180

Wolf, M.W., 158
Wolfe, V.V., 119
Wong, B.Y.I., 164, 165
Wong, M.M.T., 25
Wood, A., 125
Wood, J.J., 110, 120
Woods, D.W., 194, 195
Woodside, D.B., 136
World Health Organization (WHO), 52, 170
Wortham, B., 130
Wright, J.P., 69
Wunder, J., 99
Wynn, J.W., 182

Yang, Q., 152
Yang, R., 123
Yanovski, J.A., 138
Yanovski, S.Z., 138
Yeung, P.P., 112
Yi, I., 142
Yi, P., 151
Yirmiya, N., 171
Yolken, R.H., 15
Young, B.J., 111

Young, S.E., 68–69
Youngstrom, E.A., 80
Yule, W., 66
Yurdakok, K., 86
Yurgelun-Tudd, D., 132

Zahn, T.P., 92
Zahn-Waxler, C., 65
Zakis, S., 108
Zametkin, A.J., 84
Zeijlon, L., 56, 174
Zeman, J., 99, 121
Zhang, H., 192, 193
Zhang, R., 194
Ziccardi, R., 176
Ziegler, D.A., 176
Zigmond, N., 179
Zill, N., 45
Zimmerman, B., 92
Zimmerman, E.H., 158
Zimmerman, J., 158
Zoccolillo, M., 66
Zollo, L.J., 111
Zubenko, G.S., 121
Zupan, B., 62
Zwakhalen, S., 100

Subject index

Note: Page references in **bold** indicate boxes, figures and tables.

health ramifications, 131, 133
medications, 142
prevalence, 132–133
psychological factors, 133–135
treatment, 141, 142–143
see also bulimia nervosa
Anterior cingulated cortex (ACC), 140
Antidepressants, 142–143, 179
Antipsychotic medications, 160, 179, 185,
194
Antisocial behavior, 40, 68, 70, 71, 72
Anxiety disorders, 99–113
age of onset, 104, 106
assessment, 106–108
behavioral explanation, 110
causal forces, 108–111
classification, 102–106
cognitive explanations, 109
comorbidity, 111, 112, 119
and culture, 108
emotional development, 100–101, 108
family factors, 110–111
and gender, 100, 108, 109
generalized anxiety disorder (GAD),
102–103, 104, 109, 111, 112
genetic factors, 108–109, 193
medication, 112–113
obsessive-compulsive disorder (OCD),
103–104, 109, 111, 112, 134, 193
post-traumatic stress disorder (PTSD), 54,
106
prevalence, 39, 102–103, 104, 108
separation anxiety disorder (SAD), 46,
104–105, **105**, 109, 111, 112
social anxiety disorder (SocAD), 105–106,
109, 111, 112
treatment, 111–113, 158
Anxiety Disorders Interview Schedule-
Child Version (ADIS-C), 48, 52, 107
Asperger's disorder, 6–7, 187–188
Assessment, 47–52
of ADHD, 78–81, **82**
of anxiety disorders, 106–108
of autism, 169, 172–173
behavioral observations, 48, 51
of depression, 119
of learning disorders/disabilities, 163
of mental retardation, 146–149, **147**

parents rating scale, 48, 49
and prevalence of disorders, 56
reliability, 47
self-report measures, 48–49
structured diagnostic interviews, 48,
51–52
Teacher Rating Form, 49, 107
validity, 47–48
Atomoxetine [Straterra], 91
Attachment, 105
Attention-deficit hyperactivity disorder *see*
ADHD
Autism, 8, 167, 168–187
age of onset, 168, 170
assessment, 169, 172–173
biological factors, 176–177
causes, 174–177
classification, 168–173, **170**
communication skills, 177, 180–181, 182,
183–184
comorbidity, 176, 177
course, 177–178
and culture, 174
echolalia, 171
education, 179–180
environmental factors, 177
family factors, 174–175
and gender, 173–174
genetic factors, 175
medications, 178–179, 185
mental abilities, 172, 177
parent training, 179, 182–185
prevalence, 173–174
self-injury in, 170, 185–187
social deficits, 169, 170, 177–178
theory of mind, 172
treatment, 178–184
Autistic spectrum, 173
Aversive procedures, 186
Avoidance responses, 21–22, 23, 110, 134

Behavior, antisocial, 40, 68, 70, 71, 72
Behavior disorders, 55
disruptive behavior disorders, **53**
and mental retardation, 157
and Tourette's disorder, 193
see also conduct disorder; oppositional
defiant disorder (ODD)

Behavioral observations, 48, 51
Behavioral training
  for autism, 179, 180–184
  bladder control training, 196
  classroom management for ADHD, 94
  differential reinforcement of other
      behavior (DRO), 186
  extinction, 186
  habit reversal training, 194–195
  for mental retardation, 157–158
  time out, 186
Behaviorism, 18–24, 33
  classical conditioning, 18–19
  evaluating the approach, 23–24
  observational learning, 22–23
  operant conditioning, 19–22
Biological factors
  in ADHD, 84–85
  in anorexia nervosa, 135–137
  in autism, 176–177
  in bulimia nervosa, 140–141
  in depression, 120
  in learning disorders/disabilities,
      163–164
  in mental retardation, 151–154, 156
  in Tourette's disorder, 193–194
Biological models, 13–18, 200
  brain, 14–16
  evaluating the model, 17–18
  genetics, 16–18
Biomedical models *see* biological models
Bladder control training, 196
Brain
  in ADHD, 84–85
  in autism, 176
  in Down syndrome, 151–152
  in fragile X syndrome, 153
  in learning disorders/disabilities,
      163–164
  neural communication, 15–16
  neuroimaging, 14, 17, 200
  structure, 14–15
  in Tourette's disorder, 193–194
Bulimia nervosa, 137–143
  age of onset, 138
  biological factors, 140–141
  causes, 139–141
  classification, 137, **138**

cognitive factors, 139–140
course and outcome, 140
and culture, 138
diathesis-stress model, 141
family-based treatment (FBT), 141, 142
family factors, 139
and gender, 138
health ramifications, 138–139
medications, 142–143
prevalence, 138
treatment, 141–143
see also anorexia nervosa

Callous traits, 68
CAT (computerized axial tomography), 84
CBT (cognitive-behavioral therapy),
    123–126
CDI (Children's Depression Inventory),
    48–49
Cerebral cortex, 14
Child/Adolescent Multimodal Treatment
    Study (CAMS), 112
Child Behavior Checklist (CBCL), 48,
    49–51, **50**, 54, 80, 107
Childhood disintegrative disorder, 188
Childhood disorders, 1
  impact of, 39–40, 199–200
  prevalence, 39, 55–56
Children, 2–10, 12
Children's Depression Inventory (CDI),
    48–49
Chromosomal abnormalities, 151, 153
Chromosomes, 16
Classical conditioning, 18–19
Classification
  diagnostic systems, 52–54
  externalizing disorders, 55, 68
  internalizing disorders, 54–55, 66
  statistical approach, 54
Classroom management programs for
    ADHD, 94
Clomipramine, 112
Clonidine, 194
Cognitive-behavioral model, 26–27
Cognitive-behavioral therapy (CBT),
    123–126
Cognitive-behavioral treatments
  for ADHD, 94–95

Diatheses, 34
Diathesis-stress model, 34–35
  for anorexia nervosa, 136–137
  for bulimia nervosa, 141
  for depression, 121–122
  for feeding disorder of infancy, 130
  for schizophrenia, 35
  in verbal abilities, 151
DICA *see* Diagnostic Interview for
  Children and Adolescents
Diet and ADHD, 85–86 *see also* eating
  disorders
Differential reinforcement of other
  behavior (DRO), 186
Diffusion tensor imaging (DTI), 14
Disadvantage *see* deprivation and
  disadvantage
Disease models *see* biological models
Disruptive behavior disorders, **53**
Divorce: effects on children, 43–47, 71
  age of child, 44
  child's processing style, 45
  gender of child, 45
  mediation, 46–47
  postdivorce contact, 46
  predivorce conditions, 45–46
Dizygotic (fraternal) twins, 16
Dopamine, 69, 84, 91, 140, 194
Down syndrome, 151–153
  and age of mother, 152
  cause, 152
  comorbidity, 152
  course and outcome, 152, 153
  physical characteristics, 151–152
  prebirth information, 204–205
  prevalence, 152–153
DRO (differential reinforcement of other
  behavior), 186
DSM (*Diagnostic and Statistical Manual*), 53
DSM-IV (*Diagnostic and Statistical Manual*,
  4th edition), 52, **53**, 53–54
  ADHD, 78, **82**
  anorexia nervosa, **132**
  autism, 170, **170**
  bulimia nervosa, 137, **138**
  conduct disorder, 62, **62**
  depression, 116, **116**
  enuresis, **195**

learning disorders, **53**, 162
mental retardation, **53**, **146**
pervasive developmental disorders, **53**,
  167
separation anxiety disorder (SAD), 104,
  105
tics, **53**, 191
Tourette's disorder, **192**
DTI (diffusion tensor imaging), 14

Eating disorders, **53**, 129–143
  anorexia nervosa, 33–34, 130–137, **132**,
    141, 142–143
  bulimia nervosa, 137–143, **138**
  feeding disorder of infancy, 129–130
Echolalia, 171
Education
  for autism, 179–180
  inclusion, 159, 179
  mainstreaming, 159, 179, 180, 205–206
  for mental retardation, 158–159
  special education, 93, **149**, 159, 161, 162,
    179–180
Education for All Handicapped Children
  Act 1975, 158–159
Ego, 28, 32
Electra dilemma, 30
Elimination disorders, **53**
  encopresis, 195, **196**
  enuresis, 195, **195**, 196–197
Emotional development, 42, 100–101, 108
Emotional disorders, **53**
Empathy, lack of, 68
Encopresis, 195, **196**
Enmeshment, 33–34, 134
Enuresis, **195**
  causes, 195, 196
  medication, 196
  treatment, 196–197
Environmental factors
  in ADHD, 86
  in autism, 177
  in depression, 120
Escape responses, 21–22
Ethnicity *see* culture and ethnicity
Externalizing disorders, 55, 68
Extinction, 186

Family *see* family therapy; parenting and family factors
Family therapy, 58
  action-oriented, 73
  for anorexia nervosa, 142
  for bulimia nervosa, 141, 142
  multisystemic family therapy, 74
Fears
  classical conditioning, 19
  cognitive-behavioral treatments, 111–112
  and emotional development, 42, 100–101
Feeding disorder of infancy, 129–130
Fetal alcohol syndrome, 154–155
Fixation, 31
Fluoxetine [Prozac], 123
Forebrain, 14
Fragile X syndrome, 153
Fraternal (dizygotic) twins, 16
Functional MRI (fMRI), 14

GAD *see* generalized anxiety disorder
Gender
  and ADHD, 81
  and aggression, 66
  and anorexia nervosa, 132
  and anxiety disorders, 100, 108, 109
  and Asperger's disorder, 188
  and autism, 173–174
  and bulimia nervosa, 138
  and childhood disintegrative disorder, 188
  and conduct disorder, 65–66
  and depression, 117
  and effects of divorce, 45
  and encopresis, 195
  and enuresis, 195
  and fragile X syndrome, 153
  and internalizing disorders, 66
  and learning disorders/disabilities, 161
  and mental retardation, 149
  and Rett's disorder, 187
  and suicidal behavior, 118–119
  and Tourette's disorder, 193
  and types of disorders, 55

Generalized anxiety disorder (GAD), 102–103
  genetic factors, 109
  and obsessive-compulsive disorder (OCD), 104
  treatment, 111, 112
Genes, 16
Genetic factors, 16–18
  in ADHD, 83–84
  in anorexia nervosa, 136
  in anxiety disorders, 108–109, 193
  in autism, 175
  in conduct disorders, 68–69
  in depression, 120, 121
  in learning disorders/disabilities, 163
  in mental retardation, 150–151
  in phenylketonuria (PKU), 153–154
  in schizophrenia, 16–17
  in Tourette's disorder, 193
Genital stage of psychosexual development, 30
Guanfacine, 194
Guilt, absence of, 68

Habit reversal training, 194–195
Haloperidol, 194
Hindbrain, 15
Hostile attribution bias, 67–68
Hyperactivity, 79 *see also* ADHD (attention-deficit hyperactivity disorder)
Hyperkinetic reaction *see* ADHD (attention-deficit hyperactivity disorder)
Hypothalamic-pituitary-adrenal (HPA) axis, 120, 136
Hypothalamus, 14, 135–136

ICD-10 (*International Classification of Diseases*, 10th edition), 52–53, 170
Id, 28, 32
IDEA (Individuals with Disabilities Education Act, 1990), 161, 162–163
Identical (monozygotic) twins, 16
Imipramine, 196
Impulsivity, 39, 63, 78–79
Inattention, 78
Intellectual disability *see* mental retardation
Internalizing disorders, 54–55, 66

Interpersonal psychotherapy (IPT), 123
Interpersonal relationships, 31
IQ scores
  and ADHD, 79–80
  and autism, 172, 177
  and mental retardation, 146, 147–149,
    151

Latency stage of psychosexual
  development, 30
Learning disorders/disabilities, 160–165
  assessment, 163
  biological factors, 163–164
  causes, 163–164
  classification, **53**, 161–163
  comorbidity, 162
  definitions, 145, 161, 166
  family factors, 163
  and gender, 161
  genetic factors, 163
  prevalence, 161
  psychological factors, 164
  treatments, 164–165
  see also mental retardation
Learning models, 18–24, 33
  classical conditioning, 18–19
  evaluating the approach, 23–24
  observational learning, 22–23
  operant conditioning, 19–22
Leiter International Performance
  Scale–Revised, 147
Limbic system, 14

Magnetic resonance imaging (MRI), 14,
  17
Mainstreaming, 159, 179, 180, 205–206
Major depressive disorder (MDD),
  116–117, 120
MASC (Multidimensional Anxiety Scale
  for Children), 107
Masturbation, 30, 158, 178
Mathematics learning disorder, 160, 161,
  162, 165
Medical models *see* biological models
Medications, 17, 18
  for ADHD, 58–59, 91–93, 95–96, 160
  for anorexia nervosa, 142
  antidepressants, 142–143, 179

antipsychotic medications, 160, 179, 185,
  194
  for anxiety disorders, 112–113
  for autism, 178–179, 185
  for bulimia nervosa, 142–143
  for depression, 122–123, 126
  and "direct-to-consumer" (DTC)
    advertising, 202–203
  for enuresis, 196
  for mental retardation, 159–160
  psychotropic medications, 58, 159,
    202–203
  for self-injury, 185
  stimulants, 58–59, 91–93, 96, 160,
    179
  for Tourette's disorder, 194
Medulla, 15
Mental health care
  funding, 207–208
  geographic barriers, 206–207
Mental retardation, 145–160, 166
  adaptive behavior, 145, 146, **147**, 148
  age of onset, 145
  assessment, 146–149, **147**
  biological factors, 151–154, 156
  causes, 150–156
  classification, **53**, **146**, 146–147, **149**
  comorbidity, 145, 150, 157
  and culture, 148, 149
  Down syndrome, 151–153, 204–205
  education, 158–159
  fragile X syndrome, 153
  and gender, 149
  genetic factors, 150–151
  IQ scores, 146, 147–149, 151
  medications, 159–160
  phenylketonuria (PKU), 153–154
  placement, 156–157
  prenatal and perinatal environments,
    154–155
  prevalence, 147, 149
  and the right to reproduce, 203–204
  self-injury in, 150
  and social environment, 155–156
  and socioeconomic status, 149–150,
    155–156
  treatment, 157–160
  see also learning disorders/disabilities

Methylphenidate [Ritalin], 58–59, 91, 92
Midbrain, 14–15
Modeling, 22–23, 110
Models of childhood disorders, 13–37
  behaviorism: learning models, 18–24, 33
  biological models, 13–18, 200
  cognitive-behavioral model, 26–27
  cognitive model, 24–27
  diathesis-stress model, 34–35
  psychodynamic model, 27–33
  systems models, 33–34
  trends, 35–36
Monozygotic (identical) twins, 16
MRI (magnetic resonance imaging), 14, 17
Multidimensional Anxiety Scale for Children (MASC), 107
Multimodal treatment strategy, 95
Multimodal Treatment Study of Children with ADHD, 95–96
Multivariate statistical taxometric system, 54

Neuroimaging, 14, 17, 200
Neurons, 15
Neuropsychological models of treatment, 165
Neuroses, 29–30
Neurotransmission, 15–16
Neurotransmitters, 15–16
Non-suicidal self-injury (NSSI), 118
Nonconscious processes, 32
Norepinephrine, 91, 136

Object relations theory, 31, 33
Observational learning, 22–23
Obsessions, 103
Obsessive-compulsive disorder (OCD), 103–104
  age of onset, 104
  comorbidity, 134, 193
  and generalized anxiety disorder (GAD), 104
  genetic factors, 109, 193
  prevalence, 103–104
  treatment, 111, 112

Obstetrical history and intellectual development, 155
Oedipal dilemma, 30
Operant conditioning, 19–22
Oppositional defiant disorder (ODD)
  and conduct disorder, 63
  and depression, 118
  prevalence, 65
Oral stage of psychosexual development, 30
Organic models see biological models

Panic disorder, 108–109
Parent training, 58
  in ADHD, 93–94
  in anxiety disorders, 112
  in autism, 179, 182–185
  in child depression, 124
  in conduct disorders, 73–74
  in feeding disorder of infancy, 130
  in learning disorders, 165
  in mental retardation, 158
Parenting and family factors, 12, 33, 43–47, 200
  in ADHD, 80, 86, 89
  in anorexia nervosa, 33–34, 134
  in anxiety disorders, 110–111
  in autism, 174–175
  in bulimia nervosa, 139
  in conduct disorders, 69–71
  in depression, 120, 121–122
  divorce, 43–47, 71
  enmeshment, 33–34, 134
  interparent violence, 70
  in learning disorders/disabilities, 163
  overprotection, 34
  physical abuse, 69–70
  rigidity, 34
  weapons use, 70
Parents rating scale, 48, 49
Pediatric Anxiety Rating Scale (PARS), 107
Peer relationships, 44
  in ADHD, 79
  in anxiety disorders, 99, 101, 110
  in autism, 170
  in conduct disorders, 64, 72
Pemoline [Cylert], 91

SES *see* socioeconomic status
Sexism, 32–33
Sexuality, 30
Shaping, 20–21, 180–181, 183
Social anxiety disorder (SocAD), 105–106
  causal forces, 109
  treatment, 111, 112
Social environment
  and ADHD, 86
  and mental retardation, 155–156
Social learning theory, 23
Social phobia, 22
Socioeconomic status (SES)
  and ADHD, 82–83
  and conduct disorder, 66
  and mental retardation, 149–150,
    155–156
Special education, 93, **149**, 159, 161, 162,
  179–180
Specific learning disability, 161 *see also*
  learning disorders/disabilities
SSRIs *see* selective serotonin reuptake
  inhibitors
Stanford-Binet Test, 147
State-Trait Anxiety Inventory for Children
  (STAI-C), 106–107
Stimulants, 58–59, 91–93, 96, 160, 179
Stimulus–response, 19, 21–22
Straterra, 91
Stress, 34
Structured diagnostic interviews, 48,
  51–52
Substance use
  and ADHD, 88, 93
  in anxiety disorders, 99
  and bulimia nervosa, 140
  in conduct disorders, 63, 72
Suicidal behavior, 118–119, 123, 126
Summation, 15
Summer camps for children with ADHD,
  94
Superego, 28, 32
Synapses, 15
Systems models, 33–34

TADS (Treatment for Adolescents with
  Depression Study), 126
Tantrums, 20, 106

Teacher Rating Form (TRF), 49, 107
Television use and ADHD, 86
Test of Nonverbal Intelligence (3rd ed.),
  147
Thalamus, 14
Theory of mind, 172
Thorndike's law of effect, 19
Thought-shape fusion, 140
Tic disorders, 191
  in ADHD, 92
  classification, **53**
  tics, 191, 192
  transient tic disorders, 191
  see also Tourette's disorder
Time out, 186
Tourette's disorder, 191–195
  age of onset, 192
  biological factors, 193–194
  cause, 193
  classification, **192**, 192–193
  comorbidity, 193
  coprolalia, 192
  course of disorder, 192
  and culture, 193
  and gender, 193
  genetic factors, 193
  habit reversal training, 194–195
  medications, 194
  motor tics, 192
  vocal tics, 192
Treatment for Adolescents with
  Depression Study (TADS), 126
Treatment outcome studies, 57
Treatments, 2, 39, 56–59, 199, 200
  for ADHD, 90–96
  for anorexia nervosa, 141, 142–143
  for anxiety disorders, 111–113, 158
  for autism, 178–184
  for bulimia nervosa, 141–143
  child therapy, 58
  for conduct disorders, 72–76
  for depression, 112, 122–126
  efficacious treatments, 57–58
  for enuresis, 196–197
  for learning disorders, 164–165
  for mental retardation, 157–160
  multimodal treatment strategy, 95
  play therapy, 58

school-based programs, 73, 124
see also family therapy; medications;
    parent training
Twin studies, 16
  ADHD, 83
  anorexia nervosa, 136
  anxiety disorder, 109
  autism, 175

conduct disorders, 68, 71
  mental retardation, 151
Tourette's disorder, 193

Unconscious, 28, 32

WISC-IV (Wechsler Intelligence Scale for
  Children), 147, 148